COMPUTERS
IN EARLY
AND PRIMARY
EDUCATION

Douglas H. Clements
Kent State University

COMPUTERS IN EARLY AND PRIMARY EDUCATION

Prentice-Hall, Inc., Englewood Cliffs, New Jersey 07632

Library of Congress Cataloging in Publication Data

CLEMENTS, DOUGLAS H.
  Computers in early and primary education.

  Bibliography: p.
  Includes Index.
  1. Computer-assisted instruction. 2. Education,
Primary—Curricula—Data processing. 3. Education,
Preschool—Curricula—Data processing. I. Title.
LB1028.5.C5254 1985   372.13′9445   84–16588
ISBN 0–13–164013–5

Editorial/production supervision and
  interior design: *Edith Riker*
Manufacturing Buyer: *Barbara Kittle*
Cover design: *Photo Plus Art*
Cover photograph: *Douglas H. Clements*

Printed in the United States of America

10 9 8 7 6 5 4 3 2 1

ISBN 0-13-164013-5 01

Prentice-Hall International, Inc., *London*
Prentice-Hall of Australia Pty. Limited, *Sydney*
Editora Prentice-Hall do Brasil, Ltda., *Rio de Janeiro*
Prentice-Hall Canada Inc., *Toronto*
Prentice-Hall Hispanoamerica, S.A., *Mexico*
Prentice-Hall of India Private Limited, *New Delhi*
Prentice-Hall of Japan, Inc., *Tokyo*
Prentice-Hall of Southeast Asia Pte. Ltd., *Singapore*
Whitehall Books Limited, *Wellington, New Zealand*

To my wife, Holly, whose love and understanding underlies my work and life, and to my parents, who first showed me how to nurture a child, this is dedicated.

CONTENTS

Appendix, 292

Glossary, 302

References, 306

Index, 315

PREFACE

Computers in Early and Primary Education is addressed to all those concerned with the education of young children in preschool, kindergarten, and grades 1 through 3; those concerned that computers fulfill their potential for benefiting children; and those concerned that they do not affect children negatively in any way. It is based on the assumption that, considering the influx of computers into the home and school environment, there is a need for a book written for this audience that shows how computers *can* be used and raises issues concerning how computers *should* be used with young children. This, then, is meant to be a practical book. However, this does not mean that inflexible prescriptions are offered. Available computer programs are changing too rapidly to allow this. Furthermore, "cute" activities that have not been adequately considered in the light of what children need to learn and of how children learn are the bane of early education. Instead, the book is practical in that it presents guidelines for computer use along with suggestions and illustrative activities that follow these guidelines.

In past periods of innovation, education of young people has been fraught with fads, fetishes, and formulisms. So that they will not blindly endorse nor needlessly reject computer technology, teachers need to be knowledgable of its potential and applications.

The purpose of the book is to help the reader gain this knowledge—to understand how computers *can* be used to help young children learn and develop. Just as important, its purpose is to help readers think about and decide how computers *should* be used—what applications *should* and *should not* be employed. First, it is necessary to see the big picture—an overview of computer uses. Second, guidelines for their use must be established. The first chapter presents such an overview and a set of guidelines. Later chapters expand on and develop these ideas.

Many computer programs *will* be described; however, no comprehensive list of the "best" programs will be attempted. As this is read, hundreds of programs will be available that were just a gleam in a programmer's eye at the time this was written. This book will show how computers can help achieve the important goals of early education, promoting achievement in basic skills, growth in higher-level problem solving, positive attitudes toward learning and self, and social development. The teacher who understands this will be able to decide confidently which new computer programs are worth inclusion in his or her educational program. It is these teachers, making professional decisions regarding computer use, who are best prepared to direct the course of this powerful technology's role in young children's lives.

It would be nice to say that all this is based on established theory and research. Unfortunately, a young technology has little of either. Where it *does* exist, it is applied and cited. Otherwise, guidance is found in pertinent research and authoritative opinion from other related educational fields. Finally, practical observations of young children and their work with and without computers have made their contributions. For these observations, the author has drawn on his own experience teaching kindergarten in Wilson, New York, as well as teaching 3- and 4-year-olds, and several years of observing other teachers use computers to enhance the development of young children aged 4 to 9.

The book is divided into seven parts. Part I introduces computer use in early education. Part II discusses specific ways this technology is used to help educators teach and manage the classroom. Part III tells what, how, and why children should be taught about computers themselves. Part IV offers hints on setting up an educational environment that includes computers. Part V discusses computer programming for young children. Part VI describes how computers are used to teach what is in the curriculum. Part VII takes a look into the future.

1

MICROKIDS WITH MICROCOMPUTERS
The Whys and Hows of Computers in Early Education

FIRST IMPRESSIONS

To begin to examine your own knowledge and beliefs about computers and children, please answer the following questions:

_____ 1. An Apple is
   a. the fleshy, usually rounded edible pome fruit of a tree of the rose family.
   b. a spherical object, usually given to a teacher as a present by a young child after it has turned brown and soft.
   c. insufficient for warding off colds during the time of year that 17 kindergarten children cover their mouths *after* sneezing.
   d. a brand of microcomputer.

_____ 2. A PET is
   a. a domesticated animal kept not for utility but for pleasure (at least, that of the children).
   b. one of a variety of creatures let loose during every surprise "show and tell."
   c. an acronym for Parent Effectiveness Training—a course of guidance and discipline suggested to the parents of "Billy the Bullet" by every teacher he has had since preschool.
   d. another brand of microcomputer.

_____ 3. CAI is
   a. an acronym for an intelligence agency, arranged in code.
   b. the word "cat" as spelled by Billy on a good day.
   c. and acronym for Computers Are Insipid, a humanistic organization.
   d. an acronym for computer-assisted instruction.

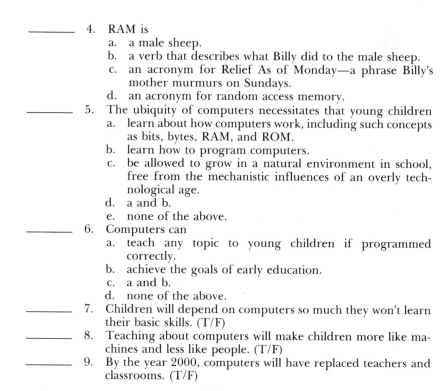

4. RAM is
   a. a male sheep.
   b. a verb that describes what Billy did to the male sheep.
   c. an acronym for Relief As of Monday—a phrase Billy's mother murmurs on Sundays.
   d. an acronym for random access memory.

5. The ubiquity of computers necessitates that young children
   a. learn about how computers work, including such concepts as bits, bytes, RAM, and ROM.
   b. learn how to program computers.
   c. be allowed to grow in a natural environment in school, free from the mechanistic influences of an overly technological age.
   d. a and b.
   e. none of the above.

6. Computers can
   a. teach any topic to young children if programmed correctly.
   b. achieve the goals of early education.
   c. a and b.
   d. none of the above.

7. Children will depend on computers so much they won't learn their basic skills. (T/F)

8. Teaching about computers will make children more like machines and less like people. (T/F)

9. By the year 2000, computers will have replaced teachers and classrooms. (T/F)

Computers are rapidly becoming as common as blackboards and pencils in classrooms, including early childhood classrooms. It is only since the late 1970s that option "d" would constitute a correct response to questions 1 through 4. It is an indication of the extent to which computers have burgeoned into the school that this option would now be the preferred choice of many teachers. More serious, though, are the concerns raised in questions 5 through 9. These address the role that computers will play in the schools.

How would you honestly answer the last five questions? Considering the topic of this book, what do you believe the "right" answers were supposed to be? It is hoped that you chose "none of the above" for questions 5 and 6. Although these questions are purposely somewhat vague, this book is based on the belief that there is no reason to *require* that children learn how computers work nor is there any reason to banish them from the early childhood classroom on the basis of a misguided humanistic/mechanistic dichotomy. The position is taken that children can learn many things working with computers—including, but not limited to, basic skills—and that computers can help to achieve many goals of early education but that not every topic or goal is best approached through technology.

You are probably wondering what *your* beliefs should be, what computers can and cannot do, and how computers will affect the curriculum you will teach and how you will teach it. To assist you in developing well-founded knowledge and beliefs, the rest of this chapter will present perspectives concerning the use of computers with young children.

PERSPECTIVES ON COMPUTERS AND CHILDREN: THE SPECTRUM OF OPINION

Both the children we teach and the computers we use are so young. They have within them an incredible amount of potential, but to that extent, they are also malleable. Each may scale heights never before reached, or each may fail to do little more than tred tired paths. It is at a precipice that they meet, ready for direction and guidance to fulfill their potential. Those who shall bring them together hold an awesome responsibility, for how they guide one will probably affect the direction and development of the other. As in so many situations, great responsibility is accompanied by great differences of opinion concerning how that responsibility should be deployed.

On one end of the spectrum, citizens' committees have attacked the idea that computers will solve the ills of the educational system ("Citizens Committee," 1982). The color at this end is deep red, the red of STOP signs and warning lights. In the middle of the spectrum, the media commonly promote the notion that computers can do just about anything. At the same time, they may give the impression that computers are too complicated for young children and even teachers—that computer technology belongs much later in the curriculum (or program). These sources emit a confusing kaleidoscope of conflicting colors. At the other end of the spectrum, viewpoints overflow with optimism and urgency. "Start early! The preschool level provides an excellent psychological conditioning period to introduce computers" (Palamara, as cited in Long, 1982, p. 312). "In fact, we believe that in five years computer literacy will be second only to reading for elementary kids" (Reagan, in Oliver, 1983, p. 64). "For children to feel that computers are approachable, that they are machines rather than frightening beings, children must have early and frequent contact with computers" (Bitter & Watson, 1983, p. 136). "It is in the elementary grades, perhaps even among preschoolers, that microcomputers may ultimately challenge and radically alter traditional instructional modes" (Martin, 1981, p. 41).

Children seem to agree. One visitor to Lamplighter School in Dallas overheard a 5-year-old "speaking disparagingly of a fellow student: 'Jonathan is already 4, and he can't do the computer' " (Fiske, 1982, p. C-1). Another child maintained "There should be a computer in every school, for each kid" (Humphrey, 1982, p. 97). Colors at this end are the pleasant blues and violets in which children are to bask and grow (producing, perhaps, vitamin D, for "development").

The spectrum of opinion is wide. How are teachers to avoid being blinded by any single color? Although there are no simple answers, we must attempt to pass the colors through a prism of knowledge and theory so that the bits of truth in each colored opinion are fused into illuminating white light. First, we will take a look at applications of computer technology both as it might be used by the early childhood educator and by the pre-school or primary school child to see if these beliefs are valid. Then, we will discuss principles that will guide the selection and implementation of these applications.

METAPHORS FOR THE MACHINES

Perspectives: How Computers Can Be Used to Enrich the Learning/Teaching Environment

The computer as tutor. Used in this way, the computer acts as a limited "teacher." It may present information, ask questions and check if the child's responses were correct, loop back and repeat lessons or branch off to a remedial lesson if the child is having difficulty, and so on. At its simplest, it may be nothing more than electronic flashcards. At a more complex level, it may provide everything a textbook provides *and* much more: interacting in speech, music, and pictures; individualizing its presentation continuously in response to the child's actions; and improving its ability to help the child learn by being "taught to do new things." Chapter 2 will provide a more comprehensive overview of this use of computers.

The computer as subject. What should children be taught *about* computers? This area, often called computer awareness, may include knowledge about the history of computers, how computers work, the components of a computer system, and the social applications and impact of computers. Some maintain that a full appreciation of the role of the computer in the life of the individual and in the world cannot be gained without study of these topics. Others argue that true literacy (such as our knowledge of telephones, automobiles, or microwave ovens) comes only through experience with the application of these devices in our lives. What and how to teach young children about the computer is the subject of Chapters 4 through 6.

The computer as tool. Probably the most effective way to use the computer is in its myriad applications as a *tool,* by having children learn by doing a task in a manner similar to the way an adult would. Rather than having them count pictured sets, the children should count the people at their table to determine how many pairs of scissors they should bring. Rather than filling in coloring book outlines, the children should draw to express their visions. Children do not, of course, conduct these activities at the same *level* as an adult, but the *nature* of the activity is the same—there is purpose and personal involvement.

Similarly, rather than interacting with the computer only as a drill master, children should use it as a tool as adults do. Adults use word processing programs to help them write; children can use many computerized tools, including simplified word processing programs, message programs, and other aids to communication, to help them communicate. Adults use computers to create graphics and art; children should use programs that allow them to scribble, design, and draw. Some adults instruct the computer to do what they want it to do through computer programming; given appropriate computer "languages" children can similarly control this powerful tool. Teachers can view the computer as

> Palette and easel
> Tinker Toys
> Communicator (storywriter, message carrier, etc.)
> Musical instrument
> Miniature world to be explored
> Center for social and emotional growth

As can be seen, the computer can be many tools. It can even be used by the teacher as a tool for managing the classroom (see Chapter 3). These many uses will be discussed throughout the remainder of the book.

Perspectives: Other Ways a Computer Can Be Viewed

The computer as pencil. Seymour Papert asks you to think of a computer as a pencil. The pencil is always there, ready to be used for scribbling, writing, arithmetic, drawing, and so on. The computer will also be used in many ways, serving education, not dictating it.

The computer as sandcastle. Jeanne Bamberger (1983) wishes us to approach the computer world as artists working with the sensory world, creating a sandcastle, a paper doll, or a design on paper. As we arrange these materials, we watch them take shape, and even as we shape them, they shape us—we learn. The "stuff" talks back to us, recreating our ideas as to what is possible. The computer can also reflect back to us a sometimes surprising, always interesting, interpretation of what we *thought* we meant. Applications of these ideas will be found throughout the book, especially in the chapters on programming and the arts.

The computer as building blocks. This last metaphor is especially appropriate to early childhood education. As are the building blocks of the classroom, the computer is limited only by the imagination of the builder. The same set of materials, worked on by different hands and different minds, can be anything from a spaceship, to a home, to a weight for papers blowing in the wind. Not limited in scope or purpose, the materials can grow with the child, ever increasing in complexity and depth. They can be used alone, but they are especially enjoyed when they are shared and used with others. And finally, although they have infinite possibilities, they can be put away in favor of other experiences, to be returned to another day.

Every new technological advance brings advantages and disadvantages. In the play *Inherit the Wind,* a lawyer was arguing that another, different, intellectual/scientific advance should be welcomed rather than censored, even though it was not without drawbacks.

> Progress has never been a bargain. You've got to pay for it. Sometimes I think there's a man behind the counter who says, "All right, you can have a telephone, but you'll have to give up privacy, the charm of distance. Madam, you may vote; but at a price; you lose the right to retreat behind a powder-puff or a petticoat. Mister, you may conquer the air; but the birds will lose their wonder, and the clouds will smell of gasoline! (Lawrence & Lee, 1961, p. 67).

Computer technology offers us a new way of thinking about learning and about thought itself. But we may have to give up some old comfortable notions and ways of teaching. In addition, we have to work so that children benefit and do *not* suffer. We need to make sure that we use these tools to extend and enrich the life of the thinking child and also that of the imagining and fantasizing child. But we also need to ensure that these are an addition to, rather than a replacement of, other experiences. We need to let the child see beyond the video arcade. To do this, we require a set of directions, or principles, to guide us.

PRINCIPLES OF TEACHING: YOUNG CHILDREN AND COMPUTERS

What are Principles?

Every teacher holds beliefs about children and the way in which they learn, about curriculum and teaching, and about the interaction of these and other facets of education. When these beliefs are used to guide and evaluate an education program, they are called *educational principles*. Every new activity and every change in the program should be based on principles that have been carefully considered and explicitly stated. Good teachers constantly think about what they are doing and why they are doing it. Stated principles serve as a reminder of this and as a framework in which this thinking and evaluating can be done.

What good are educational principles? Of major importance, of course, is that the education of young people have direction, consistency, and validity. Beyond that, however, are the principles of practical importance? Yes; they provide a blueprint for instruction that indicates what to do in any situation. Rather than wondering "What exactly do I do Monday morning?" a teacher following principles has a comprehensive perspective with which to view any situation or problem, an integrated framework to guide general planning and day-by-day improvisation and decision making.

Suggested Principles

The following statements of beliefs are examples of educational principles that might guide the early childhood educator in using computers. As a reader, you are asked to examine your own beliefs in relation to these statements with the intention of accepting, modifying, supplementing, or rejecting the statements as educational principles for your own program.

1. There are situations in which computers SHOULD be used, and there are situations in which computers SHOULD NOT be used. Computers can enrich the school environments of young children. They *should* be used when they are consistent with the general goals and principles of early childhood education (see Chapter 7), for example, when they promote the growth of a positive self-concept and when they contribute to learning without depriving children of other important experiences (Figure 1–1).

Computers *should not* be used when they *replace* other active or social experiences believed to be essential to the young child's development. Until research is more conclusive concerning what computer experiences are beneficial, controversies should usually be resolved on the conservative side. For instance, actively manipulating and counting objects may be necessary for building a firm concept of number. They should not be used when the use violates the principles of an educational program. For example, if one principle states that self-concept should be developed, computer programs that give insulting feedback should not be used. Computers should not be used as time-fillers, as workbooks too often are.

FIGURE 1–1 (Courtesy of EduWare Services.)

2. Priority should be given to computer applications that place the children in the role of active learners with some control over their educational environment.

3. Both experiential and drill (and tutorial) programs are beneficial; however, children should receive as much practice as possible in the context of higher-level experiences.

Principles 2 and 3 indicate that personally significant and meaningful experiences should be given first priority for computer use. Examples of such experiences include working together to make up stories, rearranging musical notes to create tunes, exploring mathematical patterns, and drawing.

Principle 2 emphasizes the philosophical and psychological position that children's learning is most effective when they are given some choice as to when, what, and how they will learn. Children are active learners. They decide whether or not to attend to and process what they see and hear. Tasks that children choose, or into which they have some input, are often more meaningful and motivating, and therefore more powerful as learning experiences.

A corollary of this principle, principle 3 concerns different types of computer programs. Experiential programs not only develop higher-level abilities of synthesis, analysis, and problem solving, they *also* provide meaningful practice in lower-level skills. However, information processing research reveals that reaching a level of *automaticity* in select lower skills is a prerequisite for the development of some higher-level abilities. Therefore, drill on these skills that supplements experiential work may be necessary and can also constitute a valid use of computer facilities.

For example, a major application of computers in the language arts (see Chapter 11) is to help children engage in meaningful communicative experiences through constructing stories or writing letters. However, recent research indicates that developing several lower-level skills such as quick word recognition to the point of automaticity (responding immediately without "wasting" mental processing power) is essential to comprehension; therefore, games that are designed specifically to develop fast and accurate word recognition will also benefit children (Lesgold, 1983; Perfetti, 1983). The guide should be that the right amount of practice on lower-level skills is the *minimum* amount necessary to achieve automaticity; additional time should go to higher-level activities.

4. Children's preferences should not be the *only* basis for curricular decisions. Since the time of John Dewey and the Progressive Education Movement, we have known that we cannot be governed only by what children like or want to do. Children's interests should certainly be taken into consideration, and they should be given a significant degree of control over their own learning, as noted here. However, choosing activities and subject matter solely on the basis of student's whims leads to an incoherent and incomplete educational experience.

Even common sense cannot always be trusted. For example, most currently available educational computer programs are based on the assumption that students learn more from materials they enjoy using, yet at least one study has found that children enjoy the method from which they learned the least (Saracho, 1982). It is certainly not being argued that anyone should dislike learning. However, most people will admit that it was often those ideas or abilities that were the most difficult to grasp that gave them the most satisfaction to have mastered. Motivation is essential, but there are many types of motivation (e.g., competence motivation may propel infants to their feet even after they have fallen—and cried—repeatedly). Claims that a computer can "make learning fun" should be listened to carefully, but also critically.

5. Child development should be used as a guideline. Findings of developmental psychology provide lenses that can help us to see more clearly what to expect of children at each age level in their interaction with computers. In a similar vein, they help us to view programs written for these children critically. However, recognizing that some computer applications may positively influence cognitive development, these findings should not be allowed to become blinders that limit our vision of what children can accomplish.

6. Students should experience a wide variety of computer applications. There are many reasons for diversity of computer use: (a) to enable children to become familiar with the many ways computer technology is applied in the world, (b) to expand children's conceptions of the capabilities and limitations of computers, (c) to extend children's abilities to utilize computers in performing different tasks, (d) to provide for individual differences in the aptitudes and interests of children (e.g., one child might like to compose music using the computer; another might like to write simple arithmetic programs), and (e) to provide many opportunities for explorations and learning.

7. Computer activities should be integrated into the curriculum.

8. Children can and should use computers meaningfully in ways that facilitate their intellectual, social, emotional, and creative growth.

Principles 7 and 8 both stem from one general principle—educating the whole child. As general-purpose tools, computers can and should be used to help achieve the goals of early education.

Used appropriately, they *can* contribute to the development of young children. Children will use computers; educators must ensure that they are used humanely to help children learn. However, to believe or advocate, as some do (true/false question 9 is an actual quotation), that computers can replace teachers and socially based early education is to misunderstand both the way in which children develop and the goals of early education. In accordance with principle 1, computers should be used in some situations but not in others. Children need to experience their world in a variety of ways, many of which involve large-muscle movement and social interaction, to grow successfully. This is the way they develop and learn. Similarly, many of the *goals* of early education could never be reached through machines alone. These goals include the development of social and physical skills and a positive self-concept.

Life is much bigger than working with computers, but computers can enrich many facets of life. Educators should consider these goals first and then determine which applications of computer technology will help to achieve these goals. It is these applications—creating music and art; drawing, writing, and communicating in a variety of ways; working together; solving problems of all types; locating and using information; and learning—that must be the central concern of those responsible for children's learning. If it is, the fears of losing basic skills competence or mechanizing children and their learning will be unfounded.

The last three principles might actually be the most important.

9. Every computer practice should be consonant with the overall principles of the educational program. Obviously, all the preceding principles are specific manifestations of general principles of early childhood education. These general principles must serve as the major guidelines. Because they should be used directly to evaluate every computer program, they will be discussed in detail in Chapter 7. Conversely, the adoption of specific computer applications will have an impact on the school's instructional philosophy. A discussion of how computers can be integrated into a classroom in a way that is consistent with Montessori principles can be found in Ross and Campbell (1983).

10. Learning with computers should be a *means* to achieve educational goals, not an *end*. The goals of early and primary education should be considered first. The computer is a *tool*, to be used to help achieve these goals. Although many of us adults feel that we need to cope with computers, that is not the need of children. Their need is to learn to communicate with people, to solve problems, to understand changes, and to handle information. For them, computers are a method of fulfilling their potential to grow in the world and with the world. Learning with and about computers is but one part of the optimal educational environment. Using computers in this way, the curriculum will be enhanced, not crowded to make room for "something else," and there will be more social interaction rather than less.

11. The teacher is the key to successful use of computers. The teacher is the most important variable for many reasons, not the least of which is that he or she ensures that the other principles are not violated. Therefore, teachers must integrate the classroom application of computers into their own teaching style.

You may wish to change or eliminate some of these principles or to add some that are not mentioned. What is important is that you *consider* what principles you will use to guide your use of computers with young children. The field is young and still forming. We need to go forward with enthusiasm, but with foresight—a vision of what can be—and hindsight—a recognition of what educators of the past have learned, all the while holding in our mind's eye that which we value.

FIGURE 1–2   Self-esteem can be developed through the recognition of each individual's unique creations. (Photo by Douglas Clements.)

THINK ABOUT

1. If a school had only one computer, would principle 3 change? How?
2. Name several "should" and "should not's" of computer use.
3. Reread questions 5 through 9 at the beginning of the chapter. Answer them again as you now would. Answer them as you now believe the author would. Discuss any discrepancies.
4. Is principle 3 wishy-washy? Are principles 2 and 4 contradictory? Why or why not?
5. Which two principles are most important? Least? Add one.
6. If you could only choose one, would you use the computer as teacher, subject, or tool? Why?

ANNOTATED BIBLIOGRAPHY

Grady, M. T., & Gawronski, Jane D. (eds.) (1983). *Computers in curriculum and instruction.* Alexandria, VA: Association for Supervision and Curriculum Development.

Harper, D. O., & Stewart, J. H. (eds.) (1983). *Run: Computer education.* Monterey, CA: Brooks/Cole.

Sadowski, B. R., & Lovett, C. (eds.) (1981). *Using computers to enhance teaching and improve teacher centers.* Houston: University of Houston.

Silver, S. (ed.) (1983). Children in the age of microcomputers [special issue]. *Childhood Education, 59.*

Taylor, R. P. (1980). *The computer in the school: Tutor, tool, tutee.* New York: Teachers College Press.

Other philosophical views can be found in these readings. Compare your principles with theirs.

2

COMPUTER-ASSISTED INSTRUCTION
Some Examples

HELPING YOUNG CHILDREN LEARN

When discussing the use of computer technology with preschool children, it is often overlooked that "dedicated" or special-purpose computers are commonly employed with this age group. Touch & Spell and Speak & Math (from Texas Instruments) utilize microprocessors to combine sight, sound, and touch in introducing children to basic vocabulary and number concepts. However, more and more programs are being written for young children that will run on an all-purpose microcomputer. A microcomputer with a variety of programs covering many different subject areas and ability levels is a more versatile and powerful tool.

This application of computers, often called computer-assisted instruction or CAI, can be viewed as "the computer as tutor." In this view, the computer is a sophisticated teaching machine, teacher's aide, or audiovisual device. The purpose is to teach children skills, facts, or concepts from the traditional curriculum. More elementary schools use computers in this way than any other (Center for Social Organization of Schools, 1983). We will briefly examine some of these programs, recognizing that new (and, it is hoped, even better) ones are being written every day and that teachers would benefit from trying to keep abreast of these developments. Later (in Chapter 7) we will discuss specific criteria for evaluating any computer program; however, it will be useful here to consider the characteristics of preschool and primary grade children that make them unique computer users (Kimmel, 1981; Kleiman & Humphrey, 1982):

1. Most preschoolers cannot read, and many primary grade children have limited reading skills. So the programs should have limited written prompts. This has been the standard form of communication for computers. However, different methods of feedback have been designed for

the prereading child, including simple (but effective) smiling faces, faces or robots that shake their heads "yes" or "no," "firework" displays, and sound effects. It should be ensured that this feedback is correctly understood by the children.

2. Preschool children are forming cause and effect concepts. Programs should facilitate this growth, and avoid frustrating the learner, by clearly relating the child's action to the effects.
3. Many young children have limited appreciation for competitive games.
4. Fine motor skills are not always well developed. This may demand modification of arcade game formats and programs that require complex typing skills. It should be easy for the child to enter responses.
5. Young children do not seem to be able to spontaneously practice that which is to be memorized. We may not be able to train this, but we can provide needed (and patient) repetition with good computer programs (Cleary, Mayes, & Packham, 1979).
6. Preschool and primary grade children have limited ability and interest in complicated setup. Programs should be easy to get under way.
7. Young children are easily distracted. Programs for them should avoid irrelevant graphics, color, sound, or the like that do not direct attention to what is to be learned.

All CAI programs should take these characteristics into consideration. Beyond this, their purposes and teaching strategies differ. They can be placed in one or more of the following categories: drill and practice, tutorial, simulation, and exploratory/game. Knowledge of these categories helps teachers choose the correct one for the job and keeps teachers from overusing one or two types.

DRILL AND PRACTICE

The most widely used type of computer program is drill and practice. This application is easy for most teachers to understand, as it not unlike other common approaches such as flashcards or programmed textbooks.

For example, several programs provide simple practice in counting. One places from 0 to 9 objects on the screen and waits for the child to type in the number (*Primary Math/Prereading;* Minnesota Educational Computing Consortium, MECC; see Figure 2–1). If the child is correct, a smiling face and the numeral appear. If the child is incorrect, the numeral is

FIGURE 2–1
Counting practice in *Primary Math/Prereading.* (Courtesy of MECC.)

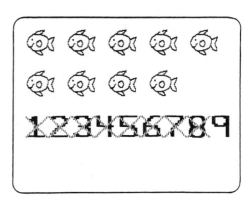

crossed off the list. Most drill and practice programs share the following characteristics.

PURPOSE:

To provide practice on skills and (usually lower-level) knowledge to help children remember and use what they have been taught.

METHODOLOGY:

1. Linear (progresses in a "straight-ahead" fashion, without branching to explanations if a child's responses are incorrect).
2. Repetitious.
3. Format: computer presents exercise; child types in response; computer informs child if answer is correct (if the answer is correct, computer goes on to next exercise; if not, the computer asks the child to try again at least once before supplying the answer).

STRENGTHS:

1. Uses efficient manner of building skills, due especially to individualization and feedback.
2. Is interactive (the child must actively respond to the program; the program responds to the child).
3. Ensures that child is practicing correct response.
4. Motivates child to perform what otherwise could be boring activity of repetitious practice, *if* well constructed.
5. Is easy to use.
6. May handle record keeping.
7. With programming experience, teachers can construct their own small CAI drill and practice routines.

WEAKNESSES:

1. Usually addresses discrete sets of lower-level skills only.
2. Has narrow range of teaching strategies.
3. May be boring *if not* well constructed.
4. May reinforce incorrect *concepts*.
5. Necessitates considerable access to computer facilities (i.e., you need to have one or more computers available for periods of time that are long enough to provide sufficient hands-on experience for each child).

While these characteristics are shared by most drill and practice programs, they vary widely in their adjunct characteristics. Some are quite simple, such as the example just given. Others either ask the child what skill level he or she would like to begin at or automatically assign the child to an appropriate level based on either (a) a set level supplied by the teacher or (b) the child's previous performance. Some programs also automatically advance the skill level minute by minute as the child improves. This can reduce the tedium for children who have mastered the skills of a particular level. Some keep extensive records of each child's skill level, and even of specific skills that he or she did or did not master. Some provide feedback in the form of elaborate sound effects and graphics (pictures), to the extent of mimicking arcade games to motivate children.

One example is the Arcademic Skillbuilders series (Developmental Learning Materials, DLM). In one program in the series, *Alien Addition*, children encounter beeping, invading spaceships, each of which has an addition problem written on it. They must load their laser cannon with the

correct answer and "equalize" the spaceships before they are exploded in an atomic cloud and a cacophony of beeps. Hits and misses are recorded at the terrain at the bottom of the screen (see Figure 2–2). The skill level (speed at which the ships descend), problem range (addends up to 3, 6, or 9), and run time can be preset by the teacher. (The teacher does not have to know how to program. The choice can be made from a "menu" that appears on the screen. As does a restaurant menu, this is a list that offers the teacher choices.) Note that in this program the teacher rather than the computer sets and resets these levels. Also, final scores are displayed, but the teacher or student must record them (a paper record-keeping system is provided). Programs that have the computer perform these functions will be discussed in detail in Chapter 3.

Other drill and practice programs may provide support for children who need it. For example, if a child responds to "3 + 5" by typing "7," the program might display a pair of die (two dice) alongside the problem.

$$\begin{array}{r} 3 \\ + 5 \\ \hline \end{array}$$

Notice that success in the *Alien Addition* program depends on the speed of a child's responses. Timing elements may provide the needed incentive for children to achieve a level of automaticity.

Approaches such as these that contain timing elements and those that provide support for children such as the pictures of the die should not be mixed. The first should emphasize correctness, *speed,* and accuracy; the second, correctness, *conceptual knowledge,* and accuracy. It is also important to point out that programs with sophisticated graphics and sound will not necessarily promote higher achievement. They may distract some children from the task at hand.

Careful readers may have noticed an apparent contradiction in that one strength of drill was that children practice correct responses and a weakness was that children may practice incorrect concepts. Actually, these situations can exist at the same time. Students in self-paced, individualized programs have been shown to have attained the ability to supply correct *answers* but have not developed an understanding of the underlying *concepts*. For this reason, CAI drill, like any drill, should complement teaching for meaning and should be balanced with other forms of practice and learning.

TUTORIAL

As you might expect, a tutorial CAI program instructs. It attempts to teach the child about some subject matter area in much the same way as a parent or teacher would do interacting with the youngster on a one-to-one basis. In fact, some of the better tutorial programs use a Socratic thinking approach to teaching. In this technique, the teacher directs children's own discovery through a carefully sequenced series of leading questions. The student then types a response. The program provides appropriate feedback based on this response and either provides more information or asks further questions. To enable the program to respond appropriately, the original questions must have a limited range of possible responses.

An example of a simple tutorial for older children is *Punctuation* (from Educational Activities). After a child types in his or her name, the computer writes the child a letter with no punctuation. The computer then prints (in large letters):

WOW!
SOMETHING IS MISSING.
WHAT DO YOU THINK IT IS,
BONNIE?

All the punctuation marks in these sentences then flash on and off several times. The screen clears and displays

RIGHT, BONNIE.
IT'S PUNCTUATION.
, ! , . ? .

The screen clears and the following is printed, one paragraph at a time.

FIRST LET'S LOOK AT PERIODS. A PERIOD ENDS A SENTENCE. WHEN YOU SEE A PERIOD, YOU CAN STOP AND CATCH YOUR BREATH. SENTENCES THAT END WITH PERIODS JUST TELL US SOMETHING. MOST SENTENCES END WITH PERIODS.

FIGURE 2–3
Punctuation. (Courtesy of Education Activities, Inc.)

IN THIS PROGRAM, WHEN YOU SEE ME POINT TO THE END OF A SENTENCE, ADD THE CORRECT PUNCTUATION
TYPE IN THE PERIOD.

This appears in Figure 2–3.

Different sound effects are used for each punctuation mark. When Bonnie types in the period, she hears a short beep.

THAT'S HOW A PERIOD MIGHT SOUND IF IT COULD MAKE A NOISE.
TYPE IN A PERIOD.

The graphic figure indicates the space after the word "noise" where a period should be placed. When Bonnie types a period again, she hears the beep and reads

A PERIOD IS NOT EXCITING
TYPE IN A PERIOD.
IT IS JUST THERE TO TELL YOU TO STOP

For the fourth time, Bonnie types in a period (each time the graphic figure points to the place a period was missing). The computer beeps, the periods all flash on and off, and the first line of the letter is displayed again, with the figure pointing at the end of the first sentence. The program then continues to guide Bonnie to insert the needed periods properly. This is only one example. Tutorials differ widely; however, the following are characteristics shared by many.

PURPOSE:

To teach the student about a particular topic.

METHODOLOGY:

1. Linear progression with various amounts of branching.
2. Progression through a series of lessons.
3. Format: Socratic dialogue—presentation of information, questioning, and feedback dependent on the child's response; branching to explanations or review if child's responses indicate misconceptions.

STRENGTHS:

1. A well-designed tutorial can effectively bring forth, or educe (the root of "educator"), the child's active involvement and understanding of knowledge.
2. Can provide individualized, self-paced instruction.
3. Ensures that the child is participating in dialogue and is responding correctly.
4. Although perhaps limited in certain ways, is more interactive than a lecture or textbook.
5. Can be an excellent means of providing students with review of concepts or helping students who have been absent to "catch up."
6. Is easy to use.
7. May handle record keeping. May diagnose, prescribe, automatically present correct lesson/level of difficulty, and store information about child's performance, strengths, and weaknesses.
8. Teachers with programming experience or specially designed programs that help teachers to write programs can construct simple CAI tutorials.

WEAKNESSES:

1. Has narrow range of teaching strategies.
2. The intelligence of present-day tutorials is severely limited, especially compared with a teacher, who has considerable knowledge and intuition on which to rely. Therefore, the program's ability to respond to the child in a maximally helpful manner is also limited.
3. Similarly, to participate in a richer, more meaningful dialogue, the program must be extensive. Most microcomputers do not have enough memory to allow this. To respond intelligently to a child's open-ended responses also requires extensive field-testing, which is another reason this type of tutorial is not often done. (Producers maintain that the programs sell without expensive and time-consuming field testing.) Therefore most tutorials follow a restricted multiple-choice format.
4. If it is overused, this type of tutorial can become a game of "find out what the teacher wants and give it to her." It can also promote a shallow and narrow understanding of concepts.
5. Necessitates considerable access to computer facilities.

It is easy to get the impressions that tutorials might be appropriate only for older primary grade children. This is not true. *First Words* is a tutorial program written for very young or very handicapped children. It has been used successfully with children as young as 18 months to teach receptive vocabulary—50 nouns that are among the earliest to be understood. The package comes with a speech synthesizer. Therefore, all directions to the child are oral. There are several beginning levels of the program that teach the child how to respond that we will not discuss here. Once the child has learned how to press a button so as to interact with the program, an adult chooses one of ten categories for the tutorial, let us say "transportation." The child might then see the "blob," a silly, bouncy, green character, move over a single colored picture, while the computer says (out loud), "Here's the train." The train then relocates to one side and another picture appears on the other side. The blob *cues* the child by cartwheeling over to the correct picture—the train. Then an orange box is shown around first one picture, then the other, as the computer intones, "show

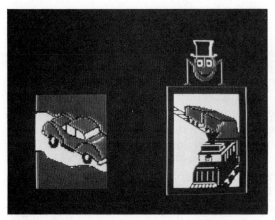

FIGURE 2–4a *First Words.* (Courtesy of Laureate Learning Systems, Inc.)

FIGURE 2–4b
Jenna, two years old, enjoys using *First Words.* (Photo by Cindy Brzuski.)

me the train" (Figure 2–4a). The child is to press the button when the box is around the picture of the train (Figure 2–4b).

The blob turns a somersault if the child is correct. If not, the picture of the train flashes and the program waits for a second response (cuing of the correct response). Again, a correct response is reinforced. If the second response is incorrect, the picture is shown alone in the middle of the screen and the child is instructed, "See the train." The program continues to present the ten pictures in the transportation category until a criterion level (preset by an adult) is reached.

Again using an on-screen menu, the adult can also set the scanning speed—the time the orange box stays on each picture before moving. In addition, the program can easily be altered so that the child moves the box with a joystick (a lever similar to that used in many computer games to move something around the screen) directly to the correct picture. With technological advances allowing computers to talk *and* to listen, tutorials for younger children should become more widely available. As with any approach, however, tutorials should be used in conjunction with a wide variety of other learning experiences.

Most presently available tutorials tell a child that he or she is wrong but they do not attempt to determine *why* the child answered as he or she did. Sophisticated programs may analyze and evaluate a child's response to an extent and branch to a lesson that deals specifically with the child's misunderstanding. This is beneficial if it is well planned. When the subject matter is not well defined, however, this is not frequently done. Indeed, because the program must have an explicit model or idea of the knowledge being taught and a psychological model of the child, it is rarely done well.

SIMULATION

Simulations are models of the world. Children who play house are simulating adult roles and activities. Although they cannot yet actually perform many adult activities, they learn a lot about them by pretending. Many popular games, such as "Life" and "Monopoly" are simulations. Computer simulations (discussed at length in Chapters 6 and 14) are also models of some part of the world. Children can learn a lot by pretending to be in that part or situation. Simulations are imaginary environments (albeit based on real-world facts) with a series of problems, often posed to a character who is under the children's control.

Computer simulations have an advantage in that they can be programmed to respond in realistic ways based on real-world information. For instance, given a player's life choices such as going to college or getting a certain kind of job, a computerized game of "Life" could tell the player what his or her future would be like based on actual population statistics. This allows them to be more realistic and more powerful as learning tools. Let us consider the following example.

Oregon (MECC) simulates a trip along the Oregon Trail in 1847. Students reenact the journey of a family of five who attempt to complete the 2,000-mile trip in five to six months. They have $700 and a wagon at the beginning of the trip. Simulations are based on the manipulation of variables. This program asks several questions. The students type in their answers, which appear beside the question mark and in a column on the right.

```
        HOW MUCH DO YOU WANT TO SPEND ON-

        OXEN? 200                        200

        FOOD? 50                          50

        AMMUNITION? 100                  100

        CLOTHING? _

        MISC. SUPPLIES
```

(At this point, the program is waiting for the students to type in the amount they want to spend on clothing.) After the students complete their expenditures, the screen shows

```
        HOW MUCH DO YOU WANT TO SPEND ON-

        OXEN? 200                        200

        FOOD? 50                          50

        AMMUNITION? 100                  100

        CLOTHING? 200                    200

        MISC. SUPPLIES? 100            + 100
        --------------------             -----
                                TOTAL= $650

                    $700   SAVED
                  - $650   SPENT
                    -----
                    $50    BALANCE

        YOU HAVE $50 DOLLARS LEFT TO
        SPEND ALONG THE WAY...

            PRESS SPACE BAR TO CONTINUE
```

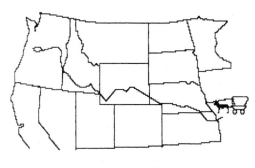

```
MARCH 29 1847          MILES  0
```

FIGURE 2–5
(Courtesy of MECC.)   PRESS SPACE BAR TO CONTINUE

The screen then shows a map of the Oregon Trail with a covered wagon at the beginning (Figure 2–5). The program then asks

```
MONDAY- MARCH 29, 1847          MILES= 0
-----------------------------------------
FOOD   BULLETS   CLOTHING   MISC.   CASH
50     5000      200        100     50
-----------------------------------------


DO YOU WANT TO-

   1.  STOP AT THE NEXT FORT
   2.  HUNT
   3.  CONTINUE

WHICH NUMBER?
```

If children choose to hunt, they must press a key in an attempt to shoot a deer. They are then asked such questions as, "DO YOU WANT TO EAT— 1. POORLY, 2. MODERATELY, 3. WELL. WHICH NUMBER? If they choose "3," the screen might show

```
MONDAY- MARCH 29, 1847          MILES= 0
-----------------------------------------
FOOD   BULLETS   CLOTHING   MISC.   CASH
38     4976      200        100     50
-----------------------------------------
```

Then a message might be displayed:

```
WAGON GETS SWAMPED FORDING RIVER - -
LOSE FOOD AND CLOTHES
```

The map is redisplayed, and the wagon moves along the trail. The screen then shows

```
MONDAY- APRIL 12, 1847          MILES= 181
-----------------------------------------
FOOD   BULLETS   CLOTHING   MISC.   CASH
8      4976      180        100     50
-----------------------------------------

YOU'D BETTER DO SOME HUNTING
OR BUY SOME FOOD AND SOON!

DO YOU WANT TO-

   1.  HUNT
   2.  CONTINUE

WHICH NUMBER?
```

If the students should happen to ignore the warning, they would read

```
YOU RAN OUT OF FOOD AND STARVED
TO DEATH.

DUE TO YOUR UNFORTUNATE SITUATION
THERE ARE A FEW FORMALITIES
WE MUST GO THROUGH—
WOULD YOU LIKE A MINISTER? ...
```

If the same students played the game again, they might encounter hostile riders, heavy rains and other bad weather, rugged mountains, injuries to daughters and oxen, fires, fog, snake bites, wild animals, and so on. If they eat too well (relative to their limited food supply) they will eventually starve; but if they eat too poorly, they may get sick. The simulation is based on historical information. For example, the frequencies of misfortunes is based on an analyses of diaries of people who actually traveled the entire length of the trail.

The simulation is designed to help students learn about the westward movement, emigration, the Oregon Trail, the effects of natural events during migration, and the economic systems during the period. Students can also learn to discuss and solve problems in groups. However, the teacher must ensure that this learning actually occurs. As with field trips, simulations can be the centers of wonderfully productive units of study if the teacher carefully plans and structures those units, or they can be pleasant excursions with little real benefit.

There are many types of computer simulations. One computer program simulates pouring some number of units of one measure (e.g., quarts) into another (a pictured gallon container). If the child specifies 5 quarts, some of the liquid spills out of the gallon container. Teachers usually are delighted with the program. What do you think?

Another simulates a swinging pendulum. Children type in the specifics: weight, length of the string, height of the weight before release, and so on. They are to find out which variables change the period (the length of time for each swing). What do you think of the program?

Despite their delightful appearance, *simulations such as these two should probably not be used with young children.* This use would violate the first chapter's principle 1 of computer use, as it would replace a valuable hands-on activity with an unnecessarily vicarious and abstract one. Children, especially young children, should pour and measure liquids themselves; they should swing the pendulum (and then only attempt the experiment described if they are ready to handle several variables at once). They benefit from the motor activity, from the sensory input of feeling and manipulating of real objects, and from the physical knowledge not included in the computer simulation (how far do you tip the quart to pour without spilling? how does liquid sound when it is poured? etc.). In some cases, careful comparison of a simulation and a real-world event is beneficial; this is indeed recommended whenever possible. However, in these two examples the computer adds little and may subtract considerably from the experience.

Simulations share most of the following characteristics:

PURPOSE:

To promote problem solving, develop an intuition or sense about a particular situation, facilitate the acquisition of skills and knowledge, and motivate interest in the subject and in learning.

METHODOLOGY:

1. Nonlinear.
2. Exploratory, discovery-oriented.
3. Format: Provides a model of some part of the world through which children can learn by pretending, exploring, and manipulating.

STRENGTHS:

1. Allows interaction with and study of events that would otherwise be inaccessible due to expense, danger, or time constraints.
2. Is motivating and highly interactive.
3. Is realistic (promotes transfer to out-of-school abilities).
4. Promotes social interaction and true discovery learning; children solve an actual problem.
5. Is individualized in terms of a project approach.
6. Enables wide range of teaching strategies (but not always built in).
7. One computer can easily serve the needs of an entire class.
8. Reflects real-world use of computers (see Chapter 6).

WEAKNESSES:

1. Does not ensure that students are responding correctly (because they are designed to allow children to explore "wrong" paths, this could be seen as a strength if properly managed by the teacher).
2. Is relatively more difficult to use effectively; is an unfamiliar approach to education for many teachers.
3. If use is not well planned, can degenerate into little more than a "beat the computer" game.
4. Does not handle record keeping.
5. Most presently available are limited in the information they include.
6. Is a copy of only *some* aspects of reality; if oversimplified and/or misused, may promote a misguided conception of real-world situations and problems. If too complex, may be inappropriate for children.
7. Does not include other important aspects of the real world, such as physical action and sensory impressions.
8. Teachers cannot easily create their own simulations without extensive instruction in programming and simulation construction.

Most presently available simulations of any quality are designed for use by older students. These include scientific experiments, social and genetic growth patterns, historical events, economic situations, and so on. However, it is certain that the future will see this type of quality simulation appearing for younger children.

EXPLORATORY/GAME

Exploratory programs and instructional games, like simulations, differ from the traditional modes of instruction with which most adults are familiar. However, early childhood teachers know that playful explorations and games are major ways in which young children learn. "Games" here does not mean low-level drill and practice exercises transplanted to outer space. In these games, the concepts to be learned are intrinsic to the structure and content of the game. These programs provide new minature worlds for children to explore and, therefore, share certain characteristics of simulations.

Bumble Games (The Learning Company) is a collections of six programs that teaches number lines, number pairs, and graph plotting to children from kindergarten to third grade. The first program, FIND YOUR NUMBER, teaches the number line from 0 to 4, as well as concepts of greater and less, by having the child guess a mystery number. The choice is highlighted on the screen and an arrow appears if the mystery number is greater ($\rightarrow$) or less ($\leftarrow$) than that guess. FIND THE BUMBLE extends children's skill with a number line to include a two-dimensional grid. The grid consists of four rows labeled A, B, C, and D, and four columns labeled 0, 1, 2, and 3. The child is to choose one letter and one number from the grid. He is then shown that this number pair corresponds to one square that is highlighted on the grid. The object of the game is to find the Bumble's secret hiding place. Clues are given (e.g., "It's down and to the right"; arrows are also provided). TIC TAC TOC, a version of the game tic tac toe, reinforces these plotting skills and expands the grid to 25 points.

These are well-designed educational games. The final program, BUMBLE DOTS, is an example of an exploratory program. Here children are asked to enter dots on a grid by typing in number pairs. As each new dot is entered, lines are drawn to connect them. In this way, children create a picture, which is named by the child and displayed with an electronic fanfare (see Figures 2-6 and 2-7). Ability to use computers, knowledge of

FIGURE 2–6 TIC TAC TOC, from *Bumble Games.* (Courtesy of The Learning Company. Photo by Mark Tuschman.)

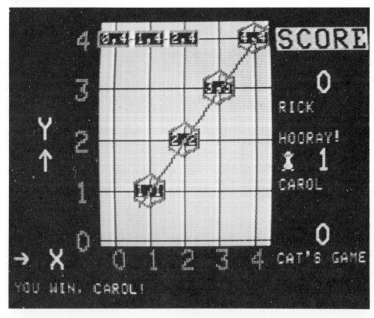

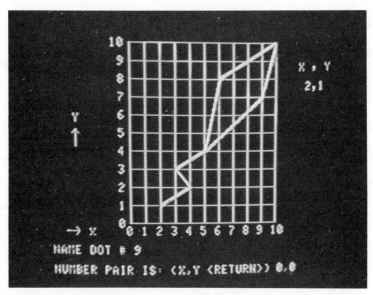

FIGURE 2–7 *Bumble Dots* from *Bumble Games.* (Courtesy of The Learning Company. Photo by Mark Tuschman.)

numbers, plotting, spatial visualization, and creativity are developed simultaneously in this exploratory program.

Another exploratory program is *Troll's Tale* (Sierra On-Line). This adaptation of the popular adult adventure games can be used by children at a reading level of third grade. The children's task is to recover the treasures stolen from the king. They move from one location to another, making decisions and predicting outcomes. Used wisely, the program could develop reading, planning, memory, problem solving, and spatial/map skills.

What about interactive stories for prereading children? They exist, although the quality varies. *Sammy the Sea Serpent* (Program Design) is a storybook on a computer for preschool children. Sammy gets into all kinds of predicaments such as being lost in a water pipe or in the middle of a city. Children listen to Sammy's story on a computer-controlled cassette player. At certain points they are asked to help Sammy by moving him around with a joystick—through a pipe, over a wall, next to bugs to eat, and so on—until he gets home. This particular program has some limitations, but the idea is powerful and new programs may be quite worthwhile.

Programs in the exploratory/game category are quite diverse in their characteristics. However, many share the following:

PURPOSE:

To develop creativity, divergent thinking, and problem solving, facilitate the acquisition of skills and knowledge, and motivate interest in learning.

METHODOLOGY:

1. Nonlinear.

2. Exploratory, discovery oriented.
3. Format: Provide a set of tools or a miniature (often fantasy) world that children use for explorations and productive play.

STRENGTHS:
1. Utilizes and develops convergent and divergent abilities.
2. Is motivating and highly interactive.
3. Promotes social interaction and true discovery learning; children solve an actual problem that they pose themselves.
4. Is individualized in terms of self-directed learning.
5. Permits a wide range of teaching strategies to be employed.
6. Can be used again and again.
7. Reflects real-world use of computers.

WEAKNESSES:
1. Goals and objectives are not always clear.
2. Does not ensure that students are responding correctly.
3. Is relatively more difficult to use effectively.
4. If use is not well planned, can degenerate into little more than "playing with the computer."
5. Does not handle record keeping.
6. Is variable on requirements for computer access.
7. Teachers cannot easily create their own exploratory or game programs without extensive instruction in programming.

The most important question a teacher should ask—about all computer programs, but especially about exploratory/game programs—is, "*Why* am I buying (or using) this program?" Not all interesting-looking games help children to achieve important educational objectives. Studies have shown that the use of games raises achievement, *if* they are carefully selected to match curricular goals (Baker, Herman, & Yeh, 1981; Kraus, 1981). Otherwise, they either make no difference or lower achievement (probably because children spend less time learning). (What principles from chapter 1 should be operating here?)

BEYOND CAI

Other exploratory computer programs stretch the boundaries of what is commonly considered CAI and better fit the metaphor of "computer as tool." As one example, Early Games for Young Children (Counterpoint Software) includes a simple, but interesting, drawing program. A 3- to 6-year-old child presses any key. If the key was toward the right side of the keyboard, one small block or square on the screen is colored in toward the right. A key (e.g., "1") to the upper left would move the drawing toward that corner and so on. The color can be changed. Pictures can be saved.

Other programs allow children to compose music; write and revise stories; choose different segments of stories and see them animated on the screen; send messages to each other, even over long distances; build minature electronic machines on the screen and watch them run; save and retrieve information, like an electronic filing system; make charts or graphs easily; and so on. These exciting applications of computers will be discussed throughout the remainder of this book.

WHAT DOES RESEARCH SAY?

Several extensive reviews of the research concerning the effectiveness of computer assisted instruction have been conducted (Billings, 1983; Bracey, 1982; Chambers & Sprecher, 1980; Edwards, Norton, Taylor, Weiss, & Dusseldorp, 1975; Fletcher, Suppes, & Jamison, 1972; Forman, 1982; Hartley, 1978; Kearsley, Hunter, & Seidel, 1983; Madgidson, 1978; O'Donnell, 1982b; Visonhaler & Bass, 1972). Most of them combine results from all grade levels; however, they provide directions for early education. There is general agreement on the following points:

1. Computers can be used to make instruction more effective; the use of CAI either improves performance or shows no difference when compared with traditional classroom approaches, regardless of the type of CAI, computers, or measurement instruments used; it is approximately equivalent to individual tutoring.
2. CAI usually yields this improved performance in less time than traditional instruction.
3. Computers can make the learning experience more exciting, satisfying, and rewarding for learner and teacher; students have a positive attitude toward CAI, frequently accompanied by increased motivation, attention span, and attendance.
4. Students given CAI lessons may not retain as much information.
5. Computers do not stifle the creative process, nor are they dehumanizing.
6. None of these benefits is inherent in CAI; rather, they depend on the abilities of the professionals involved—CAI is most effective when it is used as an adjunct under the control of the classroom teacher.
7. It is still not known *why* CAI is effective, or *how* to individualize instruction or maximize the positive effects.
8. Teacher training must be radically altered and updated.
9. There is a dire need for quality courseware and new instructional design methodologies for technological media.
10. Computers have dramatically changed the entire field of education and educational research, and yet the potential of CAI has only begun to be realized.

Some Final Points to Consider

1. Limitations are *present-day* limitations. There is progress being made in developing intelligent computer-assisted instruction (ICAI), which will have the capability to understand the learner and serve as an intelligent, sensitive tutor. The problem is complex: the computer must possess models of (a) learners and their knowledge, (b) the knowledge an expert would have, and (c) teaching strategies. However, recent interdisciplinary efforts involving psychologists, educators, and computer scientists show promising signs of progress.

2. The CAI categories overlap in many ways, and good computer programs often combine elements of each. In fact, quality programs of the future might well inject a bit of tutoring into any gamelike drill exercise, or start out with a simulation or tutorial and then provide—within the same programs—tools for children to use to solve resulting problems.
3. Each category has its own characteristics, its own strengths and weaknesses, and thus there are particular situations in which each should and should not be used. A balance of approaches is needed. Table 2–1 presents a summary of the categories, including suggestions for their use.
4. Every category of software will be used more effectively if you spend time using it alone first, getting used to it, and checking to see whether there might be interpretation problems.
5. Children need to know exactly *how* to use and *why* they are using a program. It is too easy, once you understand a program, to assume too much knowledge on the children's part. One child worked with moderate success on a same/different visual discrimination program for two days before the teacher discovered that he was pressing the key for "same" *every time*. She assumed he needed practice (he got about half correct!); actually, he did not know about the "different" key!

TABLE 2–1   Summary of CAI Categories

Drill and Practice
Purpose: To provide practice.
Methodology: Individualized, self-paced, linear, repetitious practice.
Strengths: Is an efficient skill builder, provides feedback, motivates, is easy to use, may keep records, is simple enough that teachers can create own programs
Weaknesses: usually utilizes only low-level skills, narrow pedagogy, may not develop concepts, demands considerable computer access.
Appropriate Use: For situations in which there exists a set of essential skills that necessitate intensive practice with immediate feedback. These skills should be those that have been shown to support the development of higher-level concepts, for example, basic arithmetic skills and immediate word recognition. Following the established principles, use *only as much drill as needed* to achieve the objective(s).
Suggestions for Use:
1. Drill should be used immediately *after* an understanding of the concepts has been developed.
2. Children should have the intent to memorize and respond automatically.
3. Use short, frequent sessions in conjunction with regular conceptual review.
4. Introduce only a few new facts/skills at a time.
5. Vary drill activities and ensure that enthusiasm remains high.
6. Praise children and keep visible records (e.g., simple charts). Make sure that the children develop strong self-concepts as they develop skills.
7. Make sure that the children practice only those skills on which they need practice.
8. Practice those skils that require immediate feedback.
9. If computer resources are limited, have children take turns (two or three at a time on a computer, depending on the program).
10. Ultimately, you, not the machine, should determine how much and what kind of drill is needed. Also, let the student have some control over the use of the program. Children need to begin to "learn how to learn."

Tutorials
Purpose: To teach a topic.
Methodology: Linear, with branching; Socratic dialogue.

Strengths: Promotes active involvement, is individualized, provides self-paced instruction, provides feedback, is useful for review, is easy to use, may keep records, is possible for teachers to create own programs.

Weaknesses: Has narrow pedagogy and limited range of feedback, may promote shallow understandings, demands considerable computer access.

Appropriate Use: For situations in which a well-defined set of information must be acquired.

Suggestions for Use:

1. Choose topics that lend themselves to a focused, Socratic questioning approach.
2. Use tutorials alongside other instruction and for review.
3. Do not overuse.
4. Discuss the content of the program with chldren, or otherwise ensure that the concepts they are acquiring are complete and accurate.
5. If appropriate, let children work together on the computer. Consider social and emotional goals—ensure cooperation and success.
6. Consider programs that employ other media such as tape cassettes, speech synthesizers, and video disks.
7. Be very critical of the programs you select (see Chapter 7). Use child development as a guide to appropriateness.
8. Let the student have some responsibility and freedom in directing his or her own work with tutorials.
9. Make sure that you have access to enough computer time to use the program with your students. Also ask, "Is this a high-priority use?"

Simulation

Purpose: To develop problem-solving ability, intuition about situations, and concepts.

Methodology: Nonlinear, discovery oriented, provides a model of some aspect of the world.

Strengths: Allows exploration of events not otherwise accessible, is motivating and realistic, facilitates social interaction and discovery learning, is individualized, allows a wide range of teaching strategies, requires only limited computer access, reflects real-world application of computers.

Weaknesses: Does not ensure students are responding correctly, is more difficult to use, necessitates extensive planning, does not keep records, is only a partial copy of reality, does not involve the "whole child," does not permit teachers to create easily.

Appropriate Use: to explore events and situations that are too dangerous, expensive, complex, or time consuming to experience directly. Following the established principles, *do not simulate that which can and should be experienced directly* as a replacement for that experience.

Suggestions for Use:

(Most simulations presently available are appropriate for older or more mature children. The following suggestions are made with these simulations in mind, but can easily be adapted for other types of simulations.)

1. Do not use simulations as simple games. Following the principles of the first chapter, integrate simulations into wider units of study.
2. Try out the simulation first yourself, and then with a small group of students so that you can anticipate questions and problems.
3. Introduce the simulation with another trial run with the whole class so that everyone understands the procedures and general purpose of the program.
4. Have students work in small groups for discussing the issues involved and making decisions.
5. If all students are not using the simulation at the same time, have other assignments for those not working with the computer that students can complete independently.
6. Have each group of students divide responsibilities in working with the program. Discuss what these might be and how they might be assigned. Simulations should develop social skills as well as academic skills.

7. As the unit develops, use guided questioning to lead students to develop concepts and strategies that help them succeed with the simulations. One useful strategy is to change only one factor or variable at a time to observe its effects.
8. Also have whole-class discussions comparing the strategies of different groups along with the results of those strategies, and the assumptions that lie behind the simulations.
9. Try out new strategies that have been developed by the class.
10. In general, discuss what was learned. Many children who work with Oregon maintain, "You almost can't ever make it." Their teacher explained that the program is based on the experiences of real people—most of whom did not make it.
11. Have students read more about the subject of the simulation and report on their readings. The simulation could then be checked for accuracy.
12. Ensure that students understand the difference between the simulation and reality.
13. Use child development as a guideline to assess if children are ready to learn from a particular simulation.

Exploratory/Game
Purpose: To develop creativity, problem-solving ability, and knowledge; to motivate.
Methodology: Nonlinear, discovery oriented, provides a miniature world or a set of tools for explorations and productive play.
Strengths: Develop convergent and divergent abilities, motivates, facilitates social interaction and discovery learning, is individualized, allows a wide range of teaching strategies, can be used repeatedly, reflects real-world application of computers.
Weaknesses: Goals not always well developed, does not ensure that students are responding correctly, is more difficult to use, necessitates extensive planning, use can become trivial, does not keep records, does not permit teachers to create easily.
Appropriate Use: To achieve goals related to the development of independence, self-direction in learning, creativity, problem solving, positive self-concept, positive attitude toward learning.
Suggestions for Use:
1. Know what your goals are in using an exploration/game program.
2. Integrate explorations/games into the curriculum. Match games with your educational objectives.
3. Play the game yourself first. Then demonstrate it to the whole class.
4. Establish "class experts" who can help others play the game.
5. Through questioning, lead students to develop strategies that help them to succeed with the game.
6. Also have whole-class discussions comparing the strategies of different groups along with the results of those strategies.
7. Try out the new strategies as a class.
8. Discuss what was learned. Make sure that students understand what *is* to be learned.
9. To help the whole child develop, encourage children to play games together. Make the experience a positive one socially and emotionally as well as intellectually.

THINK ABOUT

1. What are the advantages and disadvantages of using the program *First Words* with toddlers?
2. List the strengths and weaknesses of the *Punctuation* tutorial. How would you improve it? What else would you need to know to do an extensive evaluation?
3. Which categories of CAI seem the most in tune with the characteristics of young children?

4. Reexamine Table 2–1. Which pairs of categories are similar in their characteristics? What title would you give to the pairs?
5. Which weaknesses of each category are *intrinsic* to that approach? Which are results of a misuse or mismanagement of the approach.
6. Is there ever any age before which *no* simulations should be used with children? (Before answering, consider this: What is the nature of a nursery rhyme?)
7. Which category of CAI would you use to teach letter/sound correspondence? The concept of patterning? Values? Why?
8. Which category of CAI would you use with a bright student who was, because of past experiences with arithmetic, not interested in mathematics? Why?
9. Debate: "Discussing strategies used in simulations and games is too difficult for young (preschool? primary grade?) children. To do this would ignore the findings of child development research."
10. Debate: "Will arcade drill and practice promote aggressive behavior or motivate the learning of important skills?"

CURRICULUM CONSTRUCTION CORNER
11. Plan one unit around a simulation.

ANNOTATED BIBLIOGRAPHY

Anderson, R. E. (1980). Computer simulation games, exemplars. In R. E. Horn & A. Cleaves (eds.), *The guide to simulations/games for education and training* (4th ed.). Beverly Hills, CA: Sage Publications.

Roberts, N., Anderson, D. F., Deal, R. M., Garet, M. S., & Shaffer, W. A. (1983). *Introduction to computer simulation: The system dynamics approach.* Reading, MA: Addison-Wesley.

Wilson, C. (1981, February). Simulation: Is it right for you? *Personal Computing,* 5(2), 73–75.

> Anderson provides descriptions of simulations, along with some theoretical background and guidelines. The simulations are mostly designed for college applications, but the discussion should be useful. The Roberts book is a complete reference on simulations. Wilson provides an introduction.

Dugdale, S. (1983, March). There's a green glob in your classroom. *Classroom Computer News,* pp. 40–43.

> Dugdale discusses mathematical computer games that she calls "intrinsic models"—the game centers on the mathematics to be learned. The concepts are more appropriate for the intermediate grades, but the discussion of intrinsic models is significant for all ages. Could these games be adapted for young children?

Harper, D. O., & Stewart, J. H. (eds.). (1983). *Run: Computer education,* pp. 107–143. Monterey, CA: Brooks/Cole.

Olds, H. F., Jr. (1981). How to think about computers. In B. R. Sadowski & C. Lovett (eds.), *Using computers to enhance teaching and improve teacher centers,* pp. 13–29. Houston: University of Houston.

Taylor, R. P. (1980). *The computer in the school: Tutor, tool, tutee.* New York: Teachers College Press.

> Several chapters in Harper and Stewart discuss CAI. Olds and Taylor offer stimulating discussions of CAI and other computer uses.

Holmes, G. (1982). Computer-assisted instruction: A discussion of some of the issues for would-be implementors. *Educational Technology, 22*(9), 7–13.

This article raises questions and issues regarding the use of CAI and provides a good report of the available literature.

Howe, J. A. M., & du Boulay, B. (1979). Microprocessor-assisted learning: Turning the clock back? *PLET, 16*(3), 240–246.

The authors argue that programs that attempt to be surrogate teachers (drill and tutorial) will not be useful (this represents "turning the clock back") but that simulations might. Do you agree?

3

MANAGING THE CLASSROOM WITH COMPUTERS

Miss Williams was pleased. After only a week, her first grade class was working smoothly on the new reading program (*The Reading Machine;* SouthWest EdPsych). They were receiving individual help, tailored specifically for each student. She leaned back and remembered how hard it was to use that reading management system her school had tried a few years ago. It had seemed like a good idea: assign children each to an exact skill level, let them work individually on an area of need, test them every week, keep track of their progress, and record, and record, and . . . that's the main thing Miss Williams remembered—the paperwork! She couldn't recall actually teaching her students very much. Shaking off the noontime nightmare, she turned back to her work. The screen displayed a menu.

```
                    TEACHER'S MENU
     1.  ADD A STUDENT
     2.  CHANGE A STUDENT
     3.  DELETE A STUDENT
     4.  REVIEW STUDENTS
     5.  PRINT STUDENTS
     6.  CLEAR SCORES
     7.  SET OPTIONS
     8.  RUN DRILL
     WHICH? __

          60 STUDENTS MAXIMUM
          23 STUDENTS NOW USED
          37 STUDENTS AVAILABLE
```

She selected "4." The screen showed.

PSWD	NAME	O S	PL	AD	RE	AT	CO
CAR1	CARRIE	5 A	12	13	6	12	8
EDD	ED D.	5 E	20	18	21	—	—

She was used to the abbreviations by now (although she still wondered why a simple key wasn't provided). "PSWD" was each student's password. "O" was the number of the objective that student was working on, "S" was the section letter. Carrie was assigned to 5-A, "Given a picture and a target word missing the beginning consonant (C, G, D, S or Y), the student will press the missing letter on the keyboard." Ed's 5-E was the same, except that any consonant might be missing. The next three columns listed the number of Problems per Level presented to each student before the lesson ends, the number of problems each student needs to complete correctly to ADvance automatically to the next level, and the number of problems each student needs to complete correctly before being REinforced by being allowed to choose one of six computer games to play for 1 minute. The final two columns list the number of problems ATtempted and the total number COrrect.

This morning, Carrie attempted 12 problems and responded correctly to 8 of them. Reading was not a strong subject for her, so Miss Williams had set the reinforcement level at 5 to help keep her motivated and had placed the advancement number *higher* than the number of problems presented so that the program would *not* move her to a higher level automatically. In this way, Miss Williams can check to make sure Carrie is confident at level 5-A before she meets a new challenge. An avid reader (and computer enthusiast), Ed doesn't need reinforcement. He can handle many more problems in a sitting and can be expected to achieve a high level of mastery. He had not worked on the computer this morning, but Miss Williams noticed that he had been automatically advanced from level 5-D, at which he had been working yesterday, to level 5-E.

Satisfied, Miss Williams pressed the RETURN key and, in response to the TEACHER'S MENU, typed 1 to add the name of a student who just transferred into her class. The screen displayed:

```
ADD A STUDENT        STUDENT PASSWORD: JJJ
STUDENT NAME: JOHN—JOHN JONES
```

After she typed his name, the screen showed

```
OBJECTIVE LEVEL
1.  LETTER MATCH CAPITALS
2.  LETTER MATCH LOWERCASE
3.  ALPHABET SEQUENCING
4.  MATCHING WORDS
5.  BEGINNING SOUNDS
6.  ENDING SOUNDS
7.  SHORT VOWELS MEDIAL
8.  CONSONANT BLENDS
9.  LONG VOWELS
Ø.  CONSONANT DIGRAPHS
```

Miss Williams began talking to herself silently, making professional decisions as she responded to the program's requests for information.

"Based on his cumulative records, he has probably already mastered sequencing the alphabet, but because he's new, I'd rather start him out on something he'll be confident and successful with," she thought as she pressed 3. The list disappeared, revealing

```
3.  ALPHABET SEQUENCING
SECTION LETTER:  _____
A.  A–H
B.  I–P
C.  Q–Z
D.  A–Z
```

She pressed D. The program asked her for more information:

PROBLEMS PER LEVEL: 10	He could probably do more at a sitting, but we'll work up to that.
ADVANCE AFTER 10 CORRECT	Make sure that he *has* mastered this before going on.
REINFORCE AFTER 5 CORRECT	This is quite frequent; we'll get him interested in and familiar with the program and then drop the reinforcement off a bit.

Miss Williams decided to spend the rest of her planning period on the computer. First she used her computer filing system to help organize interest groups for next week's library project (Chapter 14 will discuss these systems in detail). She entered the results of yesterday's math test into her computerized grade-book program and noted the average of the class for the test and the averages of the students for math. She had been concerned about three students. Of these, two were improving consistently, but one was not. She had the computer print out progress reports for all three to share with parents. She used another computer program to generate math worksheets tailored specifically for these three children. Now that the end of the year was approaching, these programs would be doubly useful. The grade-book program would provide her with a complete report on the class and individuals for each subject.

The next day, Ed was in his glory. The scheduling program that Miss Williams used at the beginning of the day showed that it was Ed's turn to type the attendance into the computer *and* he was first for a reading lesson. After he typed in the names of his absent friends, he began to work on reading programs. In response to the program's request for a PASSWORD, he typed EDD. The program printed HELLO, ED, and asked him to place the "picture disk" in the disk drive. Automatically assigned to level 5-E, Ed was presented with a picture of a book and the following:

```
__OOK
FILL IN THE MISSING LETTER.
```

Ed typed B. A "B" appeared in the box and the program printed:

THAT'S RIGHT, ED.
YOU HAVE ONE CORRECT, ED.

Ed worked through his 20 problems quickly. When he made mistakes, the computer would print

WRONG, ED! THE ANSWER IS T. TRY AGAIN.

Talking to him later about his three errors, Miss Williams realized that the problem was not so much with Ed's phonics as it was with several hard-to-recognize line drawings. She made a note to write to the company and advanced Ed to the next level manually.

HELPING TEACHERS TO HELP STUDENTS

Miss Williams uses the computer to help her manage her classroom in a variety of ways. The reading program provides one example of computer-managed instruction (CMI), an educational approach in which a computer information management system supports the teacher's functions of directing the educational program. It actually helps the teacher to help students, unlike CAI programs (or the CAI *component* of programs that also include a management component), which help students directly. CMI programs vary in how they perform this function. Several different programs will be briefly described.

Some complex management systems test students, evaluate the tests, prescribe appropriate work, and record progress within a specific area of the curriculum. One such system, designed for students from first to third grade, manages mathematics work in basic concepts of whole numbers, addition and subtraction of whole numbers, problem solving, measurement, time, money, and geometry (Classroom Mangement System—Mathematics A Scientific Research Associates, SRA). This system tests specific skills defined by objectives. It evaluates each student's performance on the tests and locates exact areas of weakness. It then prescribes remedial work based on the objectives that each student has not yet mastered. The prescriptions are keyed to six major basal math textbooks and several SRA programs.

When first sitting down to use the program, the teacher types in his or her own name, the class name, a code word that allows only the teacher access to information, and information on each student in the class. The teacher then chooses to which textbooks and SRA materials prescriptions should refer. The teacher's own materials, games, activities, and texts can also be added to the list. At any time during the year, material can be added to this file.

Students first take a survey, a wide-ranged "placement" test. They can do this directly on the computer or, if computer time is at a premium, on reproduced paper copies, entering their responses on the computer at a scheduled time. If the survey indicates a possible area of need, the student is directed to the appropriate probe test to pinpoint specific weaknesses. If questions are missed on the probe test, a prescription is given. If, after completing the material, the student fails the probe test again, he or she must see the teacher. The teacher can also customize the system by omitting certain surveys or probes for the class or for individuals. The teacher also decides if the prescription should be given when a specific problem is missed or when the entire test is completed.

The teacher can call up the following records: class lists, survey or probe status reports, individual student reports, class records, grouping reports, graph grouping reports that provide a bar graph of the number of students working on each probe, and prescription reports.

Another drill and practice program, *Alphabetization* (Milliken), includes a fairly extensive management component. If the teacher enters her password, she is presented with the following:

```
A.   STUDENT MANAGEMENT PAGE
B.   CLASS MANAGEMENT PAGE
C.   REVIEW SEQUENCE AS A STUDENT
WHICH LETTER?
A
```

The screen then displays

```
WHICH NUMBER?
1.   ADD A STUDENT
2.   DELETE A STUDENT
3.   MAKE STUDENT ASSIGNMENTS
4.   LIST THE STUDENTS
5.   REVIEW STUDENT PROGRESS
6.   DELETE A STUDENT PASSWORD
3
```

Typing "3," the teacher sees

```
NAME OF STUDENT?
JOHN–JOHN
(PROBLEM LEVELS 1–65)
```

			JOHN			
ASGN	BEG	END	ML	FL	MP	STATUS
1.	Ø	Ø	70	30	6	NONE

```
WHICH ASSIGNMENT NUMBER?              1
BEGINNING LEVEL NUMBER?              1
ENDING LEVEL NUMBER?                15
NEW MASTERY LEVEL =                 90
NEW FAILURE LEVEL =                 50
NEW MINIMUM PROBLEMS PER LEVEL =    10
```

The screen displays

JOHN-JOHN
(PROBLEM LEVELS 1–65)

```
                           JOHN
ASGN   BEG   END   ML   FL   MP   STATUS
1       1    15    90   50   10   NONE
```

When John–John works with this program, he will be asked to type in his name and password and will be automatically started on the assignment. It will start at problem level 1 and end at problem level 15. The mastery level will be 90 percent correct. If he falls below 50 percent, he will be rerouted to an easier level. He will be given at least ten problems at each level. When he is finished, the computer will automatically update his records and assignments. The teacher can review the progress of her students. She would then see what assignments were completed, in progress, and finished. The report would include the percentage correct at each level and a simple bar graph for each assignment.

Other options allow the teacher to make assignments for entire classes at a time rather than individual students. From the menu, suppose that B, CLASS MANAGEMENT PAGE, were chosen. The teacher would see

```
B.   CLASS MANAGEMENT PAGE
WHICH NUMBER?
  1.  ADD A CLASS
  2.  DELETE A CLASS
  3.  MAKE ASSIGNMENT FOR A CLASS
  4.  DELETE ALL ASSIGNMENTS FOR A CLASS
  5.  LIST THE CLASSES
  6.  REVIEW STUDENT PROGRESS FOR A CLASS
  7.  SET OPTIONS FOR A CLASS
```

Choosing number 3, the teacher would have gone through a series of steps just like those listed, but now the assignment would have been made for the whole class. If 6 were chosen, the teacher could review the progress of the class, printing it on paper if that was desired. Number 7 is a valuable tool for individualizing the program for diverse populations, as it allows the teacher to select if the children will be reinforced by animation (cartoon-like characters more appropriate for younger or less mature students) or text.

While useful, Miss Williams's reading program has limited management capabilities. For example, she has to copy each student's records by hand at the end of each day and clear the scores for the next day. Her program does not suggest grouping patterns. Other, more comprehensive CMI systems can accomplish these and other tasks. The teacher may ask for individual performance profile reports for herself, the student, or parents. These reports can be on specific topics or on work done between certain dates. Reports for the whole class are also available. Based on the same information, this program can recommend grouping patterns. This makes it feasible for the teacher to work with *flexible* achievement, special needs, and interest groups. This is something that teachers generally want to do, but find very difficult to organize. The teachers at one school utilize the computer in this way in five curriculum areas and regroup students every two weeks in reading, math, and science. Without a computer, regrouping 200 students in reading used to require 10 hours of work from each of five teachers. The computer recommends a more complete grouping in less than 1 hour (during which time it works by itself).

The program can keep track of grades. Teachers can enter individuals' scores through the keyboard or enter a group of students' grades with a sheet scanner. Scores are automatically entered into the students' records. Each grade may be assigned a value, or weighted, for "averaging" and final marking.

Educators can enter any curriculum they wish for the program to store. Based on the curriculum, the program can diagnose students' performances and prescribe appropriate activities. Each of the objectives of a curriculum may be keyed to tests or test items. When a test is scored, a prescription or "recommended next step" is prepared automatically based on the student's performance and the teachers' previously entered description of what actions should be taken following various test scores. This information is given to the student when the tests are scored. The program stores test scores, automatically updates student records, and performs test item analyses. As each item can be keyed to an instructional objective, the results can be reported by objective.

Many programs include various features. *The Reading Machine*, described at the beginning of the chapter, also lets the teacher control other options, for example, bells and other sounds, a key clicker (the keys click like a typewriter when pressed), and even a cassette tape option that includes spoken words in the lesson. A list of some available mathematics and language arts programs for young children that include management functions is provided in Table 3–1.

What does research tell us?   Obtaining guidance on the use of CMI with young children is difficult for at least two reasons. First, results of the few studies concerning CMI are suggestive, but hardly conclusive. Second, the students participating in these studies were usually in the intermediate grades or higher. However, some implications and directions for future work can be found. In an investigation involving kindergarten to eighth grade students, Brebner, Hallworth, McIntosh, and Wontner (1980) reported that teachers, children, and parents all benefited from the teaching of reading with CMI and CAI. Teachers were freed from administering, scoring, and recording tests and used the extra time to plan individualized instruction. Studies with older children (Haugo, 1981; Lecarme & Lewis, 1975; Lutz & Taylor, 1981; McIsaac & Baker, 1981; Overton, 1981; Spuck & Bozeman, 1978) support the use of CMI, at least tentatively.

Teachers can use and modify CMI programs efficiently to match the needs of children (Kieren, 1973). CMI systems can reduce time that teachers spend on planning and on clerical tasks, such as correcting tests and

TABLE 3–1 Examples of Commercial CAI Programs Possessing a CMI Component

Language Arts/Reading

CADPP (sponsored by U.S. Dept. of Education; contact D. Glowinski, Buckingham County
   Public Schools, P.O. Box 292, Dillwyn, VA 23936)
CARIS (Britannica)
Class-Computer Learning and Scoring System (Holt, Rinehart and Winston)
CMS/Reading (Skillcorp)
Computerized Management System (Skillcorp)
Diagnostic Prescriptive Systems (Learning Unlimited)
Diascriptive Reading (and others, Educational Activities)
Dolch Sight Word Acquisition Game (Richard Cummins Courseware)
First Words (Laureate Learning Systems)
Letter Recognition (and others such as *Vowels, Consonants, Word Families,* etc., Hartley)
MicroSystem80 (Borg-Warner)
MMICRO (Educational Progress Corp.)
PAL (Universal Systems)
PAVE (and several others, I/CT)
Reading 1 (Prism Software)
Spelling Bee & Reading Primer (and others, Edu-Ware)

Mathematics

Apple-Based Elementary Mathematics Classroom Learning System (Courses by Comput-
   ers and Swift Publishing Co.)
Basic Math Skills (Learning Systems Ltd.)
Basic Math System S (Mathware)
C-AIM (contact Dr. Thomas Bishop, Dept. of Computer Science, Mathematics, and Phys-
   ics, P.O. Box 70, State University, AR 72467)
CADPP (sponsored by U.S. Dept. of Education; contact D. Glowinski, Buckingham County
   Public Schools, P.O. Box 292, Dillwyn, VA 23936)
Classroom Management System (SRA)
Computerized Management System (Skillcorp)
Elementary Mathematics (Sterling Swift)
Fundamental Mathematics and Basic Math Facts Drill (and others, Random House)
General Mathematics Diagnostic (Educational Media Assoc.)
Gulp!! (and others, Milliken)
Learning About Numbers (C & C Software)
Math 1 (Prism Software)
Math Machine (SouthWest EdPsych)
Math Sequences (Milliken)
Mathematics Assessment/Prescriptive Edu-Disks (Reader's Digest)
Multiplication Facts Diagnostic (Disk Depot)
Prescriptive Math Drill (Hartley)
Telemath (Psychotechnics)
Whole Numbers (and other PLATO programs, Control Data Publishing)

Management Systems Without Curriculum Content (curriculum content entered by user)

Class Management System (Holt, Rinehart and Winston)
Curriculum Management System (Learning Tools)
Customized Instructional Management System (Random House)
Customized Prescriptions (Random House)
Detroit 80 Diagnostics (Prescision People)
E-Z Learner (Silicon Valley System)

reviewing records, and increase the time they spend instructing students, even if the teachers are only minimally familiar with computers (Bozeman, 1979; Ellis, 1978; Spuck & Bozeman, 1978). Results comparing classroom with CMI to those without it usually favor the former, both in terms of students' achievement and, more consistently, attitude toward the subject (Chanoine, 1977; Knight & Dunkleberger, 1977; Spuck & Bozeman, 1978). However, results have not been positive in every case, and positive results have not always been statistically significant (Bozeman, 1979; DeVault, 1981; Wilkins, 1975). There is some evidence that children react favorably to the CMI systems themselves, as have parents (Brebner et al., 1980; Cartwright & Derevensky, 1976). Personal and psychological factors have been found to be important to the success of CMI programs (Bozeman, 1978).

A few caveats are suggested. Achievement under CMI may not always be better than under traditional systems. Also, if the teacher does not control the system, his or her authoi y might be undermined.

The computer has been shown to be effective in monitoring, tracking, and reporting student progress, generating tests, testing students, and managing instructional programs, freeing teachers from these tasks. The increase in the use of microcomputers should bring an increase in worthwhile research concerning CMI; certainly the whole story is not yet told. Also, increased use should bring the development of more effective programs, especially if professional educators are actively involved in demanding and evaluating such programs.

What are the disadvantages and possible misuses of CMI? There may be disadvantages of CMI. For example, it may necessitate considerable access to computer facilities. Also, software has not yet been developed for all purposes, and complex programs are often difficult to develop for small systems. However, advances in technology may eliminate most of these limitations. Possibly more important are the abuses that, while not absolutely inherent in the approach, must be guarded against in any management system.

The reader is asked to form a mental opinion of two educational programs, the first being almost totally individualized instruction. Each student works at his or her own pace, on tailor-made lessons gauged to his or her level of difficulty. Feedback is provided immediately. No student is rushed by others students, for each is working at a different place in the curriculum. Students are virtually guaranteed success, because they are allowed to master each level of the curriculum before advancing to the next. Students are given dimensions of freedom and responsibility.

The second program views the school as a factory. Teachers and administrators design and produce the product, students. These students are tested constantly. If they fall below a level of mastery, they are required to work alone until they are ready to be retested. The curriculum is teacher centered and consists of thousands of minute behavioral objectives. The students have few choices about what and how to learn.

If the reader shares many of the opinions of most teachers of young children, the first program sounds very attractive, whereas the second is an anathema to them. However, there is a problem with this interpretation. **Both descriptions are of the SAME type of program based on one set of principles.** Both describe individualized instructional programs. The first merely looks on the "bright" side, the second at the "dark" side. Which side represents "truth"?

Management systems in general, and large mainframe computer management systems in particular, are a result of the convergence of three themes of American education thought: individualization, behavioral objectives, and educational technology (Baker, 1971, 1978). They attempt to individualize instruction, provide immediate feedback, and ensure success. However, the skills management systems approach was borrowed from the business world, and many programs are based on a view of education that would offend many educators of young children—the school as a factory. Following this model, goals are specified as observable behaviors, students' initial capabilities are assessed and instruction prescribed, performance is continuously monitored, and so on. There are several consequences of this approach. It stresses assessment of observable, fractionalized behaviors. Most individualization concerns only the rate of progress. Materials can become confused with original purposes and become the ends instead of the means. The approach may tend to emphasize the content rather than the process, the logical rather than the psychological, the mechanical rather than the meaningful, and organized structure rather than room for incidental growth. The hidden strengths of group instruction—the power of working in groups, the positive pacing effect of the traditional class, and the orchestration of skills by the teacher (Lipson, 1976)—tend to be eliminated. Some professionals may trust the system rather than their own judgment and may lose control over their program. However, the bright side still shines, and although research does not unequivocally support individualized approaches, some positive results have been offered (Horak, 1981). Is there a resolution to these conflicting perspectives and research results? As usual, no easy answers exist. But thoughtful evaluation and use of CMI systems can maximize the advantages and minimize the disadvantages.

Evaluating and using CMI programs. First, CMI programs that are considered for adoption should be critically examined. The following questions should be asked. (Many of these questions are targeted toward complex CMI systems and should be adapted for smaller programs.)

MANAGEMENT PROCESSES

1. How is instruction "individualized"?
2. Does the program emphasize higher-level management functions, such as planning, organizing, and coordinating as well as higher-level educational goals?
3. Do recommendations for instructional grouping allow for teacher review and approval?

4. Are the reporting capabilities adequate? For instance, can the system produce reports on each sequence separately and on the entire program if desired? Can it produce graphs in reporting to teachers and students?

CURRICULAR CONTENT

1. Are curricula responsive and flexible?
2. Are there easy ways of developing and inputing additional curricula?
3. Are the tests valid and of high quality?
4. Does the diagnosis and prescription structure operate at a trivially low level, or does it attempt to analyze large units or patterns of responses?
5. Is diagnosis specific and clearly related to content?

STUDENT AND TEACHER CONSIDERATIONS

1. Is the approach modeled after the factory, or does it take a broader view of education?
2. Has it been tested in schools?
3. Is it sensitive to the learning styles and needs of different children?
4. Are personal and psychological factors considered?
5. Do the teachers involved *want* the system?
6. Is the teacher the manager of the system?
7. Last, but certainly not least, if the microcomputer resources are limited, what priority is given to this use?

Teachers planning to *use* a CMI system should also keep these questions in mind. No system will meet each of these criteria perfectly. The teacher using the system must compensate for any deficiencies. Most important, the teacher must use the system as a single tool, keeping the responsiblity for professional decisions with himself or herself rather than with the system. In keeping with the principles stated in this book, one such decision should be to maintain the integrity and wholeness of every domain of the curriculum, emphasizing the higher-level, meaningful aspects. Reading is *not* the development of a large number of specific skills; doing mathematics is *not* the ability to complete isolated exercises. CMI can help children to develop these abilities efficiently (which are, of course, important components of reading and mathematics); it should not be allowed to permit students, teachers, and parents to mistake these abilities for true understanding.

CMI can help teachers by providing timely and appropriate information so as to improve decision making (Spuck & Owen, 1974). The growing demand for accountability can thus be better met (Barrett & Hannafin, 1982).

However, good teachers have always found ways of preventing clerical tasks from interfering with teaching and learning. If CMI is to be used, teachers should ensure that it improves the learning environment for children and that it does not replace more valuable uses of computer resources. Used thoughtfully, CMI can be integrated into the curriculum, permitting other computer-based instruction, such as tutorials and computer programming, to be incorporated (Baker, 1981).

HELPING TEACHERS

Besides helping to manage instruction, computers can assist teachers with a variety of management tasks. Many of these uses benefit the teacher more directly than the student, although it is hoped that teachers will use the time saved to create a better learning environment for children. As usual, general-purpose computers are impressive in their ability to perform many useful functions. Table 3–2 lists some of the ways in which computers can help teachers to manage their classrooms.

Testing. From your own days as a student, you are probably familiar with some examples of computer-scored testing. Students are given standardized tests, and their answer sheets are sent to the testing service where they are scanned, scored, and analyzed by computer. Computer-prepared reports are sent back to the school. The school personnel do not deal directly with the computer. This may be convenient in some ways; however, it also means that the teachers have little control over the process and cannot use it to meet their own specific needs. Microcomputers can be used in the schools to perform a variety of management tasks, including scoring tests and administering individualized test instruments.

Commercial programs are available for scoring tests (e.g., *EXAM-ANALYSIS SYSTEM*, Microphys; *Grading a Test (The Easy Way)*, Aladdin Software; *HEI Score*, HEI, Inc.; *SATS—Stand Alone Test Scoring*, BMS DATA). Similar, but simpler, programs have also appeared in the literature, needing only to be entered by the teacher (e.g., Koelewyn, 1983).

Test-generating programs are available. (See Cavin, 1982; brief but illustrative examples are also provided by Hart, 1981/1982, and Eisenberg, 1977, although the test content is suitable for older students). Computers really "show their stuff" in administering "tailored testing" (McKinley & Reckase, 1980). The computer selects items during the testing that are appropriate for the student based on his or her previous responses. Errors of measurement are minimized, testing time is shortened, frustration is reduced, reliability is improved, and total test information gathered is increased. Some programs also provide students feedback while they are taking the test so that it is a learning experience too.

One interesting program is a self-administered computer spelling test (Hasselbring & Owens, 1983). Most spelling tests provide only grade equivalents or the like. Diagnostic tests that give an analysis of spelling error patterns require considerable expertise and a large amount of scoring time. The microcomputer can administer this type of test, analyze students' errors, and print the results. The computer drives a tape cassette that presents a 40-item word list. Students enter their responses directly on the computer. The program checks their spelling and compares any errors to each of 13 error types. After they are finished, the computer provides the teacher with a comprehensive summary of the test and a diagnostic error analysis. For instance, for one student, it might list the 20 correctly spelled words, the 20 incorrectly spelled words (including the student's spelling),

TABLE 3–2 Ways in Which Computers Can Help to Manage a Classroom

Managing Instruction
Supporting CAI programs with computer-managed instruction
Generating IEPs (individual education plans)
Planning projects
Scheduling

Managing Tests
Test scoring and analysis
Test generation and printing
Administering tests in an individualized, interactive situation

Aiding Communication
Grade contracting
Scheduling one-to-one time between teacher and student
Message handling

Organizing and Reporting Information About Students
Keeping attendance
Storing, analyzing, and reporting student records
Storing, sorting, and analyzing guidance records
Keeping class records (computerized grade books)
Generating reports to parents
Generating report cards
Detailed evaluation of instructional programs

Organizing and Reporting Information About the Classroom
Media reservations
Resource allocation
Purchase orders
Label or mailing list printing
Inventories (e.g., *School Inventory,* Bell & Howell)
Information storage and retrieval
Library circulation

the error types (e.g., 54 percent incorrect on digraphs and diphthongs), and the error tendencies (e.g., 16 letters substituted, 8 words with omissions, 5 words with order errors). *Math Doctor M.D.* (Modern Education Corporation) administers an individualized assessment on mathematics concepts and skills.

Materials generation. Several types of classroom materials can be generated by the computer. Certain printers can produce ditto masters and overhead transparencies. Computer-assisted graphics can generate slides or transparencies, with the advantages of speed of production, reduction in cost, ease of revision, and increased emphasis on design (Dayton, 1981). Other programs are capable of generating puzzles containing hidden words that are specified by the teacher (for instance, new vocabulary words from a unit of study), along with the solution, mazes, scrambled word games, spelling exercises, and word games (e.g., *Elementary Vocabulary/Spelling,* MECC; Crossword Magic, L & S Computerware), math worksheets (K–8 Math Worksheet generator, Radio Shack), or even reports to parents (*Parent Reporting,* Hartley).

Handling information. Clerical chores can often be handled by the computer. For instance, computerized grade books may assist in keeping track of absences, daily grades, and extra credit. They may provide test scores (weighted if desired), total grades, percentages, item analyses of tests, daily attendance and grade reports, notices of children who are failing, and individual cumulative records (Crouse, 1981; Hart, 1981/1982; Johnson, 1981). The following provides a sample run of such a program.

```
                        GRADEBOOK
    1.  ADD A STUDENT
    2.  DELETE A STUDENT
    3.  ENTER A GRADE
    4.  CHANGE A GRADE
    5.  LIST A GRADE
    6.  LIST A STUDENT'S GRADES
    7.  LIST A CLASS
    8.  GO TO SORTING MENU
    9.  GO TO UTILITIES MENU

    WHAT WOULD YOU LIKE TO DO? (TYPE A NUMBER)   ?1
    WHICH TEACHER?   ?MANNY
    WHICH SECTION?   ?2ND
    TYPE STUDENT'S NAME, FIRST NAME FIRST.
    TYPE 'STOP' TO RETURN TO MAIN MENU.
    STUDENT'S NAME? ?AMANDA BARKLY
    STUDENT'S NAME? ?SHARON GREEN
    STUDENT'S NAME? ?STOP
```

At this point, the computer would display the main menu again. If the teacher had chosen option number 8 from the original menu, records could have been sorted in alphabetical order by names or in numerical order by grades, a bar graph of this sorted information could have been printed, and so on. Option 9 allows the teacher to copy files, add and delete whole classes, change names and subjects, delete subjects, and so on. Averages can be obtained for one student in a particular subject or for the class on a particular subject, assignment, or test. More detailed statistics (e.g., standard deviations) are available if desired. The program can quickly generate honor rolls, class rank lists, and the like.

Numerous commercial programs are presently available. Table 3–3 lists a few. Teachers must of course evaluate these programs in terms of their performance capabilities. For example, would you like to be able automatically to: Drop the lowest grade? Make allowances for missed scores? Print out averages and standard deviations? Some, but not all, of these programs have such capabilities. A search of microcomputing journals and books often turns up listings of programs that a teacher can enter and use without purchasing "canned" programs (e.g., Doerr, 1979, pp. 141–148; Hedden, 1981; Teoh, 1981). Some teachers prefer to use a gen-

TABLE 3–3 Computerized Grade Books

Cactus Grade Book (SouthWest EdPsych)
Compugrade (Melcher Software)
The Electric Grade Book and Grading System Programs (Charles Mann and Associates)
Grade Averages (Educational Activities)
Grade Book (J & S Software)
Gradebook (Edusoft)
Gradebook (Management Systems Software)
Gradebook Supreme (Jahn Software)
Grade Computation (Life Science Associates)
Grade Keeper (Bertamax)
Gradekeeper and Multi Program Recordkeeper (Random House)
Grade Reporting (Bell & Howell)
Gradisk (John Wiley & Sons)
Instructor Gradebook (Serendity Systems)
Master Grades Program (Midwest Software)
Records: A Complete Grade System (Microsoftware Services)
Report Card (Sensible Software)
Teacher's Aid (Dr. Daley's Software)

Other companies selling attendance and/or grade reporting software include Americal Peripherals, Applied Educational Systems, C.E.R.F., Computer Resources, Inc., E.D.I.S. Systems, Educational Administrative Data Systems, Educational Connection, Educational Software and Marketing, Educational Timesharing Systems, Genesis Software, International Micro Systems, Micro-logic, Microphys, Microdynamics Educational Systems, Modern School Consultants, Mount Castor Industries, Powell Associates, School and Home CourseWare, School Management Systems, Softrend, Software Publishing Corp., Software Research Corp., and Vocational Education Productions.

eral-purpose electronic spreadsheet program (the "Calc" programs; see Lindahl, 1983).

Other articles describe lesson planning programs (e.g., Ingram, 1981). General-purpose filing systems are available that will store student records, inventories, library information, enrollment figures, budgets, and so on.

Record-keeping systems designed or suitable for use by educators include The Class Manager (SVE), Classfile (TYC Software), Notebook (*WINDOW*), Personal Record Keeping (from Microcomputers Corp.), and Rekord (Prism). Commercial programs are also available for keeping a school's attendance (e.g., Absentee Reporting 1, EDIS System, HARTS III, School and Home Courseware, School Attendance, Random House).

Finally, do not overlook the possibility of having children learn to use simple management systems. They might then use the computer to help them with their own work or to help you manage nonconfidential information such as inventories, schedules, or attendance. In keeping with the principles stated, however, the computer should only be used in these ways if students learn about powerful applications. If they see the computer as an instrument for boring, rather distasteful work, or if this experience supplants other meaningful computer experiences, this use is best ignored. Ways in which both teachers and students can use a simple but effective filing, or record keeping, system will be discussed in later chapters. Many other computer tools that are useful to teachers as well as students, such as word processing (writing) programs, will also be described in the appropriate chapter.

Whether the computer is used to help manage instruction or other aspects of the classroom, this type of application must be examined critically to ascertain if the use is compatible with the rest of the educational program and is a high priority. Given that it is, computer management can provide valuable assistance to the teacher.

THINK ABOUT

1. One professor argues that CMI will relieve teachers of tedious tasks and allow them more time for real teaching. Another maintains that good teachers have always found time for teaching and that poor teachers would not utilize the time anyway. With whom do you agree? Why?
2. What do you think about reinforcing children's correct responses by allowing them a minute of video game playing?
3. Do you agree or disagree that the research cited that was conducted with older children pertains to primary grade children? Why or why not?
4. Comment on the following statement: "Because testing could always be done with paper and pencil, computerized testing goes against this book's principle of giving priority to essential uses of the computer."
5. Do you think the computer will finally allow schools to truly individualize instruction? Why or why not? What does individualization mean to you?
6. Are there any options you would have liked to be added to those in the menus presented in this chapter? What are they?
7. It was stated that many of the disadvantages of CMI are not necessarily inherent in CMI itself. Describe *how* you would use a CMI system so you would avoid abusing it.
8. Work through the options described for one of the CMI programs and describe how (and why) you would set up the system for the following three children: a remedial child with a poor self-image, a bright but underachieving child, and a child who is achieving slightly above grade level.

ANNOTATED BIBLIOGRAPHY

Gorth, W. P., & Nassif, P. M. (1984, January). A comparison of microcomputer-based, computer-managed instruction (CMI) software programs (with an evaluation form). *Educational Technology*, pp. 28–32.

Hedges, William D. (1981, July–August). Lightening the load with computer-managed instruction. *Classroom Computer News*, pp. 34–35.

Spuck, Dennis W., & Bozeman, William C. (1980). A design for the evaluation of management information systems. *AEDS Journal, 14*, 30–44.

These authors provide checklists and models for evaluating computer management systems. *Educational Technology* features "Ed Tech Computer Programs," a column that provides programs you can type in and use. For example, the January 1984 issue contains programs for grading statistics and processing test scores.

4

WHAT SHOULD YOUNG CHILDREN (AND TEACHERS) KNOW ABOUT COMPUTERS?

"What happens when you load a program?"

"Well, what happens . . . this is the mouth [pointing to the tape cassette] and the computer eats the program off the tape. Then it goes through here [pointing to the cassette cable] like a straw, to the computer's stomach. Here's its face, [the TV monitor] like a big eye, and you can look in and see what's in the stomach. . . . Then when you say *run,* the computer's got the energy to run 'cause it ate the program. If you don't load the program, it can't run 'cause there's no energy to. . . . You know what else computers eat? Potato chips. I hear there's lots of chips in these things."

—Tony, age 8

"In the future, computers . . . will be like all the scientists in the world smushed into one."

—Ilana (Humphrey, 1982; p. 96)

"A computer is to play with. Like drawing and games . . . and you can learn from it. As long as the teacher doesn't make you, it's fun."

—Jeremy, age 5

SHOULD WE TEACH ABOUT COMPUTERS?

Should young children be introduced to ideas about what computers are and how they work? Some might argue that there is no reason to introduce concepts of high technology in the early grades and that students in these grades are not ready to understand these concepts. However, children *always* create theories about the things in their world. As the opening quotations illustrate, children form definite ideas about computers. The choice is not whether children will have impressions about computers but whether the impressions they have contribute to a full understanding of the nature of computers and their many uses. What should these impressions and ideas be and how should they be taught?

What about "computer literacy"? Should we be teaching children *about* computers because of their increasing ubiquity in our society? To help introduce a discussion of these issues, please answer the following questions yourself.

Fill in the Blank

1. What is a computer? _____

2. How does a computer work? _____

3. How many computers or computerized effects do working Americans come in contact with from the time they wake up to the time they reach their jobs? _____

4. About what percentage of workers in the United States perform jobs that do *not* involve material goods or services such as food production and delivery, selling merchandise, working on others' cars or houses, and so on, but rather involve *information* only? _____

5. What percentage of *today's* kindergarteners will work in jobs that involve the use of computers? _____

TRUE/FALSE

6. Most people do not need to know how airplanes or telephones work in order to use them; they do not need to know how computers work. _____

7. Enthusiasm about computers will come and go like every other "technological revolution" in education and society, from teaching machines to digital watches. _____

8. Talking about and using computers in school will lead children to be more like machines and less like people. _____

From the time Americans are awakened to the time they arrive at their place of work, they come into contact with at least 50 computerized devices or effects (Heller & Martin, 1982). These might include a minuscule computer mechanism in an alarm clock, microwave oven, or coffee pot; a computer-relayed telephone call; computer-controlled fuel intake in a car or computer-controlled traffic lights; a computerized watch; and so on. Once they arrive, over 50 percent of them work in information-related jobs (Molnar, 1981).

This is evidence of the latest "revolution" of the U.S. economy. The Industrial Revolution changed the country from a basically agricultural to a basically industrial society. The Information Revolution is changing the country from a producer of industrial goods and services to a provider of science, information, and knowledge. This information is increasingly handled by computers, and yet a National Science Foundation report indicates that the United States is becoming technologically illiterate.

This is a warning to our society as a whole. Furthermore, on an individual level, we must consider the possibility of human waste and suffering. Over 75 percent of today's kindergarten children will grow up to be employed in occupations involving the use of computers (West, 1983). Those children who are not able to function effectively in an information society will not be productive, happy members of that society—an unacceptable social and psychological cost. It has been said that ignorance of computers will render people as functionally illiterate as does ignorance of reading, writing, and arithmetic (Michaels, 1968). According to this line of thought, these illiterates will not only be limited in their choice of careers—three out of five of the fastest-growing jobs are in the computer industry—they will be isolated from a wealth of opportunities to gain information, new learning, social connections, entertainment, and so on. They will be denied use of the most powerful tool ever created for expanding the reach, creativity, and intellectual potential of humankind. There is a fear—all too valid—that the gap between those working creatively with computers and the rest of the population is growing. Therefore, it is no surprise that professionals have stressed the urgent need for teaching computer literacy in the schools (Molnar, 1981; National Council of Teachers of Mathematics, 1980; Papert, 1980) citing it as the next great crisis in American education (Luehrmann, 1980; Molnar, 1978).

It would appear that children must become computer literate. But to what level? Where and when should they learn this? These issues form the basis for the true/false questions presented at the outset. The opinions expressed in these questions raise important issues that deserve careful consideration; but the opinions rest on questionable assumptions. Those who believe that you do not have to understand either telephones or computers are partially correct. Each year people need to know less about the highly technical aspects of computers and more about how to *use* computers effectively. However, computers are an evolutionary step above other inventions. They do not extend human muscle; they extend human minds. They are not restricted to a narrow range of applications but, rather, are "general-purpose" machines that are almost infinitely adaptable.

Computers *will* permeate all areas of society. They *can* be used to expand children's knowledge of themselves, of others, and of the world, and they can do so in ways that humanize, rather than mechanize, education. It is the responsibility of educators of young children to use computers in interesting and developmentally appropriate ways. To do this, it is necessary to have (1) a working definition of "computer literacy"; (2) a scope and sequence of the topics and understandings appropriate for children of different ages; (3) background information, including basic understandings of the topics; and (4) teaching strategies and activities for presenting these topics to young children. The remainder of this chapter will present a definition and a scope and sequence; the next two chapters will provide background information and suggest approaches to teaching many of these topics.

What is Computer Literacy
for the Young Child?

The concept of "computer literacy" and notions about the effects of computers on education are so new that no single definition has been agreed upon. Some authorities emphasize computer *awareness,* or becoming knowledgeable about the effect of computers on our lives and our society:

> Computer literacy is "an awareness and understanding of the computer, its role in society, and its impact on education."
>
> Holly O'Donnell

> Computer literacy refers to a knowledge of the non-technical and low-technical aspects of the capabilities and limitations of computers, and of the social, vocational, and educational implications of computers.
>
> David Moursund

Others suggest that learning to control the computer through computer programming is the only way in which to achieve true literacy:

> If you can tell the computer how to do the things you want it to, you are computer literate.
>
> Arthur Luehrmann

Still others advocate using the computer as a tool in many ways and suggest that full literacy must be comprehensive in scope:

> Not only programming, computer literacy should include the use of "information" retrieval, word processing, statistics, and other application systems.
>
> David Moursund

> The ability to use suitably programmed computers in appropriate ways in accomplishing tasks and solving problems and ability to make informed judgments about social and ethical issues involving computer and communications systems.
>
> Beverly Hunter

> Computer literacy . . . is "whatever understanding, skills, and attitudes one needs to function effectively within a given social role that directly or indirectly involves computers."
>
> Ronald Anderson and Daniel Klassen

Considering these viewpoints and the principles previously described, several guidelines for defining computer literacy for young people can be constructed:

1. Computer literacy must be defined comprehensively, including two general areas: learning *with* computers and learning *about* computers.
2. However, decisions concerning what children learn about computers should be made not by asking "What can we teach kids about computers?" but by asking "What understandings about computers, their impact on our world, and their uses are *developmentally appropriate* for, and *educa-*

tionally relevant to, young children." This implies that lectures on the history of computers or rote memorization of computer components terminology should not be included in the curriculum. Only when meaningful concepts can be actively learned should they be considered for inclusion.

3. For both general areas, educators should (a) decide first how and when to use computers to accomplish the goals of early education, and (b) integrate these uses into the curriculum, while (c) remaining consistent with the beliefs, principles, and practices of the program. These guidelines have several important ramifications. For example, they imply that (a) the development of the "whole child" will be given first and primary consideration; (b) there will not be a "computers" unit that is separate from work in social studies, science, language arts, and so on; and (c) *individual children will have different needs, interests, and abilities and, therefore, will learn different things about computers and will use them in different ways.* This should be welcomed as well as accepted; no effort should be made to force all children to "master" all aspects of computer literacy. Instead of one definition of computer literacy for all, teachers should determine what computers can do to help a particular child reach a particular goal.

A *scope and sequence* of the topics, understandings, and skills appropriate for each age level further defines computer literacy for young people. Table 4–1 presents a suggested outline. The first major topic, 'Hardware, Software . . . ," involves understanding what a computer is and how it works. *Hardware* is the physical equipment of a computer system, such as keyboards, the internal parts of the computer, printers, television sets for viewing, and so on. *Software* is the name for the computer programs that actually tell the computer what to do. They are lists of instructions that might tell the computer how to present a math lesson, draw a picture, or keep track of files. Part A addresses the basic questions, "What is a computer?" "How does a computer work?" To answer these questions, students need to be provided with understandable models for hardware and software. They need to recognize that computers need instructions to operate, that they can perform many different functions, and that they work with letters, words, numbers, drawings, and so on.

Part B involves the different parts, or components, of a computer system and their functions. A *computer system* usually consists of a computer, other electronic equipment such as printers, disk drives or cassette players, television sets, and computer programs, all of which operate together. Again, what is important is for young children to actually know how to *use* these components and to acquire active models for understanding what the components do.

Part C, different kinds of computers, is more appropriate for children who are older, gifted, or intensely interested. These children may be guided to discover the similarity between early counting devices and computers and explore some early computing machines. All children can be led to compare different types of computers, for example, special-purpose computers, such as those in dishwashers or electronic toys, and general-purpose computers such as the popular personal computers.

TABLE 4–1 Teaching Young Children *About* Computers: A Suggested Outline

	PRESCHOOL	KINDERGARTEN	GRADES		
			1	2	3
I. Hardware, Software, Outerwear, and Underwear: What Should Young Children Understand?					
A. What is a computer? How does a computer work?					
1. Models for understanding hardware and software	I	I	I	D	D
2. Computers need instructions	I	I	D	D	D
3. Computers can do many jobs	I	D	D	D	D
4. Computers work with letters, words, numbers, sound, and pictures	I	D	D	D	D
B. What are the parts of a computer? What do they do?					
1. Computer systems and components (parts)		I	D	D	D
2. Models for understanding parts of a computer and what they do		I	D	D	D
C. What different kinds of computers are there?					
1. History					I
2. Types of computers		I	I	D	D
D. Capabilities and limitations					
1. What computers can and cannot do	I	I	D	D	D
2. Artificial intelligence			I	I	D
II. How Are Computers Used in the Neighborhood?					
A. Local applications of computers		I	D	D	D
B. Impact of computers			I	D	D
III. How Can *We* Use Computers?					
A. Getting started: using computers, typing, and problem solving	I	I	D	D	D
B. Computer programming: Now we teach the computer	I	D	D	D	D
C. Using computers as tools: learning what is in the curriculum with computers	I	D	D	D	D

I–Incidental, Informal, Introduction.
D–Directed activities, Discussions.

The capabilities and limitations of computers constitute part D. To understand this topic, children can discuss what computers can and cannot do. Background information and teaching suggestions for these parts can be found in Chapter 5. However, to understand computers truly, especially their limitations, children have to use programs for drill and practice, tutorials, simulations, problem solving, and programming. These uses are discussed in all the remaining chapters of the book.

The second major topic is "How are computers used in our neighborhood?" Children learn about local applications of computers including who uses them, what information the computers get from and give to the person, and how the person uses this information. The impact of computers on the neighborhood, including positives and negatives, is also considered. Background informations and suggestions for teaching these topics are also included in Chapter 6.

Only the bare outlines of the third major topic, "How can we use computers?" is presented in Table 4–1. This topic is dealt with throughout the remainder of the book. Each of the parts will be discussed in the appropriate chapter.

The extensive topic of children using computers concerns the abilities and skills necessary for the development of full computer literacy—using the computer as a tool to accomplish goals. "Getting ready to use computers" includes the attitudes, skills, and higher-level abilities that will contribute to successful use of computer technology. "Computer programming" involves creating a list of instructions for a computer. Children and adults must "teach the computer" to accomplish a specific task. These topics are addressed in Chapter 5 and more extensively in Chapters 9, 10, and 11. "Using computers as tools" includes learning how and when to use computers, learning from computer-assisted instructional programs, using utility programs for filing, keeping track of figures, and so on.

This book is based on the belief that it *is* beneficial for students to become computer literate. However, the focus is not on the machine, but on the child. Computers should be used, by teachers and children, to help achieve the broad goals of early education.

THINK ABOUT

1. It was stated that children invent their own theories about how computers work. An interpreter of Piaget might maintain that this is a necessary and healthy stage of children's growth and that it should not be disturbed by imposing adult theories and ideas. A Gesselian might argue that the less children think about machines, the better; that is, they need dolls and balls, not computers. Consider the exposure young children have to technology, especially video games. Then agree or disagree with each of these viewpoints, defending your position.
2. Many professionals believe that "computer literacy" is too loose a term to be helpful. What does "literacy" mean to you? What phrase would serve educational purposes better?
3. Do you believe that there is a need to understand computers more than, say, televisions? Why or why not? What should children understand?
4. What goals of the curriculum for your grade level would be amenable to being reached via discussions of, or work with, computers? Which would not?

5. Will all future citizens need to be able to control computers? In what sense?

ANNOTATED BIBLIOGRAPHY

Anderson, R. E., Klassen, D. L., & Johnson, D. C. (1981). In defense of a comprehensive view of computer literacy—A reply to Luehrmann. *Mathematics Teacher 74*, 687–690.

Luehrmann, A. (1981). Computer literacy—What should it be? *Mathematics Teacher, 74,* 682–686.

For those interested in a lucid presentation of opposing viewpoints, read the debate between these authorities. What are your beliefs? How would you alter the scope and sequence presented in this book?

Barger, R. N. (1983). Computer literacy: Toward a clearer definition. *T.H.E. Journal, 11*(2), 108–112.

Olds, H. (1981). How to think about computers. In B. R. Sadowski (ed.), *Using computers to enhance teaching and improve teacher centers,* pp. 13–29. Houston: National Teacher Centers Computer Technology Conference.

Zamora, R. (1983). Computer and other literacies. In M. Grady & J. Gawronski (eds.), *Computer in curriculum and instruction,* pp. 6–11. Alexandria, VA: Association for Supervision and Curriculum Development.

These references present challenging views of the place of computers in education and society.

Bitter, G. G., & Camuse, R. A. (1984). *Using a microcomputer in the classroom.* Reston, VA: Reston Publishing Co.

Hunter, B. (1983). *My students use computers: Learning activities for computer literacy.* Reston, VA: Reston Publishing Co.

Zachmeier, W., et al. (1983, March). K–8 computer literacy curriculum. *The Computing Teacher, 10*(7), 7–10.

These resources each present a fairly extensive scope and sequence for computer literacy.

Corbitt, M. K. (1982). *Guide to resources in instructional computing.* Reston, VA: National Council of Teachers of Mathematics.

This author presents several views of computer literacy and attempts to arrive at a consensus.

Watt, D. (1981, October). Computer literacy: What should schools do about it? *Instructor,* pp. 85–87.

Watt's account of the schools' need for a comprehension program of computer literacy instruction would be good reading for parents of your students.

5

TEACHING YOUNG CHILDREN ABOUT COMPUTERS
Hardware and Software

The previous chapter presented a rationale for teaching children about computers, a discussion of what computer literacy should be for young children, guidelines for determining what and how to teach children about computers, and a scope and sequence of appropriate topics. This chapter and the next fill in the scope and sequence, thus providing the last two pieces that teachers need to solve the puzzle of teaching about computers: background information and activities designed to help young children learn about the topics.

HARDWARE, SOFTWARE, OUTERWEAR, AND UNDERWEAR: WHAT SHOULD YOUNG CHILDREN UNDERSTAND?

What is a Computer? How Does a Computer Work?

An analogy. A computer is a device that takes in information, stores it, changes (or processes) it according to specific instructions and then shows the results of this processing. This may seem foreign to you or to your students. But it can become quite familiar and understandable if it is recognized that people do the same thing every day. Children (and adults!) may benefit from comparing their own "processing" to that of a computer. They not only gain a better understanding of how computers work, but they also gain a more important insight into their own thinking.

BOY	COMPUTER
1. A third grade boy looks at his math book and sees "28 − 15 = ." He is taking in visual information.	1. The computer also takes in information, often from a typewriter or disk (input).
2. His brain translates this visual image into neurological impulses and remembers this information.	2. The computer translates the keypresses or the magnetic information on the disk into electrical impulses and stores it in memory.
3. He brings to mind the steps he must follow to solve the problem. For instance, first look at the first column and subtract the 5 from the 8. Because renaming ("borrowing") is not needed, complete the subtraction, remember it, and write the result. Go to the second column, and so on.	3. The computer follows steps also. These steps, called a computer program, must be supplied by people. Once they are, the computer can follow these instructions independently. It also adds numbers and records the result in a certain memory location within the computer (information processing and information storage).
4. He shows the result. He might write the answer on the chalkboard, tell it to the class, or use it to solve a more complex problem; for example, the original problem might have been to find out how many more markers were needed by the class; he might go to the art room and get 13 markers. On the way, he has to remember the information.	4. Computers show the result in similar ways. They may print the answer on a TV screen or use a printer to write it on paper. With a speech synthesizer, they could say the answer (output). They also might use the answer to solve another problem.

Young children would not use a term such as "neurological," but they can be guided to compare the basic steps: input, processing, and output. They could also discuss the differences between the people and computers; for example, computers "remember" well, but if their program does not tell them exactly what to do with the information, they are "stuck." People forget frequently, but they can figure out different ways to solve problems. Therefore, people and computers complement each other.

Children's books provide needed illustrations and springboards for discussions. Appropriate books include Marion Ball's *What Is a Computer* and *Be a Computer Literate* (Ball, 1972; Ball & Charp, 1978), Michael Braude's *Larry Learns About Computers* (1969), and Jean Rice's *My Friend the Computer* (1981) and *Computers Are Fun* (Rice & O'Connor, 1981). Other books for children include Sally Larsen's *Computers for Kids* (1982), Donald Spencer's *Computer Awareness Book* (1978) and *Microcomputer Coloring Book* (1983), Linda O'Brian's *Computers—A First Book,* (1978), Elizabeth Wall's *Computer Alphabet Book* (1979), and *COM-LIT: Computer Literacy for Kids* (Horn & Collins, 1983). While useful, some of the books have a tendency to concentrate on arithmetical applications, reinforcing the erroneous belief that computers are fancy calculators. Instead, it should be emphasized and illustrated that computers can do many jobs working with words, pictures, music, and so on.

The carton computer: A dramatization. "I hear and I forget, I see and I remember, I do and I understand." The Chinese proverb applies especially to young children. Discussions and books are necessary and helpful, but what can they *do* to understand computers?

Children can dramatize the workings of a computer in several ways. One way involves a large classroom model, the "carton computer." Encourage children to decorate a large cardboard carton to look like a computer. Guide them to include a keyboard and TV screen at least. Cut two slots, one near the keyboard and one near, or within, the TV screen. One child gets inside the box with some markers and blank cards and plays the part of the computer. Other children write instructions for the computer on their own cards and place them in the "input slot" near the keyboard. Prereading children could speak their instructions. Some children enjoy pretending to type the instructions on the pictured keyboard, or they might use an actual typewriter. The child inside the computer must carry out the directions and show what he or she did by pushing a card out the "output slot." Encourage children to write directions—possibly copying from model cards—that illustrate basic concepts about computers; for example, that they work with letters, words, numbers, pictures, and sound. Emphasize also that the computer cannot do any job without instructions. If you are teaching children to program a computer, use words from that computer language and have the child inside the computer respond appropriately. For example, the children using the carton computer might write PRINT "HI THERE," PRINT 4 + 7, or CLEARSCREEN. The child in the computer would send out a card with HI THERE, 11, or nothing written on it.

Basic concepts about computers. Activities such as these introduce basic concepts about computers that should be highlighted in every lesson about hardware and software. These concepts are listed in Table 5–1. Books, analogies, and dramatizations are helpful; however, it is just as important that children actually work with computers in a variety of ways. Using different programs (sets of instructions) for different purposes (many jobs) such as those outlined in the first three chapters is the best way to build a firm foundation of understanding. This is also an essential time for teachers to reinforce and extend children's understanding through thoughtful discussions. For example, a teacher might ask a child who is working with the classroom microcomputer about the input he or she is giving and the output he or she is getting. Children who have these experiences will be able to describe meaningfully a computer in their own words;

TABLE 5–1 Basic Concepts About Computers

Computers can work with letters, words, numbers, and pictures.
Computers can do many jobs.
Computers need instructions.
Computers can work fast.
Computers can store a large amount of information.
Computers are dependable and accurate.

for example, "A computer lets you do math or writing or draw pictures on a TV or with a printer" or "Computers are machines that need instructions and then they can help you work."

What are the Parts of a Computer? What Do They Do?

Computer components. Figure 5–1a is a picture of one popular microcomputer system. It illustrates the "outerwear" of a computer system, or that which is visible from the outside. A computer system is a computer, other electrical and mechanical equipment, and computer programs, or software, that give instructions to the computer, all working together to input, process, and output information. This system has the keyboard attached to the box that holds computer itself; in other systems, the keyboard is separate. The keyboard and TV screen are probably the most familiar components of a computer system. The keyboard is an input device used to type information into the computer. The TV, also called a cathode ray tube (CRT) or monitor, is an output device that allows the computer to display information. A printer is another common output device that allows the information, including words, numbers, and pictures, to be printed onto paper. Other components, which are facetiously referred to by the term "underwear" in the title of this section, are less visible and less familiar. But analogies between these components and well-known objects can help children (and adults) to conceptualize, remember, and feel more comfortable about computer components and their functions.

The CPU. Inside the body of the computer is the central processing unit, or CPU. This is the "brains" of the computer, which carries out the instructions of the computer programs and generally controls and coordi-

FIGURE 5–1a (Courtesy of Apple Computer, Inc.)

nates all the components of the computer system, ensuring that they work together. It has only memory enough inside itself to hold the small amount of information it is directly working on, so it needs other memory systems. There are two basic types, primary and secondary storage.

Storage. Primary storage holds information and the instructions of computer programs in the memory inside the computer. This memory is like thousands of electronic mailboxes, each with its own location, or address. Each mailbox can store one letter, or piece of information. There are two categories of memory. First, the computer has to be able to interpret, or "understand," some words that the user might type in right after turning the computer on. It needs memory that already contains information and is permanent (nonerasable). This type of memory is called read only memory, or ROM, and might be thought of as a book describing a computer language. It contains information about the language that can be "read" the moment the computer is turned on, and this information does not disappear when the book is closed. For instance, if the CPU reads a PRINT "TGIF" command, it locates the exact steps it needs to follow to perform this command in ROM. This might involve (a) finding the letters "TGIF" in memory, (b) writing those letters on the next available space on the TV screen, and (c) going on to the next statement and doing what it says.

The CPU also needs to be able to store programs and many other types of information that are read from a disk or typed in by a person. This is the erasable random access memory, or RAM, which can be seen as "magic slates"—the self-erasing pads that can be written on and then erased by lifting the top sheet of plastic. Anything can be written on them, and then read, but when you are done with them, all the information is erased forever. It is called random access because it permits direct communication with any location in memory at any time. The amount of memory available in a computer is usually described in terms of the number of characters that can be stored in RAM. The size of a computer's memory is often stated in terms of the number of "K" (for kilo, meaning 1,000) characters; for example, "64K" means that about 64,000 characters can be stored in the computer's memory (to be exact, each K is 1,024 characters, or 2 to the tenth power). If possible, open the case of a computer and show children the CPU, memory, and other components.

Of course, the computer cannot hold all the programs and information you ever want to use in its memory at one time. There is a need for secondary storage, devices that can take information from the computer and save it. These components are easily seen and thus return us to the "outerwear" category. Disks are flat, circular plates with a magnetic surface. Often called "floppy disks," they resemble the thin, flexible phonograph records that are sometimes used for promotions. They are kept in a square paper jacket permanently for protection. A disk drive is a mechanical device, pictured to the right of the computer in Figure 5–1a, which actually stores information on, and reads information from, the disk. Disks, and to a lesser extent, tapes, are the most common devices for storing

FIGURE 5–1b
A Commodore computer system equipped with a disk drive. (Courtesy of Commodore Business Machines.)

information and programs so they are not lost. Disks have several advantages. First, they allow information to be transferred much more quickly. Second, like a phonograph record, any section (program) can be selected almost immediately. A tape cassette must run through all its programs until it reaches the one desired. Therefore, you often have to wait for a much longer time for a program to be read, or "loaded," from a cassette (see Figure 5–1b).

Other input/output devices. There are many other input/output (I/O) devices, the purpose of which is to allow people to communicate with the CPU. Some of these devices will become especially important for young children. Many of them can be understood as attempts to allow the computer to communicate as people do. For instance, people communicate by reading and writing; the computer can be equipped with a keyboard or even a scanning device that can "read" print for input and a TV set or a printer for output ("writing"). People talk, sing, and listen. Computers are increasingly being provided with speech synthesizers and speakers that allow them to produce music and humanlike speech (output). Allowing computers to "hear" (input) through voice recognition devices is more complex and expensive, but the field is developing. The use of a light pen (a device that is placed on the TV screen to indicate a word or location) for input is analogous in certain ways to the human sense of touch. So too are touch-sensitive screens and touch tablets, which allow children to draw or make choices by touching. (The author hopes that computerized tasting is not in the immediate future; he has uncomfortable visions of a mechanized voice demanding its fair share of a hot fudge sundae.) Figure 5–1c illustrates another system containing several such devices.

Is it silly to think of a machine being equipped with a sense of smell? Do you *already own* a device that "decides" to issue an alarm if it detects ("smells") smoke? People also need to communicate over long distances. A modem (*mo*dulator/*dem*odulator) allows a computer to communicate with another computer over telephone lines, passing information back and forth.

FIGURE 5–1c The NEC Home Electronics PC-6000 system. To the right is the Digitizer Touch Panel and to the left is the Cassette Data Recorder. (Courtesy of David L. Todd and Associates, Inc.)

Teaching about components with the carton computer. Children already familiar with the carton computer may want to expand its "capabilities." Have children decorate a smaller box that is placed next to the carton computer and labeled a disk drive. They can then save and retrieve programs from paper disks.

Charting the flow of a computer's communication. A diagram may help by further illustrating the way in which a computer works. Locate all the components you recognize in Figure 5–2. Notice that the central

FIGURE 5–2

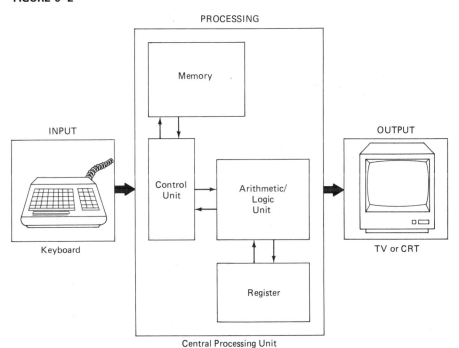

processing unit also has several parts. The control unit translates the instructions in computer programs into language the machine "understands" (can use directly) and directs the step-by-step operations of the whole computer system. The arithmetic-logic unit (ALU) performs all the arithmetic and logical operations; for example, "Does the student's spelling match the correct spelling?" Actual calculations are performed in the part of this unit called the register. The arrows indicate the flow of communication between the components.

Analogies. Provision of real-world models and dramatization of these parts and their functions can serve as powerful tools for helping students to understand the interactions of the components of computer systems. One second grade class had taken a field trip to a nearby restaurant. The class members acted out the system they had seen, relating it to their school's microcomputer system. The input, or information (data), was several children standing in line to be served, one at a time. The control unit was represented by the store's manager, who was directing his staff in serving the customers, following the owner's instructions (the program). The ALU was the staff. As each customer came forward, the manager took the order and wrote it on an erasable board (primary memory, RAM). This signaled the chef to make the food. The orders were assembled and were given in order to the customers (output). The staff (ALU) used the cash *register* to calculate the bills. At some point the manager may have to consult books on tax laws to understand how to fill out the necessary forms. This is analogous to the CPU's finding the meaning of a word in a programming language by reading the correct memory location in ROM. It also nicely illustrates other basic concepts of computers, for instance, that computers can do many different jobs following many different sets of instructions.

Notice that this simple dramatization can be expanded for older or more advanced children and additional vocabulary can be introduced. If many customers are at the counter, the board may fill with orders. This illustrates the concept of the *buffer,* a computer's temporary storage for data, that compensates for different operating speeds of various parts of a computer system; for example, between a high-speed CPU and a relatively slower printer. If the buffer board is full, the manager may not proceed. If it is not full, it is all right to proceed. Although the board was erased for each customer, the tapes from the cash register and the manager's paperwork kept a permanent record of the orders and the flow of money, which were stored in the back room by the manager (secondary storage).

At all times, the teacher took care to make the relationships between the restaurant and the computer explicit. Otherwise, many children would miss the point of the dramatization. For instance, the class compared a diagram such as that in Figure 5–3 with one such as Figure 5–2. A list might be constructed comparing the way in which the restaurant and the computer work. To illustrate such a list, and to provide yet another useful analogy, let us focus on the chef in the restaurant.

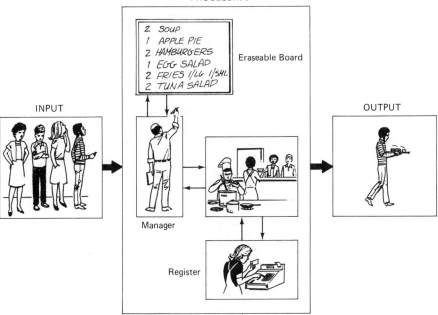

Eraseable Board

INPUT

OUTPUT

Manager

Register

FIGURE 5–3

CHEF	COMPUTER'S CPU
1. Receives orders for specific dishes, to be cooked in order in a specific order. These are written on an erasable board.	1. Is instructed to read a program that contains specific instructions (commands) to be performed in a certain way in a specific order from a disk and make a copy of it in RAM.
2. Looks up the recipe in a cookbook.	2. Locates the words (commands) that are in the instructions in ROM.
3. Reads the recipe's steps one at a time from the cookbook.	3. Reads the steps telling how to carry out each command from ROM.
4. Accumulates all the necessary ingredients and places them on the counter.	4. Accumulates all the data (information) needed from the program stored in RAM or from the keyboard and holds them in a special accumulator register, a place for information that will be worked on immediately.
5. Follows the recipe in combining and changing the ingredients to make the dishes, using a food processor, stove, etc.	5. Changes (processes) the information according to the instructions using the arithmetic-logic unit.
6. Gives the dishes one at a time to the waiters and waitresses.	6. Gives the new information (output) to the output devices, such as the TV screen or printer.

Incidental teaching. Besides leading children to see the direct connections in each of these analogies, teachers should encourage them to apply the knowledge they have gained in many different situations. For instance, one of the most effective ways of developing both understanding about computers and problem-solving ability is to pose challenging questions to children who are actively working with the computer on any of a variety of different applications. "The computer called you by name yesterday, but today it asked you to type it in again. I wonder why." (The name was stored in RAM, but not on the disk. When the computer was turned off, the memory of the name was erased.) "You have a problem. The disk drive light went on, then your program just stopped? Hmmm. What could have happened?" (The program needed more instructions or information from the disk, but the child had removed the disk from the disk drive.) Third grade children should also be able to connect the major components of the computer system and locate and fix simple problems in such connections (e.g., the TV set is not attached to the computer). There is evidence that these approaches, providing learners with concrete models of the computer and encouraging them to dramatize them and restate the information in their own words, result in broader, more effective learning (Mayer, 1980, 1981).

Learning about computers with computers. Interested second and third graders (and adults) can learn an impressive amount about the logical electronic building blocks of a computer from *Rocky's Boots* (The Learning Company), a simulation of machine parts, electrical connections, and basic circuit design elements that constitute the internal world of computers. Like an electronic Tinker Toy set, the program teaches about these elements bit-by-bit by encouraging the user to build machines and games. It will be described more fully in the science chapter.

Learning about computers with books. Children in the primary grades may also enjoy hearing or reading about the "world inside the computer" in the picture book, *Katie and the Computer* by S. Frederick D'Ignazio (reading level about 2-0). A little girl types "flower" on her new computer, falls into it (in "through the looking glass" style), and begins an adventure in the world of Cybernia, complete with Flower Bytes who live in RAM Tower, the Colonel (control), and the mean and tricky program "Bug." Katie tries, despite the bug, to get the computer to paint a picture of a flower. The story familiarizes children with the key words associated with computer components and with the major processes. The components are metaphorically represented as landmarks, and the processes appear as episodes in the story. It should be noted, however, that the allegory is not specific enough to allow children or adults to understand how computers work; teachers would need to help children understand it in other ways.

Other teaching ideas. After reading about and dramatizing the workings of a computer with her class, one teacher created a large bulletin board with a simple representation of the basic components of a computer. Children chose a problem from a pocket near the "input devices" and traced the solution through the arrows connecting the components. At each one, they had to write "what should happen here?" Different answers were compared and discussed. Other traditional methods of teaching vocabulary, while not as powerful conceptually, may also be useful: posting a computer "word for the day"; concentration games; matching words and pictures; bulletin boards with many pictures of computer components in the three basic categories of input, processing and memory, and output; and so on. Students should be able to describe the components in their own words, such as "A TV (monitor) show, words, numbers, and pictures," or "A disk drive can save information such as programs, pictures, or stories on a disk." Research has shown that providing students with a concrete model and encouraging them to "put it in their own words" can have a strong positive effect on their learning (Mayer, 1980, 1981).

What level of detail? Because hardware is changing so rapidly with technological advances, it may not be wise to study specific equipment for its own sake. Rather, as students discover the various applications of computers, it will be natural to study the functions of the parts of computer systems. Integrated study—computers in context—is more useful and more meaningful. Following the principles discussed in the first chapter, these kinds of activities help children to understand computers *and* other organizations and processes in their world, such as the restaurant in the example cited earlier.

What Different Kinds of Computers Are There?

History. Detailed investigations into the *history* and *different types of computers* will probably be undertaken only by older and self-motivated children. However, teachers may wish to develop a background in this area by reading some of the references listed at the end of this chapter. The history of computers is the story of people striving to remember and work with symbols more efficiently. The growth of computer technology, pictorially represented in Figures 5–4 through 5–8, has been summarized in a famous observation made by Christopher Evans:

> Suppose for a moment that the automobile industry had developed at the same rate as computers and over the same period: how much cheaper and more efficient would the current models be? . . . Today you would be able to buy a Rolls Royce for $2.75, it would do three million miles to the gallon, and it would deliver enough power to drive the Queen Elizabeth II. And if you were interested in miniaturization, you could place half a dozen of them on a pinhead. (p. 76)

For the motivated child, the history of computers offers an excellent opportunity to integrate computer literacy, language arts, science, and social studies as children read about these computers and give reports to the class. In a manner reminiscent of the beloved topic, "Dinosaurs," entire classes of young children have been entranced by pictures and stories of

FIGURE 5–4 Charles Babbage, in the early part of the 19th century, worked on mechanical machines, such as his Difference Engine, that parallel the design of modern computers. (Courtesy of International Business Machines Corporation.)

FIGURE 5–5 Joseph Jacquared developed an automatic loom that used paper punched cards to produce intricate patterns in cloth—an early use of data processing techniques. (Courtesy of International Business Machines Corporation.)

FIGURE 5–6 Herman Hollerith conducted the 1890 census with a mechanical system for recording, computing, and tabulating data in punched cards. He started a company that later became IBM. (Courtesy of International Business Machines Corporation.)

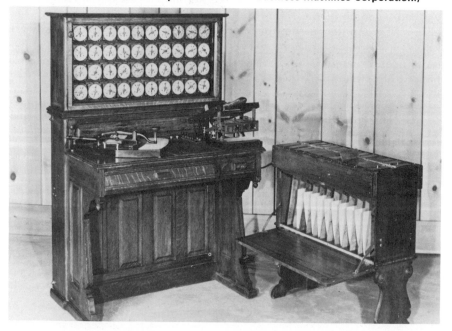

FIGURE 5-7 The fantastic evolution from vacuum tubes to transitors, to integrated circuits, and to microprocessors—large scale integrated circuits. A room full of tubes such as those pictured can be replaced by one small integrated circuit chip. (Courtesy of International Business Machines Corporation.)

FIGURE 5-8
The Intel 80286 microprocessor. It incorporates 128,000 transistors on a single square chip of silicon that measures only one-third of an inch on a side. (Courtesy of Intel Corporation.)

giant computers. Just as the young child is amazed (and proud) that he or she is smarter than the mighty *Tyrannosaurus rex,* the youngster is impressed that his or her classroom computer has more memory and more computing power than the dinosaurs of the "ancient" generations of computers.

Capabilities and Limitations

What computers can and cannot do. To understand computers and their uses fully, children must understand computers' unique capabilities and their limitations. As we shall see, this understanding not only helps children understand computers, but it may help them to understand their *own* capabilities and limitations in more depth. In this way it follows the principle of using computers as catalysts to achieve the major goals of early education.

A critical point must be made first: children should have numerous experiences with different uses of the computer, including drill and practice programs, tutorials, simulations, problem-solving applications including word processing, programming, and so on, *before* they are expected to actively engage in a discussion of the capabilities and limitations of the computer. Otherwise, the discussions will not have a meaningful foundation and will probably result in mere verbiage.

Children have a variety of ideas about the intelligence of computers:

A kindergarten girl who repeatedly lost a tic-tac-toe game asked, "How old is this computer?"
Part of the problem "may stem from defining thinking. As Chris, 8, answered, 'Think? My teacher tells me to think and I just don't know what she's saying. . . . Does the computer?'" (Humphrey, 1982, p. 98)
"Computers know just about everything, but not lots of stuff."
"Smart? It can't even talk! My brother can talk and he's only three!"

Like adults, children are not at all sure about the intelligence of computers or about intelligence itself. Teachers help children to learn about computers and about their own thinking by listening closely to their ideas and guiding them in talking to each other about these ideas. One teacher provided her students with many opportunities to use computers. She also had the class engage in a few specially designed activities. For instance, comparing the time it took the computer to print a letter 60 times with the time it took a child to do the same task. Or asking the computer and the child to recognize a word with a slight misspelling, such as PRINTT, or respond to a question such as "Are you happy today?" Of course, the computer could not match the child's performance in the last two tasks. Then, guided only by a small number of carefully chosen questions from the teacher, children can be led to list what computers can do (capabilities) and what they cannot do (limitations). One class's list is reproduced in Table 5–2.

Examine the limitations in Table 5–2 again to see if you notice any-

TABLE 5–2 What Computers Can and Cannot Do Well*

What Computers Do Well

1. Go fast	Speed: computers can perform millions of calculations or other operations per second.
2. Do many different jobs	Generality: computers can help solve a wide variety of problems.
3. Help you to write, read, do math, make drawings, and make up songs	
4. Work without making mistakes	Accuracy.
5. Remember a lot of things	Memory: computers can store large amounts of information and can search through it quickly.
6. Do just what you tell them to	Reliability: utility.

What Computers Cannot Do Well

1. Be there when you need them	This group's way of saying that there were not enough computers at school or home—an economic limitation.
2. Fix even little mistakes by themselves	Inflexibility: improvises poorly.
3. Figure things out for themselves	Limited intelligence or creativity: computers of today are not capable of solving problems requiring creative intelligence without specific instructions from people; they can think "linearly" but not divergently.
4. Love anything or have any feelings	
5. Decide what is right and wrong	Is less capable in decision making involving judgment.

*Children's ideas are on the left; the author's comments on the right.

thing about them. Did you notice that the things that computers cannot yet do well are things that people do well—that they are intelligent behaviors? Children should understand what their own capabilities are and should never feel that they are not as smart as the machine. To ensure they do not, discuss their abilities to think flexibly, creatively, and intelligently, to empathize with others, and to decide what is the right thing to do. Conversely, children may benefit from understanding their own limitations. Psychologists note that young children do not have well-developed "metacognitive" processes—they do not realize when they do not understand; they do not think of rehearsing a list of things that they are to remember; they do not have an accurate picture of the frailty of their own memories; and so on. Discussions such as these may help children to achieve these realizations.

As mentioned, actual demonstrations are effective. Races among children working with a calculator, with paper and pencil, or "in their heads" may illustrate both the appropriate uses and the unique capabilities of each. For instance, how does each perform on a test of 20 problems such as 38 + 35? (The calculator is probably the most efficient tool.) On 20 problems such as 3 + 3? (Children will see that mental addition is faster and more accurate for these types of problems.) Children who have had computer programming experience could compare similar problems, possibly including some like "Write your full name 100 times."

Also effective in developing metacognitive abilities is the use of computers in problem solving and programming (see Chapters 9–11). To give a brief example, children often overvalue the fast, "correct the first time" answer. The teacher might lead them to see that when programming computers—giving them instructions on what to do—almost no one "gets it right" the first time. Good computer programmers are usually good "debuggers"—they examine their work carefully to locate and fix errors. Children who understand this and debug programs may learn a considerable amount about their own thinking. The characteristics of the computer can help in planning for the guidance of children. With children who tend to blurt out answers, the teacher might discuss or show how a logical sequence of steps must be performed by the computer before it can come up with an answer. In the same way, students may benefit in many situations from using such a sequence. Directly working on a computer might benefit a passive child; the computer will wait forever, doing nothing until the child takes the initiative.

Some would argue that computers will never be creative or truly intelligent. However, there are those who disagree and are working on building such intelligence into computers. While it is good practice to discuss the limitations of present-day computers with students, it also behooves educators to know that these limitations may *not* be permanent. In the next section we consider artificial intelligence, the study of the "smart machine."

Artificial intelligence. The field of artificial intelligence involves computer systems and computer programs that can perform intelligent tasks, namely, computer simulations of human intellectual activities. This makes computers appear to think as people do. This type of research may help us to learn more about the way in which both machines and people "think."

Is it absurd to think that computers can think? It has been said that they cannot write novels like Hemingway or contatas like Bach. However, most of *us* would not like to be evaluated on our intelligence on those criteria. We react emotionally to the idea of a thinking machine—with distaste, anxiety, and possibly fear. This keeps us from thinking about the issue objectively, and it illustrates that intelligence is not all we are—our feelings and values are of crucial import.

Most of the activities in which the computer has appeared to be intelligent have been gamelike. A person devises a way in which to program the computer to choose the best among myriad possibilities in a game such as chess. This brings up an interesting issue. Some authorities believe that the intelligence of the computer is always only a reflection of the human intelligence of the programmer; others, like Marvin Minsky and Christopher Evans, tend to believe that truly intelligent machines can be developed in time. It is not certain which opinion is correct; however, it *is* true that Dr.

Arthur Samuel of IBM has written programs that have beaten state champions in checkers matches.

You are already familiar with several "intelligent" machines. Your thermostat makes decisions—when the temperature drops below a certain point, it senses this and turns on the heat. When a higher temperature is reached, it turns it off again. Not impressed with the intellectual brilliance of the device? You should not be, for any one-celled organism is smarter. However, in the future thermostats will be a bit more intelligent. With built-in microprocessors, they will control heat flow differently for different rooms at different times of day. They might sense the presence of people in rooms and direct infrared lights to warm them, allowing the air in the house to remain cool, thereby saving money and energy resources while keeping the people comfortably warm.

Evans (1979) has pointed out that while the computers presently are not as intelligent as humans, they are more intelligent than a tapeworm. And while humans reached their state of intelligence over several hundred million years, the computer has had only a quarter of a century of development. Evans answers common objections about machine intelligence and points out that a computer surpassed a human in solving the famous "four-color problem," *proving* that on any two-dimensional map you would only need four colors to ensure that no two territories of the same color adjoin each other. Another constructed new proofs in Euclidean geometry.

As a final argument, Evans discusses what is often accepted as the best test of computer intelligence devised up to the present time—the Turing test, after its inventor, scientist Alan Turing. Here, a person (the subject) is screened off from a computer and a normal thinking person while establishing communication to each through a terminal. The subject is to carry out conversations with each in an attempt to determine which is which. If the person cannot decide, the computer has passed the test as an intelligent machine. While no computer has passed this test absolutely yet, Evans notes that on several occasions, situations have been close to this. ELIZA, a program written by Joseph Weizenbaum to "converse" in English, analyzing the user's message and responses to it, amazes many people with its apparent "intelligence." It mimics a nondirected psychiatrist in the tradition of Carl Rogers. (Weizenbaum, 1976, pp. 3–4)

```
MEN ARE ALL ALIKE.
IN WHAT WAY
THEY'RE ALWAYS BUGGING US ABOUT SOMETHING OR OTHER.
CAN YOU THINK OF A SPECIFIC EXAMPLE
WELL, MY BOYFRIEND MADE ME COME HERE.
YOUR BOYFRIEND MADE YOU COME HERE
HE SAYS I'M DEPRESSED MUCH OF THE TIME.
I AM SORRY TO HEAR YOU ARE DEPRESSED...
I NEED SOME HELP, THAT MUCH SEEMS CERTAIN.
WHAT WOULD IT MEAN TO YOU IF YOU GOT SOME HELP
PERHAPS I COULD LEARN TO GET ALONG WITH MY MOTHER.
TELL ME MORE ABOUT YOUR FAMILY
MY MOTHER TAKES CARE OF ME.
WHO ELSE IN YOUR FAMILY TAKES CARE OF YOU
MY FATHER.
YOUR FATHER...
MY FATHER IS AFRAID OF EVERYBODY.
WHAT ELSE COMES TO MIND WHEN YOU THINK OF YOUR FATHER
BULLIES.
DOES THAT HAVE ANYTHING TO DO WITH THE FACT THAT YOUR BOYFRIEND
MADE YOU COME HERE
```

It should be noted, however, that this program has *no true understanding whatsoever*. It merely analyzes and stores phrases, manipulates them, and responds in certain prescribed ways. Weizenbaum (1976) was upset by suggestions, made by practicing psychiatrists, that the program could actually be used in psychotherapy. Nevertheless, the program does illustrate the potential of computers to carry on a conversation.

As another example, two scientists at M.I.T. were talking via the network when one left without telling the other, who carried on a conversation with the computer, unaware that it was not still his friend. Evans concludes that the difference between computers and people is one of degree, not of kind. As you might imagine, other people's opinions differ. Religious thinkers maintain that intelligence is not all there is to humanity or the making of wise decisions, and, of course, most authorities in artificial intelligence do not deny that there is more to humanity than cognition. Others have argued that it is the responsibility of humans to limit the power of any tool (Weizenbaum, 1976).

Is this branch of computer science useful in working with children? Besides its importance as content for the study of computers, discussions and activities related to intelligence can be helpful to children. They can bolster children's self-concepts, increase their awareness of problem-solving strategies or metacognitive abilities, and provide children with a "working vocabulary" of terminology about learning and understanding that will allow them to be more independent learners. Start by asking children, "What do people do that lets you know they can think?"

Another program, called ANIMAL, available in Logo (from Terrapin), BASIC (from Apple), and commercial packages (*Mix and Match* from CTW and Apple), allows young children to see a simple example of learning performed *by a computer*. Notice how the program responds.

```
?ANIMAL
THINK OF AN ANIMAL.  I WILL
TRY TO GUESS IT BY ASKING QUESTIONS.      (The child
                                           thinks "dog.")
DOES IT HAVE FOUR LEGS?
YES
DOES IT GO MOO?
NO
DOES IT WHINNEY?
NO
IS IT A PIG?
NO
OH WELL, I WAS WRONG.  WHAT WAS IT?
DOG
PLEASE TYPE IN A QUESTION WHOSE ANSWER
IS "YES" FOR A DOG AND "NO" FOR A PIG.
DOES IT BARK?
```

Has the program learned? What happens next time someone thinks of a dog.

```
LET'S TRY AGAIN.
THINK OF AN ANIMAL.  I WILL
TRY TO GUESS IT BY ASKING QUESTIONS.
DOES IT HAVE FOUR LEGS?
YES
DOES IT GO MOO?
NO
DOES IT WHINNEY?
NO
DOES IT BARK?
YES
IS IT A DOG?
YES
LOOK HOW SMART I AM!
LET'S TRY AGAIN...
```

Older children with programming experience can actually see *how* the program works, modifying it and writing their own versions. Young children could interact with the program—note that with very simple changes the *same* program could try to make guesses about *any* subject from any curriculum area. This allows them to "make the computer smarter," as one first grader put it rather than the other way around. In this way they learn about the subject matter, about computers—how they work and what they can and cannot do, and about thinking and learning. This kind of highly meaningful, integrated, and potent learning should be given high priority when choosing computer applications.

Older children might engage in a creative writing project describing their ideal "computer of the future." They could describe the jobs the computer would do and discuss if their vision were realizable. A game can be played to dramatize the Turing test, but using two people rather than one person and one computer. Two students who differ, a boy and a girl, for example, sit in a different room. Questions that the class asks are relayed to each of them by a messenger. One of the two is free to make whatever responses he or she thinks will fool the class; the other must tell the truth. Can the class tell which is which?

Children could contribute to a bulletin board that featured "smart" machines. How smart is a thermostat? Different kinds of elevators? What *decisions* and what *actions* based on those decisions do machines make?

Related to artificial intelligence—especially in the public's view—is the subject of robots. A robot is a machine that simulates human behavior and human intelligence. There are three categories of machines: simple machines (extensions of human muscle power), programmable machines (which can do a number of tasks, for example, Jacquard's loom), and robots. A robot usually consists of a programmed general-purpose computer with memory, sensing devices such as photoelectric cells, and effector equipment (which allow movement) such as mechanical arms. Thus, its actions are determined not only by programming but also from information it gets from the world that is relevant to the task it is performing; robots make decisions (Evans, 1979).

Robots have been developed as toys and for household work (D. Hunter, 1983). While still quite expensive, some can walk, sense objects in its way with sonar and "feelers," *learn* about how to get around a room, recharge themselves, talk, recognize what *you* say, see (with an infrared sensor), pick up objects (and turn itself off) with robotic arms, and even vacuum the carpet and detect and put out a fire!

Does robotics have any potential for educational use? Educators should be aware that this type of research is valuable in producing prosthetic devices for handicapped children. Again, besides being fascinating content for study and discussions, some of the robot toys provide a superb introduction to simple programming for young children. For example, the toy Big Trak is programmable.

While still somewhat expensive, simple robots that can be controlled

FIGURE 5-9
RB5X can be programmed to do your bidding. (Courtesy of RB Robot Corporation, Golden, Colorado.)

by programs written on a microcomputer by students are available (see Figure 5-9 and Turtle Tot in Chapter 10). They can be programmed to move in prescribed ways, to draw pictures, to react to objects in the environment, and to speak.

THINK ABOUT

1. Try once more to fill in the blanks. What is a computer?

   _____

   How does a computer work? _____

   _____

2. At a parent conference, a child's mother was upset because her daughter's marks on reading and mathematics were low. She blurts, "And why are you teaching them about *computers,* for Pete's sake? She doesn't need to be a computer science major, but she does need someone to teach her to read and write." What do you (remaining calm all the while) respond?

3. Review the limitations of computers. As the fields of artificial intelligence and computer technology advance, which of these limitations will be overcome? Which are inherent in the use of mechanization?

4. If you have a classroom computer, should you call it by a name? Would this make the machine less intimidating and more understandable, or will it block understanding and create false impressions?

CHOOSE A POSITION AND DEFEND IT.

5. a. "Only bright children should be introduced to the more technical language of computers" (e.g., RAM, ROM, controller).
   b. "That's not true. All my students amaze me with the language they can use and understand if they are exposed to it in nonpressured, motivating situations."

6. a. "People could not live . . . could not be the same, if they thought machines were more intelligent than they were."
   b. "Intelligence is not all there is to living! Machines are stronger and faster than we are, and we use them gladly."
   c. "It is just egotism that makes us insist that we be the 'kings or queens of the hill.' Computers will surpass us in intelligence; there is no real reason to fight it except our own insecurities."

CURRICULUM CONSTRUCTION CORNER

7. Describe an improved version of the carton computer, possibly adding other features of computer systems in a way that would be understandable for young children.

8. What would the "input" for the football team/computer analogy be (remember, it might be a combination of factors)? Secondary storage? What would the coach represent? Is this analogy a good one? Why or why not?

ANNOTATED BIBLIOGRAPHY

Asimov, I. (1962). The feeling of power. In C. Fadiman (ed.), *The Mathematical Magpie*. New York: Simon & Schuster.
   Asimov compares and contrasts human and computer capabilities in an entertaining and thought-provoking story of a man of the future who discovers that he can actually work arithmetic *without* a computer, giving him *a feeling of power.* How might you use this story with a third grade class?

Basic computing (1984). New York: Scholastic.
   The dictionary provides a good explanation of computer terms. *Basic computing* is a set of workbooks for grades 1 to 6.

Bitter, G. (1982, October). The road to computer literacy. Part II: Objectives and activities for grades K–3. *Electronic Learning*, pp. 34–37, 85.
   Bitter presents a scope and sequence model for computer literacy along with suggested activities for each grade from kindergarten to third.

Conniffe, P. (1984). *Computer dictionary.* New York: Scholastic.

D'Angelo, K. (1983). Computer books for young students: Diverse and difficult. *Reading Teacher, 36,* 626–633.
   The author found that computer books for young children were "diverse and difficult." She provides several examples that illustrate useful diversity and describes ways in which teachers of young children can ease the difficulty.

Hunter, B. (1983). *My students use computers: Learning activities for computer literacy.* Reston, VA: Reston Publishing Co.
   A set of computer literacy objectives and activities for grades K–8. The objectives are classified into six strands: procedures, using programs, fundamentals, applications, impact, and writing computer programs. Lesson plans are comprehension and well written. The book would serve as an excellent resource for teachers.

Krutch, J. (1981). *Experiments in artificial intelligence for small computers.* Indianapolis: Howard W. Sans & Co.

For the reader who wishes to pursue the area in more depth, this book provides some understandable artificial intelligence programs that can be typed into your microcomputer.

Lawson, H. W., Jr. (1981, October). Explaining computer-related concepts and terminology. *Creative Computer,* pp. 92–102.

Markle, S. (1983, September). Close encounters with the inside. *Teaching and Computers,* pp. 15–17.

Taylor, R. (1975). Computerless computing for young children or what to do till the computer comes. In O. Lecarme & R. Lewis (eds.), *Computers in education: Proceedings of the IFIP 2nd World Conference.* New York: American Elsevier.

Taylor provides additional background information and teaching activities.

Weizenbaum, J. (1977, September). How computers work. *ROM,* pp. 60–79.

If you want a more thorough understanding of how computer systems work, and ideas for teaching this to children, consult these references.

6

TEACHING YOUNG CHILDREN ABOUT COMPUTERS
How Computers Are Used

A man, well known in the neighborhood for his ability to do repairs, had helped two families fix their washing machines. They were somewhat surprised, therefore, to see him throwing out several items of clothing: a shrunken wool sweater and several distinctly red T-shirts. But their surprise stemmed from a confusion of knowledge about what a machine is and how it works with knowledge about its use. The man did not know how and when to use it—he mixed red clothes and T-shirts in hot water—and, just as important, when *not* to use it—on wool. So it is with any tool. As we read in Chapter 4, people must understand how and when computers can—and should—be used and the impact of their use on people's lives. To learn about the use of any tool, young children need to discuss its use, see it being used, dramatize its use, and use it themselves.

Of course, this chapter will center on computers. However, the impression should not be given that these ideas are to be taught as a separate unit. The best approach is to integrate these topics into the regular curriculum.

HOW ARE COMPUTERS USED IN OUR NEIGHBORHOOD?

Local Applications of Computers: Types of Applications

The first computers were designed to be used for specific purposes and were too expensive to be used by most businesses and individuals. However, with the advent of the low-cost microcomputer, almost every business, and numerous individuals, began to use this technology to solve their own problems. The myriad present applications often fit into one or more of the following categories. *Computation and data summarization* involve solving problems through the application of mathematical or statistical formulas or the tabulations of a number of pieces of information, or data, into categories. *File maintenance* involves storing, updating, and retrieving information. Like large, automated systems of file cabinets, computers can change, add, or erase information; sort it (e.g., into alphabetical or numerical order); and produce reports about it (Chapter 14). *Word processing* helps people handle written language (Chapter 12).

Simulations are simplified models of some part of the world. Children's play—with dolls, trucks, blocks, play furniture in a housekeeping center, and so on—is a simple type of simulation. Like a model airplane, simulations have characteristics in common with the real object or situation. Even though they are not the real object, models of airplane wings, in the simulated flight of an air tunnel, can tell us much about how a real airplane's wings would perform.

All simulations are models—the real objects are not in the classroom, only a simulation of them. Discussing the use of such models, or simulations, may help children to understand computer simulations, which are representations of physical situations or conditions according to a mathematical model. In the adult world, an executive might want to predict how a new advertising campaign would affect her sales. A couple wants to buy a new car but is unsure how their budget would be affected. A professor would like each student in his reading course to learn how to administer an informal reading inventory but does not know if they have the skills to work successfully with children. All these people wish to know "What if." Computer simulations can help them to answer their questions. For instance, the couple would "try out" the purchase by entering the payments into their computer's budget program, thus seeing how it would affect their financial condition for the next few years.

Teaching about Computer Applications

The supermarket. The best way in which to introduce children to such uses is to integrate the material into social studies units. For instance, one kindergarten class took a walk to a nearby supermarket. One of the goals was to find out how computers were used there. They observed the markings on products and how the computer "read" these, printing the name of the item and the price on a receipt and a display. These coded lines on products, the Alphanumeric Bar Code or ABC, also allow automatic tabulation of inventory, prices, sales, and taxes for later use. The children heard the manager explain how he used the computer to take inventory. The computer stored the information about items that were needed. At the end of the week, the manager called a larger computer on the telephone (!) and had his computer "talk" to the other, transferring his order for goods. In simple terms, the manager told how the computer helped him with the store's accounting, billing, taxes, and payroll.

Back in the classroom, the student's play store was soon overstocked with "goods" brought from home and quickly brought into the world of high technology as the children planned, constructed, and played with a "store computer." One kindergarten teacher used the carton computer, which she had previously used in the housekeeping, office, and block centers. They dramatized using it in all the ways the manager had explained. At the checkout counter, a girl slid the products over the plastic panel so the computer could read the products' codes and tabulate the inventory. Another group attached the store's "computer" to a cardboard modem and a play telephone. On the other play telephone, a group of "warehouse workers" took the order from their own computer and set about gathering the needed goods. The teachers intervened only to help them figure out who was using the make-believe computer ("We're the guys in the stockroom"), what they were using it for ("We're trying to order the food we need in our store"), what data they were putting in ("We typed in all the stuff we sold"), and what they did with the output ("The computer shows what we need to order, so we call up the warehouse and tell 'em to let our computer talk to theirs"). In a final activity, children used the classroom computer to play a simulation of buying and selling (see Chapter 14).

Transportation. Many young children love trucks, trains, cars, and planes. Through field trips, books, or other media, they can be shown that the transportation industry uses computers to plot paths for shipping, control railroad trains and yards as well as air traffic, train pilots, design safe aircraft, and construct that aircraft. Again, it will require very little effort on the teacher's part to get children to incorporate pretend computers into their transportation play. The teacher's talent is used, as usual, in extending children's understandings of the role of the computer by entering into their play or asking pertinent and often challenging questions at crucial moments; for example, "You're the air traffic controller? *How* is the computer helping you? What information are you giving it? What information is it giving you? What do you do now?" Do you recognize a pattern in these two sets of questions? In each activity, teachers should strive to help children understand and use basic concepts concerning how computers are used in the neighborhood (see Table 6–1 and Hunter, 1983).

The hospital. One urban class found out how computers were used in a nearby hospital. Nurses showed them how computers assist with such tasks as room and bed assignments, determining kinds and amounts of

TABLE 6–1 Basic Concepts About How Computers Are Used

---

1. People want to use computers to help them do what they want to do.
2. Someone instructs the computers to do what people want.
3. People use computers to do many different jobs involving *information.*
4. A person puts information into the computer (input).
5. The computer does something with the information (processing) and shows the person what it did (output).
6. The person uses the new information from the computer to do his or her job.

---

medicine, planning meals nutritionally designed for specific patients' needs, and monitoring the health of patients. In the laboratories, they found that computers helped perform tests and that new medical techniques are tested via simulations. A doctor explained the newest advance, "expert" computer systems that can make decisions in ways similar to humans and thus help with diagnoses. The doctor provides symptoms, and the computer generates possible hypotheses for the doctor to consider.

The post office. Children in another school found that computers help to sort letters, read addresses, schedule transportation, regulate the working environment, inspect mail, and even keep track of how many computers are being used! Eventually the electronic mail and message will replace paper mail to a great extent. Messages will be transported almost instantly. They will be read, replied to, sent to other parties, discarded, and filed with a flick of a computer key (Nelson, 1981).

Government is the largest user of computers. The Census Bureau and Internal Revenue Service collect and process large amounts of data from individuals and businesses. The bureau of the budget depends on computers to predict how much money various agencies will need and how much will be available. Virtually all governmental record keeping is done with computers. The court system is beginning to manage information and time with the aid of the computer. Along with the FBI and police agencies, national records are kept concerning crime.

Science. As you might expect, scientists use computers in many interesting ways. They have been used to uncover sites and facts in archaeological studies, monitor volcanic activity, analyze soil samples and movements of the earth to locate probable oil deposits, study the communication of porpoises, determine the proportion of pollutants present in water or air, and predict the weather.

Art. Not just tools for the business manager, bureaucrat, or scientist, computers have entered the world of the arts. They have helped artists to draw; create cartoons; produce graphic images, television commercials, and movies; design sculptures; compose traditional and computer-generated musical compositions; and construct multimedia pieces.

Other teaching ideas. Whatever uses can be uncovered in your neighborhood should be investigated. For other uses, vicarious experiences are useful. Books, television programs, filmstrips, magazines, newspapers, and local industries provide a variety of resources for teachers introducing computer applications and careers. Helpful books include Gloria and Esther Goldreich's *What Can She Be? A Computer Scientist* (1979) and Berger's *Computers In Your Life,* (1981) as well as those listed in the previous chapter. A class library might be created. Students can use these sources to construct collages, scrapbooks, and reports. Wall collages can brighten the classroom. A bulletin board might be divided into four sections, categorized, and labeled as the last four "basic concepts" in Table 6–1. Children, individually or in groups, could pick one computer use—supermarket, banks, business, and so on—and locate and mount pictures for that use under each category.

People from organizations and businesses—banks, stores, police, post offices, government offices, libraries, travel agencies, newspapers—will be happy to come in and speak to your class about their use of computers. They might bring in examples of computer input and output. They can help to describe the many types of computer-related jobs, such as terminal operators who type in information; technicians who service the machinery; programmers who develop, "debug," test, and implement computer programs; and operations supervisors and systems analysts who oversee or plan for the use of computer systems. A staff member from your own school might discuss the school's use of computers for payroll, inventories, and student records. Notice that the emphasis in all these studies should be on *information* and the way in which computers handle it to help people do their jobs.

Impact of Computers on the Neighborhood

Computer crime. Implicit in the all the foregoing is the notion the computers can be used to benefit people in all walks of life. However, computers can also cause problems and be misused. Problems include loss of jobs and privacy, feelings of powerlessness and mechanization, and increase in crime. Computers are also vulnerable to many types of abuse, in particular embezzlement: whereas the average noncomputer embezzlement involves about $100,000, those involving computers average over $1,000,000.

Computer crimes are difficult to uncover, in part because of the nature of the crime (i.e., little or no physical evidence is created). Can these crimes be prevented? As with all crime, the most effective prevention involves moral education along with the knowledge of computer/information ethics. That this is true is supported by the fact that many computer criminals believe that they are just playing a challenging "game" when they tamper with passwords and access others' systems. Computer crimes, in the end, are human crimes and they necessitate human solutions.

Privacy. As with crimes, the issue of privacy is not unique to the world of the computer. Yet because of the need to store volumes of information about people in computer data banks, many people fear that their privacy has been seriously threatened. While we should maintain vigilance concerning our right to privacy, at least one expert's research has led him to conclude that it is the record-keeping practices of organizations, not their use or misuse of computers, that causes the problems that occur (Frates & Moldrup, 1980).

We are an information society, and that information must be safeguarded. Active roles must be assumed by individuals regarding the use of computers. Education must play an essential role in producing a literate, concerned population.

Can young children understand these issues? They may seem very "adult" and inappropriate for your students. However, even the youngest should deal with them on a practical and immediate level that *mirrors* the "adult" issues. The following comparison describes rules that children can be expected to understand and follow and their adult counterparts (for the latter, see the right-hand column). Teachers who see the comparison will lead more meaningful discussions and will guide children to understand—bit by bit—the larger issues involved. (Detailed *positive* rules—the most important kind to use with children—are discussed in Chapter 8.)

CLASSROOM COMPUTER RULES	SOCIETY'S LAWS AND ETHICS
1. Take care not to harm the computer or computer programs because we share them with other people.	1. Respect the property of others.
2. Use the computer fairly—keep on the schedule; do not use other people's time.	2. Follow contractual agreements; be fair and considerate. It is illegal to use computer time that does not belong to you.
3. Do not erase or change other people's programs, and do not change what is on their disks.	3. Respect others' ownership of programs and data. It is illegal to tamper with others' information.
4. When using a program (e.g., a CAI/CMI program) do not try to learn or use someone else's password or "sign on" with their name.	4. Respect the privacy of others. It is illegal to use their information without permission or use codes that are not yours.
5. Do not copy programs that are someone else's without their permission.	5. It is illegal to copy or use programs or data that is copyrighted or that you do not have permission to use.

These rules deal with actual situations that make the issues concrete and real for young children. The classroom is used as a microcosm of society. In later years, these issues will be dealt with at increasingly deeper levels. Children should be given positive procedures to follow and told why these procedures are necessary, or the teacher might lead a brainstorming session or two to determine rules democratically. Later discussions should reiterate the rules and ask children to explain their justification. Older children should be led to see the connection between their classroom rules and societal laws and ethics.

Attitudes toward computers. There are many widely held attitudes and beliefs toward computers that, regardless of their accuracy, form public opinion. One of these beliefs is that computers are incapable of error, in the sense that whatever a computer "says" is correct and not open to question or change. Many think of the computer as the ultimate intelligence or brain that can operate without people and will surpass them in capability. People often feel that the computer is strange and complex—too strange to be comprehensible.

Most of these beliefs and attitudes stem from basic misunderstandings of the roles of humans and machines. There is a need for accurate, and preferably firsthand, information about computers so that the citizens of tomorrow will neither be intimidated nor misinformed about computers and their potentials: for societal good, for misuse, and for personal growth and enrichment.

HOW CAN WE USE COMPUTERS?

As was emphasized in the previous chapter, children will not fully understand how computers are used only by learning about how others use them. We will now turn to what is probably the most important use of computers in education—use by children. Most of the remainder of this book will illustrate how children can use computers to solve problems, write programs of their own, learn subject matter, and generally use the computer as a tool to realize their full potential. Also included is information that teachers need to open up this exciting world for their students.

THINK ABOUT

1. Should children explicitly discuss the connections between their classroom rules and adult laws?
2. Does every child have a right to access to a computer at home and at school? Would you deny anyone access to a pencil, book, or news source? Do you ever learn much about anything or from anything that is not close at hand? For example, would you look up an interesting word you came across in a dictionary that was upstairs? In the library across town? Right next to you? What about if you could (verbally) ask a computerized dictionary to answer you instantly?
3. Computer crimes, it was concluded, are human crimes. What does this mean for a computer literacy curriculum? Should we teach ethics within such a curriculum? Or should such ethics be dealt with in other, specifically designed coursework (or, should this be the domain of schools at all?).
4. What attitudes would you *want* your students to have toward computers? What are your attitudes? Do you feel leery, anxious, even a bit resentful? Try to examine those feelings. What could you do to discover if these feelings are valid.
5. Undoubtedly, computers will eliminate jobs, especially those that are timeconsuming, tedious, and laborious. There is disagreement as to whether an equal number of service or knowledge-oriented jobs will be created. Leisure time may, by necessity, increase. Will educators need to prepare children both for the future's careers and its leisure time?
6. Do you think that students who are not computer literate will be significantly disadvantaged in our society at the time of their graduation?

CURRICULUM CONSTRUCTION CORNER

7. Plan a field trip emphasizing computer uses. Make sure that you use the structure in Table 6–1.
8. Integrate understanding of computer uses into a curriculum unit in social studies.

ANNOTATED BIBLIOGRAPHY

Billings, K., & Moursund, D. (1979). *Are you computer literate?* Beaverton, OR: Dilithium Press.

Frates, J., & Moldrup, W. (1980). *Introduction to the computer: An integrative approach.* Englewood Cliffs, NJ: Prentice-Hall.

Rothman, S., & Mosmann, C. (1976). *Computers and society* (2nd ed.). Chicago: Science Research Associates.

Sanders, D. (1977). *Computers in society* (2nd ed.). New York: McGraw-Hill.

To increase your depth of awareness of the role of computers in our lives, read one of the many worthwhile books on the subject.

Moursund, D. (1981, October). Introduction to computers in education for elementary and middle school teachers. *The Computing Teacher, 9*(2), 15–24.

Information and activities can be found in this reference.

Quick scan of computer careers. (1982, June). *Changing Times,* pp. 50–51.

Kennedy, J. L., & Winkler, C. (1982). *Computer careers: The complete pocket guide to America's fastest-growing job market.* Cardiff, CA: Sun Features.

Mandell, P. L. (1982). Computer literacy, languages, and careers. *School Library Journal, 28*(8), 19–22.

Other sources provide more extensive listings of computer careers.

7

CHOOSING SOFTWARE AND HARDWARE

CHOOSING SOFTWARE

Miss Marong was miserable. After all that effort to get a computer into her kindergarten class, it had only increased the number of frustrating experiences that her students had and headaches that she had. She had been so excited about buying it that she had ordered software quickly through the mail. But now most of it lay scattered on her desk, unused, and very few children even asked to use the computer for any reason. One program was advertised to teach shape, number, and visual discrimination. When it came, she and the children had a terrible time figuring out how to run the activities since there were no directions. Finally stumbling on the solution, they discovered that the program showed pairs of shapes or numerals at 3-second intervals. When they matched, the child was to press any key. Unfortunately, there were still many problems. Most of her students already could discriminate between such elementary shapes. The numeral 0 looked like a rectangle. And the worst was that her children got bored just sitting there with nothing to do most of the time. This was interactive learning? Now what was she to do, with the funds spent for the year?

Unfortunate circumstances like these are common when teachers do not follow sound software evaluation practices. There are a few simple procedures that can keep this from happening to you and ensure that you will purchase programs that meet your children's needs. Many useful checklists have been written to assist teachers in the evaluation of software. However, early childhood educators generally agree that teaching the young child is different in important ways from teaching older children. Therefore, the software will be evaluated from two perspectives, each of which considers the needs of the young. The first is a broad view. Principle 9 in the first chapter stated that computer practices should be consonant with *another* set of principles—those of early childhood education. Therefore, the first view provides guidelines to use in examining whether various programs—even those that look "flashy" on first inspection—follow these general principles. The second view focuses on important facets of the medium itself and provides a checklist designed to be used to evaluate individual programs to be used with young children.

EARLY CHILDHOOD EDUCATION PRINCIPLES AND COMPUTER PROGRAMS

In a flurry of activity, various producers of software are generating numerous programs for the young child. These programs are becoming increasingly easy to use and more sophisticated graphically. But are these programs beneficial to children? Many features of educational computer programs—interactivity, for example—are consonant with early childhood educational principles. Other features are not. Does the novelty of the medium and the "flashiness" of computer graphics blind many of us to practices that might conflict with principles of early childhood education that we use as guidelines for evaluating other facets of the program? If we allow this to happen, we will do a disservice to our students, and we may needlessly reject computers when we finally recognize the conflict, *after* we have used the programs. We might even conclude that computer use is not appropriate for young children, when actually it was only the software, unwisely purchased, that was inappropriate.

Principles of Early and Primary Education

Although there is no single list of accepted principles of early childhood education, there is a great deal of agreement. The following represents some of those often cited (Fowler, 1980; Frost & Kissinger, 1976; Leeper et al., 1974; Nimnicht, McAfee, & Meier, 1969).

A. Provide opportunities for social growth and the development of a positive self image.
B. Provide for intrinsic, rather than extrinsic, motivation. The curriculum grows out of the personal interests of the child; play is an important vehicle for learning.
C. Provide a minimally restrictive environment that encourages autonomy and exploration and is responsive to the child.
D. Provide for feedback that is a natural consequence of the child's activity.
E. Emphasize the child's active participation rather than passive reception in planning and executing the activity.
F. Provide practice in setting realistic goals and in predicting and confirming events.
G. Provide for exploration of problems involving real situations and concrete materials.
H. Encourage multiple solutions and alternate routes to any solution.
I. Use techniques to ease the learning of complex material; teach general rules about regularities instead of collections of unrelated facts.
J. Encourage transfer by allowing the children to discover relationships by themselves and by providing them the experience during learning of applying principles within a variety of tasks.

K. Provide many opportunities for children to express themselves freely and creatively.
L. Develop aesthetic interests, skills, and values.
M. Provide many opportunities for learning without pressure for mastery.
N. Allow for the adjustment of learning opportunities for children differing in intellectual abilities, interests, and ways of learning.

Several computer programs designed for young children will be described. As you read, consider how well these programs follow these principles of early education.

Computer Practices

One technically sophisticated package designed for young children teaches several mathematics concepts. One lesson on seriation graphically presents five unordered bars of different heights. The child must place a marker under each and type in a number (1 through 5) corresponding to that bar's place in the series; that is, the shortest bar is number 1, the next taller is number 2, and so on. If the child succeeds, a face smiles and a point is added to a running total of the number correct. If the child makes an error, the face frowns and a point is added to a total of the number incorrect.

Certainly, several of the educational principles are in evidence in this program: the child receives feedback concerning the correctness of the response and self-discovery may take place (principle J of this chapter). However, in our initial appreciation of the cleverness of the programming, we may overlook other principles that are not upheld and are possibly violated. For instance, consider the nature of the task. The child is not actually actively manipulating concrete materials to solve a problem (principle G). For Piaget, it is just this manipulation that is essential for cognitive growth. The many possible solution strategies that children use in ordering objects (e.g., Young, 1976) are not only not encouraged, they are not possible (principle H). When a child orders blocks, the feedback he or she receives is real and meaningful—the blocks either form "steps" or they do not. In the computer program, the frowning face feedback is not a natural consequence of the child's activity (principle D). This feedback may emphasize extrinsic, rather than intrinsic, motivation (principle B). The score keeping may place undesirable pressure for mastery on the child (principle M). Finally, it would seem that neither this program nor the program described at the beginning of the chapter will encourage autonomy, active planning, setting goals, self-expression, aesthetic interests, and true individualization (principles C, E, F, K, L, and N).

The Story Machine (Spinnaker) is a program designed to allow children to compose stories. The child types in sentences and watches as they are graphically portrayed. One boy typed, A GIRL RUNS TO THE TREE. A small figure and then a tree appeared on the screen. The girl then ran over to the tree. Feeling silly, the boy typed THE TREE RUNS TO THE BOY. Obligingly, the tree turned to the side and, on its newly discovered legs, ran to a boy who had appeared on the other side of the screen (Figure 7–1).

FIGURE 7-1 A child's sentences on *The Story Machine.* (Photo by David Barnett.)

Young children can "teach the computer" rather than being taught by it if they use one of the several computer languages that allows them to program the computer to draw pictures using simple commands. They draw by directing a triangular pointer around the display screen. Shortly after being introduced to Logo, Kristen drew the picture in Figure 7–2. (See Chapter 10 for an extensive discussion of Logo.)

These two programs, although quite different, share some educational attributes that are consistent with early education principles. Both tend to encourage socialization and the development of positive self-concepts (principle A). The motivation is intrinsic; children have sentences to write and pictures to draw (principle B). The open nature of these activities encourages active exploration, provides practice in setting goals and predicting and confirming events, and encourages transfer by requiring the child to discover relationships and concepts (principles C, E, F, H, J). Logo, however, is less restrictive and more amenable to multiple solutions. The

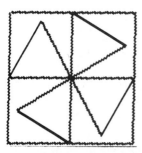

FIGURE 7–2
Kristen's picture, programmed in Logo. (From Terrapin.)

vocabulary and syntax accepted in *The Story Machine* are extremely limited (thus, principles C and H may be partially violated).

The problems that are explored in both programs are real and concrete to the child (principle G). Some may question the latter term; however, the animation of a child's story or the creation of a drawing *is* concrete to the child; indeed, Papert (1980) maintains that Logo can "concretize" thinking processes and lead children to "think about their thinking." The child receives feedback based on her own activity—the tree runs to the boy, the square is drawn (principle D). However, *The Story Machine* may not accept some sentences that are perfectly valid without telling the child why. Powerful, generalizable ideas are taught (within the limitations discussed): syntax, subject/object relations, directionality, breaking a problem into manageable pieces, and so forth (principles I and J).

Opportunities for free expression and aesthetic appreciation for art are provided in Logo without pressure for immediate mastery (principles K, L, and M). *The Story Machine* allows for some such expression, although within a much more restricted range. Finally, Logo encourages individual explorations by children who differ in abilities and interests (principle N).

Neither of these programs represents a computing panacea (nor is the seriation program totally without merit—in addition, other lessons in the same package are quite worthwhile). Limitations of *The Story Machine* that could lead to a violation of some of the principles have been mentioned. It might be viewed as being partially compatible with the principles. Also, it is the responsibility of the teacher to create a balanced Logo environment. On one hand, children need to be guided and challenged. On the other hand, if the individual project approach degenerates into the imposition of a required curriculum, the activity will violate the principles and will represent one more area in which children will feel anxious and pressured. Therefore, teachers are still the most important factor. Nevertheless, Logo does represent an *idea* or conception of educational software that is consistent with most of the principles listed.

Eyes of the beholder. These comments are but one person's view of the match between the programs' characteristics and educational principles. As a teacher of young children, you must look beyond the "bells and whistles" and examine *with your own eyes* to what extent the goals and methodology of these programs are consonant with the principles of *your* program. This will ensure that the computer programs you use will be pedagogically consistent with your overall program and will benefit your students. The principles upon which your program is based may be different from some of those listed. That is to be expected, and it is the reason that this level of evaluation was kept separate from the upcoming, more specific evaluative criteria. The intent of this section is not to convince you to adopt these principles of early education—although it is hoped that you give them some thought. Rather, the intent is to persuade you that *you should evaluate any software in terms of the principles upon which your program is based.*

CRITERIA FOR EVALUATING SOFTWARE

Evaluation according to specific criteria is even more necessary for software than for printed or manipulative materials. With the latter, teachers and children have some control over sequencing, use, and modification. There is much less possibility for this kind of control in most computer materials.

Table 7–1 is a software identification and evaluation checklist appropriate for materials designed for young children. Notice that the rating scale to be used ranges from 0 (the characteristic is not present in the

TABLE 7–1 Software Identification and Evaluation Checklist

I. *Identification*
    Name _____
    Producer _____
    Address _____
    _____

    Hardware required
    Brand _____
    Memory required _____
    Operating system _____
    Special language required _____
    Disk/tape/cartridge _____
    Equipment required (peripherals, number of disk drives, color monitor, printer, speech synthesizer, paddles or joystick, etc.) _____
    _____

    Backup policy _____
    Cost _____
    Subject/topic _____
    Objectives _____
    Prerequisites _____
    Age/ability level _____
    Description
    Instructional strategy _____
    Management system _____
    Program structure _____
    _____

    Grouping _____
    Average time of student interaction _____

		RATING* COMMENT
II. *Evaluation*		
A. Content		
1. Appropriateness of content		
a. Does it match your curriculum?		
b. Is it educationally significant?		_____
c. Is it suitable for young children?		_____
2. Is the content accurate?		_____
3. Are the values explicitly or implicitly presented those of your program?		_____
B. Instructional considerations		
1. Is it consistent with the principles of your educational program?		_____

2. Instructional design
   a. Are the objectives and purpose well defined? _____
   b. Are prerequisite skills listed? _____
   c. Are the learning activities well designed? _____
   d. Are the assessments viable? _____
3. Can it be modified for individual students? _____
4. Appropriateness of characteristics
   a. Is the teaching strategy appropriate? _____
   b. Does it stimulate convergent and/or divergent thinking appropriately? _____
   c. Does the child control the rate and sequence appropriately? _____
   d. Is the feedback appropriate? _____
   e. Does it employ graphics (color and animation) and sound appropriately? _____
   f. Is the management appropriate? _____
5. Is field test data available? _____

C. Social/emotional
   1. Will the program motivate and sustain interest? _____
   2. Will it build self-concept? _____
   3. Is there an appropriate balance of cooperation and competition? _____
   4. Does it encourage social problem solving? _____
   5. Does it encourage sharing? _____

D. Performance/operation
   1. Ease of use
      a. Can it be used with little effort? _____
      b. Are instructions simple? _____
      c. Is input appropriate? _____
      d. Are directions, menus, and on-line help available? _____
      e. Is the level of difficulty appropriate? _____
      f. Is the presentation clear and consistent? _____
   2. Error handling
      a. Is the program reliable (free of bugs)? _____
      b. Are keys that are not used disabled? _____
      c. Can children correct mistakes? _____
      d. Does the program limit the number of errors it allows before offering help? _____
      e. Can the program handle diverse input? _____
   3. Is the operation fast (i.e., loading before and during operation)? _____

E. Is the documentation for teachers and students adequate?
   1. Are clear directions for load the program included? _____
   2. Is there a full description of the program, including objectives, background, prerequisite skills, etc.? _____
   3. Are support materials supplied? _____

F. Global evaluation (1 to 5) _____

G. Comments (strengths, weaknesses, potential):

_____

_____

---

*Rating scale: 0–5

0 Characteristic does not exist in program	3	No opinion
1 Strongly disagree	4	Agree
2 Disagree	5	Strongly agree

program) to 1 (program possesses the characteristic, but receives a very low rating) to 5 (the highest rating). This rating scale has been found to be quite useful as is or as entered into a computerized filing system for easy storage, sorting, ordering, and retrieval. Explanations of the various categories on the checklist follow.

I. Identification

This portion of the checklist enables teachers to find the program that they need. Beware that most programs developed for one type of computer will not run on any other type. That is why it is essential to know exactly what *hardware* is required to run the software. As an illustrative example, one package requires brand, Apple II; memory, 48K; operating system, DOS 3.3; special language, none; disk drive; and color monitor. In the future, more "emulators" may be produced that allow software designed for one machine to run on another. Manufacturers may someday agree to adopt universal standards. For now, however, listen to claims critically and check them yourself.

Young children have a tendency to believe that "being careful" with a fragile disk means yanking it away from a friend and protecting it by hugging it closely to the body. It is therefore especially important to have a backup copy of the program. A few producers of software for young children are beginning to allow teachers to make their own inexpensive backup copies to use with the children (the original is then stored safely away in case of mishap). Most, however, still "copy protect" their software; that is, they make it difficult to make a copy by normal means. If this is the case, make sure that you can purchase a backup copy for a reasonable price.

As are the names of the program and producer, categories such as subject/topic, age/ability level, objectives, and prerequisite skills should be self-explanatory and familiar to most teachers. The description adds detail to these general categories. Instructional strategies include those discussed in Chapter 2: drill and practice, tutorial, simulation, exploratory/game, and so on. The presence of a management system, such as those described in Chapter 3, should be noted. Program structure includes such characteristics as the sequence of activities, branching, and timing—the general "flow" of the program. Grouping asks whether the program is intended to be used by individuals, small groups, or the whole class. Used in that grouping pattern, what is the average time it would take a student or group of students to use the program each day?

Evaluation*

A. Content.

1. Is the content appropriate for use with young children? It must first match the content of your curriculum. Miss Marong was disappointed in that the visual discrimination program utilized simple shapes that were

*Letters and numbers refer to the corresponding sections of the checklist in Table 7–1.

already easily distinguished by her students. She knew that a computer program that has school-aged children discriminate among a circle, triangle, and square is not *educationally significant*. If the activity is to be a prereading exercise, students should discriminate between letter and word forms—the "stuff" of written language.

As another example, there are several inappropriate ABC programs on the market. First, they contain a poem or other reading material. If the child is reading, what is the sense of his working with an alphabet recognition program? More important, some programs utilize pictures that make it nearly impossible for the prereading child to make the correct letter/sound connection. One uses mythical beasts, many of which were unknown to adults. This content is not *suitable* for independent use by most young children. Another uses "rabbit" for "R" (many children say "bunny") and "airplane" for "A" (many children say "plane"). Most children never even approach the correct labels for the pictures of quilt, parrot, and night.

2. Accuracy, or integrity, of content should be checked. Some reading material contains spelling and grammatical errors. Many times these are not immediately obvious. One teacher worked with a word discrimination program a long time before she discovered that if a child answered only one of several questions correctly, he was informed, "THERE ARE ONLY 1 WORD IN THE GOOD BOX." Information should be authentic and up to date. Accurate directions are also required. One math program for primary grade children printed, "PRESS ANY KEY TO CONTINUE," but only the RETURN key worked.

3. Values of a program may be obvious or hidden. Games based on violence are an anathema to many educators of young children. Activities that emphasize the view of the world as basically competitive would conflict with many teachers' programs. Materials containing racial, ethnic, or sexual stereotypes should be avoided just as biased materials in any media should be avoided.

B. Instructional considerations.

1. The primary consideration is whether the software is consistent with the principles upon which the educational program is based. This, of course, was discussed in the first section of this chapter.

2. Every piece of software used in the classroom should follow the rules of instructional design. It should have an identified purpose. The objectives need not be strictly behavioral; most teachers of young children know the value of open-ended, exploratory activities. However, justifications that a game is "fun" and promotes "eye-hand coordination and some thinking abilities" are insufficient. Prerequisite skills should be listed, so it can be determined what skills or knowledge the child must already possess before using the materials.

The learning activities must be well designed. For drill and practice and tutorial programs, that means that the activities should follow from the objectives and be carefully sequenced and well organized. Young learners should know what they are to learn. The program should focus their attention on the material, provide guidance, ask for a mental and physical response for the children, provide appropriate feedback, and assess the performance. Tutorial programs should branch to appropriate material if a common mistake is made. For instance, if in response to "4 + _____ = 9," a child types "13," a tutorial program should explain the structure of the problem, not present more practice on number facts. Assessment should be frequent. Provisions should be made in both types of programs for progression in the level of difficulty. Management and record keeping should be available.

Other types of software are evaluated according to different criteria. Simulations should be selected primarily on the grounds that they allow children to explore a situation that they otherwise could not or, conversely, that they do *not* replace that which would better be experienced directly (recall the examples in Chapter 2). Considering the children's age, determine how many variables are manipulated within the program. The younger the children, the fewer the variables they should manipulate. There should not be a single strategy that works every time—this would be unrealistic and unchallenging; however, younger children should not be overwhelmed with a great number of possible strategies. Realism and challenge are also heightened if the program contains at least some random events, such as the weather in *Oregon*. Documentation is a particularly necessary component of a simulation package. It should include a description of the program and the variables, a list of the assumptions, background information, suggestions for teaching, and other support materials.

Games should be based on the material to be taught rather than on an artificial situation such as a space battle. The game itself should embody the concepts within an environment that can be explored at several levels of difficulty. The instructions for playing the games should be less complicated than the content the games are to teach. Cooperation as well as competition should be involved. Players should be active participants, without waiting long periods between turns. Choice in the level of difficulty should be provided; it should progress as the child gains skill. Feedback should be clear and related to conceptual errors.

Assessments, if included in the program, should be expected to meet the same standards as any other tests. They should be reliable, yielding results you can trust. They should be valid; that is, they should actually measure what they purport to measure.

3. Programs can be "individualized" for students in many ways. Some, discussed in Chapter 3, involve computer management of the assignments given to students. This is similar to versions of "individualized education" such as IPI (individually prescribed instruction) and is appropriate for tutorial and drill and practice programs. However, there is also the type of individualization that teachers employ when they provide rich environments for learning that can be explored at many levels of complex-

ity and difficulty, for example, painting, working with blocks, or writing. Many computer games and exploratory environments are designed to be individualized in this way. For example, children working with a drawing program bring different abilities and interests to it and create different pictures with it, just as they do at the easel.

4. All programs should follow the rules of instructional design. However, it is a mistake to believe that all good programs should be identical in every way. Some characteristics are appropriate for one type of program but not for another (Roblyer, 1981).

The teaching strategy should be matched to the goals and objectives of the program. As was discussed at length in Chapter 2, a drill and practice format is appropriate for building essential skills that require intensive practice with immediate feedback. Convergent, automatic responses should be encouraged. However, to foster divergent or reflective thinking, a guided discovery strategy is more appropriate.

Divergent thinking is developed significantly when the child interacts frequently with the program and makes many decisions. These programs are often open-ended, provide for many "spin-offs," and anticipate a wide range of responses.

These two teaching strategies also necessitate different degrees of student control. If mastery of a predetermined set of skills is desired, such as recognition of the letters on the keyboard, it is better to allow the machine to control the sequence and pace of instruction, assigning practice on needed material and gradually increasing the rate at which items are presented. A tutorial on reading for the main idea, however, should allow the child to read and reread at his or her own rate. Children also vary. Some, especially the bright and motivated, work well when they are given control over what and how they will learn. Others need more guidance.

Appropriate feedback will vary according to several factors. Younger children may enjoy cartoon graphics that would seem childish to their older schoolmates. Several commercial programs allow the teachers to select the type of reinforcement. Drill and practice programs designed to depelop automatic responses should not employ the same type and extent of feedback as, say, a tutorial. Generally, incorrect responses in the former should *not* be met with elaborate animation or verbal messages such as "WRONG, JOHNNY. THE ANSWER IS C. COOKIE STARTS WITH C." These types of feedback waste a student's time and interrupt the required fast pace of the lesson. It is more effective and just as informative for the program to make *no* response. For a correct answer, moving to the next problem is reinforcement enough for most students while still providing adequate feedback and increasing time on task. However, in a more complex tutorial program, it may be appropriate to branch to a simple explanation of a child's error. No matter what kind of program is being used, few children benefit from messages such as that on one math package, "NO! NO! TRY AGAIN."

Another consideration is the reinforcement value of feedback. In one counting program, a train chugs onto the screen containing a different number of cars each time. The child counts them and types the number. If correct, a new train chugs on; if not, the train falls apart. Which do you think young children would rather see? What does that encourage?

There are several levels at which more elaborate feedback is presented. At the first level, a simple verbal message or picture is presented, as in the programs already described. At the second level, the student is offered a more interactive external reward. Recall the reading program described at the beginning of Chapter 3, which allows a student to play a video game for 1 minute after answering a preset number of questions correctly. At the third level, the child is rewarded by being allowed to participate in an activity that is related to the original activity. In *Arrow Graphics* (from Edu-Fun), children who solve three of the program's graphic design problems correctly are allowed to create their own design. At the fourth level, the feedback is inherent in the activity. Children who compose a simple song and then listen to it as it is played back are receiving this type of feedback.

What level of feedback is best? Although each type is necessary in specific situations, the feedback that is related to content of the program is probably most powerful educationally. If the program teaches what Piaget calls "social knowledge," such as the names of letters, it should simply tell the child the correct answer. If the program is designed to facilitate development of "logical-mathematical knowledge," such as understanding if the same number of objects is added to two equal sets the resulting sets are also equal, the program should guide the student to discover the answer, possibly through questions and animated graphics. Feedback can often be effective by utilizing increasing levels of prompts or hints.

Similarly, graphics, color, animation, and sound are valuable components *when they support learning.* When they help to illustrate concepts, especially dynamic concepts, they are important aids. However, research has not shown that elaborate color graphics increase learning in every situation. Color has potential disadvantages—color monitors are more expensive, and some children have color blindness to certain shades. Quality software has options for those without color monitors, such as different black-and-white shadings. In addition, peripheral enhancements may draw the attention of many young children away from that which is important. For prereading children, for drawing programs, for programs that illustrate vocabulary words, and the like, graphics are, of course, essential. There should be an option to turn off sound that is not essential.

C. Social/emotional

1. The program should be interesting to children. Malone (1980) investigated the characteristics of computer games in an effort to discover what made them intrinsically motivating. He found that three elements were especially important: challenge, fantasy, and feedback. This is especially interesting for early childhood educators who have long recognized the important place of these elements in children's development.

They can serve as guidelines for evaluating the potential of software for generating intrinsic interest. In addition, many children are motivated to use programs that address them in a personal style, have a friendly tone and employ simple humor, use graphics and other computer capabilities in creative ways, allow for a variety of responses, include a high degree of active involvement and control, provide appropriate, helpful feedback, and illustrate children's progress.

Another concern is that programs sustain children's interest. Teachers are often delighted by a variety of ABC or numeral identification programs when they first use them. They touch a key and the letter or numeral appears, along with a picture illustrating the letter (as an initial consonant of the name of an object) or numeral (as a set of objects). After about the sixth key press, however, they get a bit bored. After the tenth, they start wondering if their students will get bored. Programs that are more complex or sufficiently open-ended have more potential for sustaining the interest of adults and children alike.

2. Programs that motivate children and sustain their interest are more likely to build the child's self-concept. Whenever possible, programs should also assure a positive balance between success and failure, encourage the child to invent his or her own ideas, and allow each child to express his or her own creativity and personality.

3, 4, and 5. Programs can be designed and used in ways to encourage, rather then discourage, interaction among children. Competition may be used effectively on occasion, such as between groups involved in a simulation or between students and the computer. However, both these examples also involve cooperation among children. Simulations that *necessitate* cooperation among children in a group have been written for older students; such materials undoubtedly will become available for primary grade children.

D. Performance/operation.

1. The program should be easy to use for both students and teachers. It should start effortlessly and continue to run without complicated setup or frequent changing of disks. Instructions and routines should be simple enough for the age level. Reminders should be included in the display. Help should be offered in using the program. One educator reported that his son was typing numbers into a coordinates game such as the one described in Chapter 2. The boy typed in a space between the numbers again and again. His father finally had to help him. A simple screen prompt such as "Are you typing a comma?" would have solved the problem. The input for the program should be simple for the young, often involving hitting a single key or *any* key as a response or manipulating objects pictured on the screen with a joystick. The level of difficulty should be appropriate also in terms of other requirements: reading level, attention span, level of reasoning, and so on. Menus and help should be offered and readily accessible.

The screen presentation should be well planned and consistent.

Layouts should be easy to comprehend and uncluttered. Voice synthesis should provide an invaluable aid for giving instructions and help to young children. Their teachers should lobby for this.

To determine the ease of use, run through the program yourself and observe students as they use it. Do not tolerate poor materials, but avoid giving up on a good program too soon. For example, quite often primary grade students can use programs written for older children if they are given support. If the goals and activities of a program are sound, young children are amazingly able to tackle required keypresses or other aspects.

2. Obviously, programs should be free of programming errors. But they should also handle errors by users. If someone enters a word instead of a number, or inserts extra spaces as young children often do, does the program freeze or fail ("crash")? Quality software does not allow young children to inadvertently stop the program just by pressing an inappropriate key. In one program, children were asked to type in "yes" or "no." When they typed "y," the program accepted this as the answer and went on. This is normally helpful, as it eliminates unnecessary typing. However, in this case the program still accepted the "es" and used it as the child's answer to the *next* question. Because the response was to be a number, the program froze (the children didn't; they merrily hammered on keys at random until the teacher intervened).

Keys that are not to be used should be disabled; that is, nothing should happen if they are pressed. In one math program, this was not done. Children who entered a letter repeatedly got the computer-generated response "REENTER," which was not helpful. Children should be able to correct typing mistakes before the program analyzes their answer. The program might allow erasing with the "backward arrow" key or might ask the child, "You want the block A, 1. Is that right? (Y/N)." If the child types "N," he is allowed to type his choice again.

If children do not know an answer, the program should not make them try again and again until they get it right. This can generate frustration and encourage random hitting of keys. The program should be able to accept "8" or "eight," or possibly even the misspelling "eigth" if that number is the answer. To encourage children to use the appropriate keys, programs should supply simple directions; guides as to which keys are to be used, including picture clues; and clear menus.

3. The program should load from a disk or tape quickly, both at the beginning and at points where this is needed within the program. Young children's attention span cannot usually tolerate long delays with nothing to do. A message that something *is* happening should be given.

E. Documentation. Documentation, the written materials accompanying the program, should list the objectives and prerequisite skills. It should supply a basic description of the content and structure of the program, including all the information described under the "Identification" portion of the checklist in Table 7–1. Clear directions for using the program should be included, such as directions for loading, special keys and commands, and information about program flow and on-screen menus. Sample "runs" are helpful. Support materials should offer suggestions for introducing, integrating, and following up on the program. Background information and resources are useful. When appropriate, the materials should be tied to specific chapters in widely used textbooks. Some programs include a student workbook. Possibilities for program modifications should be described in detail. Some teachers want lengthy, detailed documentation. However, this is not always necessary for simple programs. The best often combine an extended discussion with short summaries and charts to serve both needs.

STEPS FOR EVALUATING SOFTWARE

I. Establish goals first. Make sure you know exactly what you want the program to do, and insist that it does it.

II. Look into the organizations and journals listed in the appendix dedicated to helping teachers locate and evaluate software. If you have any access to a computer, there may be a computerized *data base* that will allow you to search quickly for the programs you want.

III. When locating software, ensure that service is available (including someone who will answer questions).

IV. Obtain the basic documentation and program.

    A. If you cannot obtain the program for preview, check the following:

        1. Did you attempt to submit a purchase order with "on approval" written on it? Make sure that the company must take back the program if you do not approve the purchase.

        2. Are there demonstration disks or tapes available?

        3. Was field testing done? (Some, e.g., Psychotechnics, do conduct field tests. Write to the sites.)

        4. Are reviews available? (Check who the reviewer was: the closer they are to your situation, the better.)

        5. Is it a reputable company?

        Note: Many organizations, such as the Educational Products Information Exchange (EPIE), believe that educators should refuse to buy materials from producers who do not allow preview.

    B. If you can obtain the program,

        1. Go through the program as a successful student would. Test the "intelligence" of the program by making creative or different responses.

        2. Go through the program as a less successful or more "active" student (like "Billy the Bullet") would. Respond incorrectly, not only by making mistakes but also by typing numbers instead of words, hitting the RESET (or RESTORE, BREAK, RUN/STOP, etc.) key, not following directions, and so on. Repeat the same incorrect responses and try different kinds of incorrect responses. What happens? Is the program "bullet-proof"?

        3. If possible, observe several students using the program. Are they interested? Do they understand the program? Do they have any difficulties?

        4. Read the documentation, running through other parts of the program as needed.

V. Complete the evaluation checklist.

VI. Make a decision. Share evaluations with other teachers. If you decide not to purchase the program, return it promptly to the producer with a copy of the evaluation—a valuable way for educators to influence the quality of software.

There are many excellent general checklists and guides for the evaluation of computer software. Many provide an in-depth discussion. If you wish more information, contact any of the organizations listed in the appendix. Most of the magazines and journals listed in the appendix also review software. Remember that no single software evaluation form fits every type of program and that no software evaluation is satisfactory for all teachers. Educators must decide what their needs are and use the information available to help them meet those needs. Teachers following these suggestions will select high-quality programs for their students and will positively influence the field of software development.

HARDWARE EVALUATION

"Why does the section on evaluating hardware come *after* the section on evaluating software? Isn't that putting the cart before the horse? How can you pick software before you have the computers to run it on?"

Of course, you do need hardware to run the software you select. However, the question is, "Which is the horse?" The answer is that actually that *software* is the source of the power of educational applications of computers. *It* is the horse that will give movement and direction to computing; the hardware is merely the vehicle. If either must be considered first, it should be the software. However, because no one gets very far without both the "horse" and "cart," it might be more accurate to say that the evaluations should be made together, looking at software, then at the machines that run it, then at more software, and so on.

Before discussing the evaluation of hardware, it should be stated that there is no research that indicates that one computer is better than another or that any particular characteristic such as color enhances learning. Instead, the general question that must be answered is, "Which machine will do what I want it to do for the least cost?" Taking the following steps should help you answer that question.

Steps in Evaluating Hardware

1. *Determine desired uses of computer.* Every potential user of the computer should list the jobs they would like the machines to do. This list will be constantly revised, but at this stage "pull out the stops" and consider every application for the present and near future.

2. *List computer system features required.* What features are needed to accomplish these aims? Different applications require different features. Table 7–2 gives a brief example of the features required for several educational computer uses. This summary chart cannot be completely specific, however. Programs and computer languages you wish to use may differ,

TABLE 7-2 Required Computer Features for Different Applications

	SUBSTANTIAL MEMORY	LOWERCASE	GRAPHICS	SOUND	DISK STORAGE	SPECIFIC LANGUAGES	PRINTER	SUBSTANTIAL ACCESS TIME
Drill and practice	R	P	R	P	P			P
Tutorials	R	P	R	P	R		P	R
Simulation	R	P	R	R	R		P	R
Exploratory/game	R				R		P	
CMI				P	R		P	
Computer awareness		P	P			P		
Programming								
Logo	R		R	P	R	R	P	R
BASIC			P	P	P	R	P	R
PILOT	R		R	R	R	R	P	R
Word processing	P	R			P		R	R
Utilities (filing, graphing)	R		R		R		R	P

Notes:
R—Required.
P—Preferred.

and you must determine the exact requirements. In addition, requirements differ for different children. For example, tutorials for preschoolers or handicapped children may require speech output.

3. *Survey the field.* If you have little experience with computers, visit a few computer stores and other teachers who are using computers. Try out some computers and software programs. Read about different types and talk to those who have experience using them. While this is not the time to purchase, because it is recommended that you deal locally, you should be aware of the quality and quantity of assistance dealers provide.

4. *Set priorities.* Weight the importance of the features required. Determine the highest priorities of use. Consider especially the time per student required for each use (see the category Substantial Access Time in Table 7–2). Make a decision to implement *only* the highest-priority applications at first. It takes time to get even a limited computer program successfully under way, and a successfully implemented program is the best argument for future program expansion.

5. *Evaluate different computers.* Do a detailed analysis of the computer systems you believe would be suitable, using your goals, the basic criterion of availability of desired programs, and the checklist in Table 7–3 as guidelines. Articles in the suggested references provide mathematical methods for weighing the importance of the requirements, if this appeals to you.

6. *Determine the best buy.* Once the computer system is selected, determine which vendor will give the best price, service, and so on.

Evaluating Hardware: Some Suggestions

1. *Buy from local dealers.* You may be tempted by lower prices offered through mail order. However, once a helpful dealer has provided advice on how to get your word processing program to do what you want it to, or has provided quick repair on an errant electronic device, you will appreciate how important it is to have this assistance immediately available. It is, of course, necessary to ensure that maintenance will be performed at the store and that they are willing to provide the needed assistance.

2. *Look for local users.* It is helpful to have others in your area who use the brand of computer you are buying. Local clubs are usually based on one type of computer and can provide help and ideas for that type.

3. *For a large purchase, consider a consultant.* If your school system is considering purchasing many computers and there is a lack of experience within the system, it would be wise to hire a consultant after the initial goals have been outlined.

4. *Do not necessarily buy "small systems" for small children.* It seems to many that young children require only a limited, inexpensive computer. "They can't do that much, they can use those little computers." Actually, the younger the children, the *more* sophisticated support they need to in-

TABLE 7–3 Hardware Evaluation Checklist

I. *Identification*
   Name _____
   Producer _____
   Address _____
   _____

II. *Evaluation*

	DESCRIPTION	RATING
A. Features		
1. Memory	_____	_____
2. Keyboard	_____	_____
3. Text	_____	_____
4. Graphics	_____	_____
5. Color	_____	_____
6. Sound—music, effects	_____	_____
Sound—speech	_____	_____
7. Power-up diagnostics	_____	_____
8. Storage medium	_____	_____
9. Systems software	_____	_____
10. Languages available	_____	_____
11. Peripherals	_____	_____
B. Durability	_____	_____
C. Allowance for expansion	_____	_____
D. Networking	_____	_____
E. Documentation	_____	_____
F. Ease of use	_____	_____
G. Maintenance	_____	_____
H. Training/assistance	_____	_____
I. Cost:		
Computer (CPU and keyboard)	_____	_____
Monitor	_____	_____
Storage device	_____	_____
Printer	_____	_____
Other peripherals	_____	_____
Sound/speech	_____	_____
Languages	_____	_____
Maintenance	_____	_____
Other supplies (disks, paper, ribbons, etc.)	_____	_____
Other (classroom space or outlets, additional personnel, electricity, insurance, etc.)	_____	_____
Total		_____

Rating scale: 0–5
   0   characteristic does not exist in program
   1   very low
   5   very high

teract with computers on anything but a trivial level. It is the *older* students who have the ability to do interesting things with a restricted machine. We provide young children with the materials and support they need to learn, be it materials such as blocks, paper, clay, and other manipulatives or carefully structured language in activities, questions, and discussions. In the same way, we must supply them with computers capable of providing the support they need. As an analog to materials, the computers should provide easy-to-use graphics, sound, and so on. As an analog to the supportive language/questioning environment, computers should be capable of providing "friendly" programs that help children to succeed by offering helpful, understandable feedback and interact with them in intelligent ways.

5. *Be wary of the "newest breakthrough."* Avoid buying a new product in an effort to own the most technologically advanced machine *if* that machine has not yet "proved itself." Two problems that often plague these computers are (a) mechanical bugs that are not yet worked out and (b) a lack of software. Be somewhat skeptical of promises that a whole line of educational software will be available "real soon now."

6. *Take your time.* The urge to "get going" is strong, but it should be resisted. It is often valuable to buy one computer and explore its capabilities and uses before buying several for a school. Do not be discouraged by delays.

Using the Checklist

Table 7–3 provides a checklist designed to help you evaluate computer systems. The first section involves a brief identification. The evaluation section has spaces for a description and a 0 to 5 rating similar to that used on the software evaluation checklist.

A. Features.

1. Memory. How much memory is available for (a) programs you wish to load into the computer, (b) computer languages such as Logo, or (c) programs written by you and your students in whatever computer language you plan to use? Make sure that the number you hear (such as "48K," meaning about 48,000 characters can be stored) is "user available RAM"; that is, some memory may be taken up by the computer itself to control its operations and thus be unavailable to the user.

2. Keyboard. Are the keys large enough and separated enough to be used easily by young children? Are the figures printed on them clear? Does the keyboard allow typing a full character set (ASCII character set)? Does it include graphic keys if those are desired? Do the keys have the capability to repeat? Are keys that allow movement on the screen (cursor control keys) available and clearly marked? Are the interrupt (BREAK or RESET) keys that disturb a program placed away from the other keys so as not to be pressed accidentally? Can they be disabled manually or are they under the control of computer programs? You may want extra features such as user-defined, or function, keys that permit a key to have a special function in a program, special overlays, or a numeric keypad.

3. Text. Are upper- and lowercase letters available? Do they require an extra expenditure? Are letters clear and readable? How many characters fit onto a single horizontal line?

4. Are graphic images (pictures) clear and distinct? Are special graphic characters or other enhancements available?

5. As mentioned, there is little evidence that color enhances learning. However, you may wish to use this feature for any of several reasons: (a) color recognition is a desired goal, (b) the software you wish to use necessitates color, or (c) you believe that color will motivate your students. If so, make sure that the computer *and* the TV or monitor have color capability.

6. Sound.   Does the computer have the capability to produce music and other sound effects? This feature is built in to many and can be added to others. Obviously, this feature is especially important to music applications. Is a speech synthesizer to provide voice output available? This feature will be increasingly important to young learners.

7. Power up diagnostics.   Can the computer run a "check" of its own functioning when turned on?

8. Storage medium.   Although a cassette-based model is less expensive, it is not recommended, for several reasons. (a) Young children have little patience for long loading times. Worthwhile programs are often complex and require substantial time to load from a cassette. (b) Most quality software programs, including many computer languages such as Logo, are often only available on disk. (c) Disk-based programs are generally easier for young children to use. Hard disk drives, which are faster and store much larger amounts of information, are not feasible financially for most single classrooms at the present time, but they may be in the future.

9. Systems software.   This includes the programs that come with the computer, usually including a computer language and the disk operating system (DOS). The quality and capabilities of these programs vary widely. Are they fast? Easy to use? Use the *software* evaluation checklist in determining their relative merits.

10. Languages available.   Make absolutely certain that the computer has the languages that you wish to use. Logo and other educational computing languages are not available on every machine. Just as important, the *kind* of Logo "dialect" that is available on each computer varies. Some just include graphics, whereas others are full programming languages offering much more potential.

11. Printer and other peripherals.   There are different types of printers. Thermal printers use heat and heat-sensitive paper. They are inexpensive and often quiet, but special paper is needed that costs more than standard paper. If you expect to use the printer frequently, an impact printer is probably more cost-efficient. It strikes a typewriter-style ribbon with pins to form letters and graphics constructed out of dots. The quality of the printing is usually higher than that of the thermal printer. Even higher quality is the printing of the letter-quality printer, which uses formed letters just as a typewriter does. Many of these cannot produce pictures, however, and considering their greater price, they are usually not chosen for classroom applications. There are many possibilities for other peripherals, such as a modem for telephone communication, light pens,

graphics tablets, touch tablets, voice recognition systems for audio input, and so on.

B. Durability. The reliability and durability of a computer system for young children is obviously a concern, but it is difficult to assess. Ask others who use the systems, and read journals that review them (see the appendix).

C. Allowance for expansion. Almost all educators, once they see the potential of the computer, wish to expand their use of the machine. Look for a computer that is expandable or one that has the capabilities to meet demands that you will probably put on it in the near future. This includes the addition of other devices such as graphics tablets, paddles or joysticks, plotters, speech synthesizers, light pens, storage devices, prosthetic devices for the handicapped, and so on.

D. Networking. This refers to the connection of several computers to a central computer with disk storage, often a hard disk system with a large storage capability. It links computers together to allow them to share programs and other information. Often a larger computer with a more powerful CPU (e.g., "16-bit") is preferred with this type of system.

E. Documentation. Documentation should be judged by the same criteria as that for software documentation. It should be well organized and informative.

F. Ease of use. This includes its simplicity of operation, size, portability, number of cords, and so on. Can the system be moved if necessary? How much does it weigh? How much protection from hazards such as heat, static electricity, and dust is necessary?

G. Maintenance. What is the warranty period? Who will service the computer? Is a service contract available? If so, is it worth the investment? Maintenance costs must be figured into the cost of computer programs.

H. Training/assistance. Does the dealer provide training? Will assistance be available as needed?

I. Cost. A common mistake in planning for computer acquisition is to negect to consider hidden costs. Several are listed in Table 7–3. Others include (1) staff time in planning for the purchase and use of computers, (2) teacher training, and (3) additional software requirements.

As a final reminder, evaluate your needs first, then the software, then the hardware. Be critical of, but open to, appropriate compromise. If you follow the guidelines presented in this chapter, you will be well on your way to selecting worthwhile computer materials. The next chapter provides some hints on getting started with them.

THINK ABOUT

1. Situation: A fixed budget. Solution 1: Many inexpensive machines with limited software. Solution 2: Fewer, more powerful machines with more software. Debate.
2. What instructions should be included in paper documentation, which on-line in the computer program? What kind of help should be available to young children within the program itself?

3. What questions in Tables 7–1 and 7–3 should be given the highest priority? Which are not really necessary or important?
4. "A school should delay purchasing hardware and software as long as possible because new technological advances are always just around the corner." What do you think?
5. Should producers of software for children—especially young children—be pressured into allowing or providing backups?

ANNOTATED BIBLIOGRAPHY

Coburn, P., et al. (1982). *Practical guide to computers in education.* Reading, MA: Addison-Wesley.
  See Chapters 4 and 5 of this book for additional suggestions on selection of hardware and software. Chapter 6 contains suggestions on funding the purchases.
Countermine, T., & Lang, M. (1983). Assessing the hidden costs of a personal computer. *Child Development, 59,* 248–250.
  A checklist and discussion of computers and costs can be found in this reference.
Heck, W. P., Johnson, J., & Kansky, R. J. (1981). Guidelines for evaluating computerized instructional materials. Reston, VA: National Council of Teachers of Mathematics.
International Council for Computers in Education. (1982). *Evaluator's guide for microcomputer-based instructional packages.* Eugene, OR: Author.
Riordon, T. (1983, March). How to select software you can trust. *Classroom Computer News,* pp. 56–61.
Sanders, R. L., & Sanders, M. E. (1983). Evaluating microcomputer software. *Computers, Reading, and Language Arts, 1*(1), 21–25.
  These represent several sources of guides and suggestions for software evaluation. Compare several of these to Table 7–1. Is there anything that you would like to add to this chapter's checklist? What items on the checklists do you believe are of primary importance?
Harper, D. O., & Stewart, J. H. (eds.) (1983). *Run: Computer education.* Monterey, CA: Brooks/Cole.
Microcomputers in education. (1982). New York: Scholastic.
  Several articles in Harper and Stewart provide guidelines and checklists for evaluating hardware. In one, Braun presents an interesting mathematical model you may wish to use. *Microcomputers in education* contains a similar model.
Moore, O. K. (1983). Guidelines for choosing hardware to promote synaesthetic learning. *Child Development, 59,* 237–240.
  The author provides guidelines for selecting software specifically for (a) young children and (b) the purpose of promoting his vision of learning done for its own sake.
Roblyer, M. D. (1981, October). When is it "good courseware"? Problems in developing standards for microcomputer courseware. *Educational Technology,* pp. 47–54.
  This article discusses problems in developing standards for microcomputer courseware, two courseware philosophies, and three categories of courseware criteria: essential characteristics, aesthetic characteristics, and differential characteristics.
The software yellow pages: A minidirectory to software reviews (1982, October). *Electronic Learning,* pp. 56–58.
  Many other sources are listed in this article. While not providing critical comments, directories can be useful in locating software; many are listed on page 57 of this reference.

8

GETTING STARTED

If you have decided to use computers in your classroom and know how to select the appropriate hardware and software, you are ready to get started. It will be helpful to plan your computer environment with care.

SETTING UP A COMPUTER ENVIRONMENT OR HOW DO YOU GET THE JELLY OUT FROM BETWEEN THE KEYS?

First, relax. Remember the metaphors from the first chapter and view the computer as merely another learning tool. This will allow you to bring into play the planning skills you already possess. Second, consider the following steps.

1. *Become familiar with the computer.* Of all the uses of computers, which appeals to you the most? Sit down with a friend or colleague and the appropriate hardware and software and "mess about" with this computer application for awhile.

2. *Select goals.* One principle in Chapter 1 stated that computers should be a means by which to achieve educational goals rather than an end. Start small. Select one or two applications that you believe hold considerable promise for helping children to achieve significant goals.

3. *Choose suitable software and hardware* as discussed in the previous chapter.

4. *Involve administrators and parents.* With your means and goals firmly in mind, encourage your administrators and parents to observe what you are doing. It is especially important to have this support with regard to (a) the purchase of additional software and hardware and (b) the way in which you plan to use computers—for example, as a means of increasing problem-solving ability and humanizing the classroom.

5. *Plan how computer resources are to be managed.* How will the equipment be stored and used? This important step is discussed fully in the next section.

6. *Introduce the computer gradually.* Start to implement the one or two applications with which you decided to begin.

7. *Spread out to other applications and other teachers.* Slowly expand your computer use to other applications that have high priority. Start sharing ideas with other teachers.

Classroom Management of Computer Resources

Step 5, "Plan how computer resources are to be managed," is a particularly important one. Asking yourself the questions that follow will help you to take that step successfully.

1. Where will the equipment be stored? It should be safe, dry, clean, and easily accessible. The following are suggested guidelines. Few classrooms will have an ideal spot; do the best you can.

Keep it away from radiators or other heat sources.

Keep it away from glare from sunlight or overhead lights.

Keep it away from dust and liquids. These can quickly damage hardware and software. Do not place computer materials near chalkboards. Cover computers when not in use. Close the doors to disk drives when not in use. Store disks upright in containers.

Keep it away from magnetic fields such as televisions, stereos, tape recorders, or radios.

Static electricity can damage computers. If the equipment is set on carpeting, special sprays or mats should be used. Humidifiers might also help.

Sufficient grounded electrical power must be available. This source should not be connected to other heavy power-consuming equipment (power drops or surges can be damaging) or to televised instruction (the computer can interfere with the quality of signal). It is useful to have an extension cord or strip with its own switch.

It is generally useful to place the computer so that (a) you can monitor its use and (b) one to three children can work with it at a time, not distracting others. Many school systems have found it advantageous to mount the computer systems, including extension cords, on portable carts, to facilitate moving as needed. Note that mechanical components—the disk drive and printers, for example—can be harmed by jarring.

2. How will children be grouped? Depending on the application, children should work in groups of two or three or individually. Working alone is generally only necessary when one child is developing an intensely individual project such as a song or working on a diagnostic-prescriptive program.

3. When and by whom will the computer be used? There are several different methods that teachers have used successfully to schedule computer use. As with all routines, it is well worth giving extra time at the beginning to ensure that children understand and follow simple rules.

In one school, two kindergartens shared a microcomputer and several computer programs. One teacher "loaded" a different program into the computer every day, just before "free play" time (in which children chose activities from the many interest centers about the room). Because the computer activity was always popular, the teacher challenged the children to invent a fair way in which to take turns. They decided to make a list every day. It was each child's responsibility to cross off his or her name and then, when finished, figure out who was next, and tell that child. Computer literacy, socialization, writing, and reading all in one! As children became more accustomed to the microcomputer, it lost a bit of its power to provoke arguments, but never its attraction as a place to play and learn.

The second teacher created a creative computer center, partitioned off from the rest of the classroom and located next to another carrel where volunteer parents and her "hour-a-day" teacher's aide worked with children individually. The parent or aide checked whose turn it was to work with the computer next and made sure that the child was off to a good start. Questions or problems the child had were dealt with as they arose. With this system, the teacher utilized the computer every minute it was in her classroom and also kept track of which students were working on what programs.

In another school, a primary grade teacher allowed her students to sign up for one half-hour session per week. Two 2-hour blocks of time were set aside for makeup and whole-class sessions. Whenever possible, it is advantageous to have students responsible for the scheduling, including making-up sessions. One third grade teacher had students draw computer times from a hat. If their time fell during a peak instructional period such as a reading or math lesson, they could either take the time *and* the responsibility to make up the work or wait to choose another time.

Other schools have housed the computers permanently in a computer laboratory, often located in the media center. Children come as a class or half a class at a time or individually. Reservation and circulation of materials are handled through the media specialist. Advantages of this arrangement may include (a) efficient use of limited computer resources and (b) availability of enough computers for group lessons with a hands-on component. Disadvantages may include (a) need for additional staffing, (b) scheduling problems, (c) lack of integration with classroom work, and (d) teachers' feelings that they are not in touch with the computer program.

If you decide on a computer lab, consider the following suggestions (see also Ragosta, Holland, & Jamison, 1981):

a. Utilize parent helpers.
b. Consider networking several computers, connecting them to one disk drive and printer for efficient loading of programs.
c. Have specific schedules, rules, and responsibilities and stick closely to them.

While this procedure may provide a temporary answer to scarce computer resources, to integrate computers totally into the curriculum, one computer housed in each classroom is an absolute minimum. In addition, arrangements should be made to allow for lower computer-to-student ratios when necessary. The ideal situation is to have one computer for every two or three students. Teachers and administrators must work toward these minimum, and eventually maximum, goals. The main goal is to provide students with the access to computers they need to develop their full potential.

One computer, 30 kids: other suggestions. There are, then, several ways in which to manage even minimal computer resources. In addition to those already suggested, the following may be helpful:

a. Teach the whole class. Hook up the computer to a large classroom television monitor. Use simulation programs with large groups of children deciding their next move together.

b. Assign blocks of time.

c. Set up a management system during small-group instruction. An important aspect of good teaching is to engage children in meaningful activities when you are engaged in small-group instruction. For example, you might teach several reading groups during which time other pupils are working on activities independently, so that your group will not be interrupted. Using a timer (some computer programs include one; a kitchen timer will suffice), a CMI program, and a list of names, students can work independently for a preset period and alert the next student on the list when their time is up. The next child resets the timer and the program and does his or her work. Once set up, this organizational scheme can run for several weeks without requiring additional teacher time or effort.

d. Promote children's use of the computers during noninstructional time. This may include time before school, during breaks, after school, and the like.

4. How long should each child spend on the computer? As discussed in Chapter 2, a drill and practice program might best be used for 5 to 15 minutes per child. However, larger blocks of time should be planned if the computer is to be used for simulations or programming.

5. Who will help students use programs? Introduce most programs by demonstrating their use in front of the whole class. However, some children will still need help as they use the program. Unless you know that you will be available, have a list of "consultants" or "experts" for each program displayed near the computer.

Consider using parent volunteers and older students to help with this as well as other facets of your computer program. In one successful program, several sixth graders taught to operate the school's computers each teach one weekly computer class to children in the first through third grades.

6. How should the computerized instruction itself be managed?

Do not allow computers to become a male activity. Many teachers tend to believe—often unconsciously—that boys will enjoy and excel at computer activities. They then inadvertently reinforce boys for their computer work more strongly than girls and even permit boys relatively more access to computer facilities. Also, do not let computers become a math activity. Even recruiters for businesses say that it is not just technical skills that they value; rather, it is familiarity with the use of computers for problem solving, logical thinking, and working independently.

Value all computer learning and use. In a similar vein, the child who is just learning to turn the computer on should be reinforced just the same as the child who is programming on his or her own. Who is contributing more to society—the knowledgeable computer "hacker" who works at a computer all day, breaking into the programs of others, or the artist who, knowing very little about how computers work, nevertheless uses them to produce a great work of art?

Set up rules or guidelines for computer use. Each teacher and each setup will require slightly different rules. The following suggestions may help you to determine what rules you wish to use. Of course, younger children will do better with a small number of essential rules.

(1). Use the computer fairly—keep on the schedule, do not use other people's time. Or you can use the computer for _____ minutes.

(2) _____ people at a time can use the computer.

(3). Talk, but do not bother others.

(4). Help, but do not tell. Offer help to others, but do not just give them the answers. Let them do it themselves.

(5). Take care of others' programs. Do not erase or change other people's programs or data, and do not change what is on their disks.

(6). When using a program (e.g., a CAI/CMI program), use your own name. Do not try to learn or use someone else's password or "sign on" with their name.

(7). Take care of the computers. Press keys, do not pound them.

(8). Take care of the disks—use the rule of thumb (pick up the disk only with the thumb on the label). Touch them only on the label, do not bend them; keep away from magnetism, heat, and cold, and keep them stored vertically in their envelopes.

(9). Use clean hands and keep only pencil and paper near the computer (no food, liquid, or small objects).

(10). Put away everything when done.

A related idea that has worked well for some teachers is to use "computer licenses" that are given only to students who have demonstrated knowledge of how to use the computer. This assures that children using computers will be competent in their use, and allows these students to serve as resources for others.

Stick to the rules and schedule.

Promote a positive attitude.

Keep communication open among yourself, your students, and any helpers such as older students, parents, and teacher's aids.

7. Was the plan successful? Evaluate the application of computer resources. Were the goals achieved? What could be done to increase utilization? Should the emphases be changed? What components of the program should be kept, which should be altered or dropped?

QUESTIONS ON USING COMPUTERS

Is computerized instruction cost-effective? Concern about the cost of computerized education is often the major obstacle to its widespread acceptance. A review of this research (O'Neal, Kauffman, & Smith, 1981–1982) indicates that CAI is cost-effective. Compared with certain aspects of conventional instruction, it already appears *more* cost-effective and comparable in terms of student achievement. Educators must consider that conventional instructional costs will continue to rise, whereas CAI costs will continue to drop. This engenders another popular question.

Will computers replace teachers? Some say that computers will eventually replace teachers; others say that computers will release teachers from tedious jobs, allowing them more time for teaching; still others say that any teacher who *can* be replaced by a computer deserves to be. Which is true? Probably none of these. None actually addresses the complex problem of computers in education. Computers will not replace teachers if the goals of education are respected. However, the position taken here is that computers should not be used merely to release teachers from boring tasks.

The goal is to design a complete and powerful educational environment for children, including good teachers, meaningful computer applications, and much more. Teachers will need to orchestrate the myriad elements of the environment and provide the "human touch." The question of "replacing teachers" is, in the last analysis, overly simplistic.

Will computers change education? Teachers should not be replaced by computers, but education will be changed by them. Educators have the responsibility to ensure that education is changed in ways that benefit children.

Can teachers who do not "get along" with technology use computers? Most teachers who follow the steps we have outlined are impressed with the range of classroom applications of the computer, often remarking that they are not sure how they got along without them. "Humanistically oriented" teachers recognize their power to fulfill human potential and increase social interaction.

Do you have to learn how to program? Many worthwhile activities do not require programming on the part of children or teachers. The computer is a tool; if you want a job done, it is likely there are programs written to help you do it. However, new computer languages for programming are available that make the venture easier and more meaningful for children and other beginners.

Must you choose programming or CAI? There is a myth that teachers must take a stand for one computer use or the other. There is no reason why the two computer uses cannot be combined.

Should children be required to use the computer? When is it better to accept a child's preference for other activities? For the earliest years especially, this is an important philosophical issue. It is suggested that you accept a child's preference but simultaneously seek out other computer applications that will interest and benefit the child. However, there is a thin line between avoiding harmful pressure and giving the impression that computer-related activities are unimportant. The latter can be interpreted by children as a lack of concern on the part of the teacher or as a signal that only some children—often boys—are expected to enjoy and succeed at computer activities.

What if children avoid the instructional aspects of a program and choose to use only its "play" elements? First, ask, "Is the program structured correctly?" Recall that computer activities should be *intrinsically* rewarding. If interest is generated in an artificial manner, the program is probably at fault. Check if children understand the purpose of the program. Discuss the program with them and challenge them appropriately, possibly through modeling. Finally, remove programs that are wasting students' time and computer resources.

What about typing skills? Should young children be taught to type? Touch type? How can their typing be improved? There would seem to be little reason to teach correct finger placement to very young children with limited access to computers and/or other keyboards. However, O. K.

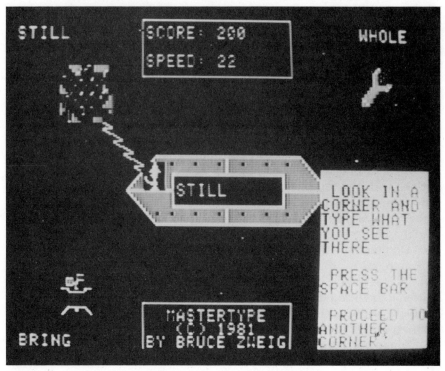

FIGURE 8–1   Children can practice keyboarding skills with the popular *Master Type*. (Courtesy of Scarborough Systems, Inc.)

Moore's work with the "Talking Typewriter" of decades ago showed that even children just entering school can enjoy learning correct finger placement with the proper guidance. Given the increased importance of keyboarding, it would seem that teachers with enough access to computers can help children learn to use the proper fingering when typing.

Moore color coded the keys and children's fingertips. This has worked successfully for many teachers. In addition, several computer programs are designed to teach typing. *MasterType* (Scarborough) is a drill and practice program that utilizes a game format to hold student interest, contains a number of preprogrammed lessons, and allows teachers to create additional lessons. Children fight off invading letters or words by typing them in before they launch missiles toward the defending planet. Speed of presentation can be controlled by the teacher, and special lessons can be designed (Figure 8–1). Other programs are *Type Attack* (Sirius Software), *Microcomputer Keyboarding* (SouthWestern Publishing Co.), *Microtyping II* (Hayden Software), and *Typing Tutor* (Microsoft Consumer Products). It is not suggested, however, that typing programs should have a high priority. (The February 1984 issue of *Teaching and Computers* contains a three-step process for teaching keyboarding skills.)

Is it important that home and school work together?   Yes. The more unstructured atmosphere of home learning should be guided by collaboration with the better planned learning environment of the school. Cooperation and coordination are essential if computer learning is to be optimized. Schools should help parents to learn about computers and how computers can benefit children and should share ideas and software suggestions.

Can I do anything to fix a computer?   Actual repairs, of course, need to be conducted by trained personnel. Schools should ascertain the value of service contracts and build repair costs into their budget. Nevertheless, there are a few simple steps that teachers can take:

1. Check the manual.
2. Check the power supply to each component being used.
3. Check all the connections. If some connections are inside the computer, *turn off the computer, ground yourself* (on the power unit; see the manual), and gently push down any "interface boards," or "cards," that are inside. The gold-colored contacts of boards can be cleaned with cotton wetted with denatured ethyl alcohol.
4. Check if the problem is in the hardware or software. Use the program with a different computer, or use a different program with the computer.
5. Clean the disk drive heads. Kits are available for this purpose, but those interested can use much more cost-efficient methods.
6. Think ahead: Make or purchase backups of all software and store originals safely in another location; have duplicates of every computer component within the school.

Getting started is a necessary first step, but the rest of the journey is more challenging and enjoyable. The next chapters discuss how this computer environment can benefit children.

THINK ABOUT

1. What kinds of things might teachers inadvertently do that would reinforce computer usage on the part of certain children more than others?
2. Would involving administrators and parents in your computer program increase its effectiveness or decrease the freedom you have to direct it?
3. Which of the plans concerning "when and by whom" the computer is used would you consider best? Why?
4. Which is better, a computer lab with 16 computers, or 16 classrooms with one computer each? Why?

   CURRICULUM CONSTRUCTION CORNER
5. Develop a plan for introducing computers into a classroom, including the physical setup and the first lessons with children. Share it with your peers.

ANNOTATED BIBLIOGRAPHY

Chaffee, M. R. (1982, March/April). Viewpoint. *Classroom Computer News*, pp. 17–18.

Coburn, P., et al. (1982). *Practical guide to computers in education.* Reading, MA: Addison-Wesley.

Chapter 6 of this book provides suggestions on introducing computers into the school, including the politics of computer acquisition (the advantages and disadvantages of centralized, decentralized, and shared planning approaches) and preparing faculty for computers.

Fisher, G. (1983). Developing a districtwide computer-use plan. *The Computing Teacher, 10*(5), 52–59.

Grady, M. T. (1983, May). Long-range planning for computer use. *Educational Leadership, 40,* 16–19.

Joiner, L. M., Miller, S. R., & Silverstein, B. J. (1980). Potential and limits of computers in schools. *Educational Leadership, 37,* 498–501.

These authors raise some important questions that should be asked by those responsible for planning a school or school system's use of computers, and provide suggestions for developing such a plan.

Ray, D. (1983, January/February). How I learned to stop worrying and love the microcomputer. *Classroom Computer News,* pp. 40–42.

Ray shares her experience of introducing an entire elementary school to computers with only one machine.

Sherman, S. J., & Hall, K. A., (1983). Preparing the classroom for computer-based education (CBE). *Childhood Education, 59,* 222–226.

Nine steps for preparing your classroom for teaching with computers are provided.

Zaks, R. (1981). Don't (Or how to care for your computer). Berkeley, CA: *Sybex.*

A good reference for do's and don'ts of using hardware and software.

9

PROBLEM SOLVING
AND READINESS
FOR PROGRAMMING

What is a problem? Is "What is 3 times 4?" a problem? For a third grader it might be only an exercise, even if it is couched in a verbal format such as "Three friends each have 4 toy cars. How many toy cars do they have in all?" If the student could simply multiply and say "12," he has not solved a problem—there *was* no problem. Can it ever be a problem? Yes; give a set of toy cars to a group of kindergartners and ask them the same questions. Let them figure out the answer among themselves in any way they can. Some may act out the situation. Some may count on their fingers or out loud without objects. *Even if they make a counting mistake,* if they discover a solution, they have engaged in problem solving.

A problem is a situation in which a person wants to reach a goal but does not know immediately what actions he or she can take to achieve it. Notice that 3×4 can never be a problem for a person *unless* he or she wants to know the answer. Also, the problem does *not* have to involve mathematics.

A PROBLEM-SOLVING FRAMEWORK

Although solving a problem necessitates the simultaneous use of many skills and abilities, it is useful to examine several categories separately for two reasons. First, it allows a more intensive examination of the separate abilities to identify and organize them. Second, it is appropriate for children to engage in activities that highlight one ability at a time, although it is essential that real problems constitute the mainstay of the problem solving program. The categories are memory, convergent problem solving, and divergent problem solving. These abilities have been found to be present in good problem solvers (Lester, 1983).

Memory

To solve a problem, children first need to remember the information involved. There is evidence that young children do not spontaneously use memory strategies such as rehearsal (Cleary, Mayes, & Packham, 1976). *Memory: A First Step in Problem Solving (K–2)* (Sunburst) is a set of lessons, some off and some on the computer, that are designed to develop these strategies. Specifically, the strategies are sequencing/chaining, quantifying the task (noting the number of items to be remembered), auditory aids (associating rhythms, rhymes, or melodies with the task), regrouping, personalization (remembering jobs you have to do, forming a mental picture of yourself doing the jobs), creating a context (such as a story), self-testing (mental rehearsal and attention focusing), whole to part (simplifying a task by dividing it into smaller parts), visual association (visually relating something unfamiliar to something familiar), and mnemonic systems (using an external order to facilitate the task). A few illustrations might be helpful.

Chaining is a way of remembering a sequence of items in order by reviewing a partial sequence and extending each review by one more item (i.e., A, AB, ABC, . . . , as in the "I'm going on a vacation and am taking . . ." game). The *Memory* package suggests several activities. One off-the-computer activity introduces a puppet called Teddy. Students must remember and repeat a number of movements Teddy makes, adding one each time. For practice with this strategy, they use a collection of computer programs, "Teddy and Iggy." In TEDDY, a teddy bear is shown making his bed step by step. The children must remember the order in which Teddy makes his bed. In the next game the children must remember which shape was stacked first, second, third, and so on (see Figure 9-1).

WHAT'S IN A FRAME? provides practice in using the "quantifying the task" strategy. Children are shown a picture of a frame with a number

FIGURE 9–1 (Courtesy of Sunburst Communications, Inc.)

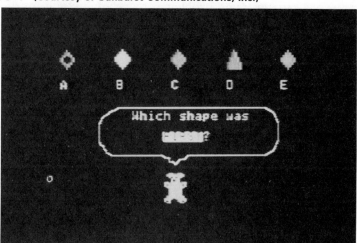

FIGURE 9-2
(Courtesy of EduFun, Milliken Publishing
Company.)

of objects in it they have to remember. The class discusses the fact that it is helpful to count the number of items and remember the number. They also discuss other helpful strategies such as creating a context or regrouping. Children should be engaged in the process of examining a problem and deciding on a plan to solve it, that is, choosing appropriate strategies.

Another example of a memory game is *Tracer* (*WINDOW*). A path is created in a grid a bit at a time. The children must recreate it each time until it reaches the other side. *Facemaker,* discussed later in this chapter, also contains a memory game. Others include *PAVE* and *Word Memory Programs* (I/CT).

Convergent Problem Solving

In convergent problem solving, reasoning is logical and structured. The goal is to find and identify the one *best* answer. Usually, it is a deductive process—going from the general to the particular, wherein success depends on the application of relevant general principles to the problem.

Discriminating and classifying. Discrimination is the ability to determine differences between objects or events. Numerous programs develop children's ability to discriminate simple shapes, colors, and the like (e.g., *Children's Carrousel,* Dynacomp, *Early Games,* Counterpoint Software, *Early Childhood Learning,* Educational Activities, *Ernie's Magic Shapes,* CTW, *KinderComp,* Spinnaker, *Kinder Concepts,* Midwest Software, *Learning with Leeper,* Sierra On-Line, *PAVE,* I/CT, *Preschool IQ Builder,* PDI).

Chaos (EduFun) uses a video game format to practice classification skills. The children's spaceship must capture alien satellites that match the shape and/or color of the satellite in the center square (see Figure 9-2).

Programs can go beyond simple discrimination practice and lead children to solve classification problems and develop logical thinking skills in interesting ways. In *Gertrude's Secrets* (The Learning Company), children move to any of several puzzle rooms. There they must solve different types of classification problems. For example, in the "one-loop puzzle room," they find a box and a group of shapes of different sizes and colors. They must discover the rule of classification through theorizing and experimenting. It might be that all the pieces of one color go in the box or that all the pieces of one shape go in the box (Figure 9-3). More of these will be described in the chapter on mathematics, as will another classification and logic program, *Moptown* (from Apple Computer). In *Big Bird's Special Delivery* (from CTW) children must help Big Bird deliver packages by considering and comparing objects according to form, class, and function.

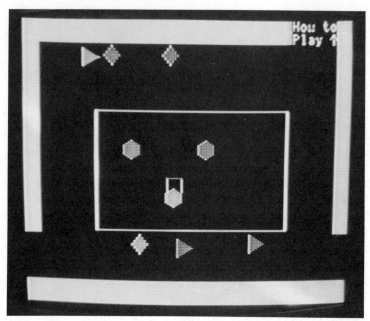

FIGURE 9–3 (Photo by Bill Milheim.)

Following the *Memory* package in the problem-solving series from Sunburst is *Discrimination, Attributes, and Rules: The Second Step in Problem Solving.* Teddy provides practice with attributes. In "Iggy's Gnee's" students must discover Iggy's secret and build a gnee as proof. A third program shows children groups of pictures, words, letters, or numbers and asks them to find the "Odd One Out." In "Gnee or Not Gnee" children are given examples that do or do not apply to a rule and then must guess the rule. Finally, they try to choose more examples of the rule. Another program has one child think of a "secret rule" and then use a simple vocabulary to create examples that do and do not apply. Other children try to prove they have guessed the rule by creating a matching example.

Deduction: applying principles to new situations. This strategy can be developed in several ways. *Code Quest: Practice in Problem Solving* (Sunburst) encourages children to solve problems by understanding, selecting, and applying rules appropriate to given situations. *Reverse* (EduSoft) is a strategy game using a list of scrambled digits. The object is to get them in order through a series of moves called "reverses."

In *The Incredible Laboratory* (Sunburst), children choose and mix "crazy chemicals" that produce various features of a monster. The students' job is to discover each chemical's effect through trial-and-error or other strategies.

Using multiple strategies in combination. One simulation, *Rocky's Boots* (The Learning Company) also challenges children to build a machine. Here, however, the possibilities are nearly endless, and because the parts are based on computer logic/electronics, the program teaches important computer science concepts. This will be discussed in more detail in Chapter 14. This simulation also encourages divergent as well as convergent thinking, an area emphasized in the next section.

Divergent Problem Solving

Convergent thinking is an important ability, but it alone does not constitute problem solving. Divergent problem solving also needs emphasis, especially considering its increasing importance in the future (Quinn, Kirkman, & Schultz, 1983).

Induction: working from incomplete information. In one type of divergent thinking, the intuitive/inductive reasoning process, many new facts—some complete, some incomplete—are organized and related to what is known and a new whole is formed. Creative solutions are demanded. Who uses this rather odd-sounding process? Anyone who makes important decisions. In most "real-world" problems—especially in a world exploding with new information—people must make decisions in situations in which they do not know everything there is to know and where several solutions are possible. Children must learn to make intuitive decisions that are supported by available information. Two computer applications are especially pertinent. Simulations involve just this type of interpretation of data. On the basis of limited information, children must make decisions, enter these into the computer, evaluate the computer's response, and revise their decision-making strategies on the basis of new—but still incomplete—information.

Another powerful learning situation is the use of simple filing, or data-base, programs. People will have to organize, retrieve, and use a glut of information to solve their problems. Computers are the most effective tool for this purpose. Children can begin learning and applying this process in the early years by using simple data-base programs to solve problems that interest them. Examples of such use are provided in Chapter 14.

Our world *will* be increasingly inundated with data. Data are raw facts. We will have more raw facts than we can handle. These computer applications should allow children to transform these facts. Alone, data have no meaning. If children interpret it, they give it meaning and transform data into information. But one more transformation is necessary. Information must be analyzed, synthesized, and evaluated. As Piaget would tell us, to act on something is to know it. When children do this—when they think about, organize, and reflect on information, cognitively acting on it—they have gained knowledge. Television and other sources may fill children with information. Our goal as educators should be to help children gain not just information, but knowledge. "Turning information into knowledge is the creative skill of the age, for it involves discovering ways in which to burrow into the abundance rather than augment it, to illuminate rather than search" (Smith, 1980, p. 326). We must set our sights on no less than this—the creative search for meaning through the acquisition of knowledge.

Dragon's Keep (Sierra On-Line) is an adventure game appropriate for young children. Its purpose is to develop children's ability to solve a series of problems by predicting outcomes, making inferences, and drawing conclusions as well as to develop skills in reading, identifying details, and map reading. Children's task is to free 16 animals held captive in the dragon's magic house. After a few lines of introductory text (second grade reading level), children are shown a picture of the house and are offered three choices—they can walk in the front door, climb up a ladder to the second floor, or walk around to the back of the house. If they choose to walk around the back, the screen shows a pond with a fish in it. They can choose to move the fish to the river or go somewhere else. The game continues in this way, with children free to choose where to go and what to do at different locations in and around the house.

One reason adventure games are so popular is that there are few other situations in which you can actually be the main character in a fantasy-adventure story. They have to make decisions based on limited information in situations where no single decision is necessarily better. Children can explore alternate paths and solutions freely. Therefore, both convergent and divergent problem solving are brought into play. It should be noted that these abilities will be used by some, but not necessarily all, children, unless the teacher introduces and discusses the programs to encourage this.

Thinking creatively. Teachers of young children include many activities designed to promote creativity. But, as they say, Is it art? More relevantly, Is it problem solving? Yes, on both counts. Young children's creative efforts involve divergent thinking in the solution of problems of expression. Using the computers as a tool to compose stories, poems, or music, or to draw pictures or designs, is problem solving of the highest order. Some of these programs involve mostly intuitive, creative thought. Others, such as computer programming, combine creative and logical thought. Another example of this is *Patternmaker* (Scarborough), in which children design and explore patterns and symmetry. They view patterns artistically and mathematically. They take a pattern and perform, transform, and move it in certain ways to produce a larger pattern. These applications, discussed more fully in Chapters 10 and 15, should be given serious consideration when planning for computer problem-solving activities.

Strategies to Encourage for All Problem Solving

Several strategies and skills are important to the development of both convergent and divergent problem solving *and* readiness for computer programming, the topic of the next section. They should be used in problem-solving activities on and off the computer, even with young children. They fit within a general framework for teaching problem solving: (1) present a problem, (2) help students to develop and implement a plan for solving the problem, and (3) discuss the problem and the solutions, as well as the necessity for checking work and evaluating solutions (Lester, 1983).

Talk it out. Children need to talk about their problem-solving processes to develop them and to understand what problem solving is. Problem-solving strategies can be translated into sets of self-statements that are modeled by a teacher, puppet, or peer, are discussed, and then are rehearsed. For example, in working with a drawing program, one child was heard to mumble a version of the self-statements that his teacher had modeled: "What am I trying to do? Put this square on top of the mountain. How can I do it? I'll move the cursor over here and . . .". Children should also be encouraged to restate the problem in their own words, "making it their own" (support for this approach is provided by Piaget, 1973; and Meichenbaum, 1977). Computer programming, the subject of the next chapter, offers a fertile ground in which abstract thinking interacts closely with concrete results (see Figure 9-4).

Some people warn that not all situations can or should be "talked out." This is often argued with regard to psychomotor skills. (The centipede was happy quite/Until the toad in fun/Said, Pray which leg comes after which?/This wrought her mind to such a pitch/She lay distracted in a ditch/Considering how to run.) Papert (1980) discusses how even these skills, such as juggling, can be learned more easily if properly thought and

FIGURE 9–4 Two first graders, Elizabeth and Christine, "Talking It Out." (Photo by Douglas Clements.)

talked about. The author hopes that the admission does not damage his intellectual credibility, but confesses that every so often, while in a hurry, he forgets how to tie his necktie—his hands just will not cooperate. So he takes the time to talk it out—"Up from the back and over to the right . . .". Now when the hands forget, the verbal brain assists easily and effectively.

People only really know an idea when they say it. Children should be led to be explicitly aware of their own solution strategies. Ask children what they are doing and why.

Act it out. For young children especially, it is important to visualize what is involved in a problem. By dramatizing the essential actions, the problem and the relationships in it become clearer and more concrete.

Write it down. Sometimes acting out a problem is difficult. Other times, information has to be organized so that patterns can be found. In either case, it is helpful to write it down, in pictures or words and numbers. Like talking it out, writing also forces children to become more explicitly aware of the thinking and serves as a record of problem-solving efforts so that unproductive paths are not retraced.

Make it up. When children pose their own problems, they gain insight into the nature of problems and problem solving. Many of the applications of computers in the "creative" category possess this characteristic, but children can also be encouraged to make up their own convergent problems to share with each other.

Make it your own. There are two ways in which to make something your own. Try to compare the problem to another situation that is similar and more familiar. Relate what is new and to be learned to something you already know. Use analogies, such as those suggested in Chapters 5 and 6. This could be called "make it your own by making it familiar." If the idea is a very new one, "mess about" with the problem or idea until you are familiar with it. Play with it and build with it until you are its master. This could be called "make it your own by exploring."

Look for a pattern. Patterns are the basis for mathematical, scientific, and logical thought. They also exist in human behavior, nature, and art. Looking for patterns should become an active search rather than merely a passive observation. Patterns should be found, interpreted, and used to solve problems.

Solve it again. Rather than having children solve three problems one way, have them solve one problem three ways. Multiple-solution strategies and multiple representations of problems should be encouraged.

Plan it out. Without teaching a pedantic process, encourage children to (1) think about exactly what the problem is, (2) brainstorm as many alternative plans as possible and then choose what appears to be the best one, (3) carry out the plan, and (4) look back and see if the plan worked adequately.

Break it down. When faced with a large problem, it is often helpful to tackle just part of it. Children should be led to see how they can identify a subgoal and work toward that first. This involves *procedural thinking,* which, as an essential component of readiness for computer programming, will be discussed in the following section.

Applied problem solving. While these general problem-solving strategies can be valuable, it must be remembered that good problem solvers use powerful strategies that are directly related to the content of the problem. Help children to understand the problem qualitatively from the beginning.

Young children using problem-solving strategies: An example. Two children were working with "Layer Cake" (on *Body Builder* from CTW). A three-layer cake rests on a small plate labeled 1. The children were to move the whole cake to one of two bigger plates (2 and 3) one layer at a time, *without* ever placing a larger layer on a smaller (this is a version of the famous Tower of Hanoi puzzle). Theresa decided to move the small layer (S) to plate 3 and the middle-sized layer (M) to plate 2. She placed S on top of M on plate 2. She then moved the large layer (L) to plate 3. Then she was stuck. It may appear at first that Theresa has limited problem-solving strategies. But she has already shown evidence of being able to recognize that she needed to use subgoals, moving plates to other than their desired final position to serve the end goal.

Her teacher asked her to talk it out. They discussed that she had solved part of the problem. She was encouraged to look for a pattern, solve it again (use the same strategy again on a similar problematic situation), and write it down. Theresa drew a few pictures and figured out that to "move a bigger piece that's covered, you've got to get the other pieces out of the way by using the extra plate." The teacher asked her which piece she wanted to move. She indicated M. The teacher encouraged her to use her plan to move it. Theresa started the puzzle again. She moved S to plate 2, M to plate 3, put S on M, and L on plate 2. Then she murmured, "now I'll move you out of the way," while moving S to plate 1. She quickly moved M onto L and S onto M, and the problem was solved. She broke the problem down—because she could not move the whole cake, she moved parts of it at a time. She used means-end analysis, planned, talked out her solution strategy, and found a pattern of movements that led to a solution. Research shows that even preschool children consistently use some problem-solving strategies (examples of 4-, 5-, and 6-year-old children using such strategies to solve a Tower of Hanoi task can be found in Klahr & Robinson, 1981).

READINESS FOR PROGRAMMING

Why teach programming? There are basically three justifications offered for the teaching of programming: (1) to provide children with an early start on a skill that will be as important as reading and arithmetic in their later lives and occupations, (2) to promote computer literacy, and (3) to use programming to develop problem-solving skills. The first two reasons are important and deserve consideration:

Who is in control of the computer may be one of the critical issues of the next few years. I believe that citizens of the 1980's and 1990's must understand the ways in which they can control computers and the ways in which computer systems and programs can be and are being used to control and manipulate *them*. . . . But one thing is certain, given the right programming language to use, children should learn to control the computer just as they now must learn to read and write in the earliest grades. (Watt, 1981, pp. 85–86)

However, by themselves these reasons might not justify computer programming in the early years. The third justification is the most powerful, and it is in this area that programming may have the most impact on education. It has been claimed that programming has the potential of expanding the intellectual capabilities of learners, making them inventors of their own intellectual tools (Molnar, 1981; Olds, 1981), amplifying the powers of humanity and liberating human potential (Dwyer, 1980). Marvin Minsky of M.I.T. has said, "Eventually, programming itself will become more important even than mathematics in early education" (1970, p. 205). The following chapter will view the research evidence testing these claims. However, teachers often must make pedagogical decisions on limited evidence. Such is the case with programming. We must decide if programming and related activities will help children to reach educational goals. These goals might include the development of computer literacies, but, given that it is not at all certain that all children will need to program computers, the main goals should be to develop skills in problem solving, reasoning, communicating, and the like.

What is computer programming? Programming is giving a computer a set of systematic instructions so that it can perform a certain task. This task might be drawing a picture, giving a quiz, writing a poem, playing a game, or the like. A common misconception is that doing computer programming is somehow similar to doing arithmetic. This is not accurate. The early childhood activities that are most like programming are block building and making up stories. Like block builders, programmers combine a small number of elements in a fairly structured way to reach a main goal. As discussed in Chapter 1, these building blocks may become anything the child can imagine, from the simple to the complex. Like the story maker, the programmer uses a strict coding scheme to express his unique ideas. He may need to work on the mechanics a bit at first and may sometimes ignore the overall structure, but with development and practice, he can concentrate more and more on the overall message and form. Alan Kay from the Atari research department has said that to be good programmers, people should first spend a year writing plays. Both analogies express the ideas that no one program is "right," that modifications are necessary, beneficial, and interesting, and that programming is essentially a creative activity, developing divergent as well as convergent thinking abilities. Blocks, language, and programming are also general-purpose tools, not restricted to any single subject matter area.

Teaching readiness for programming. First, answer this question: "Have you already used activities designed to prepare children for programming?" If you answered "no," consider "Have you tried to develop your students' ability in following directions, sequencing, classifying and reclassifying, and locating and fixing mistakes?" Then you should have answered "yes." Most good developmental programs are *already* doing a lot to develop the same skills that children need to solve problems and learn to use a computer effectively. If you recognize these interrelationships, however, you will increase the power of your teaching. How? You will lead children to see new connections and relationships. Your conception of these skills will be deepened by a new perspective on their importance. Additionally, you will learn about new activities and ways of thinking about problems that will enrich your educational program.

Computer Thinking Without Computers

Learning problem-solving strategies. Wasn't that the subject of the last section? Absolutely—this is just a reminder that developing children's ability to solve a variety of problems is the most important readiness activity for computer programming.

Readiness for computer information handling. Taylor (1975) has provided examples of some activities that can help solve the problem of "Computerless Computing for Young Children, or What to Do Til the Computer Comes." He suggested that teachers conduct activities that prepare children for the types of thinking computer programming will demand. This is necessary if computers are not available, but it is useful even if they are, in that it develops problem-solving abilities and integrates computer activities into the curriculum. For example, classifying and reclassifying sets of foods might help children to see how computers can sort and resort information. Children might "put all the foods together that go together" by color, type (fruit, vegetable, cereals, etc.), preference, texture, sweet/sour, origin, how eaten, when eaten, and so on. This will build important readiness skills for understanding how a computer filing system would work—the computer could also sort any information it has stored by a variety of attributes and could very quickly tell the user all the foods that were, for example, fruits, or yellow fruits, or yellow fruits that were smooth.

It is important for children to begin to realize that *if* information is sorted one way, it *excludes* any other sorting. This means that the way in which information is classified determines how it can be retrieved. Other classification activities facilitate the growth of these understandings. Sort objects as many ways as possible. Children's disagreement on the placement of an object ("This should go in the blue pile." "No! That's green!") is a valuable opportunity to have them vote, but discuss that either decision would have been all right. Children should understand that *there is no single correct answer*. People create categories for their own purposes.

Creating and following directions. Teachers have developed the ability to construct and follow specific directions by playing games like "May I," scavenger hunts, or "Simon Says" (". . . all the children with red pants hop three times and then sit down"). Students can give and receive directions in the "Step-on Game" in which foam rubber shapes differing in shape, color, size, and thickness are placed on the floor. One first grader told her classmates to first step on only the shapes that were large squares, then only the shapes that were not green circles and not thin. One preschool teacher had pairs of children sit on opposite sides of a partition with matching sets of beads. One of each pair placed all his beads on a string, then told his partner how to make a string exactly like his. After the description (which was often a dialog—"Now put on the ball." "*Which* ball?" "Oh, the large red ball.") was finished, they took down the partition to check if their strings were identical. Both following directions and multiple classifications are exercised in lessons like these.

Children also enjoy "playing robot" as they simultaneously learn how to give precise directions and learn about some of the characteristics of robots. One student plays the robot, one the programmer. The programmer directs the robot to do some task (say, getting paper for a class project from the cupboard). The instructions must be precise or the robot should not follow them. For example, "go to the cupboard" is not in the robot's repertoire; it must be told exactly how many steps to take in what direction. Similarly, even the directions "open a space between your fingers and thumb" is not sufficient . . . right or left is not specified. You can equip your classroom "robot" with sensing devices ("look to see if anything is in front of you"), but you must remember to give it detailed instructions on what to do in *each* case; for example, "if there is nothing there, take one step forward; if there is, turn right," and so on. Another variation—better left to experts—is to blindfold the robot and direct him or her to walk around obstacles. One teacher asked the "robot" to stand on the tiles of the floor. Other children directed the robot with such commands as "forward 4 tiles, turn left, forward 2 tiles," and so forth, so that the robot would reach some goal, such as the housekeeping center.

Older children might write directions such as "how to make a peanut butter and jelly sandwich"—a favorite among students and teachers (the activity, not the sandwich!). Younger children might speak the directions into a tape recorder. In either case, it is fun and enlightening to have someone follow the instructions exactly as they are given; for example, putting the jar of peanut butter on the bread because the directions did not include opening the jar. This kind of specific exposition of a sequence of instructions is precisely what is required in computer programming. Seeing others attempt to follow their directions precisely helps children lose their egocentric point of view and helps them correct, or "debug," any errors. This ability to locate and fix errors is an important problem-solving and programming skill in and of itself.

Debugging.   Treasure hunting games can also help develop skills of following directions and "debugging" or finding and fixing mistakes in directions. If children can be led to create a set of "treasure hunt" directions to swap with another team, both teams will discover where their directions were incomplete or erroneous. They can "debug" these directions for another team. Like many of these activities, this one employs several of the problem-solving strategies such as talk it out and act it out.

Have children play the "shape detective" game. Place several figures on a felt board that vary by shape, size, and color. Tell the children they are to discover a hidden shape that is just like one of the figures on the board, and they can find out which one by asking questions about it. If they ask, "Is it red," and the answer is "No," all the red figures are removed from the board. As the game progresses, the child who asks relevant questions gets to take down the figures that were not correct. Guide children to use effective questioning/searching strategies that eliminate the most figures (the most effective strategy is that of a "binary search" that repeatedly categorizes the remaining figures into two groups). Children will learn to "debug" their questioning strategies when they see that a particular type of question does not remove any figures from the board.

Procedural thinking.   Procedures are step-by-step instructions on how to do a specific task. People follow procedures all the time without being aware that they are doing so, but computers need exact instructions to operate. These instructions are procedures. Considered as such, they are similar to directions, such as those already discussed. However, they are more than simple directions in two ways. (a) They describe a specific and limited set of directions that accomplish a specific task (mathematicians refer to "algorithms" in much the same way). In this sense, the peanut butter and jelly sandwich activity was an example of a procedure, but Simon Says was not. (b) They can be combined in various ways to perform quite complex tasks.

The first characteristic can be introduced to children by having them describe a familiar activity in procedural form. For example, one child came up with the following procedure for writing the first letter of her name: "First you put your pencil on the top line and draw a line straight down to the bottom line. Pick up your pencil and put it down again where you started. Now draw a half circle on the right side of the straight line going from the top of it to the bottom. Stop! See? D for Darlene!"

The dual benefit—better understanding of procedural thinking and better understanding of the task itself—can be obtained in virtually all areas of the curriculum. A kindergarten teacher often had her classes order wooden rods from smallest to largest as a mathematics readiness activity. To extend the activity and develop procedural thinking and problem-solving abilities, she decided to ask children how they solved the problem. Here are some of their solutions, which also illustrate young children's real ability to solve problems.

You pick up any one and if it's not right [i.e., if it breaks the uniform increase of the "stairs"] then you put it back and get another one.

See, you get one and then you try to see where it goes. If it doesn't go at this end or this end you have to move some of the others over.

You pick any one and then you've got to find just the right place for it. Like this, see, it has to be bigger than all these, and, uh, like not as big as any of these.

Easy. Find the smallest one, then the very next smallest one, and keep going like that.

All these students had found a solution. Some were more sophisticated than others; however, they all gained from having to describe their own method in terms of procedures and in comparing their procedure to those of others. Note that this process of ordering actually has many similarities to computer programming. First, it is accomplished by carefully following a logical series of actions or steps. Second, it involves repetitive use of these steps. Third, at certain points it involves making decisions. Fourth, different procedures are equally successful at solving the problem. This teacher also enriched her pupils' understanding by having a puppet, "Mr. Mixup," order rods . . . incorrectly. She had the puppet ask the children to find the "bugs" in his procedures and—with words—tell him how to fix, or "debug," his method. (The rich variety of methods children use is described in Young, 1976).

A third grade teacher combined within one lesson work with alphabetization and with procedural thinking. She asked students to not only put a list of words into alphabetical order but to try and describe as best they could *how* they did it. Different methods were compared and evaluated in terms of their efficiency. A bit later, when they had the computer in their room, the teacher challenged them to describe a way the computer might perform the same task. Would it be just like their way? Some students wrote several different programs that were tested, discussed, and contrasted. The children were quite amazed that the computer, too, could do the job in more than one way, yet each time do it correctly. They discussed the differences in the computer's methods, for instance, that it did not "jump around" as they sometimes did when they saw a quick way to place some words in order.

Other teachers have involved their students in similar investigations concerning sorting and classifying, graphing results of investigations, finding references in a library, and even planning a report to the class or planning group activities. Most of these are best done utilizing the second characteristic of procedures, that they can be combined in different ways to perform complex tasks. How might this idea be first developed with children?

One class wanted to make a dinosaur diorama. The teacher guided them in planning the main procedure ("superprocedure") as

TO MAKE A DIORAMA
1. Make the background
2. Make the scenery

3. Make the dinosaurs
4. Put it all together

They decided to break down 1, 2, and 3 into smaller procedures ("sub-procedures"). For example,

3. Make the dinosaurs
   a. Make a *Tyrannosaurus rex*
   b. Make a brontosaurus
   c. Make an ankylosaurus . . .

At this point, different groups of children chose to work on one of these subprocedures. Each group then had to break its procedure down into more manageable procedures, such as

b. Make a brontosaurus
   (1) Find a good picture
   (2) Make papier-mâché paste
   (3) Make a big wad of paper for the body
   (4) . . .

Of course, this too could be subdivided. The teacher supplied them with the procedure for making papier-mâché paste, which in turn involved procedures for measuring and, because the recipe had to be doubled, for adding fractions. The teacher wisely spent a math period on that procedure. She knew that the children were catching on when one girl said, "Hey! Even that can be broken down into procedures. See . . . you need two times 1/4. You add that to get 2/4. Then you can look at the measuring cup and see that's 1/2." Following this procedurally based format helped the children to work together, increased their knowledge of problem-solving strategies, prepared them for computer programming, developed their convergent and divergent thinking abilities, and extended their knowledge in several subject matter areas, including science, math, language arts, and art.

There are actually three subcategories of knowledge within this view of thinking: conceptual knowledge, procedural knowledge, and executive knowledge. Conceptual knowledge is knowing *what* to think, similar to subject matter knowledge. Procedural knowledge involves knowing *how* to think or solve problems, for example, knowing a series of actions that will place a set of sticks in order or solve an arithmetic problem. Executive knowledge involves knowing *how to think about thinking* or how to regulate the internal, personal structure of thinking itself. This might include thinking of appropriate problem-solving strategies and then deciding which to use or monitoring progress to know if you are on the right track. The last two types are essential to effective problem solving. Many teaching suggestions offered earlier in the chapter (e.g., talking it out, acting it out, writing it down, making it your own, solving it again, and planning it out) will help to develop these types of knowledge. Breaking it down, or procedural thinking, is another powerful strategy for children to use. Techniques such as this help children to view problem solving as a complex set of processes requiring many different solution methods (see Lester, 1983).

Conditional thinking. All computer languages have a way of expressing conditionals—"IF something, THEN do something." Children need to express and hear many examples of this type of thinking. They might brainstorm to fill in the blank: "If it is raining, then _____ _____." Point out to children whenever conditionals are used in the classroom: "So, José, you are saying that *if* it is not too cold, *then* we should play outside; *otherwise*, we should play in the gym. Does everyone agree?" Or "That's another IF/THEN statement: *if* I put two more pencils in the can, *then* there will be just enough for each person."

Coding. An important part of understanding and using computers is understanding and using the various codes they employ, translating back and forth from human language to computer code. Children like "secret codes," clues, and puzzles. They could be encouraged to extend this interest by creating and using simple codes. For example, one group of second graders sent messages to each other like "20 8 1 20/9 19/9 20" using the code A = 1, B = 2, C = 3, and so on. What is the message? *CompuCrypt* (from *WINDOW*, Vol. 1, no. 3) is a computer coding game children can play. Not every child will be interested in such activities, but teachers *can* emphasize to all children that the work they do in reading and writing also involves decoding and encoding. This encourages children to approach literacy tasks in both human and computer languages with a spirit of adventure and challenge. In addition, it helps children to understand the relationships between thought processes and the written word.

READINESS FOR PROGRAMMING ON THE COMPUTER

Given appropriate computer languages, most children can begin programming computers almost immediately. However, there are several software programs that are designed to provide children with a gentle introduction to giving commands to the computer.

Children working with *Facemaker* (Spinnaker) first build a face by choosing from a series of menus of noses, mouths, eyes, ears, and hair types. As each choice is made, it is added to the face. Then they program the computer to animate the face. For instance, they might make it wink two times, smile, wiggle its ear, frown, cry, and finally stick out its tongue three times. They would do this by writing the following *program* or set of instructions for the computer face to follow: W W S E F C T T T. They could then see the face repeat this program as many times as they like. *Facemaker* also includes a game that provides practice in visual memory. The computer animates the children's face and they have to remember what the face did. As with the previously mentioned games designed to teach the chaining strategy, one new motion is added each time to the list they have to remember. Several activities in the *Early Childhood Learning Program* (Educational Activities) are excellent introductions into such concepts as directionality, sequencing, directions, part-whole relationships, and so on. Children aged 3 to 8 use single keystroke commands to explore simple but interesting computer environments. For example, they may move different shapes around to construct pictures.

There are several other software programs and programmable toys that are designed to introduce children to programming. Because they have their roots in the computer language Logo, and are basically modifications of it, they will be discussed in the next chapter.

The very young child. For preschool children, just the realization of a cause and effect relationship between their actions and the responses on the screen are a developmentally appropriate place to begin. Therefore, programs in which children draw (e.g., *Early Games,* Counterpoint Software; *KinderComp,* Spinnaker; *Learning with Leeper,* Sierra On-Line; *Magic Crayon,* C & C; *Paint,* Reston; *PictureWriter,* Scarborough Systems) create bodily amalgamations (*Ernie's Quiz* and *Body Builder,* CTW; *Alphabet Beasts & Co.,* Software Productions), or otherwise make something happen (*Children's Carrousel,* Dynacomp, *First Words,* Laureate Learning Systems; *Run, Robot, Run,* Educational Teaching Aids; *Space Waste Race,* Sunburst), can all be viewed as first steps to programming. The *Early Childhood Learning Program* (Educational Activities) has several activities that are good examples of each of these steps. Obviously, these programs should be used only if they are judged worthwhile for other reasons as well.

Creative Problem Solving, Creative Teaching

You may have noticed that some of the computer activities were similar to traditional classroom problem-solving activities in that there was one right answer. This type of activity has merit, but the more powerful use of computers involves solving problems in which there is no single answer. In many, there is no wrong answer at all. This type makes many teachers uncomfortable. They do not know the answer to the problems and the problems are complex and difficult. People who use computers learn to jump right in and begin working, trying out different strategies, and welcoming mistakes as opportunities for learning. We must allow ourselves to experience these new approaches to teaching and learning if computers are to realize their full potential in the most important area of education for the future—problem solving.

THINK ABOUT

1. How can creativity be taught without sacrificing disciplined inquiry?
2. Recall the "warning" in the centipede poem. Read Papert's (1980) discussion of this issue, in which he disagrees with Bruner's position that some problems should *not* be "talked out"? What do you think?
3. "'Off-computer' activities have little or no relationship to real computing. They will allow administrators to avoid buying them and teachers to avoid using them, while each maintains that they are developing computer literacy in children." What do you think?

4. What problem-solving strategies do you believe are most powerful and useful. Why?

CURRICULUM CONSTRUCTION CORNER

5. List five ways in which you have already helped students to get ready for programming. How could you alter these activities or lessons to make them even more productive?
6. Make up a lesson for teaching procedural thinking in an appropriate area of your curriculum. The procedure itself should be an important part of the subject area.

ANNOTATED BIBLIOGRAPHY

Lochhead, J., & Clement, J. (eds.) (1979). *Cognitive process instruction: Research on teaching thinking skills.* Philadelphia: Franklin Institute Press.

The reader who is particularly interested in the teaching of thinking skills will find interesting information here.

Silvern, S., & Countermine, T. (eds.) (1983). Children in the age of microcomputers. *Childhood Education, 59.*

This special issue includes several articles concerning the use of computers to enhance the problem-solving and creative abilities of young children.

10

PROGRAMMING IN LOGO

Tammy had experimented enough yesterday to know firmly what she wanted to do today. She typed TO SNOWFLAKE. The screen cleared, and the computer got ready to "learn" how to make a SNOWFLAKE. Tammy looked at her notebook and typed

```
TO SNOWFLAKE
  REPEAT 6 [POINT RIGHT 60]
END
```

Tammy typed "CTRL-C" to tell the computer she had completed her idea. She typed DRAW. A small triangle appeared on the screen. She typed SNOWFLAKE. The triangle began moving and drawing lines, producing the picture seen in Figure 10-1. "Yes! Now, I want a lot of 'em." She typed

```
TO SNOWFALL
  REPEAT 5 [PENDOWN SNOWFLAKE PENUP FORWARD 65]
END
```

She typed SNOWFALL and watched the triangle create Figure 10-2.

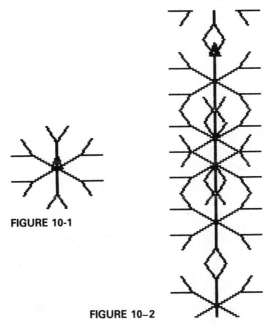

FIGURE 10-1

FIGURE 10-2

"Noooo . . . ! They're all on top of each other. Let's see. I have to turn them to keep them from piling up. That will be prettier anyway. And I have to start up at the top." She typed EDIT SNOWFALL and, with a few simple keystrokes, added one command:

```
TO SNOWFALL
    REPEAT 5 [PENDOWN SNOWFLAKE PENUP LEFT 35 FORWARD 65]
    END
```

She moved the triangle into position and the triangle drew Figure 10-3. Tammy was pleased. "Hey look, Paul!" She showed her friend.

"That's pretty. But snow falls all over at the same time, not in a line."

"I couldn't do that. They just go on top of each other."

"Hey, I have something called ROWS that I used to put balls all over the screen. Maybe it'll work."

The two friends used Paul's ROWS procedure with Tammy's SNOW-FLAKE. Called BLIZZARD, the final program produced Figure 10-4.

FIGURE 10-3

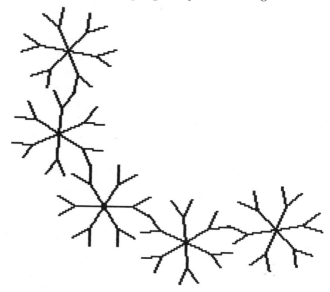

FIGURE 10-4

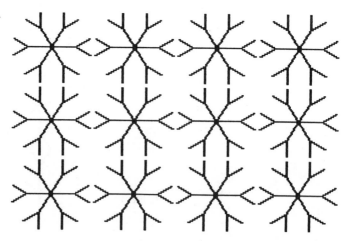

WHAT IS LOGO?

Tammy and Paul have been working with the computer language Logo. What is Logo? First, Logo is a computer language, a program that translates commands and instructions that people understand into electronic signals that the computer can "understand"; in other words, into instructions that the computer can follow. In this way, Logo is like a translator in a foreign country who helps you to say what you want to say but does not ever tell you *what* to say.

Second, Logo has been called "a language for learning." Other languages such as BASIC were written for computers from the 1960s that had small memories. Therefore, primitives, the basic words the computer understands, were kept to a minimum, and the languages were kept concise in every way. Often, the small number of basic words was taken as an advantage. Wouldn't that make the language easy to learn? To answer that question, answer another: Could you express yourself more easily with a language limited to a 100-word vocabulary?

Not accepting these limitations, Seymour Papert and several of his colleagues developed a language that is at once simple *and* powerful; that can be used by preschoolers and college graduates; that allows a person to create interesting programs almost immediately; and that, according to its creators, can help children to develop problem-solving skills, convergent and divergent thinking abilities, and an explicit awareness of themselves as thinkers and learners. Therefore, Logo is not just a language you learn; it is a language *with which you learn.*

Turtle Graphics

Let us explore that part of Logo that often serves as an introduction to the language, "turtle graphics." The triangular pointer in the middle of Tammy's screen is called the turtle. This is because the first turtle was an actual computer-controlled robot, called a tortoise or turtle, that scurried around on large sheets of paper, drawing shapes.

The turtle responds to a few simple commands. If you type FORWARD 50, the turtle moves forward (in whatever direction it is pointing) 50 turtle steps (about one-fourth of the height of the screen). RIGHT or LEFT rotates the turtle a given number of degrees; the turtle turns "in place." RIGHT 90 commands the turtle to make a "right turn." PENUP and PENDOWN tell the turtle to stop and start leaving a trace of its path on the screen. Interesting drawings can be created just using these commands. Figure 10-5 shows the work of one kindergartener. But the truly beneficial

FIGURE 10-5

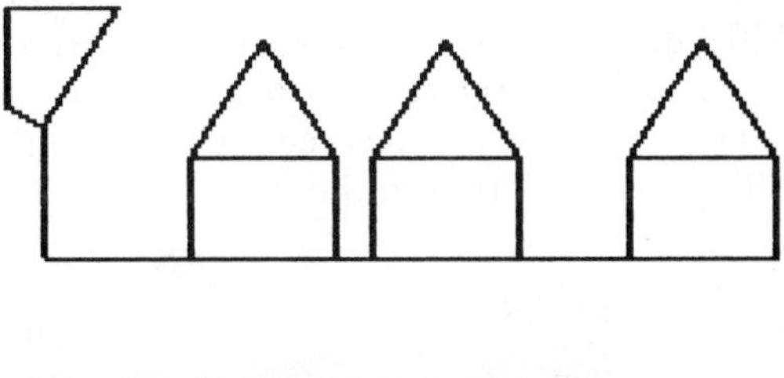

explorations come from teaching the computer new words. For instance, one second grader taught the computer how to make a square:

```
TO SQUARE
   FORWARD 30
   RIGHT 90
   FORWARD 30
   RIGHT 90
   FORWARD 30
   RIGHT 90
   FORWARD 30
END
```

SQUARE is now a new Logo *procedure*. The first line specifies the name (which did not have to be SQUARE—it could just as well have been called BOX or HI.) The rest tells the computer how to carry out the procedure. It is a list of instructions. SQUARE tells the turtle to go forward 50 steps, turn right 90 degrees, go forward 50 more steps, make another right turn, and so on. But this square can only be one size, unlike the more versatile FORWARD, which takes an *input* that determines how far the turtle should move. Procedures can also have "inputs." For example, SQUARE might be written this way:

```
TO SQUARE :SIDE
   FORWARD :SIDE
   RIGHT 90
   FORWARD :SIDE
   RIGHT 90
   FORWARD :SIDE
   RIGHT 90
   FORWARD :SIDE
END
```

Or as

```
TO SQUARE :SIDE
   REPEAT 4 [FORWARD :SIDE RIGHT 90]
END
```

Now the person that types in SQUARE must specify a certain length for the side. If she does not, Logo "complains":

```
SQUARE
SQUARE NEEDS MORE INPUTS
```

The :SIDE is a *variable*. A variable is a bit of information with a name. The name is SIDE. The colon in :SIDE means "the bit of information whose name is . . . SIDE. The information stored under that name will depend on what the user types in. SQUARE will draw a square, and the length of each side will be that number (see Figure 10-6). The information stored can easily be changed or *varied;* that is one reason for the name *variable*.

Sprites

Many implementations of Logo employ sprites, "invisible beings" that "carry" shapes in varying directions and at varying speeds across the screen. With little effort, the Logo-controlled computer can be programmed by a child to create a world. He can put a yellow circular region in the sky. He can make it travel leisurely across the clouds. Cars, trucks, people, and so on are all moved the same way, and they keep moving while

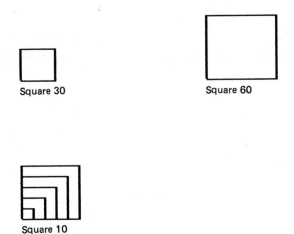

Square 30

Square 60

Square 10
Square 20
Square 30
Square 40
Square 50   **FIGURE 10–6**

the child creates more of his or her microworld. The possibilities are almost endless—the effects on reading, thinking, and self-concept potentially quite powerful.

WHY LOGO?

> The first computer language you learn has a lifelong effect on how you think, computerwise. Thus, the computer language we choose for use in the schools becomes vital. . . . Logo is a much better language to use for introducing children to computers than, say, BASIC. (Morgan, 1982)

It is difficult to understand people's excitement about (and often overzealous advocacy of) Logo without experiencing the language first-hand. The ease with which even beginners can create interesting programs is an important advantage of Logo, one that can only be appreciated with hands-on experience. Therefore, *you are advised to make a real effort to get some actual hands-on experience with Logo* and to try out some of the ideas in this chapter and the references at the end of the chapter. If you cannot, at least follow through the programs presented, trying to "map out" what is happening. In either case, resist feeling that you do not understand either the language or its uniqueness until you have given it a chance.

Characteristics of Logo

Let us look briefly at some of Logo's characteristics and then more examples.

1. Logo is procedural. The previous chapter discussed procedural thinking and its importance as a problem-solving strategy. The structure of Logo, like Pascal and other modern languages, is procedural. Instead of the long lists of commands you see in the commonly used BASIC language, Logo programs consist of small, understandable procedures, each of which has a specific job to do. Therefore, built into the language is the tool that children need to *break it down*. In Tammy's program, SNOWFLAKE draws a snowflake. This procedure helped her to write the procedures SNOW-FALL and BLIZZARD more easily.

One procedure can call another. In Tammy's program, SNOW-FLAKE called POINT six times.

```
TO SNOWFLAKE
  REPEAT 6 [POINT RIGHT 60]
END

TO POINT
  FORWARD 20
  LEFT 30
  FORWARD 15
  BACK 15
  RIGHT 60
  FORWARD 15
  BACK 15
  LEFT 30
  BACK 20
END
```

Try to "walk yourself through" them to understand how they work. Remember, the SNOWFALL procedure called the SNOWFLAKE procedure and so on. (Go back and look at those procedures and walk through them, too.)

Another example is provided by three boys' procedure. Guided by their teacher to plan it out first, and then break it down, these children started by writing

```
TO E.T.
  THROAT
  HADE
  EYE
  EYE
  EYEBROWS
END
```

Then they taught the computer how to draw each part, defining the throat, "hade" (head), eye, and eyebrows separately. This finally produced the drawing in Figure 10-7.

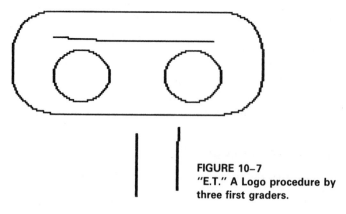

FIGURE 10-7
"E.T." A Logo procedure by three first graders.

It can be seen that this process allows children to look at the "big picture" first, planning what they want to do and then breaking this large plan down into "mind-sized bites." In this way, children can "divide and conquer" problems as they begin to see, in a concrete fashion, how tasks can be broken down into procedures, how procedures can be combined to form superprocedures, and how procedures interact. Also illustrated is a powerful idea: *You can "teach" the computer new words.*

2. Logo is interactive. Unlike Pascal, another modern, procedural language, the Logo programmer can type in a command or program and see it executed immediately.

3. Logo is recursive. A procedure can "call itself." Look at the procedure SUN, which Tammy wrote.

```
TO SUN
  POINT
  RIGHT 15
  SUN
END
```

It is a bit tricky at first, but "walk it through." SUN begins by drawing a POINT. (Note that Logo encourages children to build up and modify ideas, to play and experiment. This is the same POINT that created a snowflake.) Then it instructs the turtle to turn right 15, and then it "calls" SUN. This means that it generates another copy of itself, which in turn draws a point, turns right 15, and generates yet another copy of SUN. . . . This produces the design in Figure 10-8.

FIGURE 10–8

4. Logo is a language for learning. It has been specially designed, with features such as turtle graphics, to encourage learning and problem solving in children. Instead of typing coordinates on a grid to produce pictures, children use commands such as FORWARD that they already understand from their everyday lives.

Logo is "user friendly." Instead of getting a message such as "SYNTAX ERROR," a person might be told, THERE IS NO PROCEDURE NAMED FOWARD 10" (because the "R" was forgotten).

Logo has "no threshold and no ceiling." It is used by 3-year-old children who are first learning to use a computer and write simple, but interesting, programs and by M.I.T. mathematics and physics graduates.

Logo was also designed as a "language for learning" in a more profound sense. Papert studied with Jean Piaget and based the philosophy of the computer language on the psychologist's research and theories concerning how children develop thinking skills. Rather than the aspect of Piaget's theory that discusses stages of development and their limitations,

Papert emphasized the notion of *constructivism*—that children are not passive learners but are active creators of their own intellectual tools. Most teachers of young children subscribe to a similar view; for example, they know the value of play to young children's development. Logo allows children to play with the turtle, with designs, and, most important, with their own ideas.

We will look at these and other characteristics in more depth as we go on. For now, notice that because children can "play" with the turtle, they can solve more abstract problems by using their intuitive knowledge. For instance, they can ask, "If I were the turtle, what would I do next?" Working with turtle geometry, they can develop this intuitive sense even further, laying a foundation for later studies in geometry, trigonometry, calculus, and physics.

BEYOND THE TURTLE

The turtle may be Logo's best friend, but paradoxically, it also tends to limit people's perception of Logo's potential. The attention given to turtle geometry leaves many believing that Logo is "just a drawing program for kids." Unfortunately, they have missed two essential points. First, as discussed, Logo is structured to aid learning in a profound sense; that is, Logo is based on and embedded within a well-developed theory of learning. Second, although Logo is an interesting and useful language for explorations of graphics and geometry, its power does not stop there. Logo can deal with numbers, words, and sentences. Children might first write simple commands and procedures that print on the screen. For example, REPEAT 20 [PRINT [HI THERE, HOW ARE YOU?]] will print the sentence 20 times. Children might use the PRINT statement to label their pictures. Extending the SQUARE program would yield

```
TO SQUARE :SIDE
  REPEAT 4 [FORWARD :SIDE RIGHT 90]
  PRINT SENTENCE [THIS SQUARE'S SIDES ARE ] :SIDE
END
```

Logo can be used to write interactive procedures—programs that "talk" to the user. The following is a "run" of a program written by two third graders, called DISAGREE.

```
DISAGREE
WHAT DO YOU LIKE?
STRAWBERRIES
I DON'T LIKE STRAWBERRIES.
WHAT DON'T YOU LIKE?
WASHING THE DISHES
I LIKE WASHING THE DISHES.
WHAT DO YOU LIKE?...
```

Instead of handling data as numbers or "strings" of characters like BASIC does, Logo uses *lists*, composed of *words*. In Logo, a word is a group of characters such as letters and numbers, like CORRECT, 135, OR R2D2. A list is a sequence of words, numbers, *or* other lists. How is this different from a character string as in BASIC? In the latter, the string must be manipulated on a character-by-character basis. In Logo, lists can be manipulated as wholes or on a word-by-word basis. Let us look at some other Logo programs that use lists, which must always be in brackets. Notice that Logo has many more commands than BASIC, and recall that you can define and add your own original commands.

```
TO FADEOUT :MYLIST
  IF :MYLIST = [] THEN STOP
  PRINT :MYLIST
```
(If the list contains no words, stop. Print the list.)

```
  FADEOUT BUTLAST :MYLIST
END
```
(Call another copy of FADEOUT, *but* without the *last* word.)

Here are sample runs—the person types the first line, giving a list to the procedure FADEOUT and thus asking FADEOUT to do its job using that list.

```
FADEOUT [I AM GOING FAST!]
I AM GOING FAST
I AM GOING
I AM
I

FADEOUT [A B C 1 2 3]
A B C 1 2 3
A B C 1 2
A B C 1
A B C
A B
A
```

This defines a procedure that takes a list as input: :MYLIST means "the information [a list of words in this case] that is called MYLIST." If the list is empty, it stops. Otherwise, it prints the list. Then it does something powerful. The procedure calls itself (recursion). But when it does, it uses a list that is the list it started with *minus* (BUTLAST) the last word. It generates another procedure called FADEOUT, which is instructed to "do its job" on the list [I AM GOING]. That list is printed, and the procedure calls itself again, with a list again shortened by one word. When the list is empty, the procedure stops. Now let us combine some procedures:

```
TO DISAPPEAR
  FADEOUT [I AM THE DISAPPEARING SENTENCE!]
  PRINT [XXXXX POOOOOOOF!!! XXXXX]
END
```

Now all you have to type is

```
DISAPPEAR
I AM THE DISAPPEARING SENTENCE!
I AM THE DISAPPEARING
I AM THE
```

The first line of DISAPPEAR calls FADEOUT, instructing it to "do its job" given the list I AM THE DISAPPEARING SENTENCE! When FADEOUT has ended, DISAPPEAR prints its final list.

Of course, these simple examples only touch on the capabilities of

Logo. Because lists can consist of words *or other lists*, hierarchies can be created that mirror the hierarchies of human language and thought. This reflects Logo's roots in LISP (LISt Processing), an artificial intelligence computer language designed to help program computers to respond to situations like a person would respond. Recall the ANIMAL procedure that was written in Logo (Chapter 5).

WHAT CAN BE LEARNED FROM LOGO PROGRAMMING?

1. Learning to Use Computers

Logo allows children to develop self-confidence and abilities in controlling the new technology. They gain firsthand knowledge of basic concepts about computers as discussed in Chapter 5. By instructing computers to do what they want them to do, they also gain knowledge of how computers are used (Chapter 6).

2. Learning to Solve Problems

Children may benefit by developing problem-solving strategies that they can apply to many situations. First, Logo problems are *real* problems. Unlike the typical assignment or arithmetic story problem, the pictures that the children create or the stories that they write are problems they themselves have set. They have therefore accepted the problem and have an emotional investment in solving it.

Second, Logo programming is structured to promote the development of problem-solving strategies. In programming, children put down their thinking in concrete language and action. Their solutions and strategies are right in front of them. This facilitates *writing it down* and *talking it out,* putting their ideas in precise language, or rather, two languages, the exact coding of the computer language and the child's rich natural language. Children programming computers *do* solve problems and, in manipulating and debugging their programs, also reflect on "how the doing was done."

As children set their own problems, they are practicing two other strategies: *making it up* and *making it your own.* In figuring out how to get the turtle to go where they want it to go, children frequently *act it out*, walking the path themselves, tracing the figure with their fingers, turning their bodies or heads so that they can discover which way an upside-down turtle might turn. Finally, in writing Logo programs, children are *breaking the problem down* into "mind-sized bites," learning to analyze *and* synthesize.

Logo programming thus has the ability to combine opposites. In writing programs to draw pictures, write a poem, or compose a song, children are developing convergent and divergent abilities simultaneously. Also, children express their ideas in a highly abstract code. However, the results of their efforts are concrete and visible. Thus abstract thinking is tied closely to concrete results. This has the additional advantage that children *know* when they are right. The feedback they receive is inherent in the activity, not imposed from the outside.

3. Learning Subject Matter Content

Even though they believe that Logo has interesting possibilities, many teachers feel anxious: "Where will I fit this into my already full schedule?" There are two answers to this. First, it is important to set priorities. Are there areas of the curriculum that are less important and could be replaced? This is generally difficult for educators, but it is paradoxical that computers are used, for example, to teach long division to intermediate grade students, *even as they are making the skill itself nearly obsolete.*

Second and more important, it is not necessary to push subject matter aside to make room for programming. Too often, especially in early childhood, it is said, "I don't concentrate on the academics; I believe emotional and social growth is more important." Similarly, in the primary grades, reading is often taught disconnected from content. Children *should* develop emotionally, but they do not do it in a vacuum. They develop self-confidence and cooperative skills as they work with others, mastering some task. They do not just read; they read about something. In the same way, children should not just "program"; they should program the computer to do interesting things in art, music, language, and the sciences. Logo allows children to learn about content more deeply and in ways impossible in other formats. Illustrations of this will be provided in the appropriate chapters. Logo offers opportunities to present the core subjects—reading, language arts, math, science, social studies, music, and art—in new and exciting ways. Instead of asking, "Where will I fit Logo programming in my crowded day?" teachers might better ask, "How can I improve the learning/teaching in my classroom so as to take advantage of the new approaches to subject matter content, skills, and problem-solving abilities offered by Logo?"

LOGO AND THE YOUNG: SUPPORTING CHILDREN'S FIRST PROGRAMMING EFFORTS

"My kids can draw with crayons, and they probably cannot do *real* programming!" This teacher's comment has some truth in it. Without specially designed assistance, using Logo may be either too frustrating or little more than graphic play for many young children—more expensive, but not any better, than drawing with crayons. Unless they learn to think about their own thinking, young children may indeed be better off with physical objects—crayons or blocks (Barnes & Hill, 1983).

Can Young Children Really Learn to Program?

Even with an accessible language like Logo, research indicates that full procedural programming is a complex task for children as old as 8 years (Pea, Hawkins, & Sheingold, 1983). However, if given *support* in their efforts, even preschool children have been reported to be successful. Perlman (1976) constructed a machine with slots that allowed children to choose from a limited number of pictured commands. Such an elaborate system is not readily available to teachers; however, there is another way (the following is adapted from Clements, 1983).

Providing Support

Three levels of procedures can be typed in by the teacher to support young children's initial programming efforts. These programs give children what good teachers often give—just enough, but not too much, support. They provide the "scaffolding" that allows children to reach what would have been beyond their grasp. As children's abilities develop, parts of this scaffolding can be gradually removed. Level 1 removes many of the mechanical obstacles such as typing, spelling, and estimating distances as well as the obstacles of planning a sequence of instructions. It permits children to use single keystrokes in moving the turtle, defining procedures, and combining these procedures. Level 2 removes only the difficult demands of abstract planning and ordering instructions. It allows children to write and define new programs in the full Logo language *while* the turtle simultaneously carries out each command. Level 3 provides only a set of procedures that children could use as "black boxes" in their programming (i.e., tools they use by understanding what they do but not how they do it).

Level 1. This is a single keystroke program, which permits children to move the turtle, define procedures ("teach the turtle new words"), and combine these procedures by pressing only one key for each major command. These commands included the following (the regular Logo command that each key duplicates is in parentheses): F (FORWARD 10), B (BACK 10), 1–9 (FORWARD that number), R (RIGHT 30), L (LEFT 30), T ("Tiny Turn"; i.e., RIGHT 3), U (PENUP), D (PENDOWN), C (asks you what pen color you want), E (erases last command), W (wipes the screen clean), S (saves your picture as a procedure), P (asks what picture you want the turtle to draw), and N (names the pictures you have). Unwanted "primitive" (e.g., R or F) commands are erased directly, without making the child wait for the picture to be redrawn. That is, the turtle can just "back up" and erase an unwanted line or turn right to erase an L command. Additionally, pressing "?" (or "/") displays a "help" screen.

A child who has drawn a triangle and a "stump" (rectangle) with the F and R commands, and has saved each with the S keystroke, might combine them into a tree. Typing P, she would be asked,

She might type STUMP and, after the turtle drew this, move to the top of the rectangle, turn right, and press P and then TRI. Her tree would be complete (see Figure 10-9). She could then press S and Save the picture named TREE. At every step, she is provided useful information. For example, if she typed in a name of a picture that was not defined, the program would not stop, or "crash," but would merely respond YOU DON'T HAVE A PICTURE CALLED STUNP. Likewise, if she tried to label a new procedure with an old name such as "tree," the program would print YOU ALREADY HAVE A PICTURE CALLED TREE.

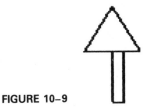

FIGURE 10-9

The level 1 program is an extension of several so-called "instant" programs. Teachers wishing to use such a program can find suggestions in the October 1983 issue of *The Computer Teacher*. This program allowed children to teach the computer new words, or procedures and to use these procedures to build other procedures, which is probably necessary to fulfill Papert's vision. To do this, a more complex program is needed. Interested teachers should consult Abelson (1982).

Level 2.   Here children use the usual Logo commands, but in addition they utilize several powerful programs provided by the teacher. Typing TEACH allows children to define a procedure. As in level 1, the turtle carries out the commands one by one as the children enter them, permitting them to use their intuitive visual strengths in creating their programs. If the children type E, the turtle erases the last command entered. If a command is entered that is unknown to the turtle, the program informs the children of this and does not enter it into the program being defined. For instance, if they type FORWARD50, the program responds: DID YOU FORGET A SPACE? THERE IS NO PROCEDURE NAMED FOR-WARD50. Typing END instructed the computer to define the procedure. A listing of this TEACH program, which you can type in, can be found in Clements (1983).

Level 3.   At this level, children use the Logo editor (or TEACH, depending on their preference) along with special procedures supplied to them. These include CIR.RT (draws a circle curving to the right; the child must specify a radius), CIR.LT, CUR.LT (a quarter circle to the left), CUR.RT, MOVE.UP (moves the turtle up without drawing; the child must specify a distance): MOVE.DOWN, MOVE.RT, MOVE.LT, POLY, and

POLYFILL (draws a polygon and fills it with color; the child must specify the number of sides and the length of each side).

Some teachers may feel that the reading and writing required by levels 2 and 3 mean that they are not appropriate for their students. However, it often does not take children long to learn to do something when they really want to do it. If a small thing like reading a few words is all that is between a child and making a computer do what he wants, watch him begin reading those words! This is a meaningful reading experience, too: the child gets immediate feedback, it is interactive, it is purposeful, it puts the child in a position of power. Take advantage of peer teaching here, too. The amount of knowledge, techniques, words, and skills that children pass about when they are intensely involved is amazing. So do not dismiss the programming that can be done with words; it just might serve as a teacher's aide for reading/reading readiness instruction.

Given the proper support, children's capacity for creative and logical thinking constantly surpasses adults' expectations. The programs just cited provide the support young children need to substantiate their ideas and visions.

LEARNING AND TEACHING LOGO

The Logo Philosophy

Logo is not just a computer language. It is a philosophy of education. Whatever our own individual philosophies and methods, it is often beneficial for us to add exploratory, problem-solving activities. This is the heart of Logo programming and Logo learning. The following paragraphs briefly describe the philosophy of Logo and some classroom suggestions and activities based on this philosophy.

Papert (1980) has argued that the most beneficial learning is what he calls "Piagetian learning," or "learning without being taught." Papert recounts his own early involvement—intellectual and emotional—with gears and the way they meshed and worked together. He learned to understand many concepts, especially mathematical ones, by asking, "How is this like gears?" Gears, for him, became tools for thinking and learning. He believed that computers could provide such a tool—albeit a more powerful one—for children.

Instead of the computer teaching the children through CAI, Papert maintained that children should teach the computer through programming it. He has proposed that computer programming can allow even young children to learn ideas previously believed to be too abstract for their level of cognitive development. Computers can make the abstract concrete and personal as they help children learn better by helping them think about their own thinking. By programming the computer to do what they want it to do, children must think about how one might do the task oneself and, therefore, on how they themselves think (Papert, 1980). In this way, Logo programming holds the promise of being an effective device for teaching *how*, rather than *what*, to think.

Papert, along with Harold Abelson, Andy diSessa, Wallace Feurzeig, Marvin Minsky, and others at M.I.T. and Bolt, Beranek, and Newman designed Logo based on three principles: (1) continuity—the language children use to program a computer should be continuous with their personal knowledge—(2) power—it must empower children to perform personally meaningful projects that could not be done without it—and (3) cultural resonance—it should be useful and should make sense in the larger social context. These principles gave birth to the turtle "microworlds." (As Papert freely admits, the turtle microworld is only one, albeit a good one. Others are needed. They need to embody other important ideas from mathematics, science, social studies, and the arts.) It is Papert's hope that these microworlds can help children to think more concretely about their own mental processes. According to Papert, human thought is structured in procedures. Therefore, if Logo can make procedures concrete and manipulatable, children can "play" with and explore their own thinking processes. As they name, define, store, retrieve, use, combine, analyze, and synthesize procedures, children are learning about thought and problem solving. ("Logo" stems from the Greek word *logos*, meaning thought or word.)

Of course, these ideas must be examined cautiously. For example, some of Piaget's ideas would actually seem contradictory to this optimistic view. For example, he writes that you cannot teach young children to deal with abstract concepts before they reach the period of formal operations. Also, Piaget maintains that biologically determined development, not learning, must come first, that learning cannot explain development but that developmental level can in part explain learning. There is, for him, no good reason to accelerate this development too much. Piaget did believe that people develop cognitively from interactions with their environment, however, and the interactions children have with Logo can be exciting.

Also often ignored are some lessons from history, notably the Progressive Education Movement, which demonstrated that children in complete control of their own learning may limit themselves to a relatively narrow range of interests. Finally, for very young children, two more questions must be addressed. What is the effect of computer use on their development? Are other, possibly more valuable, experiences supplanted?

The following suggestions are offered to help you use Logo with children in such a way as to maintain a continuous connection between the children's personal world and the turtle microworld and to facilitate children's acquisition of the "powerful ideas," while maintaining a balance between free explorations and guided discovery and between challenging children and meeting them at their developmental level.

Activities: Off the Computer

These activities are designed to introduce young children to Logo programming and learn about directionality, giving and following instructions, and problem solving. They are especially useful for teachers with relatively little access to computers. It should be noted that many important off-the-computer preprogramming activities were discussed in the previous chapter.

Turtle walks.   Classroom turtle walks are an effective way of introducing Logo programming. Have one person be the turtle while one or more others give directions. It is a good idea if an adult is the first "turtle,"so that he or she can model following directions exactly without interpreting them, even if they have "bugs." Children also enjoy "ordering around" the teacher. Then let children be the turtle. Lead the children to discover that the most useful directions involve telling the turtle to walk forward or turn right or left. Some children like to pretend that they are the "control tower" and the child-turtle is an airplane on a foggy day.

You might then have children specify the number of steps, possibly defined by floor tiles. LEFT and RIGHT could represent 90 degree turns at first or have 90 "tiny turtle turns" be right angles. If a large space is available, map out a maze on the ground and have the children direct the turtle through it. Children who need more experience with circles and degrees may benefit from playing "turtle turns" in a large circle laid out on the floor and marked in degrees (possibly in 12 sections, similar to a clock's face). The child-turtle at HOME is facing 0 degrees (i.e., 12 o'clock). Turns of different degrees can be commanded by others. This can later serve as the basis for more complicated designs, such as the FLOWER procedure.

One kindergarten teacher has her students work in pairs in the sandbox with smooth, wet sand. The children take turns telling the other how to manipulate a toy car or boat through a maze of objects to reach a goal. The path of the route left in the sand allows retracing and "debugging" solutions if dead ends are reached.

After a couple of gamelike practice sessions, have the computer available. While one child acts out the commands, have the Logo turtle do likewise on the screen. Let the activity itself emphasize that the turtle does exactly what the programmer(s) tell it to do. By using their own movement, show them that direction is *relative* to position. Have them imagine that they are the turtle. This will take advantage of their own knowledge of their bodies in space and encourage them to continue using this knowledge in their explorations of pictorial and geometric ideas. In other words, it will help them to develop the ability to "make it their own" through "acting it out."

The Turtle tells.   In this version of "Simon Says," one child gives commands to the others, involving turns and steps. The traditional game "Mother, May I?" may be modified to practice turtlelike commands.

Grid games.   Give each pair of children two grids such as centimeter-squared paper, small pictures of a turtle that fit in the squares, pencils, and a partition. Each sits on one side of the partition. They both start their turtles at the upper left-hand square of the paper, facing down. One child draws a path while describing it in "turtle talk" to his partner. The partner tries to follow the instructions. At the end, papers are compared.

Turtle clocks.   Using masking tape, draw a large clock face on the floor. Have one child stand at the center, another at 12 o'clock, and another at 9 o'clock. Have them stretch a piece of yarn between them. Talk about what shape they have constructed. Have the child at 12:00 move to 11:00 and the child at 9:00 move to 8:00. What happened? Re-create these shapes on the screen, asking children to specify each step. Then provide a board with 12 nails placed in a circle and one in the center. Children use rubber bands to make shapes and figure out angles. A regular geoboard with a 5-by-5 rectangular arrangement of nails can also be used to construct new designs. These materials are just as useful to supplement and aid on the computer activities.

Off-the-computer activities not only prepare young children for programming, but they ensure continuity between the more abstract turtle programming and the physical world. They also provide a concrete model for children to use in tackling more difficult programming challenges and for finding elusive bugs in their procedures.

Activities: On the Computer

Level 1.   Tell children that they are going to use the computer to draw. Explain that the triangle is a turtle and that it knows only certain words. They can draw by "talking" to the turtle with those words. Discuss the commands and display a color-coded chart that pictures the key, its effect, and its place on the keyboard. (Alternatively, have children experiment to discover what keys have what effect.) The actual keys might have matching colored stickers. After an initial period of exploration, engage children in a group process of (a) thinking of a picture, (b) telling one child who "played turtle" how to walk the picture, and (c) simultaneously typing the commands into the computer. Allow children ample time just to scribble and generally familiarize themselves with the commands (keys) and their effects. Then challenge them to draw pictures of their own choosing. Preschoolers might spend the whole year experimenting at this stage.

The next step is planning specific movements, or procedures. Have the children tell the child-turtle and the Logo-turtle (simultaneously) how to walk a square or other simple shape. Write down the program at the same time. At the single keystroke level, a procedure for a square might be

```
F F F F
R R R
F F F F
R R R
F F F F
R R R
R R R R
```

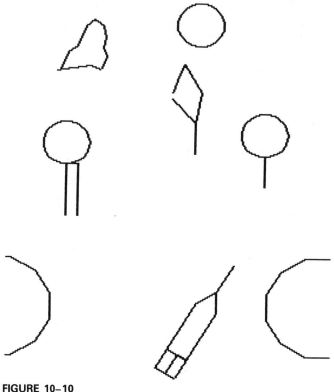

FIGURE 10–10

"Debug" the procedures as necessary. It is through this debugging (re-thinking) process that people become reflective, precise thinkers. Children can then experiment with building more complex programs based on these procedures. For example, the programs in Figure 10-10 were written by kindergarteners.

Level 2. Introduce the regular Logo commands (e.g., FORWARD 36 or LEFT 45) as new words the turtle understands. Demonstrate the commands. Discuss that the RETURN (or ENTER) key must be pressed to make the turtle follow the instructions. Some teachers explain that this is like saying, "I'm RETURNing control to you." Others relabel this key the "DO IT" key. Read and discuss common error messages. Again let children "play" or experiment with them freely for a time ("make it your own by exploring"), preferably in pairs. To give children practice with distance and angle estimation, use some of the following games and activities.

Hit the spot. Children work in pairs, taking turns. One places a finger or small sticker anywhere on the screen. The other types in as few Logo commands as possible to place the turtle directly beneath the other's finger. A later, related game involves having one child create a list of commands off the computer. His partner puts a sticker at the place on the screen he believes the turtle will stop. The prediction is checked by typing in the commands.

Sporting turtles. To play Logo baseball, place one small square sticker over the turtle in its HOME position in the center of the screen. Place three others on the screen to form a baseball diamond. Children take turns instructing the turtle to go to each base. If the base is reached with three or fewer commands, the child can try the next base; otherwise, the child is "out." (Did you recognize the conditional thinking here? Talk to children about it. IF you reach the base with one, two, or three tries, THEN you may try to go to the next base, or ELSE you are out and it is the other player's turn.)

Logo football requires a playing field that can be drawn on acetate and taped over the screen or drawn by the turtle. The defense places 11 stickers on the field. The offense has four attempts to write procedures to run a touchdown with the turtle without running into any defensive players. Extensions of these ideas can be found in Beardon, Martin, and Muller (1983).

Mazes. Draw a maze on acetate and tape it over the screen. Children direct the turtle through it. Or write Logo procedures that draw the maze.

Shoot. A variety of games, written in Logo, are available that are similar to those just described; that is, children are challenged to hit a target drawn by the turtle by turning the turtle and telling it to travel a specified distance.

How far? Have students explore the length and width of the screen in turtle steps. Also explore turtle turns.

Children can then begin to choose their own pictures and plan and program the procedures that will draw these pictures. To help them plan and program each separate procedure, children can be encouraged to draw over distinct parts of their picture with a pencil that has a paper turtle mounted on it. They would move and turn the pencil while describing their actions to a friend, who would write them down. This kind of planning and group work encourages not only social interaction, but also "planning ahead." It helps students to become better problem solvers, *and* it allows more students to get more programming experience on limited computer resources. Many children can be acting out the turtle, making small paper cut-out turtles act out their programs, drawing their designs with pencils as they study the movements they make, writing their procedures, discussing solutions to problems, and so on while one or two are actually typing in and executing their programs.

Encourage children to talk it out so as to bring their thinking to an explicit level of awareness by asking questions such as "What does the turtle have to know to draw this piece?" or "What did you tell the turtle to do? What *did* it do? What did you *want* it to do? How could you change . . . ?" and so forth. Children should come to understand that (1) the computer needs instructions, (2) you can teach it new words by naming a procedure and describing it, (3) new procedures can be used in other procedures, and (4) when programming, almost no one gets it right the first time—debugging should be expected and can be a learning experience. Specific strategies can be helpful (such as the following).

Chalk it, walk it, talk it. If children are having difficulty writing a procedure, encourage them to return to "acting it out." They might go outside on a large concrete surface and draw the desired design with chalk (inside, use masking tape on the floor). Then they walk the design and finally talk it out and write it down, describing exactly what they are doing and recording these steps so that they can type them into the computer. On paper, children can use small pictures of turtles.

Plan and predict. Encourage children to plan what they are going to do. When they are about to try something new, ask them to predict what it will look like. Structured prediction activities can also be beneficial. Write a simple program on the board in the morning. Challenge children to draw what they think the picture will be. Have one student enter and run the program to check. If appropriate, feature programs the children have written.

Encourage "breaking it down." To help children engage in "top-down" planning, have them draw a sketch of what they want the turtle to draw. Then they should decide how to break down this picture into manageable pieces and, with tracing paper, trace each piece onto a *separate* piece of paper, labeling each piece. Each of these pieces is written as a separate procedure. For example, two girls decided to write these parts of their GIRAFFE picture: GRASS, LEG, BODY, HEAD, TAIL, SPOTS, and BIRD. Using the level 2 TEACH program, they wrote a procedure for each piece and finally wrote a superprocedure that combined them. Figure 10-11 illustrates their program, GIRAFFE.

FIGURE 10–11

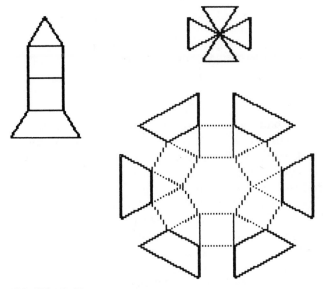

FIGURE 10–12

Turtle turners. Place a cardboard turtle on a nail in the center of each of two square pieces of wood so that it can spin. Write the degrees from 0 to 360 around the edge of a circle drawn on the wood, clockwise for the right turner, counterclockwise for the left. Children place one of the turners so that 0 degrees matches the screen turtle's directions. The cardboard turtle is spun to match the desired direction. The required turn is read off the circle.

Pattern blocks. Have children create a design by tracing around pattern blocks and then reproduce their pencil's movements with the turtle. They use the basic procedures to create drawings (Figure 10-12). (If you do not have pattern blocks, you might want to instruct the computer to draw and print out basic geometric shapes that could be duplicated for the children.)

Activity cards. Make up a chart of Logo commands and laminated cards giving the commands and their definitions. Other cards could present procedures for turtle graphics or sprites, programming challenges, or list processing projects. Commercial cards and books are available; many are listed at the end of this chapter.

Logo bulletin board. Just as valuable as commercial sources, have children mount and hang copies of their own work.

Simple editing. Logo has many useful editing commands. However, it is usually advantageous to allow children to become proficient at using only three at first: RUBOUT, move the cursor forward, and move the cursor backward.

Logo logs. Have each child keep a log of his or her Logo explorations, including printouts of their pictures, records of their procedures, ideas for future programs and the like.

Dramatization. Keep on dramatizing the programs, even after actual programming has begun. This can take place in groups *or* individually—children often turn their heads around to align with the TV turtle to determine whether the next command should be RIGHT or LEFT.

One teacher had the children who wrote the E.T. program dramatize it for the rest of the class. Each procedure was anthropomorphized as a child who held a sign with the procedures name and a list of the procedure's instructions. In this way, each procedure had one job to do. One boy pretended that he was the procedure E.T. He stood up, looked at his list of instructions, and called THROAT. This request caused another boy, who was playing the part of THROAT, to stand up. He looked at the commands that made up his procedure. The first thing he was to do was to call FORWARD and tell her to push the turtle forward 40 steps. FORWARD walked over to the turtle (another girl) and pushed her forward. The turtle left a trail with tape. FORWARD told THROAT that she was done and she sat down. THROAT then asked PENUP to do his job. PENUP walked over to the turtle and broke off the tape, placing it in the turtle's hands. PENUP told THROAT that he was done and he sat down. THROAT called RIGHT and said her input was 90. RIGHT stood up, walked over to the turtle, turned her 90 degrees to the right, told THROAT that she was done, and sat down. THROAT continued to call other commands until he was done, then informed E.T. of this, and sat down. E.T. then called HADE. HADE stood up and looked at his instructions.

The dramatization continued in this way. After being called by THROAT, HADE called CUR.LT who in turn called REPEAT, and so on. This type of activity helps children to understand procedural thinking, how procedures interact, how computers work, and how complex even "simple" programs can be. Recursive procedures can be dramatized, such as the following "pretend" procedure:

```
TO NOW
STAND UP
SIT DOWN
SAY NOW
END
```

Every time they hear "now" they should do the three actions. Of course, the procedure will never end, because they say "now" at the end. Students should give other examples, such as TO WALK/PUT RIGHT FOOT FORWARD/PUT LEFT FOOT FORWARD/WALK. Verbalize the procedure to help students understand it. "Pretend that we gave the WALK command to a computerized robot. It would do three things: put its right foot forward, then its left foot, then WALK. The computer has to check if it knows how to WALK. Yes it does. To WALK it must do three things. . . ."

After talking through a few, children might be ready to understand a recursive Logo procedure such as

```
TO SQUARE
FORWARD 40
RIGHT 90
SQUARE
END
```

The most accurate way in which to dramatize such a recursive procedure is to have one child be SQUARE. As before, he calls on FORWARD and RIGHT. *Then he calls SQUARE. This is not actually calling himself, but another copy of himself.* In other words, SQUARE calls another child who is also SQUARE, who stands up and calls FORWARD and RIGHT, who sit down after doing their job. She then calls another SQUARE. Notice that neither SQUARE has yet been told that everyone they called is done, so they cannot sit down. This continues as long as desired or until the class runs out of children! *If* there had been a "stop" rule, then one SQUARE could have ended. He would have told the SQUARE that called him that he was done and sat down, that SQUARE would have told the SQUARE that called her that she was done and sat down, and this dominolike process would have continued until everyone was sitting.

Analogies.   One potent problem-solving strategy is "make it your own by making it familiar." We have already discussed how to make the FORWARD, BACK, RIGHT, and LEFT commands real to children by acting them out. This strategy can also involve making analogies between Logo commands and children's real-life situations. For instance, the PRINT command instructs the computer to act like a typewriter and print a list of words on the screen.

We use the idea of a MAKE statement every day. "Who's the leader in line today?" "Jackie" (MAKE LEADER JACKIE: another day, MAKE LEADER PAT). LEADER is the *variable name*—the people who are the leader *vary* day by day. When dramatizing procedures with variables, say, MAKE KIDS [TOM ERNIE LINDA], have children take a box, write the name of the variable on it (KIDS), and place a strip of paper in it with a list of the three names written on it [TOM ERNIE LINDA]. If a later command is PRINT :KIDS ("print the thing associated with the name KIDS"), have them find the box labeled KIDS, read the list, and print it on the chalkboard. Later in the procedure, a command might be MAKE KIDS [BILL CICI JOHN]. The children would find the box labeled KIDS, throw out the list of names, and put a new list in it [BILL CICI JOHN]. More advanced would be the command MAKE KIDS BUTLAST :KIDS. In this case, children would find the box labeled KIDS, take out the list previously associated with that name [BILL CICI JOHN], and then put the same list back in the box *after* cutting off the last name (BUTLAST). Therefore, the list would be [BILL CICI].

The REQUEST command can be thought of as a person who asks, "What do you think?" and waits for an answer. It instructs the computer to print a "?" on the screen, wait for a response to be typed in at the keyboard, and give that response to whatever procedure called REQUEST. Similar analogies can help children make meaningful models for other commands.

Inventing games. Encourage children to invent their own Logo games. One second grader's game is "Make This a Picture." One player makes a few lines on the screen. The other must connect them in some way to make a picture.

Continuing Logo. At this point teachers might stock the Logo learning lab with disks for students to store their programs; rulers and graph paper; printouts (or hand-written records) of projects; and challenges. The day could be divided into 20- to 30-minute periods in which children can sign up for Logo time on the computer (each is responsible for leaving on time and quietly informing the next person that it is his or her turn). Each student should receive three or four turns per week if possible.

When she is free during these periods, the teacher can ask "What are you working on? What does this procedure do? Tell me exactly what you want the turtle to do. You need to. . . . How do you think you could do that? Do you have an idea about why that did not work? What did you try already? How could you test your idea? You could ask Sandy; she had a similar problem." Students often ask others without their teacher's suggestion. Some teachers have certain students (interestingly, not always those with the highest grades) serve as weekly "turtle tutors," resource people for other students needing assistance.

At specified times, the class gathers together around the computer and discusses students' programs, problems, and solutions. Interaction is guided by the teacher. "What does that make you think of? What else?" "What else could be made from that figure?" "Can you figure out what made Holly's program work?" "Chantz, would that help you with your program? How?" "Could Holly make her program different? How?" "Holly, are you going to build more onto your work? What?" "Class, how might he do that?" "That's a tough one. No one seems to have an answer. Let's put tape on the floor to draw the design. You tell Terry how to walk the pattern while I write what you say on the board." "How is this similar to other programs we have made? How is it different?"

This is an excellent time for the teacher to note strengths, areas of need, directions for future work, interests, and the like. She notices that Holly is growing in self-confidence and initiative, that Chantz might profit from working a bit with Holly for her to get him "over the hump," and that several students may be ready for an introduction to random selections. She makes a note to conference briefly with these students tomorrow. Maybe she can suggest a project that will require this; with the right hints, they just might discover the need for it themselves! She observes that several students are still enjoying just "fooling around" with variations of their procedures, whereas some are planning elaborate projects and two others seem hesitant to experiment. Maybe showing them pictures and descriptions of programming projects will help.

FIGURE 10-13   Big Trak. (Courtesy of Milton Bradley Company.)

Sons of Logo

Programmable toys.   One particularly concrete way in which to introduce young children to programming is through computer-controlled vehicles such as Big Trak (Figure 10-13). These toys respond to directions in much the same way as does the Logo turtle. You might set up obstacle courses or paths with string or tape. Program the toy to deliver messages to different parts of the room, or to the room next door. Keller and Shanahan (1983) provide a comprehensive list of objectives for using Big Trak, involving estimation, directionality, addition and subtraction with the toy on a number line, and working with mazes.

There are also robots that can be controlled through your computer and Logo (see Figure 10-14). Another, Topo, is a 1-meter-tall robot.

Other turtle graphics languages.   The popularity of the turtle has led to the hatching of many Logo offspring, many of which are less expensive than most versions of Logo. Several are similar to the single keystroke level described earlier. Some, such as *Delta Drawing*, have additional features such as a *F*ill command that allows children to fill in any section of the screen with color.

Another set of exploratory activities, the *Early Childhood Learning Program* (from Educational Activities) can be used with 3- to 7-year-old children. They learn to control the computer immediately, using modifications of turtle graphics and sprites as well as shapes to draw, build pictures from premade shapes, and create microworlds. Others have the capacity for controlling multiple turtles at the same time (*Color Logo*), and so on. Some of the available turtle graphics packages include *Color Logo* (Radio Shack),

FIGURE 10–14 (Courtesy of Harvard Associates, Inc., Somerville, Mass.)

CyberLogo (Cybertronics International), *Turtle Graphics* (HES), *Turtle Tracks* (Scholastic), and many versions of the PILOT language.

Most of these programs are well designed, and the special features of several are attractive. However, their limitations must also be considered. Some only allow 90 degree turns. Others do not allow shapes to be rotated but only drawn at different places on the screen. Perhaps the most important limitation is that the programs are not as extensible as the full Logo language. Children, therefore, cannot advance as easily into a more powerful language, as described in the levels of Logo in this chapter. Just as important, teachers cannot use the list processing capabilities of Logo to provide children with "black box" procedures to support their programming efforts.

Most of these programs, then, should not be compared directly with Logo. They are different in purpose and abilities. As always, teachers must first decide what their goals are, and how they want to go about achieving them. They then should try the programs out themselves before purchasing.

Enrichment for Advanced Children

Of course, many advanced children will virtually challenge themselves with programming projects that are extensions of those listed. Music explorations are also fruitful (see Bamberger, 1982). Logo can be used to implement a programming language that is a generative grammar—a set of rules that can be used to describe, manipulate, and explore languages, drawing, chemistry, music, and so on (see N. Rowe, 1978). There is no limit to the learning that Logo can generate (college students have used it to investigate Einstein's theory of relativity; one can hope that we teachers of young children will not have to get quite that sophisticated!). References listed at the end of this chapter will provide you with a wealth of explanations, descriptions of activities, and examples. Other suggestions can be found in Chapter 16.

Guidelines for Teaching Computer Programming

1. *Maintain a balance*—among *brief teacher-directed lessons* (on specifics of the language), *group problem-solving discussions,* and *student-planned and executed projects.* Most teachers have found that undirected, unstructured activities alone are not sufficient. One pair of teachers found that their first directed lessons were too long; children tended to copy exactly what they had demonstrated. They then virtually eliminated these lessons but found that children were not learning new commands. Finally, they settled on a pattern of (a) a 3- to 5-minute directed lesson on some new concept, (b) 5 to 10 minutes of group problem solving based on the new concept, and (c) 20 to 30 minutes of self-directed work several times a week, supplemented with weekly 5-minute conferences with each student about their Logo work. Try to provide a lot of individual attention during the self-directed work when children are first learning keyboarding and the commands. Aides and older students might be used effectively.

2. *Let children choose their own projects.* You may want to use commercially prepared activity cards and books to get children started or to generate new ideas. But avoid allowing your class's work with programming to be limited to working through a curriculum or copying the procedures and ideas of others. Children should enjoy the challenge and responsibility of setting their own goals and tasks. However, *help children to choose simple projects at first.* This does not mean that you choose the task; but children often need guidance in appropriately limiting the scope of their initial efforts.

3. *Maintain a balance*—between *allowing children to choose what and how much they want to do* and *encouraging children to approach programming as a significant endeavor.* Avoid pressuring children to program and yet avoid acting *so* nonchalant that children (often girls) come to believe that you do not care about their programming efforts and do not think they are important.

4. *Maintain a balance*—between emphasis on *process* and *product.* Both are important—learning to control the computer and producing interesting drawings and programs; also, learning skills such as keyboarding and mathematical concepts and learning problem-solving strategies.

5. *Figure out how the children are thinking.* Children's errors are reflections of their thoughts. These thoughts are not "wrong," they are a result

FIGURE 10–15 A belated birthday greeting, programmed by two first-grade girls.

of children's reasoning in their own unique way, experimenting with ideas and trying out their own self-constructed theories. Watch them work, learn about them, and *then* teach.

6. *Assist children, but only just enough to get them going again.* Sometimes, a well-planned question is all that is needed. It is difficult, but essential, to know when to intervene and when to wait.

7. *Allow children sufficient time* to develop their projects. Allow children to overlearn the methods at each level before moving to the next higher level. Recognize that building procedures and procedural *thinking* is a developmental process. Two girls wanted to write a program for a friend's sixth birthday party. With their teacher's encouragement, they did. They created a separate procedure for each letter and picture of their program (see Figure 10–15). Unfortunately, because the project *was* complex, their friend was 6 years, 1 month old by the time they finished! But the present was appreciated anyway, and the product and process were worth waiting for.

8. *Accept different learning styles.* As much as you encourage planning and "top-down" thinking, children will differ in the styles of learning and programming. Some children will delight in planning, copying down procedures, and thinking ahead. The first grade girls who wrote GIRAFFE programmed in this way. Others will use "bottom-up" thinking. Like block builders who start putting blocks together until they "recognize" something, these children tend to draw quite a bit before they combine procedures into a larger picture or other program. Some children, especially the very young, tend to scribble, drawing lines in what appears to be a

FIGURE 10–16

random fashion, experimenting and exploring with ideas such as cause and effect, direction, and color. Each style should be accepted, even if you also plan to encourage children to adopt other styles when appropriate.

Also, some children use analytic thinking, such as evidenced in the OUTSIDE program (Figure 10-16). Here two 6-year-old girls figured out how much larger each half-circle in the rainbow had to be based on the distance between the vertical lines. Similarly, two third graders analyzed spatial relationships closely to produce their COMPUTER (Figure 10-17). Others use intuitive thinking, like the 7-year-old boys used in designing the FLOWER (Figure 10-18). They used visual approximation and some good guessing. "I think it will take about 15 half-circles to get around . . . . No, how about 20?") Both approaches are valuable.

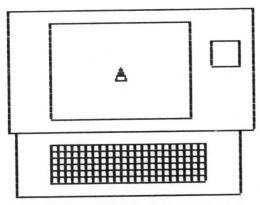

FIGURE 10–17 Two third graders programmed COMPUTERS using systematic analysis in their planning.

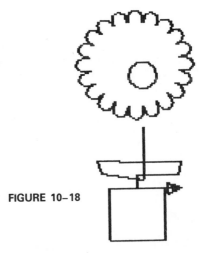

FIGURE 10–18

TABLE 10-1 Powerful Ideas

1. You can control the computer.
2. You can teach the computer new things.
3. You can use any name you want for these things.
4. You can break a problem down and solve it one part at a time.
5. You can build up a drawing or any solution to a problem from parts.
6. Everyone finds "bugs" in their programs and their thinking. Bugs can help you learn.
7. To figure it out, do it yourself (acting out a procedure).
8. To understand it, make it your own ("playing with" something unfamiliar, exploring, adapting, and modifying it).
9. To solve a problem, look for something like it that you understand.
10. Do it again (REPEAT—rotating drawings, etc.; also use recursion—solving a problem through solving only the first part of it).
11. Do it differently (modify procedures slightly).
12. Variables (information with a name).
13. A procedure can call itself (recursion).
14. You can program the computer to make a decision (IF/THEN conditionals).
15. Deliberately thinking like a computer can help you to solve some problems. It also helps you to see what mechanical/logical thinking *is* and what it is *not*.
16. The most powerful idea is that there are powerful ideas—certain ideas can be used as tools to think with for your whole life.

9. *Encourage children to learn from each other.* Whenever possible, assist children by saying, "I think Mike has a procedure that will help you do just what you want to do. Why don't you go ask him." Children should work together and be led to resolve disagreements by working them out together rather than relying on the teacher as an arbitrator. Recall how Paul helped Tammy by providing his ROW procedure, which allowed her to create BLIZZARD.

10. *Highlight powerful ideas.* The powerful ideas are best taught within the context of children's work with programming, rather than separately. A few of these powerful ideas are listed in Table 10-1 (see also Papert, 1980).

11. *Encourage divergent thinking* as children generate, elaborate, modify, and name procedures. Ask them, "What else could you make?" (or do, or name and so on). "How could you change that? What else could you make with that?"

12. *Celebrate bugs.* Bugs in procedures should be welcomed, not avoided. They lead children to reflect on their own thinking processes and reveal valuable misconceptions, sometimes in surprising ways (Figure 10-19)! Just as important, they bring serendipity. When Tammy was composing her SNOWFLAKE procedure, she changed the first FORWARD

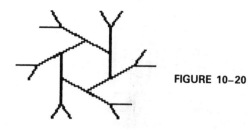

FIGURE 10-20

command to be twice as long as it had been. But she forgot to change the matching BACK command simultaneously. This bug led to the drawing in Figure 10-20. Tammy loved it and explored and defined other possible procedures before returning—with a new awareness—to fix up SNOWFLAKE.

13. *Keep the machine metaphors in mind.* Remember that, like a pencil, Logo programming is a tool, to be used for drawing, writing, doing math, or whatever you want it to do. As with a sandcastle, we learn from working with Logo, constantly recreating our ideas. We engage in a conversation with the computer. Like building blocks, Logo can be used to put pieces together in unique ways, limited only by our imagination (Figure 10-21). We can create new blocks as needed.

A GENERAL CURRICULUM GUIDE

Presenting a detailed scope and sequence for learning Logo would not be appropriate, for several reasons.

1. Logo programmers create their own words for their own purposes. Therefore there is no set sequence that each should follow.
2. Some second and third graders have been observed programming at higher levels of sophistication than some intermediate grade children. No predetermined grade level placement would be universally appropriate.
3. The Logo educational philosophy is not based on a strict sequence of skill acquisition. To capture the power of the Logo guided discovery approach, most teachers do not prescribe instruction.

Often, however, a general guideline helps teachers to begin to place a curriculum into perspective. With these caveats, Table 10-2 presents suggestions for a Logo curriculum.

FIGURE 10–19 (Photo by Douglas Clements. Originally appeared in *The Computing Teacher.*)

FIGURE 10–21 Using Logo as building blocks: Putting the pieces together. (Photo by Douglas Clements.)

TABLE 10–2 A General Curriculum Guide for Logo

| | | | GRADES | | |
	PRESCHOOL	KINDERGARTEN	1	2	3
Off the computer activities	I	D	D	D	D
Programmable toys	I	D	D	D	D
Level 1—single keystroke					
Drawing (scribbling)	I	D	D	D	
Naming pictures (procedures)	I	D	D	D	
Using procedures in other procedures	I	D	D	D	
Level 2—TEACH program					
First commands: DRAW (CLEARSCREEN), FORWARD, BACK, RIGHT, LEFT	I	D	D	D	D
Simple editing ("RUBOUT")	I	D	D	D	D
Using TEACH	I	I	D	D	D
NODRAW (TEXTSCREEN), PENUP, PENDOWN, PENCOLOR, BACKGROUND, HIDETURTLE, SHOWTURTLE	I	I	D	D	D
Rotations	I	I	D	D	D
Saving programs and pictures on disk	I	I	D	D	D
Sprites	I	I	D	D	D
REPEAT		I	D	D	D
Simple list processing (PRINT)		I	I	D	D
Variables, introduction			I	D	D
Arithmetic, introduction			I	D	D
Simple recursion			I	D	D
Level 3—full language					
Using circle and arc procedures			D	D	D
Editing procedures			I	D	D
Processing lists			I	D	D
Variables			I	D	D
Arithmetic			I	D	D
Recursion			I	D	D
Conditionals (IF/THEN; STOP)			I	I	D
Music procedures				I	I
TRACE			I	D	D
Interactive programs and other list processing commands			I	D	D

I–Incidental, informal, introduction.
D–Directed activities, discussions.

    To expand your collection of Logo activities, consult the references at the end of the chapter. Journals that include regular Logo columns include *Compute, The Computing Teacher, Creative Computing, Logophile, The Logo and Educational Computing Journal, The National Logo Exchange, Softalk, Turtle News,* and *99'er Magazine.* Issues dedicated to Logo have included *Byte* (1982, August), *Classroom Computer News* (1983, April), *The Computing Teacher* (1982, November, and 1983/1984, December/January), and *Micro-*

computing (1981, September). Many other journals have frequent articles (see the appendix).

Criticisms of LOGO

Is Logo an educational panacea? Based on what is frequently published about the language, it is easy to get that impression. However, criticisms are also made, from a variety of perspectives.

1. It is too expensive for many schools, considering the hardware and software required.
2. There is an inadequate number of knowledgeable teachers and curriculum materials.
3. Logo is not compatible with most schools' educational approach (because it is discovery oriented) and computer use (because it is not drill and practice and it is not the more familiar BASIC).
4. Several Logo properties are not easy to learn (Tinker, n.d.).
5. Logo may facilitate the learning of certain abilities, possibly better than any other educational experience. But it cannot teach in a highly efficient, directed manner, which may be required for some skills and some learners (Steffin, 1983).
6. It is not an absolutely *necessary* condition for the accomplishment of any educational goal (Steffin, 1983).
7. Preschool children are not ready for work with computers; they need real-world experiences instead (Barnes & Hill, 1983).
8. Despite the promises, programming computers has yet to show a major impact upon problem solving or achievement.

Criticisms 1, 2, and 3 are significant blocks to implementation, but basically they call for effort on the part of educators to obtain sufficient resources and provide sufficient training for teachers. Criticism 4 is a reminder that no language—or approach to education—is complete or perfect. We have seen several packages that attempt to provide something Logo does not. Other languages, SMALLTALK, for example, also hold potential but they are not yet widely available. However, the remaining criticisms are more serious.

Criticisms 5 and 6 should be considered when planning for computer use. No one program can "do it all." However, whereas no software could be said to be necessary, any computer curriculum without a turtle graphics/Logo–type component is certainly deprived of a powerful tool.

Consider the concern that computers will replace experiences with real events and objects: "Young children sitting at microcomputers are being shortchanged in terms of fulfilling those needs which are fundamental to learning and to their optimal development" (Barnes & Hill, 1983, p. 13). Of course, the position of this book is that computers themselves, much less one computer application, cannot and should not constitute the range of educational experience. It has been stressed that computer activities that simulate events should be used cautiously. However, it should also be noted that the author has yet to have met a teacher of young children who actually believes that computers *should* replace other experiences and *could* manage the majority of a child's education. The warning needs to be made—it is an important one. But emergency sirens should not be sounded prematurely.

The argument is also made that preschool children in Piaget's preoperational stage are not ready to use computers, due to limitations in reasoning abilities. As we have seen, however, Papert maintains that optimal computer environments can help children to develop these reasoning abilities sooner and more easily. Which view is correct? The next section reviews research relating to these issues. Before we do this, it is appropriate to summarize. The criticisms deserve serious consideration. But most involve problems of *using* or *misusing* Logo, not problems inherent in Logo itself. Used appropriately, it would appear that Logo has a definite place in the educational world of young children.

RESEARCH ON PROGRAMMING AND PROBLEM SOLVING

Initial Considerations

Which programming language should be used? It is relatively easy to answer the question, "Which programming language *is* being used?" Of the schools that teach programming, 98 percent teach BASIC and 5 percent teach Pascal, Logo, and FORTRAN (Center for Social Organization of Schools, 1983b). Papert (1980) maintains that other languages such as BASIC cannot provide an environment that facilitates the kind of epistemological reflection that Logo can. Others believe that *any* language, taught correctly, can enhance logical thinking. However, no definitive research exists regarding whether a certain computer language *should* be taught. There are only hints. Wexelblat (1981) suggests that as one's native tongue may alter one's thinking and view of the world, so the first programming language affects one's view of programming and computers. He conducted a survey on the matter and concluded that programmers tend to favor their first language and persist in using its style or structures, even in other languages, and the effects of poor teaching are as important as the effects of a poor first language. In a paper on presenting computing concepts to novices, du Boulay, O'Shea, and Monk (1981) suggest that programming languages require simplicity and visibility. They cite research that provides empirical support for the teaching strategy of describing and providing a concrete model of the programming language. They argue that while each language has faults, some (Logo, Solo, etc.) are best suited for novices.

Benefits of Programming

Can programming change what children know? There is slight evidence that working with programmable toys (e.g., Big Trak) can make a difference in the degree to which children master skills of directionality and sequencing (Harris, 1982) and to which first graders learn listening and mathematics skills as measured by subtests of the Iowa test (Keller & Shanahan, 1983).

Some research has been conducted measuring the effects of programming on the knowledge states of older children. Case studies appear to indicate that children exposed to programming profit intellectually (Papert, 1980; Papert, diSessa, Watt, & Weir, 1979). However, other studies show no evidence that intermediate grade children improved in achievement. Research from Bank Street (Pea, 1983) indicates that children who learned Logo for a year still possessed fundamental misunderstandings concerning the workings of the language and that few mastered important aspects of Logo's "powerful ideas" such as the concept of a variable and recursion. On the other hand, Hines (1983) found that 5-year-olds exposed to Logo programming improved their ability to conserve numbers and understand the relative sizes of numbers, to understand the nature of a computer, and to program.

Can programming change HOW children think? Advocates of computer programming by children have made convincing arguments concerning the potential of this activity for expanding the intellectual capabilities of the learner. Although this is a relatively new area, some research has been done. Gorman (1982) reported that third grade children who worked for 1 hour a week on Logo programming performed significantly better on a test of rule learning than did those with a ½-hour weekly programming experience. There has been some evidence that programming can increase problem-solving ability (Billings, 1983; Milner, 1973; Soloway, Lochhead, & Clement, 1982; Statz, 1974); however, it is not conclusive, and other attempts have showed no significant effect. Seidman (1981) found no significant gains on tests of conditional reason abilities for fifth grade children trained in the Logo language and warned that the Logo conditional (IF/THEN/ELSE) may teach logical fallacies. Other reports indicate that considerable variability in skill levels attained by individual children exists and that children's programming ability is often limited to specific contexts (Pea, 1983; Pea, Hawkins, & Sheingold, 1983). Pea (1983) found that two classes of 25 children, after a year's experience in programming in Logo, did not display greater planning skills than a matched group. Pea expressed deep doubts about the current optimism concerning the cognitive benefits of programming. Most of these studies have been conducted with intermediate grade or older children. One study, conducted with first graders, tends to have more positive implications.

Clements and Gullo (in press) provided instruction and exploratory activities in the Logo computer language to nine randomly selected first grade children and, for an equal period of time, CAI exposure to nine other children. Posttesting revealed that the programming group scored significantly higher on measures of reflectivity (thinking before answering) and on two measures of divergent thinking or creativity, whereas the CAI group showed no significant pre- to posttest differences. Reflective thinking is often observed in a Logo environment. After a procedure failed to work satisfactorily, one trio of Logo programmers expressed this need to take time and think: "We've *got* to get organized!"

The programming group outperformed the CAI group on measures of metacognitive ability (realizing when you do not understand). In this task, children heard directions to a game that omitted an essential step. They had to realize that they did not understand and inform the teacher of this. This skill—realizing when you do and do not understand—is encouraged in Logo programming. One girl mumbled to the turtle, "*One* of us doesn't understand this!"

Finally, the Logo group surpassed the CAI group in their ability to describe directions. No differences were found on measures of cognitive development. Thus evidence was provided that computer does not change children's basic cognitive ability. Rather, it may affect their cognitive style, the way in which they utilize the cognitive abilities they possess.

Final Words

It would appear that all the facts are not yet in. However, given that Logo is a relatively new phenomenon, the positive results that do exist seem to indicate that there is promise. It is unfortunate that many innovations in education have been rejected before they were even adequately implemented. The innovation might have had great potential, but teachers did not know how to realize that potential. For that reason alone, evaluative studies revealed no differences and the innovation was discarded. We need to learn *how* to utilize computer programming to fulfill the promise it holds. This will demand the cooperation of teachers, psychologists, researchers, and computer scientists.

As a teacher, you know the truth in the old saying that to truly understand something, you must teach it. In teaching Logo's new procedures (new words, shapes, tasks, ways of doing things, etc.), children also build stronger understandings. Working with Logo can combine teaching, learning, and programming into an integrated, personal experience.

THINK ABOUT

1. Read Barnes and Hill (1983) and Papert (1980) and take a stand on the use of computers with preschool children. Participate in a class debate on the issue.
2. Do you think that Papert is correct in assuming that proper programming experiences can change the way in which children think? Is he too optimistic? Does he forget Piaget's warning that learning cannot precede development, or can powerful experiences change the "natural" course of development? Will children still need drill and practice in the "basics," or will they learn these effortlessly as they pursue more meaningful projects?

CURRICULUM CONSTRUCTION CORNER

3. Read the August 1982 issue of the journal *Byte*. Of the applications in the schools described by Daniel Watt ("Logo in the Schools") and R. W. Lawler ("Designing Computer-Based Microworlds"), which do you think would fit your situation the best? Write a short description of a Logo application for your classroom. For additional ideas, see D'Angelo & Overall (1982) and any of the resources listed in the Annotated Bibliography.

ANNOTATED BIBLIOGRAPHY

Bearden, D. (1983). *1, 2, 3, my computer and me*. Reston, VA: Reston Publishing Co.
This book is intended as an introduction to Logo for children. Sources for Logo classroom activities also include Abelson (1982), Papert (1980), Papert et al. (1979), and Perlman (1976).

Bitter, G., & Watson, N. (1983). *Apple Logo primer*. Reston, VA: Reston Publishing Co.
Besides being a primer for learning Apple Logo, this includes a brief exposition of the Logo philosophy and a description of the use of Logo in schools. Parallel editions are available for several other versions of Logo.

Burnett, J. D. (1982). *Logo: An introduction*. Morris Plains, NJ: Creative Computing Press.
The author provides a brief introduction to Logo as he discusses some powerful ideas and their educational implications.

Harris, L. (1982, May/June). Which way did it go? *Classroom Computer News*, pp. 35–36.
Harris describes how she used Big Trak and a BASIC computer program (which is supplied for you in the article) to teach directionality.

Minnesota Educational Computing Consortium. (1983). *Apple Logo in the Classroom*. St. Paul, MN: MECC.
MECC's book is intended for higher grades, but teachers might use it to learn Logo themselves.

Riordon, T. (1982). Creating a Logo environment. *The Computing Teacher, 10*(3), 46–50.
The author provides thoughtful suggestions for creating a Logo environment. Make an outline of his questioning techniques.

Thornburg, D. D. (1982). *Every kid's first book of robots and computers*. Greensboro, NC: Compute! Books.
This book is written for children who wish to begin programming Big Trak or Logo. It provides a method for outfitting Big Trak with a pen.

Torgerson, S. (1983). *Logo lessons: Ideas for the classroom*. Eugene, OR: International Council for Computers in Education.
Ideas for implementing Logo activities in the classroom.

Watt, D. (1983). *Learning with Logo*. New York: McGraw-Hill.
This is designed to teach Logo to children and teachers. It highlights "powerful ideas" *and* has "helper's hints"—suggestions for teaching Logo to others. It also contains a single keystroke program for young children. Recommended.

11

OTHER COMPUTER LANGUAGES

BASIC

BASIC, Beginners All-purpose Symbolic Instruction Code, was developed by Professors Kemeny and Kurtz in 1963 to help college students write programs. It has since become the most widely used language on microcomputers. Yet in recent years, there has been much debate concerning the appropriateness of teaching BASIC to young children. Why?

BASIC has several disadvantages:

1. It is not procedural. Each BASIC program is a single list of numbered instructions. Programs cannot be easily broken down into "mind-sized bites" with one procedure calling another. Children cannot "teach the computer new words," and teachers cannot supply younger children with "black box" procedures. It is not a well-structured language—BASIC programmers usually do not start with the general and work toward the specific, in a "top-down" planning style.
2. It is not recursive.
3. It does not organize data in a hierarchical fashion, in the way that languages and subject matter content are organized.
4. Most important, BASIC was not designed for young children. It lacks the feature of turtle geometry. Its error messages are less "user friendly." It was not based on a theory of learning and thinking or designed to promote problem solving.

There *are* advantages to BASIC:

1. It is the most widely available language on microcomputers. Usually, it is the only language that is "built into" the machine and thus available when the computer is turned on.
2. It is interactive.
3. Many programs are written in BASIC. Therefore, a teacher who wishes to modify programs for her use, or wishes to use one of the many published programs, would find knowledge of BASIC useful.
4. It has not been empirically proven that any one language is superior. In fact, Luehrmann (1982b) has argued that the important thing is not using any particular computer language, but teaching children to think carefully and write clearly for the computer in whatever language is available. How can this be done in the early grades?

Making BASIC Meaningful

Analogies. Analogies drawn to familiar situations help children to understand computer statements ("make it your own by making it familiar"). The following are brief introductions to BASIC statements and suggestions for drawing such analogies (where applicable, corresponding Logo commands are written in parentheses).

The PRINT (same word in Logo) statement is relatively easy to understand. It instructs the computer to act like a typewriter and print something on the screen. The quotation marks mean "Don't change this; just print it on the screen."

As discussed in the last chapter, we use the idea of variables every day. BASIC's command is LET (Logo uses MAKE). LET N = 4 tells the computer, "Find the box with 'N' on it (if there is none, label one). If there is a number in it, throw it out. Put the number 4 in the box." Later, PRINT N would instruct the computer to print whatever is in box N—4, in this case.

10 LET N = 4	Creates a "box" labeled N and puts the number 4 in it.
20 LET M = 3	Creates a box labeled M and puts the number 3 in it.
30 LET S = N + M	Creates a box labeled S. Adds the number it finds in the box labeled N to the number it finds in the box labeled M and puts the sum in the S box.
40 PRINT S	Finds the box labeled S, and prints the number it finds there on the screen.
RUN 7	Instructs the computer to "do" the program.

INPUT allows the computer to ask the user for information (Logo uses REQUEST or READLINE). In a program, INPUT N$ instructs the computer to (1) print a "?" on the screen; (2) wait for one or more words (the $ means that the variable is a "string" variable, that is, the information is a string of alphabetic and other characters, rather than a number) to be typed on the screen, followed by the pressing of the RETURN key; and (3) put that number in the "box" (memory location) named "N$." A first grader wrote this program.

1 PRINT "WHAT IS YOUR NAME?"	Prints the message.
2 INPUT N$	Waits for the user to type in a response and store it in box N$.
3 PRINT "HELLO, "; N$	Prints HELLO and then the name stored in the box N$.
RUN WHAT IS YOUR NAME? LAURA HELLO, LAURA	

GOTO and the IF/THEN can be thought of as traffic police. GOTO 100 instructs the computer to "drive" immediately to line 100 and do what it says ("Do not pass GO, do not collect . . ."). IF A = 5 THEN GOTO 100 is a bit more involved (Logo and some BASICs use IF/THEN/ELSE). *IF* A equals 5, then the program goes immediately to line 100; otherwise, it does not (and the program continues uninterrupted). Our police officer is now doing some checking: *IF* the man broke the law, THEN he must "GOTO" jail; otherwise, he does not. (Or as one second grader said, "Yeah. *If* you washed your hands, *then* you can eat. If not, get the soap!")

```
10 PRINT "ROBBIE IS GREAT!"
```
Prints the message.

```
20 GOTO 10
```
Instructs the computer to return to line 10. There it prints the message and goes to line 20, which instructs it to GOTO 10, and so on . . .

```
RUN
ROBBIE IS GREAT!
ROBBIE IS GREAT!
ROBBIE IS GREAT!...
```

Here is a program written by, as you might guess, Tom (third grade).

```
10 PRINT "WHO IS THE BEST PROGRAMMER?"
20 INPUT A$
30 IF A$ = "TOM" THEN 60
```
Checks if the information stored in box A$ is the name "TOM." If so, goes to line 60.

```
40 PRINT "NO! TRY AGAIN."
50 GOTO 10
60 PRINT "YOU'RE RIGHT."
70 END
```
If not, "falls through" to here.
And eventually returns to line 10.

```
RUN
WHO IS THE BEST PROGRAMMER?
DEBBIE
NO! TRY AGAIN.
WHO IS THE BEST PROGRAMMER?
ME
NO! TRY AGAIN.
WHO IS THE BEST PROGRAMMER?
TOM
YOU'RE RIGHT.
```

Table 11-1 presents a brief list of some BASIC commands and statements. When you begin to learn a computer language, create analogies, personifications, and the like that you believe will help the children in your classes. In this way, age-appropriate models and lists of rules or procedures for each command can be provided for students.

Graphics: A good place to start. Perhaps the best way to introduce programming to children is to have them write graphics programs, creating pictures on the screen. This is true even though BASIC pictures are created by plotting numerous points on a coordinate grid rather than directing the movements of a turtle. However, the statements that generate graphics have not been included in the preceding brief discussion. This is simply because different microcomputers use different statements. Therefore, rather than confusing readers, it is wiser to recommend reading the manuals that come with each particular type of computer. Regardless of the particular version of BASIC used, children enjoy and learn from copying, modifying, and finally writing and debugging graphics programs.

Students in a third grade wrote the programs that drew the pictures shown in Figure 11-1. They used only statements that place a rectangular region or a vertical or horizontal line on the screen. After their initial introduction to computer programming, they learned to color their

TABLE 11-1   Fundamental BASIC Statements and BASIC System Commands*

STATEMENT	INSTRUCTS THE COMPUTER TO
PRINT	Display information.
LET	Give a bit of information a name.
REM	Do nothing—REMark is used to explain parts of a program to people reading the listing.
INPUT	Print a "?" and wait for the user to type in something.
GOTO 90	Jump to line 90.
END	End the program.
IF . . . THEN	Make a decision. If the first statement is true, then the second statement is carried out.
FOR-NEXT	Set a "counter" and "loop," or repeat a part of the program, a set number of times.
READ, DATA	Specify information within the program (DATA) and READ it.
GOSUB 1000,	Jump to line 1000, and then
RETURN	RETURN to the starting place.

COMMAND	INSTRUCTS THE COMPUTER TO
NEW	Clear its memory.
LIST	Display all the numbered statement lines in the program.
RUN	Execute the program in its memory.
SAVE	Record the program in its memory on the memory device such as a disk or tape.
LOAD	Retrieve a program from a disk or tape and place it in its memory.

Remember, the simplest way in which to edit a BASIC program is to merely retype the line, including its number, with the corrections. The computer will replace the old line with the new one. Use the back arrow or DELETE key to erase mistakes on the line you are typing.

*Instructing a computer what to do with the program.

intended design on a grid their teacher copied for them. Then they translated this into a computer program that would reproduce the design on the screen. Finally, they typed in and "debugged" their programs. Not only did this encourage "thinking ahead," it allowed computer access to more students, because only one part of the procedure had to be conducted "on the computer." The teacher pointed out that the more planning and thought was put in beforehand, the less computer time was wasted.

FIGURE 11-1
Graphics programmed in BASIC by primary grade students.

Dramatizing computer programs. There are many activities that teachers can use to help students understand these BASIC statements and computer programming. Here is how one class dramatized a FOR-NEXT loop. The author, Bobby, LISTed his program

```
10 REM  BOBBY'S ADDING PROGRAM
20 FOR N = 1 TO 10
30    PRINT N" + "N" = "N+N
40 NEXT N
50 END
```

And ran it:

```
RUN
  1 +  1 =  2
  2 +  2 =  4
  3 +  3 =  6
  4 +  4 =  8
  5 +  5 = 10
  6 +  6 = 12
  7 +  7 = 14
  8 +  8 = 16
  9 +  9 = 18
 10 + 10 = 20
```

A classmate asked it if could go higher. Bobby typed in LIST, and the screen showed

```
10 REM  BOBBY'S ADDING PROGRAM
20 FOR N = 1 TO 10
30    PRINT N" + "N" = "N+N
40 NEXT N
50 END
```

He then typed

```
20 FOR N = 1 TO 100
RUN
```

The class broke out in spontaneous squeals of delight and admiration as Bobby's program proceeded to add every number from 1 to 100 to itself. The teacher suggested that they dramatize the program. She asked several children to pull their oval rug to the middle of the room. She placed the box on which the class had written "memory" for a previous computer dramatization near the edge of the rug. Several children drew a picture of the monitor on the chalkboard. Others, under Bobby's directions, wrote each statement (with the line number) on a separate strip of tagboard. An ordered deck of cards (1 through 10) was placed near the rug. The arrangement looked like that shown in Figure 11-2.

Children took turns taking the role of the computer. Ignoring line 10 ("That's just a remark, it doesn't do anything"), the students would go to line 20, pick up the next card off the pile, deposit it in the memory box, and print the correct number sentence on the board. Then, passing line 40, they would have to check if they had reached the last number. If not, they headed back to line 20. When card 10 had been processed, the loop was finished. They then went on to line 50, which told them to END. Everyone had a chance to participate, especially as the class experimented with changing lines in Bobby's program.

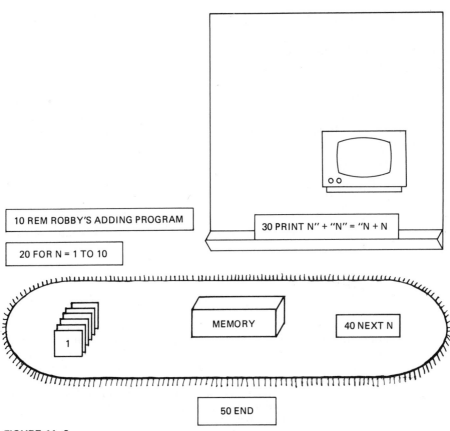

FIGURE 11-2

Learning More About BASIC

More BASIC for you. You can learn a lot about BASIC programming from one of many books that are available. Find one that makes you work a little, figuring out how to solve problems for yourself. It is also beneficial to find written sources of good programs. Studying them and typing them in can teach you a lot about good programming practice. And, as an additional reward, you end up with a usable program. For example, you might enter some instructional programs and games that have been published that you would like to use with your students or type in a gradebook program like those mentioned in Chapter 3 for yourself.

More BASIC for your students. Books have been written for children that teach programming in BASIC; several are cited at the end of the chapter. They range widely in quality, but generally the offerings are improving. Be sure to have enough copies so that students can refer to them even if they are not sitting in front of the computer. Do not feel you have to know everything about programming to work with your children on it; you can learn alongside them. This gives them a *reason* for reading (books) and for reading carefully. Their self-concept is given a boost if they can help to teach you something.

BASIC Hints on Teaching

As a teacher, you are an expert in children's learning. Many of the lessons we have learned from other areas apply to the learning of programming too. The following reminders may help you plan for positive experiences.

1. Have children engage in different levels of computer programming experience:
   a. Typing in, running, and modifying programs to investigate how commands work.
   b. Predicting how a program will operate, then running it to check.
   c. Duplicating the output of a program they have seen run, but have not seen listed.
   d. Locating and correcting bugs in programs.
   e. Solving programming problems that they choose or create themselves.
2. As with any skill or ability, children need to *use* and practice programming to achieve competence. If possible, provide at least to two or three sessions of about 1 hour (½-hour minimum) every week for elementary grade students. This is best done throughout the year, but if it must be done as a unit, try to provide at least nine weeks of hands-on experience.
3. Remember, too, that some children will need additional challenge, that some will need an extra bit of empathy and encouragement, and that some may need a slower pace. *All* students should understand that the great speed of computers does *not* mean that programming is a quick endeavor—it takes time. We certainly do not want to place pressures on students, producing a whole new phenomenon—"learning disabled programmers!"
4. Children learn best when they do things for themselves. Encourage them to write their own programs, solving their own "problems." Challenge them to predict what a program will do before they run it. Encourage the use of graphics at first. Conduct art and design "shows"; invite parents.
5. Keep a list of "BASIC experts," students who want help, sign up for a tutorial. The list can be quite popular. They can help with organization, and everyone involved may benefit. Those tutored learn what they wanted to know from someone who understood intuitively what was "bugging" them and their attempts at programming. The tutors (several of whom may not be especially high ranking in math or reading) gain feelings of self-confidence and competence. They will also learn a lot themselves. The teacher gains time to work with other children and groups of children.
6. A growing list of BASIC statements that have been learned might be posted. Other lists might include the computer's rules for performing each statement, such as described earlier. As another illustration, the computer's rules for another pair of commands, GOSUB 200 and RETURN, would be
   a. When GOSUB is encountered, remember the line number of the statement after the GOSUB statement.
   b. Go to line 200 and do what it says there.
   c. RETURN to the line number remembered in "a."

7. Utilize active, understandable models, such as those described in this and previous chapters. Research indicates that they are a powerful aid to learning (Mayer, 1979, 1981).
    a. Develop an understanding of the series of steps each single command involves.
    b. Use dramatizations and discussions that translate computer programs into English language equivalents.
    c. Do not neglect the "big picture." Use "chunking" in discussing programs and sections of programs as wholes. For example, "This program will ask you a riddle, wait for your answer, check if your answer is the same as its answer, then tell you if you're right."

Guidelines to Programming

To promote good thinking and problem-solving skills might take more effort with BASIC. The following guidelines can be modeled for and discussed with children. Older students can perform most of the steps; younger children can be introduced to the main ones.

1. *Plan it.* Begin with paper in front of you rather than a computer. Then make a plan, which might be a drawing or an outline.
2. *Break it down.* Using the plan, write down the program in more detail, in pictures or in English. Begin with the major steps. Then, through a process of "stepwise refinement," break each of these steps into their component parts (and these parts into smaller parts as necessary) until no more refinement is necessary (i.e., when each part is easily translated directly into a statement in computer language).
3. *Name variables if needed.* Decide on the variables you need, if any. List their names, content, and purpose.
4. *Act it out.* "Walk" through this program following each command just as the computer would. Return and take every branch, if possible.
5. *Write it down.* For the first time, translate the plan into computer language. If this is overly difficult or unclear, go back and revise your plan.
6. *Type it in.* Enter the program into the computer. With this kind of preparation, debugging should be minimized.

A General Curriculum Guide

Table 11-2 presents guidelines that two schools used that you may wish to adapt. Many grades use the same commands. The difference among these grades is the way in which the commands are used. Students in kindergarten and grade 1 may not memorize or fully understand the commands, but they can create short (one- to three-line) programs; students in grade 2 may create four- to six-line programs; and students in grade 3 may start experimenting with their own programming ideas.

It is the author's belief that Logo and other child-appropriate languages are more desirable than BASIC. However, creative teachers use the tools they have to construct challenging and enjoyable experiences for their students. The educational emphasis for teaching any programming language should be on (in increasing order of importance) (1) understanding the capabilities of the computer. (2) developing the ability to make the

TABLE 11–2 General Curriculum Guide for Teaching BASIC

	PRESCHOOL	KINDERGARTEN	GRADES 1	2	3
PRINT	I	I	D	D	D
NEW		I	D	D	D
LIST		I	D	D	D
RUN	I	D	D	D	D
GOTO	I	I	D	D	D
LET			I	D	D
SAVE		I	D	D	D
LOAD		I	D	D	D
Graphics	I	I	D	D	D
INPUT		I	I	D	D
FOR-NEXT		I	I	D	D
Strings			I	I	D
IF-THEN			I	I	D
REM			I	D	I
Problem solving	I	D	D	D	D

I–Incidental, informal, introduction.
D–Directed activities, discussions.

computer do what you want it to do, (3) gaining wider knowledge about subject matter, and (4) developing problem-solving abilities.

WRITING CAI PROGRAMS:
AUTHORING LANGUAGES AND SYSTEMS

Most teachers do not write their own mathematics textbooks or basal readers; most will not write a significant amount of their own CAI programs. Developing good software is time consuming and costly. When you want a particular program for a particular job, it is generally advisable to search for an available program first. However, there are several situations in which commercial materials might not be the best answer. Sometimes, a focused topic that is taught every year has not been addressed in commercial materials, at least for a specific make of computer. Sometimes, local situations are involved. Examples might be a map lesson on one's town (population $517\frac{1}{2}$—somehow large software producers have yet to write a program for it) or practice with children's telephone numbers and addresses.

Still, is it absurd to think of learning *another* computer language? Naturally, that depends on your needs and situation. Some teachers use such a language themselves and also teach it to their students and, therefore, get full use of the investment of money and time. To justify learning an authoring language, you would probably need to use it a considerable amount. However, there are levels of difficulty of these languages, and there are authoring *systems* that are even easier to use. Brief descriptions may make the choices more clear.

What Are Authoring Languages and Systems?

An *authoring language* is a special computer language that attempts to help a person who is not familiar with the intricacies of programming write courseware for use in the classroom. Using statements of only one or two letters, you can present information, ask questions, accept and store responses, and branch to different parts of the lessons depending on those responses. A particularly useful feature of many authoring languages is their ability to provide special methods of drawing graphics, special characters, and music and integrate these into the lesson. An *authoring system* provides more structure. It asks you a series of questions: what information you want to present, what questions you want to ask, what the correct answers are, what feedback to give, and so on. The system then creates the lesson for you.

Examples. The following is a list of the capabilities of several systems and languages. Table 11-3 provides a more extensive list.

1. This package allows teachers to develop lessons immediately upon sitting down at the microcomputer. The program asks the teacher for the information it needs to create and present the material. The teacher types in the information to be presented to the student, questions to be asked, hints to be given, correct and incorrect answers and responses to these, and so on (Courseware Development System, Bell & Howell).
2. In this sytem, the teacher constructs lessons from modules consisting of text pages, graphs, and graphics. Hints can be offered. Revision questions, presented if the student responds incorrectly on the main question, can be inserted. Student records can be maintained (Zenith Educational System, Avant-Garde Creations).
3. This system consists of a series of "shells" in which teachers can create their own quizzes. Three forms are available: multiple choice, matching, and true/false. With no programming knowledge, teachers can substitute their own quiz material into any of these formats (The Shell Games, Apple).
4. This system has a tutorial format with drill and practice quizzes, fill-in-the-blanks, matching, multiple choice, or true/false to test the material taught. Teachers can preset lesson branching patterns for students based on their performance on the quizzes, or they can assign specific sequences of lessons for students. Management (CMI) is available (AIDS, Instructional Development Systems).
5. This authoring language allows a teacher to type in short commands and write interactive CAI lessons. This authoring language, PILOT, is available from several companies for most major makes of microcomputers.

Using an Authoring Language

On first using PILOT, you would notice that some commands seem easier than those in other languages. To print a line of text, you need only type T: (for "type")—there are no quotation marks or the like to worry

TABLE 11–3 Authoring Systems and Languages

Representative Authoring Systems
Adaptable Skeleton, Micro Power & Light Company
Blocks Author Language System and Graphics Library, San
  Mateo County Office of Education
CAI-Manager, Mathware/Math City
CAIWARE, MicroGnome
Create (series), Hartley
Custom Ware, Random House
Educators' Lesson Master, Aquarius Pub.
Eureka Learning System, Eiconics
GENIS, Bell & Howell
Learning System, Micro. Lab Learning Center
Magic Spells, the Learning Company
Micro Test Administrative System, SRA
Microteach, Compumax
Professor, Monument Computer Service
Quick Quiz: A Mini-Authoring System, Radio Shack Outlets
Square Pairs, Scholastic
Super-CAI Authoring System, Fireside Computing, Inc.
Teacher Authoring System, Kyd Tyme Project
Teacher Utilities, MECC
T.E.S.T. and Individual Study Center, TYC Software
Test Author, Educational Curriculum Software
TRS-80 Author I, Radio Shack Outlets

Representative Authoring Languages
COMAL (COMmon Algorithmic Language)
PETCAI (i.e., CAI authoring for the PET microcomputer)
PILOT (many versions for most microcomputers)
SuperPILOT

about. To instruct the computer to stop and allow the student to type in a response, you type A: (accept child's answer and store it). One of the nicest features is the M: (match) command. It allows you to match the student's response to any of several possible answers. Depending on whether or not a match is made, you can program the computer to type appropriate responses, branch to appropriate sections of the program, compute the number of (in)correct responses, and so on. If you type

```
T: CAN YOU TELL ABOUT
T: IMPORTANT PLACES IN OUR TOWN?
T: WHAT IS THE NAME OF THE STREET
T: THAT OUR SCHOOL IS ON?
A:
M: LINCOLN,LINKIN,LINCILN          Match any of these.
TY: LINCOLN, THAT'S RIGHT!         Type this if there was a match; Y = Yes.

TN: OUR TOWN HALL IS ON LINCOLN    Type only if there was no match.
```

The M: match command instructs the computer to attempt to match the student's answer with any of the three spellings. Even if a bright and poetic student typed "IT'S LINKIN, I'M THINKIN," the program would respond, "LINCOLN, THAT'S RIGHT!" This not only comes in handy

184 Other Computer Languages

where alternate spellings can be expected, but also in situations where a student is asked to respond yes or no. The following:

M: YE,SURE,ABS,DEF

would match YES, YEAH, SURE, ABSOLUTELY, DEFANATELY (sic), and it should be noted, it would match YELLOW and ABSURD. This kind of matching, essential to natural language interactive programming, can be cumbersome at best in other languages. In your program, if the student typed MAIN STREET, the response would be "OUR TOWN HALL IS ON LINCOLN."

Many other options are open to you following a match. JY: *NEXT means "Jump to the part of the program labeled *Next (asterisks mark labels for sections of your program) if a match is made." U: (use) branches the program to a subroutine—a module, or piece of the program, with a specific function or job to do. After finishing the job, the subroutine returns the program to the line right after the U: command. In this way, a job (e.g., giving positive feedback and keeping track of the number of correct responses) that has to be repeated can be done by the same section of your program without retyping it each time.

As her first project, one teacher wrote a shape recognition program in a version of PILOT that features a drawing with a pointer, similar to Logo's turtle graphics. A listing of parts of the program, with explanations of the commands, can be found in Figure 11-3. A student using this program would read

```
        TRY TO NAME THE SHAPES
        THAT I SHOW TO YOU.
        TYPE THE NAME AND
        PRESS RETURN.
               GOOD LUCK!
        PRESS <RETURN> TO GO ON.
```

FIGURE 11-3

A Section of a PILOT Program

Program	Explanation
R: *** NAME THE SHAPES ***	A Remark is not printed.
T: TRY TO NAME THE SHAPES	Type these lines on the
T: THAT I SHOW TO YOU.	screen.
T: TYPE THE NAME AND	
T: PRESS RETURN.	
T: GOOD LUCK!	
U: TRNPAGE	Use a special section labeled TRNPAGE which asks the child to press return to go on.
T: WATCH ME DRAW THIS.	
G: COLOR 1	Graphics commands let you
G: DIRECTION 0	draw with the pointer. These
G: DRAW 20	set the color and direction,
G: LEFT 90	then draw a rectangle.
G: DRAW 40	
G: LEFT 90	
G: DRAW 20	
G: LEFT 90	
G: DRAW 40	
T: WHAT IS THE NAME OF THIS SHAPE?	
A:	Accepts the child's answer.
M: RECTANGLE,RECTANGEL	Matches the child's answer to any of these words.
TY: CORRECT!	Type if Y--if there was a match, prints CORRECT!
TN: NO, THIS IS A RECTANGLE.	If not, this is printed.
U: TRNPAGE	
*TRNPAGE	This is a label for this section of the program.
T: PRESS <RETURN> TO GO ON.	
W:	Wipes the screen clear.
E:	Ends this section and returns to the previous point in the program.

When the child pressed the return key, he would read WATCH ME DRAW THIS, and the invisible turtle would draw a rectangle on the screen.

```
WHAT IS THE NAME OF THIS SHAPE?
TRIANGLE
NO, THIS IS A RECTANGLE.
    PRESS <RETURN> TO GO ON.
```

The lesson would then continue.

PILOT is well suited for lessons with a lot of text. This would seem to limit its use with young children. However, newer versions, such as Super-PILOT have the capability to control video tapes and disks, allowing a range of lessons to be presented with quality pictures and speech.

Using an Authoring System

An authoring system takes advantage of the fact that many lessons follow the same format: information is presented, questions are asked, and feedback is given based on the student's responses. Authoring systems ask the teacher questions based on this format; that is, the teacher is asked what information is to be presented, what questions are to be asked, and so on. Then the system is able to create a lesson automatically. Systems vary in format. Some use multiple-choice questions, others blocks of text followed by questions, some have specific game formats such as a matching game or a TV show game. Some allow branching, or hints to be offered if a student gives an incorrect response. Some permit several correct answers, for example, to allow for an incorrect spelling or either "true" or "t."

For example, *The Game Show* (Computer Advanced Ideas) is a take-off on the TV show "Password." Given a set of clues, each player attempts to guess a word or phrase. A number of possible subjects to choose from is already provided; however, teachers and students can insert their own subject area, words, and clues. The program asks you for the name of the subject, the "target" word or correct answer, and a set of clues. You type these in, and a new game is ready to be played. Many more authoring systems are listed in Table 11-3.

Criticisms of Authoring Systems and Languages

While the idea of writing instructional programs using a language designed specifically for this purpose is appealing, criticisms can be made. Most languages such as BASIC, Pascal, and Logo have very similar commands. While they usually consist of more than one letter, they may not be that much more difficult to learn to use, if the programmer wants to become proficient in a language. Additionally, learning such a high-level language might be more useful to the teacher in a variety of settings and applications than would learning a more limited-application authoring language. Finally, many versions of authoring languages require extra hardware and storage.

Much of the simplicity of use of an authoring language is achieved through the reduction of the number of commands. This makes the program easy to use, but it restricts the range of possibilities. Some commands, such as the M, or match, command, are quite helpful and are unique to authoring languages. However, commands for other functions may not be available.

In an authoring language, commands are included that are designed specifically for instructional applications. While this can be helpful, it can also encourage users to adopt and utilize only one instructions strategy—presenting content, questioning, checking answers, giving feedback, going on to the next section, and so on. If programs end up as technological page turners, or as endless sequences of the same pedagogical approach—even good Socratic questioning can be tedious if there is no other approach—they will not lead to increased student achievement or positive attitudes. Variety is possible, but the nature of the language and commands tends to encourage repetition of this limited approach.

In authoring systems, the user fills in material to be presented, questions, examples, answers, hints, and so on in response to computer prompts. Therefore, the order and method of presentation is preset—programmed into the computer. While this gives the user more help, it should be noted that they also reduce the possible teaching strategies he or she can use.

Maximizing the Advantages and Minimizing the Disadvantages

Questions to ask. Therefore, a potential user of an authoring system or language might want to ask the following questions.

1. Would I benefit from taking the time to learn a more powerful computer language with a wider range of applications?
2. Are the commands available in the system I am considering adequate for the type of courseware I want to write?
3. What are the teaching strategies that are "built into" or encouraged by the program? Are these too limiting? Do they match the teaching strategies I would want to employ?
4. Could my students also learn the language?

Avoiding the pitfalls. When writing computer programs with an authoring language, the following suggestions may keep you from the pitfalls:

1. Start with a consideration of what you want to teach and how you intend to teach it. Before beginning programming, a well-developed model should exist that includes content and teaching strategies. Where appropriate, have the learner attempt to figure something out for himself or herself. This planning, or design, stage is actually quite extensive. Specifically, it should involve
   a. Analyzing the instructional needs of your students.
   b. Stating the instructional goal.
   c. Outlining the instructional program.

d. Designing a detailed plan for the program. Depending on the program, you may wish to (1) perform a task analysis, (2) specify objectives and entry behaviors, and (3) develop testing strategies. You will want to plan and sequence specific learning activities and plan how the instruction will be conducted; that is, what teaching methods and strategies will be used. Remember the public speaker's advice: "Tell 'em what you're going to tell 'em, tell 'em, then tell 'em what you told 'em."

2. Use "structured programming techniques." Using the model as a guide, break down the project into "mind-sized bites." First, develop structured outlines or flowcharts detailing the sequence of activities. Second, lay out the screen presentations or "frame storyboards." Review and revise as necessary. Plan each of the sections in detail as well as the order and branching sequences of the various sections.

3. Document the program adequately.

4. Develop each section on the computer as a first draft. Try to
   a. Use simple menu selections when presenting options.
   b. Let the student determine the pace of the program; for example, by pressing "RETURN" to go on.
   c. Use a variety of types of presentation.
   d. Avoid overusing sound or graphics.
   e. Avoid too much print on the screen at any one time. Double space.
   f. Design the activity so as to involve the learner as often as appropriate. Make requests for learner input clear.
   g. Avoid feedback for incorrect answers that is "fun."
   h. Highlight main concepts and ideas.
   i. Debug each section before going on.
   j. Ensure that the learner cannot cause the system to "crash" by typing in an unexpected or unusual response. Check what happens if the learner presses RETURN without entering any information.
   k. Ensure that the sequence you plan—branching and looping back for slow learners, branching ahead for fast learners and those who already know the material—determines to a large extent the effectiveness and efficiency of the lesson. About 80 to 90 percent of the students should correctly answer the mainline questions on the first try.
   l. Plan how performance will be monitored, if that is desired. You may want to plan an assisted quiz with lots of feedback, followed by a lesson summary and a final quiz.

5. Ask colleagues to try out the program and offer suggestions for improvement. Note that, if possible, it would probably be beneficial to use a team approach to the development of the lesson. Flaws tend to be caught sooner. The variety of suggestions given usually enriches the material. Ideally, one member of the team may be a subject matter expert, another a programming expert, and the third an authority on instructional design.

6. Formatively evaluate first-draft materials. Revise as needed.

7. Field test your materials by (a) sitting down one-on-one with one or two students while they use the program, (b) using it with small groups, and (c) letting others use it with their classes.

8. Produce final product.

9. Write helpful documentation.

Most of all, be realistic. It would be far easier for most of us to write an entire student textbook for a particular subject for our grade level than to write an extensive, high-quality CAI program. However, programming in authoring languages can still be valuable for several reasons. First, it allows us to experience directly, and thus to really learn about, the thinking that should go into CAI materials. This makes us better critics—we can choose the best from among the wide variety of offerings. Second, we can write programs that we cannot find commercially. However, new courseware is being produced daily, and programs that meet your needs might now be available. Third, some authoring languages, especially those with turtle graphics, can be used with children. They are not as adaptable as Logo and should not be viewed as an exact replacement, but children can use them to write graphics and interactive programs for each other. One school has every teacher and every student programming in PILOT (Swett, 1983).

You might want to use an authoring *system* instead. With some loss of flexibility, this would achieve about similar results with considerably less effort. You need only look for one that closely matches your needs; many are listed in Table 11–3.

If you have given thought to questions such as those posed here, and have decided that an authoring language or system—properly used— would help you in the classroom, you will also undoubtedly find yourself challenged to create more and more useful applications.

THINK ABOUT

1. Would you choose to learn an authoring language or a high-level computer language like BASIC or Logo? Why?
2. What specific applications or needs do you have presently that seem to indicate that you might wish to author CAI programs.
3. Attack or defend:
   a. Computer programming should be taught to every student as a necessity for living in a technological society.
   b. If computer programming is forced upon all children, we will soon start seeing a new phenomenon: children with a learning disability in programming.
   c. Since most programming languages are evolving quickly, it makes little sense to teach a programming language to young students, especially BASIC.
   d. Learning Logo or BASIC now, and then Pascal or FORTRAN later, will confuse children.
   e. Prealgebra students cannot understand the concept of "variables"; therefore, this should be omitted from their training in BASIC or other languages.
   f. Allowing students to use preprogrammed materials, especially games, discourages them from learning how to program.
   g. Using an authoring language forces a teacher to adopt a certain (narrow?) approach to teaching with microcomputers.

ANNOTATED BIBLIOGRAPHY

Bork, A. (1982). Computers and learning: Don't teach BASIC. *Educational Technology, 22*(4), 33–34.

Luehrmann, A. (1982). Don't feel bad about teaching BASIC. *Electronic Learning,* 2(1), 23–24.

> Whose arguments do you find more persuasive? Why? Is there some truth in each position? How about for the *young* child?

Dwyer, T., & Critchfield, M. (1978). *BASIC and the personal computer.* Reading, MA: Addison-Wesley.

Jones, A., Jr. (1982). *I speak BASIC to my* . . . [versions for many models of microcomputers]. Rochelle Park, NJ: Hayden.

Luehrmann, A., & Peckham, H. (1983). *Computer literacy: A hands-on approach.* New York: McGraw-Hill.

Moursund, D. (1978). *BASIC programming for computer literacy.* New York: McGraw-Hill.

Richman, E. (1982). *Spotlight on computer literacy.* New York: Random House.

> BASIC tutorials for adults and/or older children are numerous. The best idea is probably to check a local computer store or bookstore to find one that you like. This is but a brief list of offerings.

Carlson, E. H. (1982). *Kids and the Apple.* Reston, VA: Reston Publishing Co.

Larsen, S. (1982). *Computers for kids.* Morristown, NJ: Creative Computing Press.

Richardson, K. (1982). *Everybody's BASIC.* Indianapolis: Meka Publishing Co.

VanHorn, Royal. (1982). *Computer programming for kids and other beginners.* Austin, TX: Sterling Swift.

> This is a partial listing of BASIC programming books for children—few are available that can be used independently by primary grade children, but they supply ideas that teachers can adapt.

Hirschbuhl, J. J. (1980–1981). The design of computer programs for use in elementary and secondary schools. *Journal of Educational Technology Systems, 9*(3), 193–206.

Roblyer, M. D. (1981). Instructional design versus authoring of courseware: Some crucial differences. *AEDS Journal, 14*(4), 173–181.

Spitler, C. D., & Corgan, V. E. (1979). Rules for authoring computer-assessed instruction programs. *Educational Technology,*

12

THE ABCs AND BEYOND
Language Arts and Reading

Five-year-old Maria gazes at the screen of a plastic toy. She leans forward over the connected keyboard and types CAT. A small animated cat slinks into the center of the screen, and a built-in speaker intones "cat." Maria types BIG. The mechanized voice says "A big cat" as the cat grows in size on the screen. In response to Maria's next message, JUMP, the cat leaps to a higher corner of the screen. Her interest wandering to a suitable name for the stout feline, Maria types FATE CATE. The toy asks, "fate cate?" Maria frowns slightly, mumbles with poorly disguised impatience, "No . . . maybe like mommy", and types FATY CATY. Maria listens; her smile indicates that the toy's pronunciation has improved. A new idea gleams through her eyes as she bends over the keyboard once more.

Futuristic? The technology to build such a toy is here. Several computer programs *already* provide young children with experiences similar to those described. Teachers are recognizing that computers are *not* complicated "number machines"—that the area in which they may have the *most* profound impact on children's learning is the language arts.

One of the most reliable messages of theory and research in language arts education is that the language arts are interrelated and interdependent (Moffett & Wagner, 1983; Petty, Petty, & Becking, 1981). Experiences that help children to write also help them to read. Activities that develop speaking vocabularies of students simultaneously develop their ability to comprehend the oral and written communication of others. Teachers who try to teach children to read without recognizing their deep desire to write may meet with frustration and may fail to take full advantage of the relationships among all the language arts. This message, which is a reflection of the principle of integrating all areas of the curriculum, tells us that the best computer language arts activities will involve reading *and* writing, *and* speaking *and* listening. In doing this, programs do *not* overemphasize breaking down language into pieces—letters, words, and isolated sentences. They deal with communication that is meaningful and functional for children.

SUPPORTING YOUNG CHILDREN'S WRITING

Guided Writing

In *Story Maker* (Bolt, Beranek and Newman), children construct stories by selecting which path of several should be followed. Marko chose the "Haunted House" story. He read the first phrase, "Lace opened the front door and. . . ." He then was presented with three possible ways to complete the sentence. The options from which he could choose are contained in the boxes at the second level of a "story tree"—a branching story design (see Figure 12-1). Marko chose the second option. The computer then completed the sentence on the screen: "Lace opened the front door and slipped into what looked like a bowl of spaghetti." It then offered Marko the two options below the middle box in Figure 12-1. The whole story was constructed like this, with Marko choosing the paths he preferred from each level of the "story tree." Each choice branched him to another set of choices, and so on. When the story was finished, he instructed the computer to make a copy of it on the printer.

The choices Marko made determined not only the next sentence, but also what future paths would be available. His decisions had important consequences. He had to think about high-level aspects of the story such as story structure, the flow of the narrative, and the characters' plans. Often, when children tackle new and complex challenges in writing, other areas in which they had been competent, such as handwriting and spelling, suffer (Graves, 1979; Rubin, 1982). *Story Maker* frees children of these details (information processing psychologists would say "reduces the processing load") and allows them to concentrate fully on the meaning of their stories. Even children who are not yet reading have been observed working with *Story Maker*. Several kindergartners became fascinated listening to older children discuss what options to choose. They gravitated to the computer and started making suggestions—good ones! They watched and listened intently as the older children acted on their advice and read the resulting story. Everyone participated and learned at his or her own level. The

FIGURE 12–1 A story tree from the Haunted House.

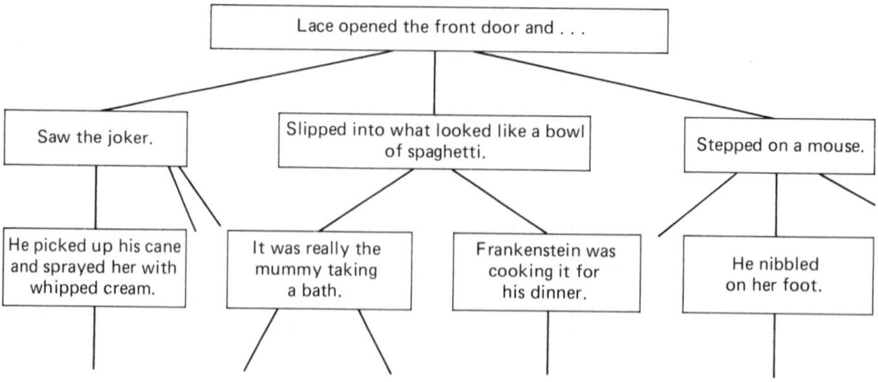

prereaders learned a lot about composition and stories and the fun that they can provide. Teachers could plan for just these types of learning situations in their own classes.

Children have been known to spend hours with *Story Maker*, printing out every possible story line. However, the computer program can challenge children in new ways. There is no "right" and "wrong." Like programming with turtle graphics, children receive a meaningful response, but not correction, from *Story Maker*. If a more specific response *is* desired, children can elect to be given a goal at the beginning of the story. For instance, for the "Haunted House" story, the program might ask

```
WRITE A STORY IN WHICH
(1)  LACE GETS A LION
(2)  LACE MEETS CATWOMAN
```

If Marko had chosen the "saw the Joker" option but then chose the "whipped cream" and thus did not reach this goal, the program would have responded

```
WELL, MARKO, YOU HAVE PARTIALLY SUCCEEDED.
YOU HAVE WRITTEN A STORY IN WHICH
(2)  LACE MEETS CATWOMAN
BUT YOU HAVE NOT WRITTEN A STORY IN WHICH
(1)  LACE GETS A LION.
IN A MOMENT, I WILL GIVE YOU A CHANCE TO TRY THIS STORY AGAIN.
```

To reach the goal successfully, children must continually read for meaning, apply knowledge of story structure, infer, evaluate, and make predictions. Teachers can challenge children with other goals, for example, to construct a story that keeps the reader in suspense. Class discussions could be held in which children describe *how* they figured out how to reach the goal ("I thought that Catwoman would be in the story with the Joker, so I picked that branch first")

Included with this program is another, *Story Maker Maker*, which demands that children create, plan, predict, and evaluate. Children add their own original story segments to an existing story tree or they can make up a completely new story tree. Teachers who use this program successfully encourage small groups of students to brainstorm about their story and write down all their ideas, often on index cards. They then lay these cards out, trying out different arrangements, and finally type in their best ideas. Some complex and fascinating stories have evolved from whole-class stories in which different groups contributed their own branches. Elementary children have been observed to carry on conversations independently concerning story structure after one remarked that another's effort was "not a story."

Students in classrooms face many obstacles to writing (Rubin, 1980). They usually write alone. Class discussions rarely concern *how* to actually write; instead, they center on low-level skills such as punctuation and grammar. Writing is usually isolated from reading, and there is no real audience for children's writing. Like *Story Maker,* other programs have been designed to remove these obstacles. (The point is *not* that *Story Maker* is perfect. Its programming is not sophisticated, for example. The point is that this and other programs such as *That's My Story* from Learning Well have been designed to emphasize meaningful, large sections of text.) Some of these are appropriate for use by children at the very first stages of writing and reading.

Very young children can place objects anywhere they wish through one-word commands in "World" (in the *Early Childhood Learning Program* from Educational Activities). They create a picture or design on the screen. Children can create stories and sentences which are animated in the *Story Machine* (see Chapter 7) and CARIS (see Chapter 16). In CARIS, for example, a 4-year-old might select a noun such as "dog" and a verb such as "falls." She would then read "The dog falls" and see a picture of a dog falling over a cliff. One teacher discussed this after her students had a chance to experiment with the program, to let them know that just because their sentence was not "accepted" did *not* mean it was wrong. She used the discussion to introduce concepts of syntax—in this program, the only acceptable sentence contains an article, a noun, a present-tense verb, a prepositional phrase if you want it, and a period (for additional suggestions, see *Teaching and Computers,* September 1983, pp. 30–31). A child showed that he understood the discussion when he later explained to a frustrated friend, "The computer just can't think of all the sentences *we* can!" The teacher did not overuse the program, and she planned to keep her eye out for similar programs that were even more powerful and flexible. Some large systems have already been similarly programmed to accept over 250,000 different sentences (Yeager, 1977).

These programs exemplify a powerful approach to meaningful writing and reading on the computer. They provide support and structured guidance in a way that helps children fully comprehend written language, even at an early age. To develop mature literacy, however, children also need to write freely, using their own ideas, vocabulary, topics, and structures. Computer programs can support this type of writing as well.

Aids

Pretend that a student of yours, Edwin, has just finished his composition. He turns in his "good copy" and his "scrap copy" (you know Edwin; he did the good copy first in ink and then wrote the scrap copy in pencil, writing in the lines, arrows, and cross-outs that he thinks will impress you). As you glance at it, you notice that he needs a good opening sentence, two sentences are out of order, and he misspelled one word several times. Dare you ask him to rewrite it (again)?

With computerized writing tools, you can feel free to confer with

Edwin about his writing, suggesting changes (or better, guiding him to suggest them). Rewriting will be welcomed. Even better, Edwin will have neither the need nor the desire to fake an early draft. The following section describes some of these tools.

Research by Graves (1979, 1983) shows that writers, whether beginners or professionals, follow the same steps in composing: prewriting, writing, and revision. Computers can support children's writing at each of these steps.

Prewriting. Before considering computer prewriting programs, let us remember that the most important prewriting activities for young children are talking, drawing, and imagining. In line with our principles, computers should not replace these valuable activities, but may supplement them. How? Children may respond to questions posed by a computer program, or they may use the computer to respond to fellow students. Questions that the computer could pose might concern the topic, characters, the setting, and so on. The program might ask the children to brainstorm, identify the intended audience, and organize their ideas into a story structure (even if this is merely having a beginning, middle, and end). Various "story starter" techniques have been used, such as providing a basic story structure and having children fill in the blanks *or* choose "defaults" if the child cannot think of anything (Levin, 1982a).

Perhaps more powerful is the use of the computer to facilitate children's responding to each other's early drafts. Students "sign on" to the computer, using a pseudonym if they wish, and read through other students' drafts, leaving comments. Or they may look at their own piece to read the comments others have made concerning their first ideas. Several "story starter" programs are being developed.

"The Planner" (in *Quill*, D. C. Heath, developed at Bolt, Beranek and Newman) prompts students regarding planning the structure of the kind of composition they are writing. If they are writing a book report, the program might ask them the name of the book, some of the characters, what type of book it was, whether they liked it, and the reasons they felt that way. "The Planner" is especially useful as teachers—or better yet, teachers and students—can brainstorm a list of prompts on questions appropriate for any writing task. This list will be added as a new planner.

Writing. The most powerful component of a computerized reading system is a child-oriented text editor, or word processor. A word processor is merely a special program that, when loaded into the computer, allows the student to type in text (letters, words, sentences, etc.), delete, insert, or move around portions of text, save it and retrieve it later (just as music is stored on magnetic tape), and so on. This allows children to "play" with written words just as freely as they play with oral language. Instead of chiseling words out of granite, a painstaking, error-prone, irreversible process, word processors make writing more like sculpture with clay. Writers gradually shape and form their ideas, try out different ways to express themselves, and revise freely. The product is always neat and professional looking. Paper copies can be printed up easily at any stage of the writing process.

To use word processing for teaching writing, you should first try out different programs to find one that is appropriate for your students. One such program, the *Talking Screen Textwriting Program* (*TSTP*, Computing Adventures Ltd.), is discussed in the following paragraphs. There are others, including *Bank Street Writer* (Scholastic), *Magic Slate* (Sunburst), and *Blackboard* (CTW).

The *TSTP* is especially appropriate for young children due to its speech capability. It can pronounce each letter as the child types it, read aloud each word as it is completed, and read the entire sentence or composition as many times as desired. The child can fix, or change, the way any word is pronounced (for those words that are not in the synthesizer's "dictionary" and are exceptions to phonics generalizations; e.g., "Sheri"). This can lead to meaningful explorations with letter-sound relationships.

First become familiar with the program until you can write more easily with it than with paper and pencil. While learning, you might wish to make a poster and duplicated sheet for your students listing the major editing commands.

Introducing writing on the computer is often most successfully done as a whole-class language experience story (Stauffer, 1980). As each of the major commands is needed, tell clearly why it is needed ("What do we need to do? Right, erase that letter."), how to remember what to do ("Let's see, how do I do that? I can press the ESC key so the program will tell me how or I can look on the poster."), and exactly how to do it ("So I press CONTROL-B to erase a letter going *backwards*.") Work intensely with a small group to develop your first "experts." Their names will be posted with the instructions for using the program so that others can ask for help.

For the next few weeks, continue presenting short, direct lessons to the class followed by work on the computer in pairs—an expert and a beginner. In this fashion, children can start writing and saving their work on a disk within the first week. When students are using the program independently, they are ready to concentrate on their compositions. If computer time is limited, the children may have to write their first draft in pencil. When they are done, they can sign up for a 20- to 30-minute session at the computer. Working in pairs, one student types in her own composition as her friend reads it, suggesting changes along the way (if possible, try to work for just a minute with students during this time—it is exciting to be a coach during the writing rather than a critic afterward; see Figure 12-2). Then they switch places. One teacher who had only one computer every third week had a parent volunteer type in the students' work after school during the two weeks in which the class did not have access to the computer. On the third week, students would read and revise their programs. Although these methods are compromises, students can still benefit from using the computer, especially in reviewing and revising—the final, crucial step in writing.

FIGURE 12–2 A five-year-old with an adult composing with Computing Adventures Talking Screen. (Photo by Fred Adrian. Compliments of Computing Adventures, Ltd.)

Revision. Because students find themselves writing more, and writing more easily, on word processors, their work may be less organized and *more* in need of revision than paper and pencil writing. Fortunately, this process—free, continuous writing followed by reflection and revision—is one of the best ways in which to compose. And the computer can help with the revisions. With the *TSTP*, children can instruct the computer to read their whole composition. Then they can fix the pronunciation of any word, insert or delete words, and so on. With the *Bank Street Writer,* words, sentences, and paragraphs can be moved, exchanged, deleted, or inserted.

Many word processors either contain or can be expanded by spelling programs. These programs usually check every word in the composition against a dictionary. Words they do not recognize are shown to the writers. They must decide if the word is misspelled. Some programs suggest what the correct spelling might be. Other programs check punctuation, uncapitalized first words in sentences, unbalanced quotes, and so on (Collins, n.d.). Possible mistakes are pointed out to the writer. There might be lists of reminders on the computer for each student, carefully chosen by the teacher, that suggest areas to check in their text.

What about teachers using a word processor alone? The computer is still a great help. Compositions can be reviewed either as paper printouts or on the computer's screen. "Reviewing" should mean that *both* the teacher *and* other students read and react to a child's writing. The real advantage for students is the ease of making corrections. Rather than messy erasures, confusing lines and arrows, and unwelcomed rewriting, editing on the computer is quite gamelike. Press a key and poof—a paragraph disappears. Move to an earlier spot in the composition and press another key—

the paragraph reappears in its new location. Or press a few keys and, in less than a second, every "din't" becomes "didn't."

Whether on paper or on the computer screen, there are techniques that should be used in conferencing with students about their work. First, structure the environment. Sit next to the children at eye level. Avoid taking the child's paper away from him or her. Instead, have the student read his or her writing to you; then respond. All students need to hear their words and ideas reflected back to them. This is called "receiving the work" (Graves, 1983). If the child wrote, "My dog is bad. He jumped on the bed all muddy" you might say, "Oh your dog *is* bad, jumping on the bed when he's dirty!" Then ask questions. "What does your mom say?" Later, more challenging, searching questions should be asked as well as questions concerning the process of writing. "Is it important to tell the reader how you felt about that?" "How are you going to tell about that?" "Where could you put that sentence?"

Listen closely. Try to "get a feel" for what the child is trying to say, who the audience is, and so forth. Reflect this in your questions. Then wait. Most teachers wait less than 1 second after asking questions. Much more is accomplished if teachers wait just 3 seconds (M. Rowe, 1978). For such a complex activity as writing, even more waiting time is needed. At the *later* stages, help the child to focus on a *single* problem in his or her writing—be it organization, development (keeping on the topic, etc.), or mechanics (grammar, spelling, capitalization, etc.)—and make the appropriate revisions on the computer.

Finally, have students print out two copies of their compositions, one to take home and one for a folder that will hold all their writing. After students are writing longer stories, they should pick one of every four or five to "publish"—print copies on quality paper, draw pictures for illustrations, and bind in hardcover form. These books are placed in the class library (Graves, 1983). Younger writers not producing long stories should select one out of every three or four short "stories" (sometimes just a sentence or two: "I love my grampa. I help him in the garden") until they have a collection of about ten, which are bound as "collected works."

Does word processing make better writers? Research is only beginning to accumulate, but researchers and practitioners tend to agree that writers using computers write more, are less worried about making mistakes, take increased pride in their writing because text looks better (one honest writer said, "The computer makes my writing look better than it is"), have fewer fine motor control problems, give more attention to finding errors, and revise more, correcting punctuation and spelling (Daiute, 1982; Watt, 1982). These beneficial effects seem to transfer to later paper and pencil work: children make twice as many deletions and eight times as many insertions in later pencil compositions. Children who have the most difficulties in writing may benefit the most (Collins, n.d.).

Disadvantages have been noted, too: word processors are expensive and not portable, they are complicated, the size of the screen limits the amount of text writers can see at one time so text coherence may be affected negatively, and the attraction of "gadgetry" may distract some writers.

Choosing a word processing program.   Like any software package, a word processing program should be selected with regard to the criteria discussed in Chapter 6. In addition, consider the following points (several of which were discussed earlier and are summarized here for the reader's convenience):

1. Are the commands simple ("English," not jargon), logical, and generally limited to a single keystroke?
2. Does it include an on-line tutorial and easy-to-use menus and help screens?
3. Are upper- and lowercase letters available? Are they easy to read?
4. Is the documentation easy to use for students, yet complete enough for you?
5. Will it allow stories to be printed on paper?
6. Does it include (if you want them) such features as windows or a "split screen" (a student can see his outline in one part, his composition in another, or two parts of a composition at the same time), "wrap around" (in a way that words that do not fit on one line are brought down to the next line automatically), indentation, "invisible lines" (for comments; they are not printed), "search" commands, and so on?
7. Can it be used at several levels of difficulty—with children using only simple commands at first, then gradually learning additional powerful commands? For example, the ability to search for specified words or phrases, changing them if desired; to move around to different spots in the text quickly; to rearrange paragraphs and sentences; to view separate sections of a piece of writing simultaneously by having a "split screen"; and so on.
8. Does it have speech capability? (A program that *does*, such as *TSTP*, may *not* contain other more advanced capabilities, such as those already mentioned.)

Check other sources for up-to-date lists of available programs and reviews (e.g., Boudrot, 1983).

Environments

In all its uses, the computer is a powerful educational tool because it can create challenging, stimulating environments in which to learn. Computer programs are being developed to provide writing and reading environments that allow children to communicate with one another. One program, *Quill* (from D. C. Heath, developed at Bolt, Beranek and Newman) contains several communication aids.

Publication systems.   Several projects have employed publication systems in third grades to produce classroom newspapers. These programs enable students to type in text and specify a particular format. For instance, the computer could automatically set up columns, headlines and bylines, a masthead, indexes, and so on for a newspaper. Likewise, for a book it would set up a title page, a table of contents, chapters and chapter headings, and an index.

The publishing system could also produce different kinds of letters, such as invitations, friendly letters, requests for information, thank-you letters, and so on. The computer, however, makes it easy for these activities to be continuous, year-long endeavors that are time efficient and beautifully organized.

Information retrieval systems.   The Library is an information retrieval system (in Quill, D. C. Heath) that allows students to store and retrieve information about any subject in which they are interested. One class used it to create files of game reviews. A description of each game was stored under several descriptive categories: video, arcade, home, board, sports, and so on. Any child who wanted to find out about an "arcade" game would type in that descriptor, and the system would list all those games. Then the child could type in any particular game to get a full description.

Message systems.   In one project (Levin, 1982a), third and fourth grade children in New Jersey will communicate with children in Alaska. Students will write messages that will be sent over phone lines via computers in each school in the middle of the night (and, therefore, inexpensively). The messages might be to "all video game lovers," to a list of people, or to a single person. Students are notified of messages that they have received when they next use the computers. They can then peruse the messages, read them, print them out, or send them to someone else. Classes could use such a system to leave messages for other classes in the same school or in other schools or to engage in such projects as interschool clubs; computer bulletin boards; a computerized version of the "personal problems" columns of newspapers and magazines; or a group epic, a long adventure story written by many children in different schools (Collins, n.d.). The advantage of this system is that children must make themselves understood *in writing,* or others who are far away are sure to ask them what they mean! A limited message program can be typed into your computer (Muller & Kovacs, 1983).

WRITING COMPUTER PROGRAMS THAT WRITE ENGLISH

The Logo computer language is a natural for language applications. For very young children, adults can write computer programs in Logo to provide language arts–oriented "microworlds" for children. For instance, the favorite computer activity of a 4-year-old named Jonathan is a simple graphic microworld that he controls with single word commands. A visitor might see him watching a planet intently on a TV set. Soon, the observer notices that rather than being a passive viewer, Jonathan is quite active. He moves forward to the keyboard attached to the television and types SHIP. A rocket ship appears. Typing UP, he watches the ship lift slightly off the planet's surface. He types UP repeatedly, watching the ship rise to the top of the screen. FLY. The rocket turn to the right and begins to move slowly. He types FASTER; the ship responds. Jonathan reflects a bit on his world. It is good . . . but not complete. He lean forward and types MOON. A yellow circle appears.

To tell the computer how to write syntactically correct, but random, sentences, the child has a deeper, more demanding purpose for understanding and using the notions of parts of speech. One third grade teacher knew that her students were not yet ready to construct such a project on their own but thought that they would benefit from modifying such a program. The teacher wrote most of the program by adapting one she had read in a book. She told her students that they had to (1) tell the computer what words to use as nouns, verbs, and so on; and (2) write a procedure to write phrases. The class tackled this together first, writing

```
MAKE "NOUN.LIST [DOGS ROBOTS ALIENS GIRLS ELEPHANTS BOYS]
MAKE "VERB.LIST [WALK EAT RUN FIGHT CRY PLAY READ]
TO SPEAK
 (PRINT NOUN VERB)
END
```

When the class typed SPEAK, the computer printed

```
GIRLS EAT
ALIENS RUN
ROBOTS READ
ROBOTS RUN
ELEPHANTS CRY
DOGS READ ....
```

Children then used the program on their own. Several children more or less repeated what the class had done, but they did have to create noun and verb lists correctly. However, with their teacher's encouragement, other children wrote rather different procedures.

```
MAKE "NOUN.LIST [RATS E.T.S BLOCKS TRUCKS CARS DINOSAURS]
MAKE "VERB.LIST [KILL RUN EAT CRASH SLEEP]
MAKE "ADJECTIVE.LIST [BLUE BIG NICE FAST GREEN MANY HEAVY]

TO MIKE
 (PRINT ADJECTIVE ADJECTIVE NOUN VERB)
END
```

This resulted in the following "run" of the program:

```
MIKE
BIG BLUE RATS EAT
NICE FAST TRUCKS CRASH
MANY HEAVY DINOSAURS SLEEP
GREEN MANY RATS KILL
GREEN GREEN E.T.S RUN....
```

Mike was pleased, but did not like the way in which his adjectives sounded in the last two phrases. He decided he needed two adjective lists that contained different words to avoid "GREEN GREEN." The problem with the phrase "GREEN MANY RATS KILL" was more difficult to understand. He and his teacher discussed how number words such as "many" and "five" just did not sound right after other adjectives. Mike never had thought about that before. He planned to put all the number words in the first adjective list.

One bright girl wanted to write sentences like "The girl went to the store." She and her teacher discussed what additional words her phrases should contain. At the right moment—after they had decided on starting with a word such as "a" or "the"—her teacher introduced the term "article" and added new procedures that chose random words from a PREPOSI-TION.LIST and an ARTICLE.LIST. Some of the girl's sentences were

```
THE PURPLE FROG DANCED OVER THE STORE
A NICE COOKIE ATE ON A POND
A PINK GIRL HOPPED IN THE FROG
```

Logo is almost infinitely extensible. The author has used a Logo computer program that displays an entire word along with a word space, at the touch of one key. Keys were covered with stickers bearing the name of the corresponding word. Keys were programmed to erase whole words and save finished sentences for instant replay. Another labeled key allowed children to program unused keys to display words of their choosing. Pressing another commanded the computer to print the children's stories. The boy who wrote

```
I AM A GOOD BOY
AM I A GOOD BOY
```

and then remarked, "Hey, I know how to make a question now! You can switch the first two words!" was beginning to develop a metalinguistic awareness that few other reading/writing programs—even those that include dictation—would so encourage.

After the children had 15 to 25 words in their programs, they would often choose to type the whole words in by themselves. With a simple adaptation, they could use the Logo editor as a word processor.

BOOKS THAT TALK TO YOU

The simplest, but still interesting, "talking books" are those that read aloud. *The Magic Wand Speaking Reader* (Texas Instruments) is a hand-held device that translates specially coded texts into a humanlike voice for beginning readers. The child slides the wand along tracks printed beneath the text (of the books that accompany the wand). An optical scanner converts bar codes (that can be compared to the bar codes on supermarket products) into synthetic speech. Words, phrases, sentences, songs, and sound effects are produced. This allows children to "reread" books and sentences as they wish. However, other types of *interactive texts* may be even more powerful.

In one system readers stumped by a word merely touch the word on the screen. The computer pronounces the word and underlines it so that readers can learn to read new words. On-line dictionaries providing definitions and explanations are also being constructed. They can "look up" words very quickly and can search for spellings with *any* letter(s) unknown—even the first! For the youngest children, the computer might be tied to a video disk that contains a picture dictionary. The word could also be pronounced. In the future, talking books will ask questions to ensure that readers understand their content. If misunderstandings occur, extra help might be offered, or the text itself may be automatically altered to a less difficult level.

In interactive fiction, the child takes the role of one of the characters in a story, talkng to other characters, making decisions that influence the plot sequence, and so on. As with composing, this places children in a motivating and intimate contact with the important features of a story: characters and their feelings, plot, sequences, and so on. Most of the programs presently available are written for older children, but there are increasing numbers of interesting programs along similar lines written for preschool and primary grade youngsters (e.g., *The Adventures of Oswald* or *Sammy the Sea Serpent*, see Chapter 2; *Dragon's Keep*, see Chapter 9).

TEACHING SPECIFIC ABILITIES AND SKILLS

In this category, the teacher determines the knowledge and skills to be learned and chooses computer programs designed to facilitate this learning. Many of the (better) programs encourage student input and choice; however, the intent of the programs is usually the achievement of goals set by the teacher. Available programs cover a variety of prereading and reading skills. It is important to remember that the programs already discussed *also* provide practice on these skills, and, because this practice is done in a meaningful, communicative context, it is irreplaceable. However, following the principles, specific practice is warranted as it is needed.

Readiness Skills

This category includes directionality, letter and color matching and naming, and beginning phonics.

1. In *Juggles' Rainbow* (The Learning Company) children are asked—via pictures—to push any key that is above, below, to the right of, or to the left of a simple line marker that is placed on the keyboard. Colored rectangles and rainbows with colored rain illustrate "above" and "below"; butterflies whose wings change color illustrate "left" and "right." Children also create variously colored pictures and work with lines and circles in activities designed to help them discriminate among "b," "d," "p," and "q."

2. *Children's Carrousel* (Dynacomp) is targeted for children ages 2 to 6. Nine programs teach simple cause and effect, same or different, shape and letter matching, letter recognition, and keyboard practice (children type any letters or words to see them appear as large characters on the screen).

3. The title of *Preschool IQ Builder* (Program Design, Inc.) may be a bit misleading. In it, children either indicate whether two figures are the same or different or type the letter that matches that on the screen. Other shape matching programs include "Balloon Pop" (in *Learning with Leeper*, Sierra On-Line) and *Match Maker* (Countpoint Software).

4. Taking advantage of the motivation of arcade-type games, *Bop-a-Bet* (Sierra On-Line) requests that young children move a box around a maze, "bopping" the next upper- or lowercase letter in the alphabetical sequence.

5. The early levels of *Alphabetization* (Milliken) involve seeing likenesses and differences in letter forms, recognizing lower- and uppercase forms of letters, and recalling alphabetical sequences. Teachers can assign exact sequences of instruction, via the computer program, including mastery and failure levels, to classes or individuals (described in Chapter 3). Other letter matching or alphabetization programs include *Alphabet Arcade* (Program Design), *Alphabet/Keyboard* (Random House), *Alphabet Song* (Edu-Soft), *Customized Alphabet Drill* (Random House), *Early Games for Young Children* (Counterpoint Software), *Kinder Koncepts* (Midwest), *Letter Recognition* (Hartley), and *Primary Math/Prereading* (from MECC).

6. In *Hodge Podge* (from Dynacomp), typing a letter yields a song, picture, and/or animated picture related to that letter. Children are free to explore and are presented with the opportunity to learn alphabet names, words, animals, musical scales, songs, and numbers. Many other ABC programs are available, such as *The Stickybear ABC* (Optimum Resource, Inc.).

7. The *Phonics* (SRA) series delivers instruction primarily through audio tape that provides directions and examples. The corresponding letters and words are usually shown on the screen (note that, while this is obviously valuable, it restricts the program to a "forward only" linear sequence). All letters to be included in the lesson are introduced. Each is shown in turn in several example words. The audio says the words and asks the students to repeat them. Finally, the audio pronounces each word and asks the students to type the letter whose sound is present in the word. Other word attack programs include *Fundamental Phonics and Word Attack* (Random House), *Old McDonald's Farm Vowels* (TEKSYM; audio narration included), and *Word Families* (from Hartley).

8. In *Roll-a-Word* (from CTW) children must match pictures and words to complete sentences in rhyming patterns. Teachers may select specific rhyming patterns and beginning blends.

Sight Word Vocabulary and Spelling

A variety of programs are designed to provide practice with spelling and reading words, including more advanced word identification skills.

1. One activity in *Spelling Bee and Reading Primer* (Edu-Ware) displays word/picture combinations and asks the child to spell the word after it disappears. Another presents three words and a picture; the child must identify the correct word.

2. In *Magic Spells* (Apple Computer), *Word Scramble* (T.H.E.S.I.S.), and many similar programs, students receive practice in spelling scrambled words. *My Spelling Easel* (Atari) teaches spelling skills. *Cookie Monster's Letter Crunch* (CTW) provides simple letter sequencing skills practice. *Alphabet Zoo* (Spinnaker) is an arcade-style game in which young children "chase" the

letters of a word around in a maze. For example, a picture of "candy" might be shown; the child must capture the letters, Pac-Man style. Teachers can select from among several levels of difficulty.

3. In *Whole Brain Spelling* (SubLogic Communications Corporation), words are presented one at a time in a box on the screen. Each press of the space bar changes the words in some way. The color (essential to the program) may change. Double letters may be presented in contrasting colors. The word may appear one letter at a time, it may flash, it may be printed in all upper- or lowercase letters. This is supposed to focus visual attention on the word. It is the intent of the program that children will apply the visualization techniques whenever they are trying to learn to spell a word, on or off the computer. Teachers of young children will wish to order "A Child's Garden of Words" version designed for preschool to third grade children.

4. *Spelling Package* (Teaching Tools) and *Create-Spell It* (Hartley) allow teachers to record whatever words in whatever context they desire on a cassette tape. The program plays the tape for the students, waits for them to spell the word, responds appropriately, and provides lists of words spelled correctly and incorrectly at the end. *Customized Flash Spelling* (Random House), *Do It Yourself: Spelling* (Program Design), and *Scramble Spell* (Hammett) allow teachers to make (written only) word lists that children use in various spelling activities.

5. A series of vocabulary building, arcade-style games are the Arcademic Skill Builders (DLM). In *Word Invasion,* the child is "attacked" by four columns of words. He has a magic ring that destroys the part of speech it is set for but that setting—flashed on the screen—comes up randomly. The player must find, among the approaching words, the part of speech indicated, position the ring under that column, and "fire" the ring. Other programs in the series include *Word Radar* (see Figure 12-3) and *Word Man,* vocabulary recognition games, *Verb Viper,* which teaches recognition of verb tenses, and *Spelling Wiz. Word Attack!* (from Davidson & Associates) includes a tutorial to introduce new words, two quiz/review programs, the exciting but nonviolent *Word Attack!* game itself (see Figure 12-4), and an editor that allows teachers to add their own words.

FIGURE 12–3

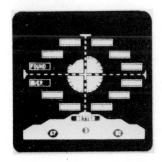

FIGURE 12–4   Word Attack! (Courtesy of Davidson & Associates.)

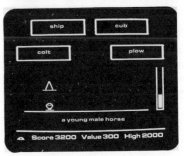

6. Teachers can assign their students to any reading skill level in *The Reading Machine* (SouthWest EdPsych; see Chapter 3). Skills cover K to grade 3, including letter matching and sequencing, phonics and vocabulary (some children may require help in identifying the drawings). Words will be spoken if an available cassette tape is purchased.

7. *Dolch Sightword Acquisition* (see Shostak, 1982) contains 219 words placed in five levels from preprimer to third grade. With a speech synthesizer, directions, words, and sentences are spoken. The word is flashed. It then disappears, and a "configuration box" takes its place. The student then types in the word, receiving feedback after each letter. Each incorrect letter is replaced by a "ghost font" or dotted version of the correct letter, which the student must mentally close and then type. If an incorrect letter is entered again, the word is written underneath to aid copying. Any words missed are stored for the teacher's information and are presented to the student the next time he or she works with the program. Tachistoscopic mastery tests are also employed.

8. *Letters and Words* (Learning Well) asks children to match words and their corresponding pictures (Figure 12-5). No spelling is required. *Kids on Keys* (Spinnaker) has several games in which children must identify the word that corresponds to a picture. In *Picture Place!* (CTW), children choose a background scene and then create a picture by using written words as building blocks. When the child decides that the word is in the proper place, it is changed into a picture.

9. In *Teach Me Words* (SVE), the child must supply a word that starts with a given letter. If the computer does not know the word yet, it asks for a definition (Figure 12-6). If it does, it will say "Mary taught me that a hat is something you wear on your head."

FIGURE 12–5 Children must decide if the word matches the picture in *Letters and Words*. (Courtesy of Learning Well.)

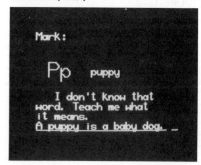

FIGURE 12–6 *Teach Me Words*. (Courtesy of Society for Visual Education, Inc.)

10. A few programs have addressed structural analysis skills. *Pet/Pit/Put* (Data Command) represents a practice game on suffixes. *Roots/Affixes* (Hartley) contains 21 lessons on multiple reading levels.

11. In the game *Context Clues* (Learning Well), children must use the context of the sentence to determine the meanings of words.

Reading for Comprehension

In these programs, children must comprehend sentences and other larger units of text to complete the program successfully.

1. One series has programs for children on each of several levels. Beginning readers may pick a picture, whereupon a corresponding story is displayed and read to them. In another program, they pick a word that correctly completes a sentence. Later, they make a story by selecting words that determine how the story develops. More advanced readers are asked to be "story solvers." Three skills are involved: determining (1) what the problem is, (2) why something happened, and (3) how characters feel. After reading stories, they are asked to respond. For example, they may be asked to choose a possible solution. They are then shown how events might have progressed if the characters had followed that path (Texas Instruments).

2. Learning Well has produced a series of games to develop comprehension skills such as predicting outcomes, getting the main idea, context clues, drawing conclusions, and so on, usually for 1 to 6 players.

3. *PAL* (Personal Aids to Learning, Universal Systems for Education) is a set of programs designed to diagnose and prescribe reading instruction for children in grades 2 to 6. Children take a computerized test on up to 40 skills and 160 subskills per grade level. They are automatically assigned tutorial lessons on the computer based on their performance on these tests. For example, a second grader might be asked,

```
WHICH ROW OF WORDS IS IN ABC ORDER FROM LEFT TO RIGHT?
A. CRUMBLE - CLIP - CITY
B. CITY - CLIP - CRUMBLE
C. CLIP - CITY - CRUMBLE
D. CRUMBLE - CITY - CLIP
```

If a child answers less than 80 percent of five questions such as these correctly, he or she receives a lesson that uses one of the incorrect responses to illustrate the correct procedure.

```
ON THIS QUESTION YOU PICKED THE ANSWER C.  CLIP - CITY - CRUMBLE
THE ANSWER TO THIS QUESTION IS B.  CITY - CLIP - CRUMBLE
ALPHABET OR ABC ORDER MEANS THE SAME ORDER AS THE ALPHABET.  IF
YOU REMEMBER YOUR ALPHABET, YOU CAN PUT WORDS IN ABC ORDER.
WORDS THAT BEGIN WITH A COME BEFORE WORDS THAT BEGIN WITH B....
IF THREE WORDS START WITH THE SAME LETTERS, LOOK AT THE SECOND
LETTER TO PUT THE WORDS IN ORDER.  THEN, THE FIRST WORK GOES ON
THE LEFT AND THE LAST WORD ON THE RIGHT.  FOR EXAMPLE, CITY COMES
BEFORE CLIP.  THE I IN CITY COMES BEFORE THE L IN CLIP.  CITY
GOES ON THE LEFT.  CLIP GOES ON THE RIGHT.  LET'S LOOK AT YOUR
ANSWER AGAIN....
```

4. Several other companies have produced (and many more will undoubtedly produce) similar software packages. Educational Activities, Inc.,

FIGURE 12-7
Diascriptive Reading. (Courtesy of Educational Activities, Inc.)

publishes *Diascriptive Reading,* a series of diagnostic/prescriptive programs in each of six areas, vocabulary, sequence, main idea, fact/opinion, details, and inference (Figure 12-7). Interested teachers may wish to check with the publishers of their basal readers. A few specific programs that feature computer management are listed in Chapter 3.

ELECTRONIC TOYS—SPECIAL-PURPOSE COMPUTERS

Numerous special-purpose computers are designed to teach the same objectives and skills as the general-purpose computer programs just described. Speak & Read (Texas Instruments; Scott, Foresman Electronic Publishing Division), designed for preschool, kindergarten, and first grade beginning readers, includes several different games. In HEAR IT, children enter any word on a word list and hear it pronounced. WORD ZAP speaks a word. Given a list of three words, children must "zap" the matching written word. In PICTURE READ, children are directed to find a specific picture in the accompanying book. They may see a large picture of the numeral "4" and, next to it, the words "four," "five," and "fish." The program asks, "What word goes here?" The child is to type in the correct word. WORD MAKER provides phonics practice. For instance, the child might add B to AT to make BAT. Comprehension practice is given in READ IT, a context clues activity in which children spell the word missing from a sentence.

Touch & Tell provides practice in simple word/picture connections (oral vocabulary development). Speak & Spell might ask children to "Spell 'earth'."

Teach & Learn (Mattel) uses records and board overlays to present several programs for very young children. The overlay for "Mix 'n Match" consists of six parallel stories illustrated in six parallel columns. If the child touches each picture from top to bottom in one column, he hears the story from that column. He soon discovers, however, that it is more fun to mix 'n match—touching the first picture in one column, then the second picture in another column, and so on, to create a wide variety of interesting stories.

Star-2 (Educational Insights), an electronic matching game, can be supplemented with 20 learning packets, including prereading (colors, shapes, letters), beginning reading (following directions, animals, alphabet sequence, number and color words, basic sight words, sounds of letters), everyday skills, and general skills.

Although attractive in appearance, these electronic toys must also be critically examined by teachers. For example, many are simply low-level drill and practice machines. If they teach essential skills well and are inexpensive, they have obvious advantages. However, if children would only need or want to work with them for a short period, their worth must be questioned.

EXAMINING LANGUAGE ARTS AND READING SOFTWARE CRITICALLY

Educational software for young children should be evaluated in terms of the criteria described in Chapter 7. This is true for all the software described in this (and the following) chapters; programs are described for illustrative purposes only—it should *not* be assumed that these descriptions imply recommendations. (Neither should this warning be taken as a condemnation; the programs described were among the best available.) Given that this evaluation is of primary importance, it is still instructive to examine some representative programs listed specifically in terms of language arts instruction.

It is the goal of several "readiness" programs to provide practice in shape matching or eye-hand coordination. Although the practices of many classrooms seem to give support to these goals, research in reading indicates that visual discrimination of *letters* and *words*, not pictures or flowers, is needed for later success in reading (Durkin, 1980; Stoodt, 1981). Similarly, there is no evidence that manipulating a joystick leads to academic success! With all materials, teachers must consider first the value of the goals and activities.

Letter naming and letter/sound correspondences are accepted goals of prereading instruction. However, the actual content of the programs must be examined carefully. In one ABC program, "U" is for "Underwear." Only children who could read the word knew that this was the word. It must be asked: If children cannot read the words, what are they learning about letters and sounds? If children *can* read the words, why are they working with an ABC program?

Critical questions should be asked about any program designed to help children spell. What is spelling? Does unscrambling a word constitute spelling? Does spelling a word after having just seen it develop the ability to spell the word from memory or from an oral presentation? Unfortunately, research does not provide complete answers to these questions. It *does* tell us that spelling should receive attention throughout the day, that both recognition and recall (or remembering) must be practiced in a cycle if new words are to be learned and the new spellings used in actual writing situations, and that a test-study rather than a study-test procedure should be used (Petty, Petty, & Becking, 1981). Teachers can ensure that the programs they use follow these guidelines, and they can use their professional judgment in addressing questions that research has not yet answered.

Consider the numerous programs that present nursery rhymes. They are attractive and might be useful. But are they better than a book/tape set or a filmstrip? The programs *can* be motivating. Introducing a kindergarten class to the *Micro Mother Goose* (Software Productions) program, the author once risked death by suffocation when it came time to choose the next child to press a key to select the next rhyme. The point is only that teachers must decide again: What should be the priorities for microcomputer use?

According to the principles, one priority should be higher-level use of language. Research shows that students learn to write and read by writing and reading, not from discrete lessons on grammar. Adult writers develop compositions through a series of drafts, with ideas developing throughout revisions. Children should use these same processes, and the same powerful tools (e.g., word processors), as adult writers use. Teachers of the youngest children must ask, "What "environments" (e.g., publications systems, information retrieval systems, message systems) could my students benefit from using? Could they be adapted? What could *I* do to support this use?"

The most effective software in the language arts will probably not only integrate instruction in writing, reading, speaking, and listening, but it will also integrate the approaches described earlier, using exploratory, communicative activities *and* programs designed to teach specific skills, each in its proper place and kept in proper perspective. A step in this direction is one extensively developed and tested program, *Writing to Read* (JHM Corp.; see Martin, 1981). It uses both activities directly controlled by the teacher and activities that put the student in control. Children are provided with up to 15 minutes of intense individualized instruction every day. The program teaches the children 44 phonemes (the program uses phonetic spelling) they will need to write everything they can say. Children are to recognize that they can recombine these to write any word (although the program is based on 30 key words). Consistent use of phonetic spelling may allow children to write more easily than if they were faced with all the inconsistencies of the English spelling system. Each cycle contains lessons on three words and the phonemes that make up the words, a mastery test, and a "make words" section giving practice on recombining sounds to make new words. Then as children learn to write, they learn to read.

At an early level, a colored picture of a rabbit might appear. The computer, equipped with a speech synthesizer, would ask the children to "Say rabbit." After a pause, they are instructed in the phonemic spelling, sound by sound. The voice asks for an "r" and waits for the children to

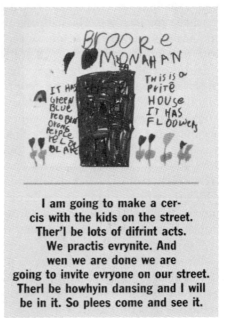

i like spring.
It is fun. I
like it so
much I couod
icsplode.

J. Henry

I am going to make a cercis with the kids on the street. Ther'l be lots of difrint acts. We practis evrynite. And wen we are done we are going to invite evryone on our street. Therl be howhyin dansing and I will be in it. So plees come and see it.

FIGURE 12–8 Actual compositions of kindergarten children from New Canaan, Connecticut. (Courtesy of *Northwest Orient,* Cathy Wilcox, *and* her students.)

press that letter. When they do, that letter goes to midscreen. The computer repeats, "Say rabbit," and again pauses for children to recite the word. This process continues until the word is spelled out.

At later levels, children play computer writing/reading games to practice skills. Two cartoon characters, a mouse and a cat, may appear on the screen. The computer intones "A cat with a hat wants to catch a mouse in a house." The cat will succeed . . . without the child's help. Every time the child correctly types "mouse," the rodent gets closer to a safe hideaway. The computer gently urges the child to type faster.

The computer is only one part of this program. Children move from it to work journals and cassettes that correspond to the lesson they just completed. They might match words and pictures. Cassette/book packages constitute the third part of the program. Finally, children write the words they have learned on typewriters, combine them into sentences, and compose simple stories. Field testing indicates that children easily adapt to 26 letters and standard spellings (see Figure 12-8).

OTHER USES OF THE COMPUTER IN LANGUAGE ARTS AND READING INSTRUCTION

Testing. In certain situations, using the microcomputer for test administration may be beneficial. For example, a well-constructed computerized test of spelling may provide error analyses that are either ignored by many spelling tests or, when conducted, require an inordinate amount of teacher time to score. Hasselbring and Owens (1983) describe a diagnostic spelling test that is self-administered by students and provides the teacher with a detailed analysis of each student's spelling problems.

Materials generation. For teachers, a useful application of the computer in language arts is to generate materials. While it is not recommended that this replace direct use by students, there are (as all teachers know) many hours in which teachers are at the school building but students are not. This is an ideal time to utilize the computer's capability to construct activities, worksheets, and so on. For example, *Elementary Vocabulary/Spelling* (MECC) includes programs that will generate mazes, crosswords from teacher-determined words and clues, a mixup game in which the student unscrambles letters to make a word, a spelling drill, word puzzles from a list of teacher-determined words, and a word game of filling in blanks with letters and guessing the word from a clue. These materials are printed out on paper by the computer. Similar programs include *Crossclues* (SRA), *Crossword Magic* (L&S Software), and *Worksheet Generator* (Radio Shack). Other uses include cloze passage generation, vocabulary list generation, test item generation, objectives production, and keeping inventories (Kuchinskas, 1983).

Readability. Matching reading materials to each student's instructional and independent reading levels is a constant challenge for teachers of reading. Counting syllables, words and sentences, checking words against an extensive word list, and substituting the numbers obtained into a readability formula is a lengthy (and hardly stimulating) process. Computers, however, are custom built for just this type of analysis. Programs to determine readability are available for purchase (Educational Activities, Hartley, MECC, Micro Power & Light, Random House, SVE, TIES,). Additionally, several programs that can be typed into a computer have appeared in the professional literature (Badiali, 1982; Judd, 1981; Goodman & Schwab, 1980; Schuyler, 1982; Walker & Boillot, 1979). Teachers can use these programs to check the reading level of commercial instructional materials, trade books, and their own tests and work sheets.

Other language analyses. Besides readability, many other analyses can be performed, either on students' writing or on commercial materials. Not many programs are available for purchase, although again some listed in the literature may be typed in (Frase et al., 1981; Moe, 1980; Pritchett, 1981). What kind of analyses? A few include the total number of words; the total number of different words; a sorted listing of words based on alphabetical order or frequency of use; the number of words consisting of one letter, two letters, and so on; the total number of sentences; the average sentence length, the number of sentences with one word, two words, and so on; the average number of syllables in a word; the number of T-units; a grade equivalent score, and so on.

Supporting a language experience approach. DOVACK (Differentiated, Oral, Visual, Aural, Computerized, Kinesthetic; Way, 1969) required very little computer knowledge yet provided much assistance to teachers using a language experience approach to beginning reading and writing. Teachers and aides helped disadvantaged children to dictate new stories every day into a tape recorder. Each evening the stories were typed into a computer. The program printed the story and a list of any words not dictated by that pupil in any previous stories. On the next day, the students listened to the tape read the new story as they said the words to themselves and followed the written words. Then they copied the story. They also read a few of their old stories and practiced their new words. Every sixth day, the program generated a word-recognition test. The program also generated complete progress reports for the teacher.

WHAT DOES RESEARCH TELL US ABOUT TEACHING LANGUAGE ARTS WITH COMPUTERS?

Although not conclusive, research results concerning the effects of CAI on reading achievement are generally encouraging. Over a decade ago, it was shown that computers could effectively teach kindergarten through third grade children to read (Atkinson & Fletcher, 1972). Since then, several studies have supported this result, although the effects are often moderate. This has held true for preschoolers (Hungate, 1982; Piestrup, 1981; Smithy-Willis, Riley & Smith, 1982; Swigger & Campbell, 1981) and elementary grade children (Billings, 1983; Bracey, 1982; Forman, 1982; Hollingsworth, 1982; Jamison, Suppes, & Wells, 1974; Kearsley, Hunter, & Seidel, 1983; Lavin & Sanders, 1983; Ragosta, Holland, & Jamison, 1981). While educators should always carefully question and evaluate new approaches, it appears that computers can facilitate the learning of the language arts and reading. One might conjecture that moderate results may merely be a result of researchers' limited knowledge concerning the best ways in which to put this tool to use.

THINK ABOUT

1. Describe several strengths and several weaknesses of one of the following: *Story Maker, The Story Machine, CARIS.* How would you build on the strengths and eliminate the weaknesses?
2. With improved voice input and output, will speech and graphics via computers replace reading? What will be gained? Lost?
3. Should reading presented on a computer be designed to ease students gently to faster and faster rates of reading? Why or why not?
4. Will children lose all the advantages of word processing if someone else types their compositions into the computer?
5. Evaluate a language arts computer program in both general terms (as described in a previous chapter) and specifically from a language arts perspective.

6. Pro: "Revision on a computer will lead to more substantial, more meaningful changes and better writing." Con: "Revision on a computer will make children lazy, like calculators did to children with regard to arithmetic."

7. Pro: "Story starters are helpful and beneficial to beginning writers." Con: "Children should be in control of the topics they write. They have plenty of deep personal importance to say, if we encourage and allow them to say it."

ANNOTATED BIBLIOGRAPHY

Blanchard, J. S. (1980). Computer-assisted instruction in today's reading classrooms. *Journal of Reading, 23,* 430–434.

Henney, M. (accepted for publication). The effect of all-capital vs. regular mixed print, as presented on a computer screen, on reading rate and accuracy. *AEDS Journal.*

> Have you worried that some programs use only uppercase letters? It is a concern; however, this study has indicated that elementary school children did not perform differently in terms of rate or accuracy of reading with all-capital or mixed print. Do you think there are other disadvantages to all-capital computer programs?

Humes, A. (1983, January). An interactive instructional program for elementary and middle school students. *The Computing Teacher, 10*(5), 60–61.

> The author describes a simple sentence combining program and uses it to illustrate how a computer matches words.

Mason, G. E. (1983, February). The computer in the reading clinic. *The Reading Teacher,* pp. 504–507.

> Overviews of computers in reading instruction along with useful references are provided.

Rowe, N. (1978, January/February). Grammar as a programming language. *Creative Computing.*

Sharples, M. (1981, February). A computer written language lab. *Computer Education, 37,* 10–12.

> If the simple Logo programs for generating English interest you, you may wish to read about programs that generate sentences randomly, transform text according to linguistic rules, and even generate sentences with meaning.

13

MATHEMATICS

Most people would readily maintain that it is quite easy to see that computers can help to teach mathematics. However, people then disagree as to the major role and impact of computers in mathematics education. Some say that computers can individualize and motivate practice on computational skills so that children will better learn arithmetic. Others argue that children will no longer need to do tedious computation because computers can add, subtract, multiply, and divide for them—after all, people will not perform these operations themselves in the future. What position would you take?

This question is important and will be discussed later in this chapter. However, the position taken by the author is that *both* viewpoints are missing the mark. Both are based on a narrow view of mathematics—it is restricted to numbers and the "basic facts." Instead, computers should be used to promote the development of *problem-solving* ability in *each* of seven topics of the early mathematics curriculum. Examples of computer applications for each of these topics are provided in the paragraphs that follow.

LOGICAL FOUNDATIONS, GEOMETRY, AND MEASUREMENT

This includes shape recognition, classification, ordering, beginning patterning, directionality, shapes, transformations, gross comparisons, and standard measurement. These concepts form a solid foundation for later mathematical and logical thought.

Shape recognition. Practice for very young children in the discrimination of same and different shapes is provided by several programs (see Chapter 9).

Classification. In *Chaos* (EduFun), the children's task is to move their spaceship to capture alien satellites that match either the shape or the color, or both the shape and color of the satellite in the center square (recall Figure 9-2). If they hit an incorrect satellite, the game ends. The game is designed to teach directionality, shape and color recognition, and simple classification.

Moptown (Apple) consists of 11 activities whose purpose it is to teach classification and logic. The inhabitants of Moptown, "Moppets," have four attributes: tall or short, fat or thin, red or blue, bibbit (big feet and big nose) or gribbit (tails). In one of the beginning activities, children see four moppets and must choose the one that is different. In another, four moppets are seen in a house. The child must identify the one thing that is the same about all of them. Other activities involve analogies and "guess my attribute" and "guess my rule" games. An example of the last is guessing the rule for inclusion in a clubhouse. Two sorting programs can be found in *Thinking Skills* (Sunburst).

Recall that *Getrude's Secrets* (The Learning Company) is another set of classification activities. Children also develop logical thinking skills through forming and testing theories. To see this theory formation in action let us observe two 8-year-olds working with the two-loop puzzle, in which two frames overlap.

The children first observe the example in which one frame is labeled "Blue" and contains blue pieces differing in shape. The other is labeled "Squares" and contains squares of different colors. In the overlapping section are blue squares. The children then move to the empty loops where they are to classify a group of shapes. They pick up a square and drop it inside one of the boxes. It falls out of the box and comes to rest beneath it. Hey! They thought squares went in this one! They have just created a theory, or idea, and had it contradicted. Maybe it's not just squares; it could be any shape (second theory). How about hexagons (third theory)? They pick up a blue hexagon and place it in the box. It stays. Elated, they assume the second box will hold a certain color (fourth theory). They choose red (fifth theory). Picking up a red hexagon, they place it in the second box. It falls out. Yellow (sixth theory)? Nope. Blue (seventh)? No. Wait a minute! There is no other color, but . . . oh! The red hexagon! It should have gone in the middle, where the boxes overlap (eighth theory and major insight). It works.

Ordering. Children are presented with five bars of varying length displayed against a measuring grid. They must press the key from 1 to 5 that corresponds to the longest or shortest bar (*Kinder Koncepts*, Midwest Software). A similar program can be found in *Introduction to Counting* (Edu-Ware). Recall the warning stated in Chapter 7 that such ordering does not involve active manipulation. A more active approach, in which children manipulate different length bars (still on a screen, of course) is provided in the *Early Childhood Learning Program* (Educational Activities).

Patterns and directionality. In *Arrow Graphics* (EduFun), students are presented with a figure created by a three-move command repeated four times. A move is a direction and a specific number of spaces; R3 is right three spaces. They must type in the three moves the computer used to draw the figure (see Figure 13-1). Feedback is in the form of a percentage of "hits." Three perfect patterns in a row gives the child the opportunity to specify the commands himself or herself and see the computer create his or her pattern.

In one of the *Moptown* activities, children see four Moppets arranged

NAME		TEST 1	TEST 2	PROJ	TEST 3	AVG
AIKENS	KENYA	85	83	72	73	78
ANDREWS	RODNEY	68	78	84	69	75
BLICK	PAULA	87	91	85	83	87
BARNES	TRISH	83	83	91	82	85
CHARLES	JOHN	94	96	90	79	90
EISEN	BECKY	85	93	87	88	88
JONES	YOLONDA	80	83	84	83	83
KNAPP	FRANK	85	79	88	81	83
LAMB	JIM	74	92	90	79	84
KUNTZ	BRIAN	72	82	78	83	79
MINIMUM		68	78	72	69	75
MAXIMUM		94	96	91	88	90
AVERAGE		81	86	85	80	83

FIGURE 13–1   Arrow Graphics. (Courtesy of EduFun, Milliken Publishing Company.)

FIGURE 13–2

in a pattern. They must discover the pattern and identify which Moppet comes next. A green frog in *The Pond* (Sunburst) helps students to recognize and articulate patterns, generalize from data, and think logically. Students must determine the patterns of lily pads that will get the frog across the pond.

Older (primary-grade) students might use an electronic spread sheet program to explore number patterns. These programs are merely an interconnected arrangement of rows and columns, filled mostly with numbers that need to undergo numerous repetitive computations. One teacher, Mr. McLoughlin, first used such a program to calculate his grades (Figure 13-2). Notice that the spread sheet automatically calculated the highest mark, lowest mark, and average for each assignment and test as well as an average, which could easily be weighted in any fashion, for each student. If students who were absent took a test late, he would simply record their scores, and the computer would automatically recompute all the averages and so forth. Mr. McLoughlin began to see how students might benefit from exploring number patterns. His first idea was to work with his class to build an addition table.

The first number in the first row and the first column was zero. Then each following number in the top row and in the leftmost column was defined simply as one more than the previous number. On the rest of the table, the intersection of each number was their sum (Figure 13-3). This allowed children to see how an addition table was generated. They also searched for patterns in the table; for example, each number only appears once in the one's place in any row or column. Reading down or to the right is like counting; any number on the upper left half can be matched with one on the lower right (symmetry and the commutative property—3 + 4 = 4 + 3). Numbers on diagonal lines heading toward the upper right are the same, numbers on diagonal lines heading toward the lower right jump by 2's, and so on. Even more interesting were the explorations that came as a result of changing the zeros that were the first numbers. One child suggested changing them to 10's; another to −10's; a third wished to see what would happen if one was 10 and the other was 0. The results of these explorations, reproduced in Figure 13-3, allowed children to find and discuss other patterns and discover additional mathematical rules and insights. What patterns can you find?

+	0	1	2	3	4	5	6	7	8	9	10	11	12	13	14
0	0	1	2	3	4	5	6	7	8	9	10	11	12	13	14
1	1	2	3	4	5	6	7	8	9	10	11	12	13	14	15
2	2	3	4	5	6	7	8	9	10	11	12	13	14	15	16
3	3	4	5	6	7	8	9	10	11	12	13	14	15	16	17
4	4	5	6	7	8	9	10	11	12	13	14	15	16	17	18
5	5	6	7	8	9	10	11	12	13	14	15	16	17	18	19
6	6	7	8	9	10	11	12	13	14	15	16	17	18	19	20
7	7	8	9	10	11	12	13	14	15	16	17	18	19	20	21
8	8	9	10	11	12	13	14	15	16	17	18	19	20	21	22
9	9	10	11	12	13	14	15	16	17	18	19	20	21	22	23
10	10	11	12	13	14	15	16	17	18	19	20	21	22	23	24
11	11	12	13	14	15	16	17	18	19	20	21	22	23	24	25
12	12	13	14	15	16	17	18	19	20	21	22	23	24	25	26
13	13	14	15	16	17	18	19	20	21	22	23	24	25	26	27
14	14	15	16	17	18	19	20	21	22	23	24	25	26	27	28

+	10	11	12	13	14	15	16	17	18	19	20	21	22	23	24
10	20	21	22	23	24	25	26	27	28	29	30	31	32	33	34
11	21	22	23	24	25	26	27	28	29	30	31	32	33	34	35
12	22	23	24	25	26	27	28	29	30	31	32	33	34	35	36
13	23	24	25	26	27	28	29	30	31	32	33	34	35	36	37
14	24	25	26	27	28	29	30	31	32	33	34	35	36	37	38
15	25	26	27	28	29	30	31	32	33	34	35	36	37	38	39
16	26	27	28	29	30	31	32	33	34	35	36	37	38	39	40
17	27	28	29	30	31	32	33	34	35	36	37	38	39	40	41
18	28	29	30	31	32	33	34	35	36	37	38	39	40	41	42
19	29	30	31	32	33	34	35	36	37	38	39	40	41	42	43
20	30	31	32	33	34	35	36	37	38	39	40	41	42	43	44
21	31	32	33	34	35	36	37	38	39	40	41	42	43	44	45
22	32	33	34	35	36	37	38	39	40	41	42	43	44	45	46
23	33	34	35	36	37	38	39	40	41	42	43	44	45	46	47
24	34	35	36	37	38	39	40	41	42	43	44	45	46	47	48

+	-10	-9	-8	-7	-6	-5	-4	-3	-2	-1	0	1	2	3	4
10	0	1	2	3	4	5	6	7	8	9	10	11	12	13	14
11	1	2	3	4	5	6	7	8	9	10	11	12	13	14	15
12	2	3	4	5	6	7	8	9	10	11	12	13	14	15	16
13	3	4	5	6	7	8	9	10	11	12	13	14	15	16	17
14	4	5	6	7	8	9	10	11	12	13	14	15	16	17	18
15	5	6	7	8	9	10	11	12	13	14	15	16	17	18	19
16	6	7	8	9	10	11	12	13	14	15	16	17	18	19	20
17	7	8	9	10	11	12	13	14	15	16	17	18	19	20	21
18	8	9	10	11	12	13	14	15	16	17	18	19	20	21	22
19	9	10	11	12	13	14	15	16	17	18	19	20	21	22	23
20	10	11	12	13	14	15	16	17	18	19	20	21	22	23	24
21	11	12	13	14	15	16	17	18	19	20	21	22	23	24	25
22	12	13	14	15	16	17	18	19	20	21	22	23	24	25	26
23	13	14	15	16	17	18	19	20	21	22	23	24	25	26	27
24	14	15	16	17	18	19	20	21	22	23	24	25	26	27	28

+	-10	-9	-8	-7	-6	-5	-4	-3	-2	-1	0	1	2	3	4
-10	-20	-19	-18	-17	-16	-15	-14	-13	-12	-11	-10	-9	-8	-7	-6
-9	-19	-18	-17	-16	-15	-14	-13	-12	-11	-10	-9	-8	-7	-6	-5
-8	-18	-17	-16	-15	-14	-13	-12	-11	-10	-9	-8	-7	-6	-5	-4
-7	-17	-16	-15	-14	-13	-12	-11	-10	-9	-8	-7	-6	-5	-4	-3
-6	-16	-15	-14	-13	-12	-11	-10	-9	-8	-7	-6	-5	-4	-3	-2
-5	-15	-14	-13	-12	-11	-10	-9	-8	-7	-6	-5	-4	-3	-2	-1
-4	-14	-13	-12	-11	-10	-9	-8	-7	-6	-5	-4	-3	-2	-1	0
-3	-13	-12	-11	-10	-9	-8	-7	-6	-5	-4	-3	-2	-1	0	1
-2	-12	-11	-10	-9	-8	-7	-6	-5	-4	-3	-2	-1	0	1	2
-1	-11	-10	-9	-8	-7	-6	-5	-4	-3	-2	-1	0	1	2	3
0	-10	-9	-8	-7	-6	-5	-4	-3	-2	-1	0	1	2	3	4
1	-9	-8	-7	-6	-5	-4	-3	-2	-1	0	1	2	3	4	5
2	-8	-7	-6	-5	-4	-3	-2	-1	0	1	2	3	4	5	6
3	-7	-6	-5	-4	-3	-2	-1	0	1	2	3	4	5	6	7
4	-6	-5	-4	-3	-2	-1	0	1	2	3	4	5	6	7	8

FIGURE 13–3

Turtle geometry. Logo was created partially as a tool for children to use in learning geometric and other mathematical concepts on their own. Papert notes that students have a difficult time learning French in school; however, if they visit France, they learn the language naturally and effortlessly. He designed Logo as a "Math Land," a place where children could explore and "talk" mathematics.

Children who are asked to find how far it is to the corners of the screen or what number turns the turtle around in a circle *are* learning about distance estimation and degrees. Just as important, however, they are learning about problem solving—that you can use a computer in many different ways to find the answer to questions, and that you can figure out how to do this by yourself.

For example, one girl learned several things "playing" with her procedure TRIANGLE. She discovered that two of them make a diamond, six make a hexagon (a "stop sign" according to her), and four of them make a larger triangle. Children who construct their own shapes learn in a more profound sense about the characteristics of those shapes, for example, that a square has four equal sides whereas a rectangle only has two sets of two equal sides. They find out for themselves that complicated pictures can be analyzed into a handful of simple shapes and that basic figures can be synthesized into myriad complex and beautiful pictures.

Children can make interesting explorations of symmetry with Logo. The teacher can suggest that they repeat a procedure after changing all the RIGHT's into LEFT's and vice versa. This is a powerful idea. The teacher can also guide children to simplify their programming task by looking for symmetry in their hand-drawn pictures before planning their procedures. Another powerful idea they must use to use symmetry successfully is to write procedures that start and end at the same place.

Recall the Logo idea of microworlds. Short procedures supplied by the teacher can be the basis for numerous explorations by children. One teacher, whose class was just beginning to work with variables, provided her children with the procedure POLYGON.

```
TO POLYGON :SIDE :ANGLE
    FORWARD :SIDE
    RIGHT :ANGLE
    POLY :SIDE :ANGLE
END
```

Children experimented with this procedure by typing in different inputs. A few are pictured in Figure 13-4. They discovered that the same angle produces the same figure no matter what the size of the side; for example, the pentagon is bigger or smaller, but is still a pentagon. After this initial discovery, the teacher guided the children to use another useful strategy: *exploring only one thing, or variable, at a time*—the angle in this case. All the other variables, such as size or position on the screen, should be held constant. Guided by their teacher, the children then discovered that triangles, squares, and many other shapes are related; they are all regular

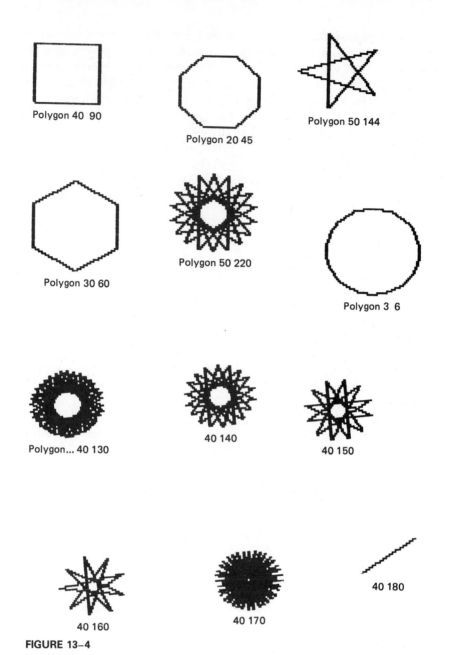

Polygon 40 90

Polygon 20 45

Polygon 50 144

Polygon 30 60

Polygon 50 220

Polygon 3 6

Polygon... 40 130

40 140

40 150

40 160

40 170

40 180

FIGURE 13–4

polygons and can all be produced by the same procedure. They discovered that a circle is really just another regular polygon with small turns.

A month later, she showed them POLYSPIRAL:

```
TO POLYSPIRAL :SIDE :ANGLE
  FORWARD :SIDE
  RIGHT :ANGLE
  POLYSPIRAL (:SIDE + 2) :ANGLE
END
```

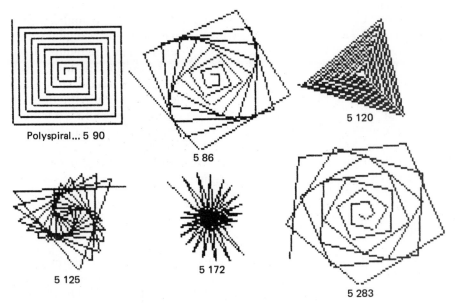

Polyspiral... 5 90

5 86

5 120

5 125

5 172

5 283

FIGURE 13-5

The class discussed how the procedure was constructed and how every time POLYSPIRAL was called the side was increased by two. Some of the results of the children's explorations are shown in Figure 13-5. One child observed "The neatest ones are not quite a regular turn, like 90. It's almost like they keep trying to be a square, but they can't quite do it" (POLYSPIRAL 5 86). Children learn that there is "magic" and logic in both the "special" factors of 360 such as 10, 30, 45, 90, 120, and so on, *and* in the "unusual" and nonfactored numbers such as 17 and 119.

Coordinate geometry.   Logo can also be programmed in terms of coordinate geometry, which involves locating or plotting points on a grid. This can also provide a meaningful exposure to negative numbers. Other programs that teach this topic include *Bumble Games* (The Learning Company; see Chapter 2) and *Elementary Mathematics,* Volume I (MECC). Geometry lessons are also included in TABS (TABS-Math Project).

Measurement.   Students are given a line segment and are asked to estimate its length in centimeters or millimeters and play a game of metric Blackjack with line segments of 1 to 10 cm in length (*Elementary Mathematics,* Volume I, MECC). *Introduction to Counting* (EduWare) has several measurement programs. Of course, most of children's measuring should not be done on computer.

Money.   Generally appropriate only for third graders, a few programs deal with money (e.g., *Elementary Mathematics,* Volume I, MECC; *Money Change,* Sunburst; *Money Master,* Med Systems and Screenplay/Intelligent Statements; and *Money! Money!,* Hartley).

Time. Learning About Numbers (C & C Software) contains a program *Let's Tell Time* that displays a conventional clock and a digital watch together. The child uses single keypresses to manipulate the hands of the clock so that it matches the time given on the watch. At the beginning level, times are presented on the hour only. As the child succeeds, more advanced problems are presented, with the highest levels stating the times in word form, using a variety of common expressions. If the child is proceeding too far in the wrong direction, the program prompts, "You are going the wrong way." *Clock* (Hartley), *Telling Time* (Random House), and *Hickory Dickory Clock* (Micrograms) are similar programs. Hartley also produces several programs that teach calendar time.

NUMBERS

Counting. There are more programs that teach counting and number-numeral correspondence than you can count. They include *Alien-counter* (EduFun), *Introduction to Counting* (EduWare), *Ernie's Quiz* (CTW), *Kinder Koncepts* (Midwest Software), *Learning About Numbers* (C & C Software), *Learning with Leeper* (Sierra On-Line), *Math Whiz Quiz* (Dynacomp), *Mathematics A, B, and C* (SRA), *Primary Math/Prereading* (MECC), and *Sticky-bear Numbers* (Xerox).

Many programs treat counting as a routine activity. Children count a set of objects and type in the number. However, counting is a complex ability which reveals deep cognitive functioning. Also, it is easy for children to harbor misunderstandings about it. It is always advisable to talk to them about their counting. One child, when asked to count, stood up and counted to 10. Praised and asked to count backward, he *turned around* and counted "1, 2, 3 . . ."! A kindergarten girl also counted to 10. She was asked if she could count higher. She took a deep breath and counted to 10 in a squeaky voice two octaves higher.

Help young children develop sound counting concepts in these ways:

1. Select programs that let the child control movement of objects.
2. Talk to children about their counting. Help them to discuss and master the basic counting rules:
   a. Say the number words in order.
   b. Count each object once and only once.
   c. Keep a one-to-one correspondence between each number word and each thing.
   d. The final number word you say represents the number of items in the set.
   e. It does not matter in what order you count the objects (Gelman & Gallistel, 1978).
3. Select programs that encourage children to count on from numbers other than 1 and to count backward as well as forward.
4. Help children to organize their counting of objects by organizing a "plan" for counting (e.g., going from left to right and top to bottom through a set), or better, by moving the objects if possible.

5. Help children develop ability in counting *and* instant recognition of the number of a small groups of objects (0 to 5).
6. Encourage children to use strategies of counting on and back from known sets "How many in all. We can see this is 4. So, 4 . . . 5, 6, 7!").
7. Make sure that the children do most of their counting with real objects in meaningful situations, such as getting enough pieces of paper for each child sitting in their row.

One program that tends to be based on recent research on counting is *Counters* (Sunburst). Children work at five levels. At the first level, a row of objects such as train engines moves onto the top of the screen. Each is accompanied by a beep and the appearance of the appropriate numeral. A horizontal line is drawn to separate the top of the screen from the bottom. One by one, engines move onto the bottom, stopping directly underneath the corresponding engines on the top. The child must press any key when the number on the bottom is the same as the number on the top. If the child is correct, the engines move together on the screen. If a key is pressed too soon, the program places the correct number of engines on the bottom, then highlights the engines that were omitted by the child, and finally demonstrates the correct correspondence by changing the color of pairs of engines—one from the top and the matching one from the bottom—one pair at a time. If a key is pressed too late, a similar sequence is followed, except that the extra objects are first crossed out.

The second level is similar, except that the objects on the bottom are not placed directly under the matching object on the top. At the third level, objects move onto the top, but are then erased and are replaced by a numeral. At the fourth level, objects move onto the top, and the child must press any key when a written numeral incrementing at the bottom matches that number (Figure 13-6). If the child is incorrect, the answer is crossed out and the program shows the numerals and the objects "count" together. The fifth level is similar, except that the objects on the top are randomly arranged. This program is not perfect either. For example, it would be better if some activities allowed the child to create a number such as 5 by pressing a key five times—to *feel* the action of "5." However, it does contain developmental levels.

FIGURE 13–6
***Counters.* (Courtesy of Sunburst Communications.)**

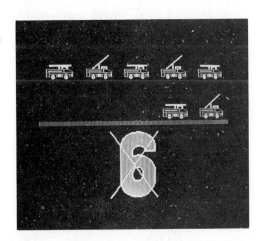

Number sequence. Programs that engage the child in guessing a number, providing feedback on whether the guess was too high or low, include the *Bumble Games* series (The Learning Company; for the youngest children), *Elementary Mathematics,* Volume I (MECC), *Guess the Number* (Edu-Soft), and *Number Sequencing* (Sunburst).

Several programs provide practice in matching numerals or "filling in the missing numeral" (e.g., *Children's Carrousel,* Dynacomp; *Early Games,* Counterpoint Software; *KinderComp,* Spinnaker; *Letters and Numbers,* Teaching Tools; and *Number Sequencing,* Sunburst).

Place value. The counting in *Face Flash* (EduFun) is based on groups of 10, and therefore could promote awareness of place value (see Figure 13-7). Other similar programs include *Numbers: Drills and Games* (Sunburst) and several public domain programs from Commodore. Tutorials on place value can be found in *Elementary Math,* Package I (Micro Learningware), *Getting the Basics,* (NTS), *Expanded Notation* (Hartley), and *Numeration* (Scott, Foresman).

Kiri's *Hodge Podge* (Dynacomp) is a collection of many small programs, each of which is activated by pressing a single key. If "N" is pressed repeatedly, the numeral displayed is increased by one, and one more block is added to a stack. For 14, two stacks are presented next to each other. The stack on the left has one block ("one 10") and the stack on the right has 4 ("four 1's"). The main activity—incrementing numbers by adding one again and again—is conceptually solid. Unfortunately, the method of representing numbers larger than 10 is not appropriate for young children, as it presupposes an appreciation of place value—the one block on the left *represents* 10 of the unit blocks on the right. It would be better for these children to be learning *about* place value by seeing 10 units placed together in a "10's stack."

COMPUTATION

Consider again the two positions concerning computers and computation discussed at the beginning of this chapter. Should computers teach children to perform the four basic operations—addition, subtraction, multiplication, and division—proficiently? Or is the availability of computers replacing the need for these skills? As is so often true, the best answer lies partially between and partially beyond these two positions. First, children still need to become proficient in the basic operations, especially with the "facts." Computers can help children to achieve automaticity in their

FIGURE 13-7
Face Flash. **(Courtesy of EduFun, Milliken Publishing Company.)**

mastery of these skills. Following the principles discussed in Chapter 1, however, children should receive as much of this practice as possible in the context of higher-level experiences. Then drill and practice programs can help them to master these skills.

Second, however, children will *not* need to achieve a level of fast performance in following such complex procedures as four-digit multiplication or long division. (When was the last time you chose to do a three- or four-digit long division problem with the typical school paper and pencil procedure?) These abbreviated algorithms were designed to help people complete large computations with the minimum of writing; however, for this reason they do not emphasize meaning. As a simple example, the algorithm on the left involves less writing, but the equivalent one on the right may be more helpful in illustrating the meaning of the process.

$$
\begin{array}{r}
195 \\
\times\ 134 \\
\hline
780 \\
585 \\
195 \\
\hline
26{,}130
\end{array}
\qquad
\begin{array}{r}
195 \\
\times\ 134 \\
\hline
780 \\
5850 \\
19500 \\
\hline
26{,}130
\end{array}
$$

Emphasis should be placed on the mathematical ideas inherent in the algorithms; for example, why is "1" (i.e., 100) times 195 larger than 4 times 195? Going a step farther, should we teach *either* of these algorithms? Beyond one- or two-digit problems in each of the four operations, we should probably concentrate on what the operations mean and how they are used. Starting in preschool, instead of teaching children to complete such involved algorithms quickly, we need to teach them the *meaning* and *application* of these operations. Third, then, we should use the computer as a tool to solve problems which involve operations . . . and other mathematical ideas as well.

Developing the meaning of computation. Several programs for young children attempt to develop concepts of addition and subtraction through a presentation such as the following:

$$
\begin{array}{c}
\bullet\ \bullet \\
\bullet\ +\ \bullet\ =\ ? \\
\bullet
\end{array}
$$

It would be better to present the addition of blocks in simple situations rather than with symbols such as $+$, $-$, and $=$. One 4-year-old read the problem as "five plus two." Another youngster counted it as seven— why not?—five blocks, one cross, and a pair of sticks! Research shows that "take-away" subtraction is easiest for young children; but $\vdots - \cdot =$ does not lend itself to this. Children may read this as "three take away one is three," or ". . . is four" or ". . . is one." The model is just not clear. A picture of one block falling off a tower of three might be more sound. There are also ways in which to involve the children actively, as the next example shows.

Teaching arithmetic problem-solving strategies. Moser and Carpenter (1982) have developed a computer program designed to relate formal mathematical representational and problem-solving skills to the informal strategies that children naturally invent to solve simple addition and subtraction problems. Children solve problems on the microcomputer by using essentially the same processes they use with physical objects. By pressing the backward and forward keys, they produce sets of squares pictured on the screen one at a time and can make a single set, or two sets, or remove elements from a set they have constructed. Then they are taught that they do not have to construct sets one at a time; to solve an addition problem, they can enter a number sentence such as $4 + 5 =$ _____. This has the effect of producing a set of 4 and a set of 5, just as the child would using physical objects. Because this number sentence actually constructs the sets, writing it becomes part of the solution process rather than an unrelated activity.

A small pilot study indicated that the program was effective. Before instruction, the children consistently wrote incorrect number sentences and generally did not use their sentences to solve the problems. After nine 20-minute sessions, three of the four children consistently used number sentences to solve a variety of addition and subtraction problems.

Counters (Sunburst) presents five levels of addition activities and two of subtraction, all similar in nature to the counting levels just described.

Although most software designed to teach computation merely presents problems, or examples, to be solved, computers can be used to provide children with a model to assist in their computations. In "The Bakery" (in *Piece of Cake,* Counterpoint Software) children read about bakers who sell some cakes: "Of their 7 cakes, they sold 4. How many were left?" A picture of 7 cakes is shown. The child has the opportunity to answer using his or her own methods. If the child errs, however, the program shows the number sentence, "$7 - 4 =$?" If the child still needs help, the computer counts out 4 of the 7 cakes. If the child still answers incorrectly, 4 cakes move away from the pile. If the child's next answer is not correct, the 4 cakes move off the screen, and the computer recounts the remaining 3 cakes. In this way, progressively more help is provided to the child, as needed, and a concrete model of subtraction is provided.

Similarly, the program provides a model for both multiplication and division. Bakers need to get just the right number of pieces from each of their cakes in "Dividacake." The program provides these hints, as needed: (1) the related multiplication number sentence, say, "2×5," is displayed; (2) a cake is cut up to show a 2×5 array; (3) the same cake is cut up into more separated pieces, with the rows and columns labeled with numerals; and (4) the pieces are counted one by one as a multiplication fact is progressively generated (e.g., $2 \times 1, 2 \times 2, 2 \times 3, \ldots$). Finally, the multiplier (5) is moved from its place in the multiplication fact into its place in the corresponding division fact. *Elementary Mathematics Whole Numbers* (Sterling Swift) also presents meaningful models in a tutorial format.

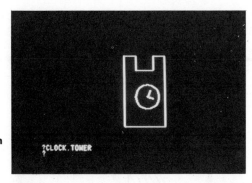

FIGURE 13–8
Two first grade boys' Logo picture, in which they applied computational skills.

Applying computational skills. Computation should be both (mathematically) meaningful and (practically) significant. This necessitates using computations to accomplish other tasks.

Children programming in Logo use computation for a purpose. Two first grade boys were writing a program to make a drawing of a clock tower in their town (Figure 13-8). Starting on the left side, they make three horizontal lines across the top. They used ideas of symmetry and equality in planning for the third line (FORWARD 10) to be equal to the first (FORWARD 10). Then at the bottom they used the mathematical concept of composition to combine the three inputs: 10, 15, and 10, typing FORWARD 35.

One of the most powerful applications of mathematics that children can experience is to use it as a tool to save them time and allow them to do something they could not do before. Some third graders were having difficulty making regular shapes with the REPEAT command. For each shape, they needed to figure out how much the turtle turned to the right or left. There are two approaches children could have taken to solve the problem. The first involves the strategy of estimating and then narrowing the limits. That worked for them at first, but it soon became quite time consuming. Their teacher then helped them to learn to use the second, an analytical approach. She discussed their successful procedures with them. She had them write out how many turns they had made in their triangle (3 × 120 = 360), their square (4 × 90 = 360) and so on, until they saw the pattern. "It's like a circle. It has to go around 360 degrees to go all the way around." This is the famous "Total Turtle Trip Theorem." She showed them a version of a table she had found in a book on Logo ideas (Bearden, Martin, & Muller, 1983; see Figure 13-9). They used the theorem, the table, and their own deductive reasoning to fill the table out and create many new shapes.

In "Diffy" (in *Arith-Magic,* Quality Educational Designs) students select four numbers that are printed on the screen as corners of a square. Then the students find the difference between each successive pair of numbers. The four differences become the corners of the next square. This continues until the number in each corner is zero. Children can be challenged to go beyond just the subtraction. Will the differences always

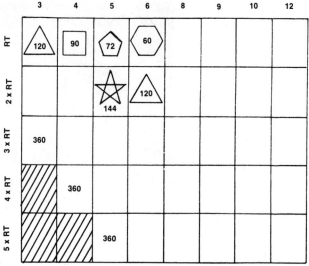

FIGURE 13-9 (Beardon, Martin, & Muller, *The Turtle's Sourcebook.*)

"diff out" or reduce to zero? Does it matter in what order the numbers are placed on the square? Can you find numbers for the corner that maximize the number of moves?

In a game from the same package, "Tripuz," the computer chooses three numbers that form the vertices of a triangle. However, these numbers are not shown to the student; instead, question marks show where the numbers are hidden. The computer *does* show the sums of each pair of vertices between the hidden numbers. The student might see

```
? 11 ?
 9 4
   ?
```

The student has to figure out the hidden numbers. Can you?

Another puzzle format is found in *Teasers by Tobbs* (Sunburst). Children must fill in the missing numbers of addition or multiplication grids. At the lower levels, there is only one correct answer.

+	4	7
3	7	10
5	9	—

+	9	6
4	—	—
8	—	—

At the higher levels, there is no unique solution. The computer tells the children "That will work" instead of "That is correct."

+	12	—
—	7	—
—	—	18

In *Cubbyholes* (Atari) children are to draw boxes (cubbyholes) partitioning off the numbers in a 3-by-3 array so that the sum of the digits in each box is equal to the number below the array.

```
┌─────────┐
│ 3  4  1 │
│ 4  2  6 │
│ 4  1  7 │
└─────────┘
    8
```

Math Mansion (in *Challenge Math*, Sunburst) combines an adventure game with practice on basic operations. Children are to escape from a haunted mansion (Figure 13-10). But to do so, they need to enter rooms and collect "possessions," and to do *that*, they need to create a problem that will produce a given answer. For example, 3 _____ _____ = 9. Students might type in either 3 + 6 = 9 or 3 × 3 = 9.

Exploring number patterns in computations: A computer programming example. Simple programming projects can lead to a host of explorations. Recall Bobby's FOR/NEXT program described in Chapter 11. The teacher wanted everyone to have a chance to participate in dramatizing the program, so he had the class experiment with changing lines in it. First they changed line 20 to read FOR N = 1 TO 7. Then they changed line 30 to print N + N + N; N + N + N + N; 2 * N. Each of these new programs was checked afterward on the computer. In this way, the children also learned to use the computer to check on their intuitive and creative ideas. They also explored the patterns that resulted. The teacher printed and posted them for discussion (columns have been labeled for the reader's convenience).

A	B		C		D		E

```
A              B                    C                        D                   E

1 + 1 =  2     1 + 1 + 1 =  3       1 + 1 + 1 + 1 =  4       1 ✗ 2 =  2          2
2 + 2 =  4     2 + 2 + 2 =  6       2 + 2 + 2 + 2 =  8       2 ✗ 2 =  4
3 + 3 =  6     3 + 3 + 3 =  9       3 + 3 + 3 + 3 = 12       3 ✗ 2 =  6
4 + 4 =  8     4 + 4 + 4 = 12       4 + 4 + 4 + 4 = 16       4 ✗ 2 =  8
5 + 5 = 10     5 + 5 + 5 = 15       5 + 5 + 5 + 5 = 20       5 ✗ 2 = 10
6 + 6 = 12     6 + 6 + 6 = 18       6 + 6 + 6 + 6 = 24       6 ✗ 2 = 12
7 + 7 = 14     7 + 7 + 7 = 21       7 + 7 + 7 + 7 = 28       7 ✗ 2 = 14
```

He asked the children to look for patterns. Identify some yourself before reading on. Here is an abbreviated version of some children's observations.

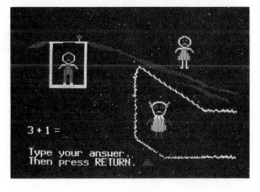

FIGURE 13-10
In *Learning About Numbers* children must answer arithmetical exercises quickly. Here, a girl is playing the part of the heroine, racing to beat the troll to the imprisoned boy. Children can also choose to help the troll! (Courtesy of C & C Software.)

3 + 1 =

Type your answer.
Then press RETURN.

The sums in the first group (column B) are like counting by 2's; column C is counting by 3's; D is counting by 4's. Guided by the teacher's questions, the children figured out that each addend was being increased by 1 each time; therefore, with two addends, the sums increased by 2's, with three addends, the sums increased by 3's, and so on. The teacher asked them what the sums for $N + N + N + N + N$ would be. The children guessed 5, 10, 15, . . . and programmed the computer to check their prediction.

They noticed that the sums across the first three groups of number sentences $(B + C + D)$ were replicated within a column starting in the second row; that is, the sums in the first row—2, 3, 4—are like the 2, 3, 4 in the very first column (A). The sums in the second row—4, 6, 8—are the same as the sums in the first group of number sentences (B) starting with 4—4, 6, 8, and so on.

Another day, they rewrote the program to print out ten sums in each series going up to $N + N + N + . . . + N$ with ten N's. This time they recorded only the sums.

N	A	B	C	D	E	F	G	H	I
(1)	2	3	4	5	6	7	8	9	10
(2)	4	6	8	10	12	14	16	18	20
(3)	6	9	12	15	18	21	24	27	30
(4)	8	12	16	20	24	28	32	36	40
(5)	10	15	20	25	30	35	40	45	50
(6)	12	18	24	30	36	42	48	54	60
(7)	14	21	28	35	42	49	56	63	70
(8)	16	24	32	40	48	56	64	72	80
(9)	18	27	36	45	54	63	72	81	90
(10)	20	30	40	50	60	70	80	90	100

Children discovered several additional patterns. The 5, 0, 5, 0, . . . pattern in column D was noticed. The digits in column A made a repeating pattern—2, 4, 6, 8, 0, 2, 4, 6, 8, 0, . . . So did the digits in column C—4, 8, 2, 6, 0, 4, 8, 2, 6, 0, . . . Interestingly, similar patterns were found in E (6, 2, 8, 4, 0, . . .) and G (8, 6, 4, 2, 0).

It should be pointed out that these lessons were conducted with only one computer for the entire class (although individuals kept modifying the programs for weeks to come) and that without the computer many of the explorations, especially those involving higher numbers, would probably not have been made. The computer also allowed the students to generate the series themselves and therefore understand *how* the series were generated. Finally, the programs encouraged them to view the mathematical operations as *processes*. Several students were motivated to learn more about mathematics and more about computer programming through writing similar programs on their own. Recall that an electronic spread sheet could also be used to generate these patterns.

Functions. One teacher used the carton computer (Chapter 5) to illustrate the important mathematical concept of function. In fact, this simple model—input, process, output—is virtually the definition of a function. If the carton computer is programmed to add, then children merely input two numbers. The person inside the computer outputs their sum.

Children might then program the real computer to be a "function machine."

LOGO

```
TO FUNCTION
PRINT [TYPE IN A NUMBER.]
PRINT FIRST REQUEST + 3
FUNCTION
END
```

BASIC

```
10 PRINT "TYPE IN A NUMBER."
20 INPUT N
30 PRINT N + 3
40 GOTO 10
```

The programs would run like this:

```
TYPE IN A NUMBER.
?4
7
TYPE IN A NUMBER.
?10
13
TYPE IN A NUMBER.
?6
9....
```

They would then run the program and let a friend play it without seeing the program itself. The friend tries to guess the "rule" or function.

Checking answers: doing computations on machines. Should computers be used to check answers to computations done by children? Should they be used to do the computations, freeing children to engage in solving meaningful math problems that require complex calculations? Yes, especially the latter. However, the smallest and least expensive "computers" we have—calculators—should be used for this purpose rather than microcomputers. Using a computer for this purpose is like using a crane to move a paper bag.

Is there truth to the concern that children will not learn their basic facts if they use calculators and computers? Research indicates that there is no ground for such worry and that calculator use can *increase* children's computational power (Shult, 1981; Shumway et al., 1981). One study found that 8-year-old children using calculators were faster and more accurate in computation (Ethelberg-Laursen, 1978). Behr and Wheeler (1981) successfully used calculators for building beginning counting skills. Another study found calculator use motivating and beneficial for children ages 5 to 7 (Scandura et al., 1978). The authors suggested that teachers not use total discovery but, rather, allow children to explore for a session or two and then build readiness for number concepts, sequences, and logic with calculator operations. Lessons should be designed to help children discover patterns, provide opportunities for estimation, provide practice in simple debugging skills, and provide opportunities for children to make up problems.

If calculators are beneficial, should children still learn their "facts"? Of course. These will always be important. They should also learn better estimation skills and learn to use technology appropriately. As discussed, they should probably not have to learn to perform abbreviated, complex computational algorithms quickly, if at all.

Basic facts—achieving automaticity.   Once meaning has been established, children profit from drill on number facts. Programs supplying basic fact drill and practice include the Arcademic Series (DLM; see Chapter 2); *Challenge Math* and *Diving into Math Drills* (and others, Sunburst), *Count and Add* (Edu-Soft), *Dueling Digits* (practice on balancing equations; Broderbund), *Early Addition* (MECC), *Elementary Math Steps* (Microcomputer Workshops or Queue), *Elementary Mathematics*, Volume I (MECC), *Grover's Number Rover* (CTW), *Gulp!* (EduFun), *Introduction to Mathematics* (Educational Activities), *Learning About Numbers* (C & C), *The Math Machine* (SouthWest EdPsych), *Math Blaster!* (Davidson and Associates), and *Monkeymath* (Artworx).

Math Strategy (Apple) allows older students to write their own math drill programs for each other. The programs are designed to improve their ability to visualize basic math equations. A program you can type in and use is provided in Hastings (1980).

ESTIMATION AND ALERTNESS TO THE REASONABLENESS OF RESULTS

Because children will be using calculators and computers to perform a large part of their calculations, it is all the more imperative that they have the ability to estimate and determine the reasonableness of results. Teachers who use calculators with their children should encourage them to use the "guess and test" method. Children predict what the answer to a computation will be, then use the calculator to check their prediction.

Working with "Digitosaurus" (in *Challenge Math*, Sunburst), children are presented with three computation problems. They must estimate which computational problem has the largest answer and identify that problem (Figure 13-11). Creating graphics in turtle graphics demands that children constantly estimate distances, angles, results of computations, and so on.

FIGURE 13–11
Children must *estimate* which problem has the largest answer in "Digitasaurus." (Courtesy of Sunburst Communications, Inc.)

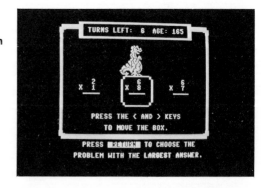

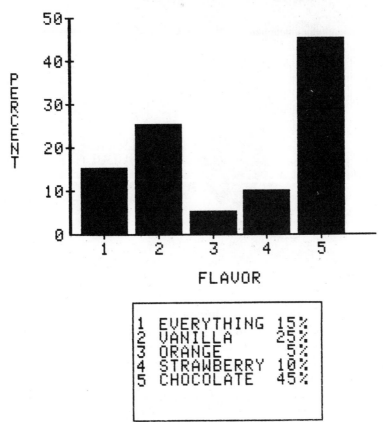

FIGURE 13–12

DATA, GRAPHS, PROBABILITY

Graphs. Children of all ages should be involved in collecting and displaying data. Several plotting programs facilitate the creation of attractive and accurate graphs. For example, one second grade classroom collected information about their friends' likes and dislikes. They put this information into a graphing program. They then could instruct the computer to use the information to construct any type of graph—bar, scatter, line, pie, and so on. The graph type can be changed in less than a minute. This group discussed the relative merits of two methods of presenting their information (see Figures 13-12 and 13-13).

The ability to quickly and effortlessly change the representation can be useful in illustrating the fact that *how* data are presented significantly affects what impression they give us. One third grade teacher showed the class a computerized graph of the progress of one student, with his permission. She asked what impression they got from it. Then she changed the

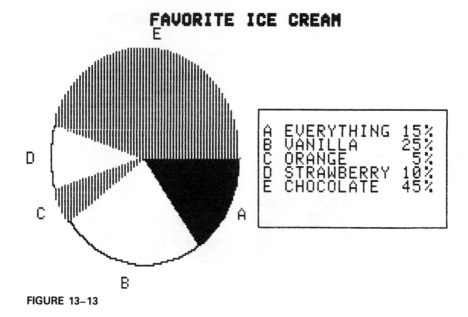

FAVORITE ICE CREAM

```
A EVERYTHING  15%
B VANILLA     25%
C ORANGE       5%
D STRAWBERRY  10%
E CHOCOLATE   45%
```

FIGURE 13-13

range of the vertical axis, and within seconds, the students were looking at the *same* information on the same type of graph, with only this one alteration. But the ensuing conversation made it clear that the children received a different impression of the boy's progress and gained a deeper understanding of data representation.

For younger children, it is usually advisable to make real graphs. For instance, have each child choose his or her favorite color block, stack them by color, and discuss the results. If young children are ready for computer graphing, make sure that their first experiences connect the real to the computer's abstraction.

Probability. This might seem an unlikely topic for young children, but at an early age, they have a notion of "chances," especially fair chances. As with the majority of mathematics topics, most work should be done off the computer. An example might be using spinners for choosing turns in a game with two people. Some of the spinners could be colored half blue and half red, some three-fourths blue and one-fourth red. Meaningful discussions are almost guaranteed. Computer activities can build on this early work. Green and gold pieces of candy fill two jars in *The Jar Game* (Edu-Fun). Children must select in which jar a buzzing fly will have the best chance of landing on a gold piece (Figure 13–14). If they score 50 points

FIGURE 13-14
The *Jar Game*. (Courtesy of EduFun, Milliken Publishing Company.)

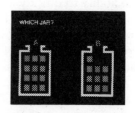

they beat the computer. *Pig* (NTS) is a game of probability and chance in which students compete to reach 100 points. They roll simulated dice repeatedly, choosing either to roll again or to pass. If a 1 is rolled, all points are lost. Older children with experience in programming computers can write simple programs that employ random numbers. One child wrote the following Logo program (FD RANDOM 20 tells the turtle to go forward some randomly chosen number less than 20).

```
TO RANDOMWALK
FD RANDOM 20
LT RANDOM 360
RANDOMWALK
END
```

Children might also use random numbers to simulate dice tossing or the like. The Worthington Schools, 752 High Street, Worthington, Ohio 43085, will provide at cost a set of computer programs that include the topic of probability for the gifted and talented.

FRACTIONS

Children are required to distinguish which of three objects is half of a target shape in *Kinder Koncepts* (Midwest Software). *Fraction Factory* (Counterpoint Software) provides guided practice on fractions and sets, equivalent fractions, and several other skills. Many programs with a large scope also provide exercises in recognizing fractions as well as other skills. These programs will be discussed in an upcoming section.

COMPUTER LITERACY

The seven basic topics of mathematics discussed in this chapter were based on several sources, one of the most important of which was the recommendations of the National Council of Teachers of Mathematics (*Ten Basic Skill Areas*, 1977). The last of their essential skill areas is computer literacy. If you have followed the suggestions in this and other chapters and have shown children how to use the computer as a problem-solving tool, then you have helped them to learn the most important component of computer literacy.

COMPREHENSIVE MATHEMATICS PROGRAMS

Several programs provide tutorials and/or drill on a wide range of mathematical topics. Many contain a diagnostic/prescriptive component. Producers of such programs are listed in Table 13-1. Recall that Table 3-1 includes a list of some commercial mathematics programs that contain a CMI component.

**TABLE 13–1 Producers of Comprehensive
Mathematics Software Programs**

Bertamax
Computer Curriculum Corporation
Davidson & Associates
Disk Depot
Educational Activities
Educational Media Association Microcomputer Software
Hartley
Holt, Rinehart and Winston
Intellectual Software
Math City/Mathware
Micro-Ed
Milliken
NTS
Orange Cherry Media
Personal Computer Art
Plato
Psychotechnics, Inc.
Radio Shack
Random House
Reader's Digest
Scandura (or Queue)
Science Research Associates
Scott, Foresman and Co.
SouthWest EdPsych
Sterling Swift Publishing
TABS-Math
Psychotechnics (Glenview, IL)
TSC (Houghton Mifflin)

WHAT DOES RESEARCH SAY ABOUT CAI AND MATHEMATICS?

In a meta-analysis (a way of combining the results of several studies) of the research on CAI and mathematics achievement covering grades 1 through 12, Burns and Bozeman (1981) concluded that

1. A mathematics program supplemented with CAI was significantly more effective in fostering student achievement.
2. CAI drill and practice were more effective at all levels with highly achieving and disadvantaged students as well as with students whose distinct ability levels were not determined by researchers; however, the achievement of average-level students was not significantly enhanced.
3. There was no evidence that results were an artifact of experimental design features.

In addition, some studies have specifically examined the affect of CAI on mathematical development of young children. The Lavin and Sanders (1983) evaluation showed highly significant results favoring the CAI group in mathematics achievement across all grades, including 1 through 4. Results from the Ragosta et al. (1981) evaluation showed the most dramatic gains for the CAI groups in mathematics. Students outperformed the control group (who received CAI instruction in the language arts) after one year and increased their gain each succeeding year. An additional pattern emerged in which students with 10 minutes of CAI exposure a day showed treatment effects about half the size of students with 20 minutes of exposure a day. These results were consistent across schools, years, and testing instruments. It included studies at grades 1, 2, and 3. It was found to be cost feasible. Hungate (1982) reported that a group of kindergarteners provided with eight months of weekly experiences with counting, visual discrimination, and other CAI programs performed as well as or better than a control group on tasks that measured these same skills that were administered the following September.

In a pilot study, Piestrup (1982a) found that children interacted with, and benefited from, software developed to help children learn early logical and geometric concepts. In another paper (Piestrup, 1982b), she reported that children as young as 3 years can use graphics editing programs and graphics-based computer learning games to gain spatial concepts.

Is the use of computer games effective in reinforcing arithmetic skills? Kraus (1981) reported that second graders with an average of 1 hour of interaction with a computer game over a two-week period responded correctly to twice as many items on an addition facts speed test as did students in a control group.

Finally, the implications of one study are important to teachers (Alderman, Swinton, & Braswell, 1979). Children exposed to a drill and practice CAI program in mathematics outperformed control group children; however, a close look revealed that the former made the same type of errors. They merely omitted fewer items. Thus they were more adept and efficient at answering questions without necessarily having a stronger grasp of the concepts. This suggests that teachers using drill and practice computer programs need to integrate closely use of these programs and classroom work on conceptual understandings. They need to make sure their students possess the prerequisite understandings necessary to work with the program correctly—practicing, in other words, procedures that are both correct and meaningful to them.

GUIDELINES FOR MICROCOMPUTER MATHEMATICS

1. *Choose computer applications that involve all facets of mathematics.* Avoid a narrow mathematics program. Engage children in a rich variety of mathematical experiences. This also means, of course, more off-computer than on-computer activities. Computer applications that integrate several topics, such as Logo programming, should be given top priority.

2. *Choose computer applications that involve both higher-level problem-solving processing and skills such as computation.* An example of this is program-

ming with turtle graphics. Also, priority should be given to those activities that promote problem solving and could not be duplicated with worksheets.

3. *Choose software that actively involves children.* Software should ask children to think about concrete experiences, should have them manipulate something pictured on the screen, and should present a valid graphic representation of a concrete mathematical model.

4. *Make mathematics meaningful.* What is meaningful to the young child is that which is connected to real life, is concrete, and is attached to something already known. Teach mathematics as a system of processes and relationships. *Computer activities should usually be accompanied by the use of concrete aids and/or paper and pencil recording of work.*

5. *Emphasize both process and product.* Activities designed to improve skills and those designed to improve understanding should be considered synergistic, not antagonistic.

6. *Practice is important, but should follow meaningful development.*

7. *Create situations in which children have to figure things out for themselves.* Do not first supply a rule. Let children discover or abstract a rule from well-planned experiences and then discuss it.

8. *Encourage multiple solutions* and all other good problem-solving strategies as discussed in Chapter 9.

9. *Talk about mathematics.* Discuss specific problem-solving processes and strategies, for everything from counting to classifying to solving a multistep real-life problem.

10. *Recognize that mathematics is developmental.* Therefore, come back to the powerful ideas of mathematics again and again, at increasing levels of complexity and depth.

11. *Use multiple representations.* Present a concept to be learned in many ways, with many different sets of materials and approaches. Use an abundance of noncomputer, movable materials.

12. *Figure out how children are thinking.* Analyze errors with the knowledge that children *have theories.* Knowing their theories helps you to know how to guide their thinking.

THINK ABOUT

1. Agree or disagree: "Being an abstract area, mathematics fits the computer screen's lack of concreteness well."
2. Consider the measurement programs described. Which are simulations and which provide actual measurement activity? What is your opinion of simulated measurement for young children?
3. Which programs were activities that—while possibly worthwhile—could nevertheless be conducted on paper or a preprogrammed calculator, without a computer. Which necessitated the use of a computer? What are the implications for the classroom?

4. Explain how you would use a simple computer programming exploration to teach mathematical concepts.

ANNOTATED BIBLIOGRAPHY

Feurzeig, W., & White, B. (1984). *An articulate instructional system for teaching arithmetic procedures.* Cambridge, MA: Bolt, Beranek and Newman.

An animated model that helps children to understand place notation, addition, and subtraction is described.

Heck, W. (1983). Teaching mathematics with microcomputers: Primary grades. *Arithmetic Teacher, 30*(6), 27, 63–66.

Heck provides a description and pictures of several arithmetic programs, mostly drill, appropriate for primary grade children.

Hill, J. (1983). Teaching with microcomputers. *Arithmetic Teacher, 30* (6).

This issue of the *Arithmetic Teacher* focused on teaching mathematics with microcomputers. What ideas could help you?

Kelman, P. (ed.) (1983, March). *Classroom Computer News.*

This issue of *Classroom Computer News* provides a look at new dimensions in mathematics software and discusses what qualities exemplary courseware should possess.

Lindahl, R. (1983, October). Electronic spreadsheets: What they are; what they can do. *Electronic Learning*, pp. 44, 46, 48, 50.

The author provides an overview of electronic spread sheets and their uses. See other ideas for their use with children in several issues of *WINDOW*.

Signer, B. (1983). *Math doctor.* Houston: University of Houston.

Signer has produced a program, *Math Doctor, M.D.* (Modern Education Corp.) that diagnoses children's arithmetical strengths and weaknesses.

Wiebe, J. H. (1983). Needed: Good mathematics tutorial software for microcomputers. *School Science and Mathematics, 83,* 281–292.

The author presents guidelines for good mathematics tutorial software.

14

NATURAL AND SOCIAL SCIENCES

As in language arts and mathematics, the computer can be used to provide drill and practice and tutorials in the sciences and in the arts (the subject of the next chapter). However, perhaps more so than in any other area, the most profound application of the computer in science and art education will be as a tool. Using child-appropriate versions of computer-based tools now used by adults in these fields, students will learn to be scientists and artists instead of learning about the sciences or arts.

POWERFUL TOOLS FOR THE SCIENCES

Simulations

As we saw in Chapters 2 and 6, simulations are essential tools used in the natural and social sciences. However, they are used infrequently in the schools. This is especially unfortunate because they can expand children's perspectives on what science is all about and they can be used effectively even if computer access is relatively low; that is, they are best used by small groups or the whole class.

There are two reasons to use simulations in the sciences. The first is to understand the concepts, relationships, and generalizations of social studies and natural science. The concepts emphasized should be process concepts and their interrelationships. These concepts are relatively high level and cannot often be shown in action. Even when they are, such as in a movie, the child cannot manipulate the variables. Simulations allow this. The second reason to use simulations is to develop problem-solving and divergent thinking abilities. To use a simulation effectively, children must explore the relationships among the variables. They should also criticize the simulation, determining its limits. This can be done most effectively by combining the use of simulations with other real-world experiences. Children should go back and forth from the mathematical, computer model to hands-on experience.

Information Management

One ability that is assuming ever-increasing importance in our world is the ability to find and manipulate information. Knowledge is becoming less a matter of memorizing and more a matter of knowing how to look up information. Computers are an ideal tool for this purpose. Children can learn how to use simple computer-based information systems.

What is an information system? Educators everywhere have to be able to store and have access to large amounts of information about students—the names, addresses, dates of birth, parents' names and place(s) of work, medical history, test scores, and so on. All this information is usually kept on cards in filing drawers or in folders in a filing cabinet. Periodically, it has to be brought up to date. It also has to be referred to for writing reports on a student; charting progress of a group of students; assigning students to classes; determining how many students, and also which students, have scored above or below a certain level; locating all the students who live in a specific area; and so on. The storage of this information, along with the method of organizing and using it in these ways, is an example of an information system.

To be useful, data must be structured in some way. Consider a list ("file") of all the names, addresses, and telephone numbers ("records") of all the children in your school system. If they were listed in the order in which they were typed, they would be almost useless. You would have to look through thousands to find the one you wanted. If they were in alphabetical order, you would not need to look at more than, say, 5 or 10. This is a data structure. Most schools would not use just this simple sequential ordering; they would use a hierarchical structure in which the records were first separated by school, then by grade, then by teacher. A computer might use a similar data structure. A computerized data-base system consists of a "base" of information and computer programs that make it easy to make needed changes in this information or to answer certain questions about the information.

Teacher's use of information management. Let us look first at a teacher's use of such a program. Mrs. Hallenbeck wanted to organize her student records for more efficient use. Using the NOTEBOOK filing pro-

```
                        CLASS FILES
                       L. HALLENBECK
                        FIRST GRADE
              DATA FILE: FIRST GRADE TEACHER
              DATE OF PRINTOUT: 1
              -----------------------------------------


NAME        BARBER AARON            NAME        JONES KENYA
READING     86                      READING     80
  LEVEL     4                         LEVEL     4
  STRENGTH  MOTIV                      STRENGTH  MOTIV
  NEEDS     BEG SOUNDS                 NEEDS     BEG SOUNDS
SPELLING    84                      SPELLING    75 REG SPELLINGS
WRITING     90                      WRITING     84
  STRENGTH  CREATIVE                   STRENGTH  HANDWRITING
  NEEDS     ORG B-M-E                  NEEDS     ORG
MATH        93                      MATH        90
  STRENGTH  PATTERNING                 STRENGTH  COUNTING
  NEEDS     COUNTING                   NEEDS     PROB SOLV
SOCIAL ST   88                      SOCIAL ST   83
SCIENCE     84                      SCIENCE     87
S-CONCEPT   4                       S-CONCEPT   4
SENSITIV    4                       SENSITIV    4
COOPERATI   5                       COOPERATI   5
INTERESTS   VIDEO GAMES CARS STAR WARS   INTERESTS   VIDEO GAMES BOOKS SPORTS
            EXCELLENT HOME-SCHOOL               FAMILY HELPFUL--KEEP IN
            RAPPORT                             TOUCH.


NAME        CHIN LU-SIN             NAME        KIMEL CAREY
READING     95                      READING     98
  LEVEL     8                         LEVEL     8
  STRENGTH  COMP BEG SOUNDS            STRENGTH  COMP SKILLS
  NEEDS     ENRICH                     NEEDS     AFFIXES
SPELLING    96                      SPELLING    95
WRITING     94                      WRITING     92
  STRENGTH  ORG B-M-E                  STRENGTH  ORG B-M-E
  NEEDS     DIVERGENT                  NEEDS     DIVERGENT
MATH        93                      MATH        94
  STRENGTH  CONCEPTS SKILLS            STRENGTH  CONCEPTS
  NEEDS     PROB SOLV                  NEEDS     NUMERALS
SOCIAL ST   93                      SOCIAL ST   94
SCIENCE     90                      SCIENCE     91
S-CONCEPT   3                       S-CONCEPT   4
SENSITIV    4                       SENSITIV    4
COOPERATI   4                       COOPERATI   4
INTERESTS   ART READING WRITING     INTERESTS   VIDEO GAMES READING
            EXCELLENT PUPIL.  NEEDS              HIGH ACHIEVEMENT ORIENTED
            SOCIAL CONFIDENCE                    HOME.  PRESSURE?


NAME        HAFTER BOB
READING     92
  LEVEL     5
  STRENGTH  COMP MOTIV
  NEEDS     BEG SOUNDS
SPELLING    82
WRITING     80
  STRENGTH  HANDWRITING
  NEEDS     DIVERGENT
MATH        97
  STRENGTH  CONCEPTS
  NEEDS     ENRICH!
SOCIAL ST   87
SCIENCE     95 MOTIV HIGH
S-CONCEPT   4
SENSITIV    3
COOPERATI   4
INTERESTS   MACHINES VIDEO GAMES
            COMPUTERS.
            LOVES SCIENCE AND MATH
```

FIGURE 14–1

gram (*WINDOW*), she created a file in which each student had a "record," or one unit of a file. She developed "fields" (the structural parts of the file) for the students' names, for each subject, for their reading level, their interests, and for various social ratings. (The records and fields that make up a file are often called a *data base*—hence the term, data-base management system or DBMS.) Printouts of parts of these records appear in Figure 14-1. This was a good way in which to store, organize, and retrieve all this information faster and more accurately than she could without the computer, but that is only half the benefit.

With simple commands, she could "call up," or display, any record. She could search the whole file by any field; for instance, she could instruct the computer to find and display the records of all the students who had not completed an assignment, who had averages in math under 80 percent, or who had completed level 8 in reading. One category was "reading needs." Here she placed specific skills in phonics, structural analysis, comprehension, and so forth. When she was ready to teach a lesson on one of these areas, she simply had the computer print a list of all the students who needed this work. This also allowed her to choose specific seatwork assignments for students that provide practice in certain skill areas. Figure 14-2 shows two lists—one of children who need work on counting, the other of those who need practice with beginning sounds. She could group children for independent study by sorting them in terms of their interests, or possibly by interest *and* reading level. In the "unstructured," or unnamed category, she would put important, but miscellaneous, information such as home-school correspondence, critical personal information, and so on.

She could also generate and print out reports. For instance, Figure 14-3 shows a list of all children at reading level 4 or higher, *ordered* by reading level. She chose to include the children's reading mark, strengths, and weaknesses in the report. She could sort her file, according to several criteria if she wanted to. For example, she could easily instruct the computer to print out a list of all the students that scored over or under a certain percentage on their final grade *and* have that information sorted in alpha-

FIGURE 14-2

CLASS FILES
L. HALLENBECK
FIRST GRADE
DATA FILE: FIRST GRADE TEACHER
DATE OF PRINTOUT: DECEMBER 10, 1985

NAME	MA	NEEDS
BARBER AARON	93	COUNTING
SAMUAL TIPPI	80	CONCEPTS COUNT
SMITH CAROL	77	COUNTING-ON
VERNY MARY	89	COUNTING SKILLS
WILLIAMS JO	88	COUNTING-ON

CLASS FILES
L. HALLENBECK
FIRST GRADE
DATA FILE: FIRST GRADE TEACHER
DATE OF PRINTOUT: DECEMBER 10, 1985

NAME	L	NEEDS
BARBER AARON	4	BEG SOUNDS
HAFTER BOB	5	BEG SOUNDS
JONES KENYA	4	BEG SOUNDS
MERRY MONICA	6	BEG SOUNDS

```
                    CLASS FILES
                   L. HALLENBECK
                    FIRST GRADE
        DATA FILE: FIRST GRADE TEACHER
        DATE OF PRINTOUT: NOVEMBER 30, 1985
        ------------------------------------------------
        NAME                 L  RE   STRENGTH         NEEDS
        ------------------------------------------------

        JONES KENYA          4  80  MOTIV            BEG SOUNDS

        BARBER AARON         4  86  MOTIV            BEG SOUNDS

        SMITH CAROL          5  82  EFFORT           COMP

        HAFTER BOB           5  92  COMP MOTIV       BEG SOUNDS

        PARKER EDWIN         6  90  MOTIV COMP       PREFIXES

        VERNY MARY           6  93  COMP MOTIV       END SOUNDS

        SAMUAL TIPPI         6  93  BEG SOUNDS       COMP

        MERRY MONICA         6  94  COMP MOTIV       BEG SOUNDS

        WILLIAMS JO          7  93  COMP MOTIV       AFFIXES

        CHIN LU-SIN          8  95  COMP BEG SOUNDS  ENRICH

        KIMEL CAREY          8  98  COMP SKILLS      AFFIXES

        LEAFGREEN SHERRI     8  96  COMP PHONICS     ENRICH
```

FIGURE 14–3

betical order by last name. Teachers have also used DBMS systems to keep track of inventories, schedules, and so on.

Students' use of information management. Using these programs with students has many advantages. First, learning to find information is one of the most important goals of education, especially in the present-day "information explosion." Students learn to use dictionaries, encyclopedias, and numerous library sources. Increasingly, computers will be used to store and retrieve information. Therefore, teaching children to use computerized sources of information teaches them an important real-world application of the computer. It helps them to understand better the subject matter they are working with. Most important, the data will have to be structured in a certain way according to set rules. In understanding this structure and applying it, students learn much about informational systems, classification, problem solving, and so on. Because these students will grow up in a world of huge data bases, it is essential that they understand that the knowledge that can be gained from them depends on the ways in which the information is structured, stored, and retrieved as well as the user's comprehension of this structure. It should be recognized, of course, that students must read to use most systems presently available. Many readiness activities, however, can be conducted with children of any age.

Several activities for introducing students to the processes of an information management system were described in Chapter 9. Other activities emphasize sorting. Have the whole class stand, with one student standing at the front of the room. Ask for words that describe that student. This word, say, "girl," is written on the board, and all girls remain standing; the boys sit down. If the next descriptive word is "blond," then that is written on the board. All those standing who are also blond remain standing, all others sit down. Continue this process until only the girl at the front of the room is left standing. The words written then form a unique description of that person. For older primary grade children, follow up this lesson by having each child write a description of himself or herself on index cards according to preset criteria, possibly sex, hair color, eye color, age, and so on. Shuffle the cards and pick one at random. Have all the students stand, and sit again as each descriptive word is read off the card. Usually, only one student will remain standing at the end, correctly identified from the data. Does it matter in what order the descriptors are read?

Children can also dramatize how a DBMS orders data. After discussing various ways in which they themselves order objects (see Chapter 9), children might act out one way in which a computer orders information (Hedges, 1980–1981). For purposes of discussion, let the letters A through E represent five children of increasing heights. The children stand in front of the room in random order: E C A B D. The first child (i.e., the child in the first, or left-most position—E) is then compared with the second (C). Because the first child is taller, the two switch places: C E A B C. The first child (now C) is next compared with the third (A). Again, they switch: A E C B D. The first child (A) is then compared with the fourth (B) and fifth (D), but because he is shorter than they, no switch is made. Next the second child (E) is compared with the third (C) and they switch: A C E B D. The second now (C) is compared with the fourth (B) and switched: A B E C D. The second (B) is compared to the fifth (D), but no switch is made. The third (E) is compared with the fourth (C) and is switched: A B C E D. The third (C) is compared with the fifth (D), and not switched; then the fourth (E) with the fifth (D) and switched: A B C D E. The children are properly sorted. Ask children to compare this method with their own.

Talk with students about how a dictionary or phone book is organized. How does one look up a phone number? An address? What do you do if two people have the same first and last names? Suppose that you are a detective who has discovered a phone number but does not know to whom the number belongs. Would the phone book help you? Why or why not? Would a computerized phone book help more? How?

Another teacher adapted several ideas that came with NOTEBOOK. Her class's INTEREST FILE got constant use. Almost daily students retrieved, changed, added, deleted, and sorted information. They used a numerical sort to find out who had the highest video game score. They used the alphabetical sort to learn the range of interests in the class. The students also kept track of books they had read in a file called BOOKFILE. Each file represents a report on one book. Students used it to find out what others were reading, locate books on favorite topics, and select their next book based on the evaluations of others. SPELLING DEMONS was a simple file that allowed students to enter the spelling words with which they were having trouble. Figure 14-4 illustrates some of the records of these files.

Systems such as these are being developed for the primary grades. They have large-type fonts, are simple to use, and handle smaller amounts of information, including symbols and pictures. They are part of a total

```
        INTEREST FILES                                 SPELLING DEMONS
    (AN EXAMPLE FROM NOTEBOOK,                      (AN EXAMPLE FROM NOTEBOOK,
     PUBLISHED BY WINDOW, INC.)                      PUBLISHED BY WINDOW, INC.)
DATA FILE: INTEREST FILE                         DATA FILE: SPELLING DEMONS
DATE OF PRINTOUT: SEPTEMBER 19, 1984             DATE OF PRINTOUT: SEPTEMBER 11, 1984
-------------------------------------            -------------------------------------

NAME        MARK HERMAN                          NAME        SHERRY SADSTER
TEACHER     MISS GOLDNER                         WORD1       BACK
PETS        MY DOG SMOKEY                        WORD2       BOOK
FAV BOOK    MY MAMA SAYS...                      WORD3       GAME
FAV MOVIE   STAR WARS                            WORD4       INTO
FAV TV      DUKES                                WORD5       HEARD
2ND TV      CARTOONS                             WORD6       KNOW
FAV MUSIC   ROCK                                 WORD7       OPEN
FAV VIDEO   PAC MAN                              WORD8       ONCE
TOP SCORE   10334                                WORD9       ALONG
COMMENT     I LIKE TO SWIM AND GO                WORD10      FEW
            SAILING. I LIKE CARS.                UPDATED     9/28/84

                                                 NAME        PAUL DOUGLAS
                                                 WORD1       KNOW
                                                 WORD2       OLD
                                                 WORD3       OVER
        BOOK FILES                               WORD4       PART
    (AN EXAMPLE FROM NOTEBOOK,                    WORD5       DEAR
     PUBLISHED BY WINDOW, INC.)                   WORD6       ASKED
DATA FILE: BOOK FILE                             WORD7       BETTER
DATE OF PRINTOUT: SEPTEMBER 25, 1984             WORD8       WITH
-------------------------------------            WORD9       WEEK
                                                 WORD10      BECAUSE
TITLE       WHERE THE WILD THINGS ARE            UPDATED     10/3/84
AUTHOR      M. SENDACK
KIND        FICTION                              NAME        TAMMY WHITE
DIFF.       PRETTY EASY                          WORD1       SIDE
RATING      5                                    WORD2       SAME
LOCATION    LIBRARY                              WORD3       NEVER
PICTURES    YES GREAT ONES.                      WORD4       TODAY
LENGTH      S                                    WORD5       THROUGH
COMMENTS    THIS IS A GREAT BOOK. THERE          WORD6       WHAT
            ARE MONSTERS AND MAX IS              WORD7       WATER
            ALWAYS DOING CRAZY STUFF.            WORD8       GRADE
REVIEWER    GREG ALSTAR                          WORD9       GROW
                                                 WORD10      HEARD
                                                 UPDATED     10/4/84
TITLE       THE SNOWY DAY
AUTHOR      EZRA JACK KEATS
KIND        FICTION
DIFF.       MEDIUM
RATING      4
LOCATION    OUR ROOM
PICTURES    EXCELLENT
LENGTH      S
COMMENTS    THE BOY PLAYS IN THE SNOW.
            I LIKED THE PICTURES BEST,
            BECAUSE HE PASTED STUFF ON.
REVIEWER    KAY BACKERLY
```

FIGURE 14–4

system that includes simple electronic spread sheets, a calculator and other tools for counting and representing patterns, graphing and charting tools, and word processors (for more information, write to the magazine *WINDOW*).

Soon, students will be communicating with data bases in school using computers equipped with a modem, a device that allows communication between computers over phone lines. These data bases will be the encyclopedias, card catalogs, and libraries of the technological society. Other tools adults use include graphing programs, calculating programs, special message systems, publications systems, and so on. Not only the program that is used, but the *way* in which computers are used, are important considerations, as we shall see.

SOCIAL STUDIES

Computers can be applied in the social studies in three basic ways: as a means of facilitating the development of social competencies; as a subject, in studying the ways in which computers are used in the world; and as a tool to develop the skills and understandings of the social studies curriculum.

DEVELOPING SOCIAL COMPETENCIES

Possibly the most important goal of social studies instruction in the early childhood classroom is not the learning of topical content, but the development of social skills and the promotion of a positive social-emotional concept. Some who warn of the dangers of using computers with children transmit an image of isolated, mechanized youngsters, dehumanized and mesmerized by the machine. Both research evidence and practical experience seem to indicate that—especially when computers are used correctly—this image is quite flawed.

Research Evidence

It has been noted that children prefer social use of computers to isolated use (Swigger, Campbell, & Swigger, 1983). Some teachers say that the greatest impact of computers in the classroom is that children tend to share more (Center for Social Organization of Schools, 1983b). Clement's (1981) review of the research indicated that computers can effectively promote positive social and emotional development.

Hawkins (1983) found that children tended to talk to each other more about their work when they were doing programming tasks than when they were doing noncomputer tasks. In addition, children engaged in more collaborative activity with computer tasks. Children did talk to each other when working on other classroom tasks (e.g., math), but the subject of their conversations was often not related to what they were doing. White (1982) reported that children socialized working with computers three times as often as they did working in the classroom. They asked many more questions working with computers.

Promoting Humanistic Use of Computers

The computer is not an adversary of humanization. If we view the computer as a tool, it is no more antihumanistic than are such tools as paintbrushes or building blocks. This applies to every application of computers. Even in drill and practice applications, the computer can promote humanization and socialization. First, it can help teachers to individualize this instruction. Students can proceed at their own pace and receive immediate feedback. Second, it may free the teacher to interact with students at a more personally meaningful level in both the cognitive and affective domains. The teacher may also intervene, cushioning any negative effects of poor performance and providing psychological support for all efforts. The teacher can become less a disseminator of exercises and information and more a guide leading children to learn, and to learn to love learning.

In this way, well-designed computer-based education may combine the best of two worlds: individualized, efficient technologically oriented instruction (often impersonal) and personal, supportive humanistic-oriented instruction (often inefficient). Educators must work to develop this ideal combination. Too often, educators developing technology have neglected the interpersonal, and those emphasizing humanistic education have viewed the computer as an enemy. The advantages of both approaches can be obtained. Learning can be personal and social, using the computer as a tool.

One important way of working toward this goal is to emphasize cooperative, rather than competitive or individualistic, learning. Have students work together to solve a task by programming the computer, to learn from a tutorial, or to work through a simulation. Not only allow, but encourage, children to talk to each other about their work. Supervise them fairly closely, to intervene as they need help and maintain their involvement with the task at hand.

Computer programs that encourage or necessitate cooperation have already been designed for older students (e.g., Jernstedt, 1983; The Search series from McGraw-Hill) and a few are appearing for younger children (e.g., *Peanut Butter Panic*, CTW, in which two players must work together to "win"). Educators should urge producers to create similar materials for younger children. Research indicates that students using these programs doubled their time on task and increased their academic achievement by 22 percent (Jernstedt, 1983).

Finally, experiential computer programs can often be used to illustrate the uniqueness and importance of each individual. If children use one of the drawing programs described in the next chapter, their teacher might point out that no drawing was exactly like any other and that each was valuable.

LEARNING ABOUT COMPUTERS IN THE WORLD

Of course, studying the impact of computers on society was the subject of Chapter 6 and will not be repeated here. Therefore, one entire chapter of this book has already dealt with computers in the social studies. One point should be stressed. This area should *not* be considered "studying computers." Rather, children should study their families, neighborhood, and world.

COMPUTERS AS TOOLS FOR LEARNING ABOUT THE SOCIAL STUDIES CURRICULUM

Skills

Although there are fewer programs available for social studies skills than language arts or reading, more worthwhile programs are being produced. As usual, the following are meant to serve only as examples.

Several programs are designed to develop map skills. *Nomad* (in *Elementary Social Studies*, Volume 2, MECC) develops map reading skills. Students engage in a simulation in which they must use a map to get to "Gramma's house." Other available programs include *Direction and Distance* and *Map Directions* (Scholastic or Micro-Ed), *Small Town U.S.A.* (Island Software), in a simple fashion, *Dragon's Keep* (Sierra On-Line), and the *Early Childhood Learning Program* (from Educational Activities; for the very young, this involves only north, east, south, and west).

One teacher working with turtle graphics gave students a map of their town. Working with small paper "turtles," the children wrote out directions for "programming" their turtles to "go from school to the supermarket" and so on. They walked their paper turtles through the map and wrote the directions as they went along.

Calendar Skills (Hartley) provides tutorials and drill and practice on months, days of the week, seasons, holidays, ordinal numbers, and so on. The program allows teachers to modify lessons, and create new lessons. *Things That Go* (Reader's Digest) is a computerized transportation puzzle for preschoolers. *The Farm* (Polytel) teaches children to recognize farm animals, spell and read their names, and write stories about them.

Geography

Several programs provide practice in associating names of the states with their shapes, and so forth. Many present a line map and ask students to identify the state, region, or whatever. Such programs include *States &*

Capitals and *Uncle Sam's Jigsaw Puzzle* (Scholastic), *Regions of the United States* (Educational Activities), and *World Polar Regions/Desert Regions* (Micro-Media). Many of these exercises are appropriate for more advanced children. It should also be noted many could be presented just as easily through a workbook, although they do provide for a degree of interactive learning and immediate feedback. Several other programs that provide tutorials on various topics, such as the community, are nothing more than transplanted books and, therefore, are not described here.

Simulations

Many other social studies topics are addressed in computer simulations. Simulations help in the social studies, a "soft" curriculum area, in that, instead of learning hard and fast rules such as those in the natural sciences, children learn to use generalizations in "best case" situations.

The Market Place (MECC) includes four selling simulations in which children must decide on the best price for a product and evaluate the effect of advertising, weather, the price of raw materials, and so on on sales. *Lemonade Stand* (also called *Sell Lemonade;* MECC) is considered an "old-time" classic of this type. Up to six lemonade stands can be run at the same time. Each child or group of children can run one stand. They are given a fixed amount of assets and must make three decisions each day: how many glasses to make (production), how many signs to make (advertising), and how much to charge (price). One group decided the following:

```
ON DAY 1, THE COST OF LEMONADE IS $.02

LEMONADE STAND 1         ASSETS $2.00

HOW MANY GLASSES OF LEMONADE DO YOU
WISH TO MAKE ?30

HOW MANY ADVERTISING SIGNS (15 CENTS
EACH) DO YOU WISH TO MAKE ?3

WHAT PRICE (IN CENTS) DO YOU WISH TO
CHARGE FOR LEMONADE ? 12
```

Results are then given for each stand:

```
$$ LEMONSVILLE DAILY FINANCIAL REPORT $$

    DAY 1                    STAND 1

    30 GLASSES SOLD

$.12 PER GLASS           INCOME #3.60

    30 GLASSES MADE

    3  SIGNS MADE         EXPENSES $1.05

         PROFIT $2.55

         ASSETS $4.55
```

Production costs may rise as the "mother" stops providing free sugar. Other random events affect sales (children have been known to play for more than an hour hoping to see the graphic of a thunderstorm). There are several values of this type of program. Children can actually manipulate variables in a model of a social-economic situation and note the effects of these manipulations. Children form theory after theory and debate these in a healthy, social, problem-solving atmosphere. "More glasses; we sold them all last time, and it's still sunny." "So what; what if nobody wants lemonade again today?" "Charge more." "No, no one's going to pay $.20 for one glass." "Well, try it out and we'll see. Keep the other things the same and just change the price." This kind of theorizing is not limited to older children. *Lemonade* is the favorite computer program of one first grade class, whose teacher uses it during her unit on economics. Several children cannot read all the beginning text, but they learn quickly how to read the necessary sentences and the results. Interested children could be led to hold all but one of the variables constant to assess its effects.

Wealth (WINDOW) is a "Monopoly"-like game in which you are pitted against the computer. You must make decisions so as to maximize your profits. With the computer doing the arithmetic *and* playing against you, you have to think.

While writing simulations is difficult even for adults, one class of third graders used the *Story Maker Maker* (see Chapter 12) to construct small sequences of historical vignettes for each other. Then they tried to find the correct paths through each other's historical stories. In a way, they were creating their own simulations.

Managing Social Information

An excellent way in which to use a filing system, or DBMS, is to have students cooperatively enter data for a major unit of study. The entire class first decides what the records and fields are to be. One class made a file of all the businesses and organizations in their neighborhood. They decided that the fields would include the name, street, type, and so on. They then typed in the information they had gathered and used the SEARCH function to look up information quickly. They could also instruct the computer to print out reports, for instance, all those on a street or in a certain area, all the supermarkets, or all the supermarkets in a certain area.

NATURAL SCIENCES

Tutorials and Quizzes

There are a limited number of programs that are specifically designed to teach scientific knowledge to elementary-age children. They involve such topics as health habits, our bodies, plants, unusual animals, cells, matter and energy, seasons, earthquakes, volcanoes, and the solar system (e.g., Educational Activities, Intellectual Software, K–12 MicroMedia, Queue, Right on Programs). However, many provide little more than reading and test-taking experience. The only value of using a computer would seem to be in the feedback given. *Micro Habitats* (Reader's Digest) allows children to choose an environment and populate it with plant and animal life. Other topics that cannot be experienced directly may be appropriate for computer presentation. Several programs have games and activities related to dinosaurs. This topic, a favorite of young children, lends itself to a graphic presentation. However, misinformation (e.g., fire-breathing dinosaurs) must be guarded against. "Solar Distances" (on *Earth Science*, MECC) uses familiar means of transportation such as walking, bicycle, car, and jet to illustrate distance as a measure of time spent traveling to various planets of our solar system.

Computer science. This topic may appear threatening and inappropriate. However, this is just a reminder that the activities suggested in Chapter 5 are designed to teach young children about how computers work and what they do—the beginning of computer science.

Simulations in Science

Imagine a laboratory of machine parts, batteries, and wires in which children can safely explore, discover, and construct mechanisms that will discriminate between hostile and friendly animals and objects and sound appropriate warnings. *Rocky's Boots* (The Learning Company) is a science microworld, just as Logo is a mathematics microworld. In this electronic Tinker Toy set, students learn about how electrical devices can be connected and about the world of logic and cybernetics, its rules, and their consequences. The building blocks are wires, machines, sensors, logic gates, flip-flops, and other electronic components—the building blocks of a computer. These can be picked up, moved, and connected. The rules are those of formal digital logic. Children might try to build a machine that kicks diamonds or circles out of a moving line of different shapes that float by (Figure 14-5).

Does it sound difficult? In field tests, third graders had no trouble learning to manipulate this environment and, while they were doing so, they learned ideas that were previously only taught in engineering courses.

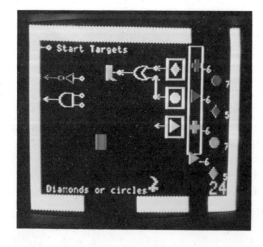

FIGURE 14–5
Rocky's Boots. (The Learning Company. Photo by Bill Milheim.)

Although written for slightly older children, some simulations of ecological environments and food chains, such as *Odell Lake* and *Odell Woods* (MECC), may capture the interest and extend the understanding of your students. Quality programs in the future will often combine simulations with tutorial or drill approaches. One first attempt, *Heart Lab* (from Educational Activities), is divided into three parts: a tutorial describes the vessels and chambers of the heart while identifying their locations in a graphic model; a drill program indicates the parts on the models and asks the student to type in the name; and a pulse simulation demonstrates how the heart responds to work. Students enter their own pulse rates before and after exercising, and the animated, graphic heart demonstrates how their hearts would function. Teachers of young children should attempt to influence producers to create similar products that match their students' developmental levels.

A good way in which to extend children's abilities in several areas simultaneously and to avoid the problem of children using and uncritically accepting an overly abstract model is to have students develop simulations themselves. Abelson and Goldenberg (1977) developed a curriculum, written in Logo, that engages students in creating Logo turtle simulations of the behavior of mealworms. Students observe mealworms, write programs that make the turtle behave similarly, and then determine how well their model fits the actual behavior of the mealworms. This is appropriate for students in or above the intermediate grades. However, two points should be made.

First, developing simulations such as this necessitates building on earlier experience. Students without previous experience with Logo, procedural thinking, and using and creating such models of the world would be handicapped in their efforts to explore this type of learning. Second, teachers could have younger children design simpler simulations in cooperation with upper-grade students. The primary grade children can observe the situations in the real world and on the computer, make comparisons, note similarities and differences, and suggest alterations to the simulation. In very simple situations, primary grade children might write their own simulations. One class constructed programs that modeled the growth of plants. They each planted marigold seeds and then had the Logo turtle draw lines of increasing length to represent the weekly height of the plants. They used these simulations to predict the next week's plant growth. As the marigolds grew, they measured them and revised their simulations accordingly.

Managing Scientific Information

One class used a DBMS to organize the information they collected on science units. For their unit on animals, the records were different types of animals and the fields were their various characteristics. One class decided on such fields as feathers/hair/other: number of legs, how they move, what they eat, how they feed their young, where they live, what they provide for humans, and so on. Individuals or small groups of students were then responsible for entering the information for specific animals. (Teachers of younger students who are reading could type in the data themselves.) After the data base was created, children could use it as a resource. For example, one student may wish to report on only those animals that live in the arctic. He could use the SEARCH function of the DBMS to quickly locate and print out reports on every animal that was entered that lives there. Of course, this information—the place of origin—would have had to have been one of the fields the class decided on. Another student might want to investigate the traveling speeds of the animals. She would instruct the system to print out a report in which all the animals were listed, ordered by running speed.

This data base could be used to answer a variety of questions: What is the largest animal? Which animals live in water? What animals weigh more than 100 kg? What about the speed of various animals? Is it true that the more the animal weighs, the faster it is? (The system could print out a report listing each animal in order of weight, including only the following information: the animal's name, weight, and running speed. Because they would be ordered by weight, it would be easy for the students to ascertain the relationship between weight and speed. Children must grapple with definitions—Are birds included?) One child discovered that animals that provide food or other materials for people often live on a farm. With the teacher's guidance, the students discovered another group of animals that provided goods for people—endangered species.

Interested and advanced children could pose other similar questions: What is the relationship between gestation period and average life span? size? intelligence? Are any characteristics related to the number of young?

Instead of introducing the word "mammals," one teacher had her students instruct the computer to print out a list of all the animals that suckle their young. They then tried to notice other shared characteristics (e.g., bodily hair). *After* they had begun to *induce* the concept, the teacher introduced the term "mammals." Thus the children went from the characteristics, to the concept, to the name. In a later unit on sea life, the teacher used a different teaching strategy. She identified the categories of open ocean fish, reef fish, and bottom dwellers and had children sort through them looking for similarities *and* hypothesizing as to the reason for them. For example, children noted that bottom dwellers are slow moving, are flattened from top to bottom, are colored like the bottom of the ocean, and may have hard shells or sharp spines. They talked about camouflage. Reef fish are brightly colored, have flattened bodies (side to side), and pincher-shaped mouths with tiny teeth. How does this help this fish live near a reef?

Similar data bases and activities could be organized alongside virtually any curriculum area, especially in science and social studies, for example, plants, dinosaurs or other animals, foods, rocks and minerals, planets, cultures or countries, cities or states, historical figures, and so on.

```
YOU THINK OF SOMETHING LIVING.
I WILL TRY TO GUESS WHAT KIND IT IS BY
ASKING YOU QUESTIONS.
CAN IT MOVE ON ITS OWN?
YES
IS IT A WARMBLOODED ANIMAL WHICH NURSES ITS YOUNG?
YES
OK, IS IT A PERSON?
NO
THAT'S NOT IT.   WHAT IS IT?
CAT

PLEASE TYPE IN A QUESTION WHOSE ANSWER
IS "YES" FOR A CAT AND
"NO" FOR A PERSON.
DOES IT HAVE FOUR LEGS?

O.K. WE'LL TRY AGAIN
I WILL TRY TO GUESS WHAT KIND IT IS BY
ASKING YOU QUESTIONS.
CAN IT MOVE ON ITS OWN?
YES
IS IT A WARMBLOODED ANIMAL WHICH NURSES ITS YOUNG?
YES
DOES IT HAVE FOUR LEGS?
YES
OK, IS IT A CAT?
YES
I GOT IT!
```

FIGURE 14–6   O.K. LET'S TRY AGAIN....

One group developed a Logo program from a framework provided by the teacher that would *learn* about living things. Figure 14-6 illustrates the program in action.

Another way of sharing information is via message systems. In one project, children participated in an interschool Dinosaur-Club. Interested children told each other about different dinosaurs and their characteristics through a computerized message system that allowed children to send messages to students in other classes within the school or around the country. Writing for a remote audience necessitated that children express themselves completely and clearly.

The Computers as a Laboratory Tool

While most are not yet appropriate for use by young children, packages are being developed that allow the computer to serve as a laboratory instrument. For example, Atari produces a package that will measure the temperature of, say, hot water and display a graphic thermometer registering this temperature. Then, as the water cools, a new picture moves out of and away from the first one, revealing a lower temperature. Time segments are also indicated. This continues as a row of graphic thermometers visually displays the phenomenon of cooling. Then, at command, the tops of the "mercury" in the thermometers are connected by lines, portraying a line graph of the process. Even very young children quickly learn to control the temperature readings (with their hands, cold and hot water, etc.) and how to read the corresponding graphs. They see the relationship between their own sensory impressions and the graph. Unlike simulations of measurement, this computer application lets children experience the process *and* extends their knowledge about it with computers. This application is superior to, say, simulations of magnetism or simple machines, which probably should be experienced firsthand.

CONCLUSION

This chapter has described how computers might help children learn about the social and natural sciences. You might be unimpressed with the range of programs appropriate for young children. This would indicate that you are evaluating computer applications critically—there *is* a serious scarcity of materials available for primary students. While most topics in the sciences *should* be experienced directly, computers can serve to help children vicariously experience those that cannot, and they can help children to organize and reflect on those that can.

THINK ABOUT

1. At what age could children first meaningfully use the computer as a laboratory tool?
2. Which of the three categories of social studies presented should be given top priority? In which would computers be used to greatest advantage?
3. Agree or disagree: "Because *Rocky's Boots* teaches about electricity, which children can experiment with, it is not an appropriate simulation."

CURRICULUM CONSTRUCTION CORNER

4. Create an outline for a data base you might use.
5. Construct a plan for integrating a simulation into your curriculum.

ANNOTATED BIBLIOGRAPHY

Barger, R. N. (1983). The computer as a humanizing influence in education. *T.H.E. Journal, 10*(7), 109–111.
   Barger describes how a computer can show people what it means to be human and help people become more human. How would you implement his suggestions in your classroom?

Debenham, J. (1978, August). Computer automated simulations: How to design one for under $300. *Educational Technology, 18*(8), 30–33.

Wilson, C. (1981, February). Simulation: Is it right for you? *Personal Computing, 5*(2).
   These authors provide guidelines for those interested in constructing their own simple simulations.

diSessa, A., & White, B. (1982). Learning physics from a dynaturtle. *Byte, 7*(8), 324.
   Even young children enjoy and benefit from playing with the "dynaturtle," a program that allows the Logo turtle to move according the principles of Newtonian physics (e.g., friction-free).

Friel, S. (1983, January–February). Lemonade's the name, simulation's the game. *Classroom Computer News,* pp. 34–39.

Several suggestions for using *Lemonade*, including analyzing it, evaluating it as a model of the world, and so on are presented.

Hodges, J. O. (1982). *A bibliography of microcomputer software for social studies educators.* Richmond, VA: Commonwealth of Virginia.

Hodges has compiled a useful bibliography of software that deals with social studies topics.

Westward expansion. (1983, Spring). *Teaching and Computers,* pp. 31–33.

This column presents ideas on how the simulation *Oregon,* described in Chapter 2, might be used.

15

THE ARTS

There is no other discipline for which microelectronics are better suited than music education.

Hofstetter, 1979

As in the sciences, there are several programs that will teach children fundamental concepts and skills in art and music. Children are led to recognize basic structural components. For example, computers can provide practice in matching colors, naming notes on a staff, or identifying whether a series of musical tones rises or falls in pitch. To the extent these programs match the goals of the curriculum, they may be valuable. However, perhaps the most interesting use of computers in the arts is as a tool, like a palette, that children can use to create pictures and music as an expression of their own creativity. The basic goal—for example, increasing musicality—must be kept in mind.

MUSIC

Teaching the Fundamentals

Many programs have been developed to teach older students the fundamental concepts of pitch and interval recognition, melody, chords, harmony, and rhythm. Students can touch a graphic display to indicate their response to musical questions. Some of these systems can be adjusted so that even young children can receive appropriate instruction. Studies indicate that this CAI is more effective than is traditional instruction (Hofstetter, 1983; Jones, 1983). MECC produces several ear training programs that play a short tune and display the notes on a clef. One note is sounded incorrectly; children must identify which one it was. Other programs have been developed specifically for younger children.

One group of programs teaches children ages 3 to 7 years pitch discrimination: between high and low, between pitch direction rising or falling, and between major seconds and major thirds (Embry, 1983). Pitches are related to graphics of a piano keyboard and correct responses are rewarded by a bird that flies up or down (in the first program), a ball that

258

rolls up or down a hill (in the second), or a character jumping up either one or two stairsteps (in the last). This is the first of a series of programs. The later ones present other concepts of music theory such as rhythm, melody, harmony, and musical expression markings.

Children playing *The Magical Musical Balloon Game* (Temporal Acuity Products) hear a short musical phrase and must determine its direction. Students must type in U, S, or D to indicate whether the phrase went "up," "straight ahead," or "down," in pitch. If the response is correct, the balloon travels forward, either rising, staying at a constant height, or falling, as the phrase is played again. Four phrases are presented one at a time; then they are played sequentially, as a tune.

Early Music for Young Children (Counterpoint Software) is a series of musical learning activities. "Guido's Quiz" is a tutorial program. On a piano keyboard, treble clef, or bass clef, all the letter names of the notes are displayed as the scale is sounded. Then question marks appear one at a time in place of one letter name, as its note sounds. The child must identify the note by typing the matching letter key. If correct, the note sounds twice; if incorrect, a buzz is heard, and the child tries again. After a succession of correct answers, the letter names begin to disappear. Eventually, the child has to identify each note as it is sounded and identified with a question mark without any letter name clues. If the child has difficulty, the program provides several levels of hints. After the first mistake, it slowly plays the scale and shows the names of all the notes except the target note. After the second, it reviews them again, quickly. After the third, it shows the target note and finally replaces all the letter names on the board, returning to the beginning level.

To play "Melody Tutor," the children choose a tune from the disk or type in one themselves. The piano keyboard is displayed and the computer plays the whole tune, as each note is highlighted on the screen. The computer then plays only the first note of the tune, highlighting that note again on the screen, and waits for the child to play it back. If the child is correct, the computer plays the first two notes, and so on. If incorrect, the computer reviews the correct notes and starts again where the child left off.

Find the Key (Edutek Corp.) introduces piano key notes and pitches. *Elements of Music* (Electronic Courseware Systems) is a series of lessons on note naming, keyboard pitches, and key signatures. *Music* (Lawrence Hall of Science) contains programs that provide practice in estimating, listening, and memory.

Creating with the Computer

The computer can be used to emulate traditional and electronic instruments. It can also be used to store, modify, build on, and play back melodies, even in several voices. Although the systems are expensive, computer-controlled synthesizers can allow people to hear a melody played by an oboe, violin, cello, organ, or an entire orchestra. Not all these projects are only for older students. David Ashton has developed a project that uses a computer-controlled organ in conjunction with a graphics scope. Children as young as age 4 have used the equipment to compose music and manipulate compositions. They see a graphic visual representation of parts of a melody. They can then redraw parts of the score and hear the effect of changes on the sound of the music represented by the line drawing.

What computers do is allow children to work on the conceptual aspects of the art without being limited, or distracted, by the technical aspects. There is a concern, of course, that children will not appreciate the years it takes to perform well on just one instrument. This should be taken into consideration; however, children should be given support on the technical aspects of composing music in much the same way that they should be given support in programming (see Chapter 10).

Early Music also contains composition programs. In one program, PERFORM/RECORD/PLAYBACK, children choose to view either a keyboard, treble clef, and bass clef. The keyboard display is a picture of a little more than an octave of a piano keyboard, from C to E. The top row of the computer's keyboard is used to play the notes. As each is sounded, its letter name is highlighted on the appropriate key in the picture. You can also choose a treble or bass clef display. As you sound each note, its letter name is highlighted on the appropriate line or space.

When you press the space bar, all the notes you play are recorded. Pressing the space bar again completes the tune, and pressing "P" plays back what was recorded. Your tune can also be saved on a disk. "Kaleidoscore" allows you to play tunes while a colorful graphic shape is displayed with each note sounded.

While these compositional tools hold potential, other applications are designed to allow children to experiment with musical ideas without being well versed in musical notation. For example, several versions of Logo also support musical programming. Children can write procedures that play music. This allows them to see the structure of music clearly. For example, Terrapin Logo has an example tune defined as follows:

```
TO FRERE
FR1
FR1
FR2
FR2
FR3
FR3
FR4
FR4
END
```

With only a little effort, you can probably figure out the song that will result and, if you hum it, what notes are in each procedure—FR1, FR2, and so on. Each procedure is defined in terms of two lists, one of the pitches, one of the durations for each pitch (40 is a quarter note).

```
TO FR1
PLAY [1 3 4 1] [40 40 40 40]
END
```

Notice how this way of representing the tune emphasizes its repetitive and balanced structure. It also encourages children to modify structures and melodies and notice the effects. For example, they may try different arrangements of the subprocedures to see which will create a meaningful tune. They might change one note of one procedure or keep the notes the same and change the duration of one or more notes. Children can easily change the command in FR1 to read PLAY [1 3 5 1] [40 40 40 40] and change the song to a major, rather than minor, key. Students can solve real problems in an environment in which they manipulate and transform musical ideas. They learn to think musically. This thinking should not replace live human music, but should serve to motivate and enrich it.

Bamberger (1983), in illustrating the "computer as sandcastle" metaphor (Chapter 1), gives an example of programming a computer to produce a clapped rhythm. Unwittingly, a pause is omitted, resulting in a totally different beat. We have a chance to say what we think and listen to what we said, translated into sound. Like the sandcastle, the computer reflects our musical thinking back to us, showing us that we did not say in our programming exactly what we did in our clapping. Logo allows people to use their intuitive powers in programming and their analytic abilities in learning about music and art. Both are valuable ways of knowing about, and doing things in, the world.

There are other profound discoveries that can be made through Logo music. Children can see the similarities between procedures in different media. For instance, a Logo procedure that draws a spiralling square, *just by changing the output from the turtle to the speaker,* will produce an ascending scale. If its output is changed to a PRINT statement, it will produce a numerical sequence: 5 10 15 20 25 . . . . This expands children's view of procedures and of music and other media while providing them with new musical intuitions and new ways of describing music. Music is a language, with syntax and semantics. Programming music allows children to experiment with this syntax and see its connection with other grammars.

A complete Logo music system can also be purchased that uses a synthesizer board connected to a stereo amplifier and speakers. It allows for extensive manipulation of more parameters and for immediate response time between typed commands and the resulting sound. It is designed to build on children's intuition about music rather than present traditional instruction on a computer (Bamberger, 1982).

Martin Lamb has developed a series of games similar to Logo music. However, no typing is required. Students use a graphics tablet and see a visual display of their compositions. Other musical composition packages that can be used with children include *Songwriter* (Scarborough System) and *Music Maker* (subLOGIC). Music can also be composed with the KoalaPad touch tablet and software sold for it.

Songwriter is especially noteworthy in that children can use it at many levels of sophistication. Composing, editing songs, and experimenting are

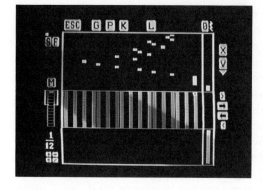

FIGURE 15-1
Children compose music and simultaneously learn music theory using *Songwriter*. Single keys add and change notes, which are represented on the screen as rectangular dots. (Courtesy of Scarborough Systems, Inc.)

encouraged through an easy-to-use editing system. Graphics and music are well integrated (Figure 15-1).

Much work still needs to be done before all these programs are appropriate for young children. However, they point to ways for students of all ages to learn that embody the experiential and exploratory approaches that early childhood educators have long advocated.

THE GRAPHIC ARTS

Teaching the Fundamentals

The fundamentals of graphic arts include skills such as recognizing colors, shapes, positions of lines, textures, and the like and developing fine motor control. Numerous programs designed to develop these skills have been described previously (especially Chapters 9, 12, and 13) and will not be repeated here.

Creating with the Computer

No longer limited to numbers or even words, computers are being increasingly employed in the creation of one of the most human of endeavors, art. The movie *TRON* and many television programs and commercials have been created with computer technology. Is this pursuit suitable for young children?

One example of an excellent art program for children of any age is *Paint* (Reston). It allows even young children to create impressive graphics, and yet it can be used at increasingly more sophisticated levels. *Simple Paint* is for the youngest child. It is limited to four colors. The child's paintbrush is the cursor, which is moved with a joystick. To paint, the child holds down the joystick button. Colors are changed by moving the cursor to a paint pot illustrated on the screen and by pressing the button. The hue and brightness can also be altered. The brush, or width of painting, can be similarly changed. Once the child has composed a picture, it can be saved on the disk, to be reloaded at a later time.

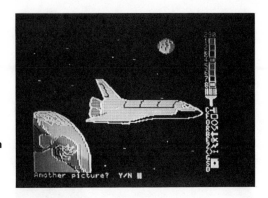

FIGURE 15–2
Children five years of age and up can create drawings using a joystick and *Picturewriter*. (Courtesy of Scarborough Systems, Inc.)

More advanced levels offer more colors and brushes; options such as textures and patterned mixes; a "Fill" feature; a "Speed" feature for controlling brush speed; a "Draw" feature, which allows the child to draw rectangles, lines and circles by marking their corners or points; and a "Zoom" feature, which allows the child to blow up the picture through two levels of magnification.

PictureWriter (Scarborough Systems) allows preschool and primary grade children to draw lines, shapes, and pictures with a joystick (Figure 15-2). They can fill areas of their drawings with color and hear the step-by-step creation of their art set to music. Pictures can be edited, colored, and saved on disk.

Other programs are available that work along similar lines, although most do not have the options of these two programs; for example, *Learning with Leeper* (Sierra On-Line), *Discovery Tool* (The Learning Company), and *Edu-Paint* (Softswap). *Finger Paint* (Nova Software) can be used by children as young as 3 years of age. Here the joystick moves a graphic hand or crayons to create pictures. Make sure you investigate any of these programs carefully before purchasing. *Color Me* (Versa Computing) is a computer coloring book in which children use a joystick to fill pictures with their choice of colors and textures. One might think that it is similar to other painting programs, but pressing a button to instruct a computer to fill in predrawn pictures is a qualitatively different experience.

Children can also draw with peripheral devices. An inexpensive graphics tablet allows children to draw directly on an electronic pad and see their drawing produced on the screen. The Koala Touch Pad contains a drawing program that allows children to draw lines, boxes, circles, rays, and so on just by touching the surface of the tablet. Children as young as three have used graphic tablets and graphics editing programs to gain spatial concepts (Piestrup, 1982b). With a light pen such as the LPSII (Gibson Laboratories), children can draw directly "on" the screen by touching it with the instrument (see Figure 15-3).

Creating pictures in Logo addresses several areas simultaneously. Children learn to construct basic shapes. They then rotate, move, and combine these shapes to create larger designs. Thus they are learning both

FIGURE 15–3
Two-year-old Jenna enjoys the creation of lines on shapes with the Gibson light pen. (Photo by Cindy Brzuski.)

the "basics" of shape, size, color, and so on, and elements of composition and design. All this takes place in an environment of problem solving, programming, mathematics, and art. Using the LPSII, children can fill in their Logo drawings with color.

One teacher has written Logo programs to produce the shapes from Ed Emberley's drawing books (Burrowes, 1983). These letters, shapes, and "things" are used as a pictorial "vocabulary" to create any of the drawings in the book. Children can also use them as building blocks for drawing anything they can imagine.

Very young children can create in this type of environment. David Alexander is working with 3-year-old children with the Logo-like language, *Delta Drawing* (see Chapter 10). He finds that children come gradually to control the program's commands. They leave the computer to go to the easel and vice versa, exploring the capabilities of each. The computer becomes an extension of what is available in the field of art. The children do not prefer either medium but seem to see them as separate. The easel painting is more motoric and filled with large circular arcs. The computer drawings are more cerebral and often consist of lines and shapes and 90 degree turns. Both are valuable. The computer has become as important a part of the children's room as the sandbox. Dr. Alexander has said that he made one mistake—not to wean himself from the computer and let children explore on their own soon enough.

Other drawing programs for young children include *Early Games* (Counterpoint Software), *KinderComp* (Spinnaker), *Magic Crayon* (C & C Software), and those discussed in Chapter 9.

Given their advantages, should computers replace other media for exploring music and art? Of course not; children need to experience creative expression in many media, the computer but one. It is, however, an effective one. In both music and graphic art, the computer can allow children of any age to explore, discover, and compose. It can create an environment in which every person is creative—and knows it.

FINAL WORDS

The arts often do not receive attention in the early years. The drive to ensure mastery of basic skills has decreased the already minuscule amounts of time granted to art and music (as well as to the sciences). This unbalanced position should be corrected, but it is more likely to be so if educators realize that the basics of reading and mathematics can be learned *as* children interact with quality projects in the arts and sciences. Computers are an especially efficacious method of integrating all subjects.

THINK ABOUT

1. Will computers mean the death of the performing arts?
2. If you program a computer to play music or draw, is it truly art? Can it be compared with that which is created by the hands?
3. Can young children benefit from composing music before they have any ear training?

ANNOTATED BIBLIOGRAPHY

Software: Side by side (1984, January). *Electronic Learning,* pp. 80–81.
　　A comparative look at music packages for beginners is provided.
WINDOW (1983). Vol. 1, no. 3.
　　This issue of the magazine-on-a-disk provides several reviews of music programs as well as *Mystery Melody,* the "world's first computer music adventure game."
Sound systems are available from Passport Designs, 116 North Cabrillo Hwy., Half Moon Bay, CA 94019; Roland, 7200 Dominion Circle, Los Angeles, CA 90040-3647; Syntauri Corp., 4962 El Camino Real, Suite #112, Los Altos, CA 94022.
　　These packages usually integrate a keyboard, synthesizers, and software to produce a complete computer music system.

16

The Exceptional Child and Computers

A victim of cerebral palsy speaks his first words through choosing words presented on the computer screen under his control. A speech synthesizer then pronounces the words. A computer-controlled robotic arm permits a quadriplegic to eat independently. Programming in Logo elicits the first active exploration and communication for an autistic child. In myriad ways, microprocessors are helping to provide support for exceptional children. The applications of this technology can be categorized as compensatory and instructional.

COMPENSATORY

Computer technology is quickly becoming the most powerful prosthetic device. It can compensate for a wide range of disabilities.

Sensing

The deaf are probably the largest group to benefit from the new technology. For those who cannot be helped by hearing aids, computers have been connected to devices that present words as vibrations on the abdomen, and thus sound recognition is learned similarly to conventional language. This is especially advantageous compared with lipreading as the latter cannot be used when the speaker is not easily seen. However, video interactive devices to teach lipreading skills are also available as well as systems that allow the deaf to "see" speech. With a modem, computers can replace telephones as communicative devices for the deaf. Researchers are also working on a bioear, which may provide hearing to the profoundly deaf. Placed behind the ear, this microprocessor would translate sound into impulses sent directly to the auditory nerve.

The blind. Because the traditional output device for the computer has been the CRT, the blind have benefited little from computer applications. Soon, technological advances should change this state of affairs.

Three of these are (1) the use of terminals that allow traditional typewriting for input but that use voice synthesis for output, (2) computerized devices that can quickly scan written material and provide either voice or tactile output, and (3) the provision of artificial vision.

One device, the Optacon (OPtical-to-TActile CONverter) produces the shape of letters under its camera on an array of vibrating pins. The camera is held with one hand and is passed over the printed page. The other hand is placed over the pins. This device is not easily used by everyone, however, and research is in progress to develop a similar device that produces spoken output. Thus, conversations with microcomputers and reading with the help of microcomputers will soon be more commonplace. Talking microcomputers are already being used by the blind in some projects. A similar simple example is the Speech+ talking calculator, with synthesized voice output.

There will be Braille printers and keyboards with Braille-to-regular print translators and/or large screens for the visually impaired. Braille printout computer terminals and printers are already allowing many blind students to graduate from computer programming programs. A Braille computer terminal that also supplies a paper copy of what appears on the screen is available (Maryland Computer Services). They are also being used to reproduce textbooks in Braille, allowing blind students to be mainstreamed more readily; less efficient methods of Brailling could not previously keep texts up to date. Of course, any material already stored on computer, such as international news and other information and computer-aided instructional materials, could be produced rapidly in Braille. In using CAI, the student might type in information on a regular keyboard but receive responses from the computer in the form of paper embossed with Braille characters continually fed from the terminal. The Durweil Reading Machine converts print into speech. These advances are currently being used at the level of higher education, but their use in all grades is not far off. One tactile vision substitution system uses photosensors to activate 1,024 electrodes that press against the abdomen. With this system, the blind can walk quickly and perform assembly tasks at a rate comparable to the sighted. Actually simulating vision seems possible by attaching a microprocessor and a video camera to the visual cortex of the brain.

Controlling

Computers also help exceptional children control the environment. The advent of computer recognition of speech will increase the applications of computer control of appliances, telephones, lights, doors, typewriters, and other everyday devices. Bed-ridden people will control any electrical device in the home from a central location. Those with severe mobility handicaps have been taught computer programming. In the near future, it will be possible for many who cannot leave their homes to be gainfully employed with the aid of communications technology.

The future will also bring aids to help the handicapped person to control the computer itself: foot controls, suck/blow switches, and specially designed keyboards to name a few. One example, the Autocom, is an electronic communication board. Items are selected by pointing with a special hand control or headset. The display is a 32-character LED array. It can be used to communicate with others or to control devices, including computers. Computer-based itself, it has a fully expandable vocabulary. Even those without speech will use input systems utilizing EMG muscle potential to control computers. Given variations in the amplitude and duration of pulses and the intervals between these pulses, complex commands may be produced by a single muscle. Thus even for spastic children, channels may be possible that allow them to output commands to a computer as quickly as a typist. Those who can produce only a few vocalizations can control a computer with an inexpensive vocal input device. Often, these children have little reason to practice these virtually nonfunctional vocal noises. With such a device, producing patterns of sounds can make a computer draw pictures, play a game, control a wheelchair, or say words the children are not yet capable of producing. The benefits include increased control of the world, meaningful activity, and incentive to learn more skills.

MAVIS. One particularly interesting development is MAVIS (Microprocessor-driven Audio/Visual Information System), a general system that offers several facilities for a range of widely differing disabilities (Schofield, 1981). It is a small suitcase that attaches to a standard television set as well as other equipment if desired. The case contains a microcomputer with a large memory and removable keyboard. Its many uses include word processing, drawing, making music, game playing, and environmental control—controlling lights, heat, televisions, telephones, and so on. Input can be by keyboard or by special switch (anything from joysticks to simple hand or foot switches to suck/blow tubes). With the use of switches, arrays of items such as characters, words, and choices are usually displayed for selection. MAVIS has the ability to modify these arrays, including their content and speed of operation.

The Adaptive Firmware Card (Adaptive Peripherals) allows physically disabled students to use the computer by pressing only one button. The card presents groups of letters. When a pointer is over the desired letter, the child presses the button to select that letter. Words, sentences, numbers, and the like can thus be entered into the computer. The best thing about this card is that it can be used with *any* program.

Those who could not use a pencil can write their thoughts. Those who had to wait to have someone else perform actions for them or be taught by someone can control their world and learn on their own, whenever they want. Computers can be designed to bridge communications gaps for all special children, even the autistic, by adapting to the child's ability to communicate rather than forcing the child to adapt to our ways. In allowing the handicapped to control their world and communicate with others, computers can hardly be seen as agents of dehumanization.

Communicating

One of the most humanizing aspects of computers in special education is their ability to allow those who could not communicate to do so.

Computer-based writing laboratories. By choosing words from computer screen menus, children who were without speech can communicate in person or over the phone. Those who could not write can have the words sent to a printer and, thus, compose letters. Advances in artificial intelligence are making it possible for the computer to anticipate input based on previous language patterns so that the speed of communication can be accelerated.

Highly motivating interactive games exist that can respond to deaf as well as standard English. These adventure games provide remarkably intelligent responses to a small range of words and sentences. Players can initiate communication rather than just respond to the computer's questions. The benefits are increased as children share the adventure, possibly through computer networks,

Communication between the deaf and the hearing world is difficult. But computers can convert normal speech into line configurations. The deaf can learn to talk by matching their own speech patterns to this pattern for a given sound. However, deaf children undoubtedly learn language best by actively operating on it, just as normal children do. Therefore, we should provide deaf children with computer-based opportunities to use and play with their language in meaningful contexts. More of these types of opportunities will be described in the next section.

Computer systems are available that greatly enlarge any text so that children with vision defects can use it.

INSTRUCTIONAL APPLICATIONS

Helping the Teacher of the Special Child

Computer technology can be an effective aid to those who work with special children. Several ways of doing this involve appropriate modification of techniques described in other chapters. We will look at these capabilities and some unique applications as they apply specifically to the needs of special children.

IEP preparation. Computers can be useful in creating mandated individualized education programs (IEPs), reducing the time needed for construction from several days to a few hours. It is, of course, still a tool—people make the final decisions as to what should be included. But it can help by analyzing the results of multiple measures and compiling the information in a usable form. It might also have access to a data bank—a large collection of goals and short-term objectives—and allow the users to match any relevant goals to the assessment information.

Software packages are available that perform many of these functions. Level I of *IEP Management Systems* (Creative Educational Services) prepares the IEP document with modifiable data files. Level II, in addition, prepares progress reporting documents for teachers and parents. Level III prints IEPs in multiple foreign languages. Level IV combines all the features in the first three levels. *SuperPlanner* (Learning Tools) is a three-part package: the Curriculum Management System serves as a resource bank for materials; the Individualized Planning System keeps records for students and interacts with the Curriculum Management System to plan goals; and the Administration Planning System updates student records for administrators automatically. *Project I.E.P.* (Evans-Newton) helps educators to meet government guidelines for special education students by issuing status reports. It also provides diagnostic and prescriptive reports, individual status progress reports, and student personal data reports (references for other programs can be found at the end of the chapter and in *Electronic Learning*, February 1984, pp. 41–42).

Data-base resources.   Once goals are established, another data base can be used—this being a collection of instructional methods, resources, and activities that are keyed to these goals. With a modem and telephone, the teachers can tie into other special education organizations to find materials, activities, and ideas from huge data banks—compilations of thousands of entries that have been found to be effective around the country (see appendix).

CMI.   CMI systems have been designed to help special educators institute and maintain individualized educational programs. CAMEO, Computer-Assisted Management of Educational Objectives, can store information on about 7,000 measurable objectives (Brown, 1982). Computers have been used to test the receptive language abilities of normal and language disordered preschool children. Children preferred the computer testing, and the results were similar to live testing (Fox & Wilson, 1982). Computers can also help the teacher in preparing reports and materials and in scheduling.

Helping the Exceptional Child

Advantages of computers.   There are four major advantages in using computers to help exceptional children learn. They help individualize instruction, in terms of method of delivery, type and frequency of reinforcement, branching, rate of presentation, and level of instruction. Computers present interactive instruction, which provides immediate corrective feedback and emphasizes the active, independent role of the children. They have the ability to hold the attention of normally distractible students. Finally, computer instruction is motivating and patient.

CMI with students.   A computer-managed instruction program may test children in broad areas. Based on their answers, it asks them other questions specifically chosen to find out just what they need to learn. It automatically keeps a record of their responses. On the basis of this diagnosis, it informs the children and their teacher what materials they should work with next. It can also print out weekly progress reports from this information. The computer-generated instructional prescription might include CAI programs that are designed to help children develop certain concepts and abilities.

CAI and the exceptional child.   Special education has been one area that has welcomed and integrated technological innovations openly. Before the advent of the microcomputer, computers had been used for instruction of the hearing and visually impaired, mentally retarded, emotionally disturbed, and disadvantaged students. Possibly their early acceptance can be traced to their compatibility with accepted practices in special education, such as presentation of carefully sequenced activities, finely tuned task difficulties, controlled provision of feedback, usually immediate elimination of as much stress as possible, patience, and the provision of a large degree of structure. It is no wonder that special educators like computer-assisted instruction. They are not alone.

Research evidence.   There is evidence that special needs children like this method of learning, too. Poorly motivated students have become more enthusiastic about their studies (Cartwright and Derevensky, 1976). They feel more "in control." They are taught in a context that is positive, patient, reinforcing, and nonthreatening. Experienced authorities report that positive effects like these are not fleeting, but continue over long periods (Joiner et al., 1982). One study offered minimally brain damaged children four individual tutorial sessions (Berthold & Sachs, 1974). For some children the lessons were presented entirely by teacher in one-to-one sessions. Others were presented the lessons by computer. The rest were presented half of the lessons by computer and the other half by teacher. The computer-only group scored lower than the other two, but there was no difference between those taught entirely by teacher and those taught half by teacher, half by computer. It would seem that computers can effectively supply up to one-half of one-to-one tutorials with the same resulting performance. In another study of CAI drill and practice, children made substantial gains in math (Fricke, 1976).

A group of ten 2- to 6-year-old deaf children demonstrated significant improvement in word recognition and identification after working with a computer program for six weeks, 10 to 15 minutes a day, twice daily (Prinz, Nelson, & Stedt, 1982). The children used an Apple computer with a special keyboard with words and pictures on it. Children might press the key labeled "flower" and see a picture, the word, and a graphic representation of the manual sign. They created sentences or phrases such as "the dog running." The benefit of computers can apparently be transmitted long distances. It has been shown to be possible to conduct interactive automated instruction with preschoolers from a central site to homes geographically dispersed across a state (Aeschleman & Tawney, 1978).

Characteristics of programs for exceptional children. Programs have often been designed or modified to meet the needs of exceptional children in the following ways (Grimes, 1981).

1. Spaces are left between printed lines of text. Teachers can often modify the program themselves to allow for this.
2. Children with learning problems sometimes have attention difficulties. Appropriate software highlights important information through visual and sound displays—color cues, music, buzzers, flashing arrows, underlining, and so on, when that is appropriate.
3. Conversely, extraneous, distracting material should be removed. Presentation should be simple and clear, in "chunks" of appropriate size.
4. Exceptional children do not always recognize their mistakes. Good courseware gives feedback when an error is made.
5. These children sometimes are impulsive, jumping to answer to quickly. Rate of presentation can be controlled by the teacher. Signals to "slow down and think" can be offered if the student response time rate is too fast. For slow-responding pupils, programs should be acquired, or existing programs modified, that allow the student to control the speed of responding, possibly providing a prompt or hint after a certain time period.
6. Programs should provide that amount of "scaffolding" or help that will allow the student to respond successfully. For example, at first a student may only be required to choose a correct answer from among three possibilities.
7. The level of difficulty should be altered frequently, if not constantly, so that the task set for the student is neither too easy nor too difficult—many small increases in difficulty are often most beneficial.
8. Programs should use a wide variety of materials and situations that are as concrete and "real world" as possible, to help students generalize what they have learned.
9. Most important, programs should follow the principles of instructional design. Thus, they should possess specified objectives and entry skills, activities that are designed to be matched to objectives and carefully sequenced, content integrity, and, usually, a management component—testing, keeping records, constructing assignments, reporting progress, and so on.
10. Program characteristics should match the needs of the specific group of children for whom they are designed. For example, Kleiman, Humphrey, and Lindsay (1983) found that hyperactive and other attention-deficient children benefited from working with computer programs providing drill in arithmetic in which (a) the level of problem difficulty was individually tailored, (b) the display was easily readable, (c) the answer format was designed to be similar to the typical paper and pencil answer format (i.e., answers for problems with three- or more-digit answers were entered right to left), (d) problem solving was self-paced, (e) motivational features in the form of graphic displays and praise statements were incorporated, and (f) there were messages specifically related to the children's problem of hyperactivity (for example, when a child answered incorrectly too quickly or made too many inappropriate button presses), the computer would print, "STOP IT!" Compared with matched paper and pencil practice, children chose to spend more time on the computer drill, working more problems. The percentage correct was equivalent.

CAI: Some Examples

MECC offers a spelling program for special needs children. *Whole Brain Spelling* (SubLOGIC) and the spelling program by Hasselbring and Owens (see Chapters 3 and 12) might also be helpful. *The Math Machine* (Southwest EdPysch) is a drill and practice program that has been shown to be effective with learning disabled students in research investigations (Watkins & Webb, 1981). Excellent reviews of other programs that are appropriate for use with exceptional children are available on paper or computer disk from the Special Education Computer Technology On-line Resource (SECTOR Project, Exceptional Children Center, Logan, Utah, 84322).

Several interesting programs are being produced by Laureate Learning Systems. *Micro-LADS* is aimed at remediating syntactic constructions frequently found to be problematic for language learning disabled children with a cognitive age of 2 to 8 years. It is a package of six disks that cover nouns, plurals and noun-verb agreement; verb forms; prepositions, pronouns, negatives, and Wh- questions (who, what, where, why, when); and passive and deictic expressions. It can also be used for reading instruction by using the speech alone, then speech and text, and finally text alone (see Figure 16-1). *Speak Up* allows teachers to build their own audible words and phrases. It can be used as a utility for facilitating the production of audible augmentative communication systems and programs and as an instructional tool. Children can build words themselves using the word processor to learn the relationship between written and spoken representations. Through building words and sentences, children can create a story that they can subsequently have read to them. A sample instructional program that comes with *Speak Up* is a tutorial program involving nouns and their categorizations. An expanded version that utilizes speech, text, and graphics, *First Categories,* includes animals, clothing, food, vehicles, body parts, and utensils.

The deaf. Studies have demonstrated that many profoundly deaf students have poor linguistic competence in comparison with their hearing

FIGURE 16–1
(Courtesy of Laureate Learning Systems, Inc.)

She is climbing.

peers. One language manipulation program provides children with the opportunity to interact more fully with a language environment, formulating and testing linguistic hypotheses (Sewell, Clark, Phillips, & Rostron, 1980). Deaf children are presented photographic slides of themselves in everyday activities. On the computer screen, they see a rearranged sentence describing the slide being displayed, for example, IS KICKING JOHN THE FOOTBALL. The words are manipulated by pressing the key corresponding to the first letter of any word on the screen. That word then moves down the screen. In this way new arrangements of words can be constructed by moving words with single key presses. When all the words have been rearranged, a smiling or frowning face provides feedback as to the correctness of the solution. After all the jumbled sentences have been rearranged, a paper printout listing all attempts is generated. If desired, entire phrases can be moved as single units. Teachers, of course, can easily add sentences to the program. For the deaf child, this provides experience in rapidly manipulating whole units in constructing sentences together with immediate feedback.

The mentally retarded. Although the research is not extensive, it does support the use of computer-assisted instruction with the mentally retarded (see Williams, Thorkildsen, & Crossman, 1983, for a review). Because of their limited reading skills, computer-controlled video tapes and especially video disks will undoubtedly provide a powerful new tool for aiding and teaching this segment of the population as well as other handicapped children. The Microcomputer/VideoDisc (MCVD) system was developed at Utah State University for the mentally retarded. It incorporates video segments into CAI lessons.

"Talking" computers have been successfully used to increase the reading vocabularies of retarded people (Lally, 1981). Students were presented with 16 words at a time. These words were placed over a matrix of 16 buttons. At first, they were free to push any word. The computer would light the word and simultaneously speak it. Whenever the child chose, he or she could go on to the second activity. Here the computer gave verbal instructions, directing the child to press a word. If correct, the word was flashed and spoken by the computer three times. If incorrect, the computer told the student what word was pressed, asking again for the correct word. If no response was made after 5 seconds, the word flashed. If the child then touched the word, the computer said, "That was right, but try again." At the end of the trials, the computer told the student how many words were correct and asked if he or she wanted to try again. After just four weeks of instruction, 20 minutes a day for four days a week, children increased their sight vocabularies by 128 percent compared with the 38 percent increase of a control group.

First Words (Laureate Learning Systems), described in Chapter 2, is a microcomputer tutorial program that trains receptive vocabulary to very young and/or language-delayed children (Wilson & Fox, 1982). It can be useful for children with a cognitive functioning level of less than a year. The training levels move from a single picture presentation with antecedent instruction, cuing and feedback to two pictures and feedback alone. Complete records are kept. Teachers can specify the content, level of difficulty, and parameters, including speed of scanning, length of time program waits before moving to next item, and criterion. This program can be used by a wide range of children with and without handicapping conditions, for example, the mentally retarded, language-learning disabled, motor impaired, autistic, and emotionally disturbed.

The handicapped. Devices that have been constructed to help handicapped children learn include touch panel terminals and computer-controlled "button boxes" that train coordination, memory, attention, and sequencing (Macleod & Overheu, 1977). Another panel displays lines and text, allows the student to "draw" by plotting points under the pressure of a pen, and thus can allow interaction with the pupil in a way that would be difficult with conventional methods. For example, children might attempt to copy a well-formed figure or line, receiving immediate feedback as to the accuracy of their effort. If they move off the line, the tracking stops and a blinking spot shows them where they should be. Thickness of line can be controlled, so graduated levels of difficulty are easily achieved. Their own tracing might also be displayed. Letters can be presented one stroke at a time so that students have to form the letters in the correct direction and order. Regardless of the number of attempts, only the well-formed example is reinforced and eventually displayed; therefore, a satisfying and accurate final product is reinforced.

A later handwriting system imparts a much greater degree of control over the process (Lally & Macleod, 1982). The student writes on a horizontal screen with a digitizer pen attached to two fine strings. A square cursor box drawn on the display indicates the calculated pen position. As students track successfully (the degree of accuracy required of them can be varied), the thin guideline they follow changes into a thicker path. If they start at the wrong place, lift the pen, or go too far off the line, path-filling stops and a small blinking dot indicates where the pen should be. In later lessons, only some portions of the outline of letters is visible. This system has been converted to the Apple II computer (Lally & Macleod, 1983).

Another important advance is reliable voice input. Voice recognition systems will have tremendous implications in special education, for CAI/CMI, for speech therapy, and for enabling special education students to control the computer for many purposes. The VBLS voice-based learning system (Instruction Systems Group, Scott Instruments Corporation) can be trained to understand almost any utterance, allowing children with speech disabilities and other physical handicaps to control the computer without using a keyboard, mouthstick, or headstick. The package comes with a miniauthoring system to allow teachers to construct individualized drills, tutorials, and tests for students.

An Activity Approach to Educating Exceptional Children

Another valuable approach is providing exceptional children with activities in which they can explore, construct, and communicate. Previously discussed tools, such as word processors (especially TSTP, see Chapter 12), serve this purpose. Other programs have been specifically designed for exceptional children.

For those with communication handicaps such as deafness, cerebral palsy, and autism, there is a need to approach language development through meaningful, purposeful communication. This approach taps the powerful motivation of communicative interaction and the effective teaching technique of integrating the language arts.

CARIS. In *CARIS* (Computer Animated Reading Instruction System, Brittanica), children select a noun and a verb by touching the CRT with a light pen. The computer then generates a brief animated cartoon acting out the meaning of that sentence. Later, the children type in the whole words. Many combinations can be explored. With the child in control and the immediate, direct visual feedback, the "best of both worlds" is achieved in facilitating reading success. (CARIS benefits very young children also.)

Logo has also been used successfully in this manner. Even children with severe handicaps have been able to explore the picture drawing, problem solving, and other general-purpose programming that the language offers. Reading-disabled children have created their own reading materials by programming in Logo to generate random sentences. Cerebral-palsied nonverbal students have drawn pictures, directing the computer to draw what they imagined. Autistic children who balked at performing upon others' requests enthusiastically explored the commands that instruct the turtle.

An advantage of Logo is the ease with which the activity or learning environment can be simplified so that children can engage in self-directed learning. For instance, physically handicapped children have worked successfully with an implementation of Logo using a scanning system. This illustrates a powerful method of working with the handicapped—letting them use their present capabilities to control a world, even if it is first the small world of computer graphics or the like and gradually expanding the range of that control. Even the repetitive behavior of an autistic child might come to have meaning if a computer sensed it and gave interesting visual feedback. As the child becomes interested in this effect, the input device might be changed to allow a greater variety of responses and a greater degree of shared meaning. This technique is similar to behavioral shaping, with important differences. The rewards are not contingent upon the observation and approval of an adult. The adult knows what the child wants, but does not give it until certain behaviors are produced by the child; the computer does not willfully withhold a reward, it merely responds to the child's commands. It may be that existing prostheses can be used to greater effect and with greater motivation in a Logo learning environment. With control via eye-tracking, even severely cerebral-palsied children may be able to "do anything the computer can do"—draw, write, compose music, communicate with others, and so on—with ease and efficiency (Papert & Weir, 1978).

Promising case studies of affective and cognitive gains resulting from Logo programming have been reported by many authorities (e.g., see Geoffrion & Goldenberg, 1981; Goldenberg, 1979; Weir, 1981). Logo demands that children try things out, be exacting, and respond to feedback— learning by doing by themselves. It emphasizes process more than product, along with the "debugging" of processes.

Priority should be given to these applications. They challenge the special child and encourage him or her to gain control, unlike programs that only use exploratory programs with above-average students, relegating the special child to the level of drill and practice.

Roadblocks

There are still roadblocks limiting attainment of many of these promises. Many teachers who deal with the special child are not knowledgeable about computer applications. Software packages are still few in number and limited in scope. No programs are optimal—modifications, including different auxiliary devices and even new languages, may help children learn more effectively. Teachers need to exert their influence on producers to create these materials, and they need to learn to use effectively what is presently available.

THE GIFTED AND TALENTED

The lack of appropriate educational programming for the gifted and talented (G/T) child borders on a national disgrace. The myths that all gifted children exhibit superiority in all areas of development and that they do not need special programs because "they'll do fine anyway" have been exploded by research; however, they still are implicit assumptions of far too many schools. The underachieving gifted child is a reality, an example of social neglect, a tragic waste of potential. Programs should meet their need for (1) increased self-acceptance, self-esteem, and love of learning; (2) rewarding intellectual stimulation; (3) genuine success; and (4) opportunities to develop social skills, including leadership (Whitmore, 1980). Special classes—at least for part of the day—are beneficial. In any setting, however, computers can aid in the provision of experiences that will help to meet each of these needs.

Gifted and talented children should learn to use the computer as a tool to extend their talents. Most of these types of applications have been described in previous chapters; the gifted child should be guided to use these programs in ways that are broader and deeper. It is especially beneficial to arrange for these children to interact with a "mentor" who uses computers in the areas in which the child is interested. Several brief suggestions follow.

CAI. *Comp-U-Solve* (from Educational Activities) is a collection of logical puzzles that can challenge bright second and third grade children. A unique aspect of this program is that the children's responses are analyzed after every move. The program "knows" whether they are progressing toward a desirable goal in an effective manner. In this way the program can coach the children. If they make the same error several times, the program will offer a hint, but not the whole solution. If the children are progressing, no special help is provided.

In "Electro-connection," children must connect four points to four matching points without going over any connecting lines. This problem is similar to that faced by designers of printed circuit boards. "Tricky Trip" is a form of the network puzzle studied by the mathematician Euler, such as the Königsberg Bridge problem, which involved traveling over seven bridges without crossing over the same bridge more than once. You must visit all the cities on a map only one time without traveling over the same road twice (Figure 16-2). Another program, "William's Warehouse Worries," is based on the classic "15" puzzle. Five numbered squares in a box must be slid around one at a time to match a given arrangement (Figure 16-3). Teachers are encouraged to introduce the programs with realia—circuit boards, maps, and the "15" puzzle. Some computer management is built in. Used properly, these programs promote the development of several problem-solving strategies: "guess and test," "finding a similar but simpler problem," pattern searching, using pictures, and working backward.

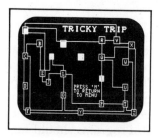

FIGURE 16-2
Tricky Trip. (Courtesy of Educational Activities.)

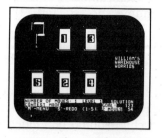

FIGURE 16-3
William's Warehouse Worries. (Courtesy of Educational Activities.)

The highest levels of *Teasers by Tobbs* (Sunburst; see Chapter 13) challenge students to use higher-level reasoning skills, see relationships, and develop both divergent and convergent thinking abilities. *Arith-Magic* (from QED) contains three games that combine computation, arithmetical reasons, and numerical theory.

CAI could also be used to compact the curriculum—helping children who are able to move quickly through the normal subject matter so as to free time for special projects. Some gifted underachievers could use *appropriate* CAI to close the gap between their achievement and their potential.

Projects. G/T programs should emphasize meaningful and challenging projects. For example,

1. Using a publishing system along with word processing program as discussed in Chapter 12 to write newspapers, reports, books, and so on. Also creating complex plots with such programs as *Story Maker* (Bolt, Beranek and Newman) and *That's My Story* (Learning Well).
2. Creating detailed information retrieval systems for use by themselves, other students in the school, and other interested and/or gifted children in other schools.
3. Programming in Logo to explore microworlds and solve problems is an excellent activity for talented children of any age, in any area—music, art, mathematics, language arts, science, and so on. Gifted children can think abstractly and can benefit from using a programming language as well as simulations and tool programs.
4. Exploring creative tools such as the drawing and music programs described in the previous chapter. Many of these children will be able to integrate this work with content from other subject matter areas, for example, investigating the relationship between the graphic and numerical representations of fractions in *Songwriter* and the musical equivalents (e.g., eighth and sixteenth notes; see the left-hand side of Figure 15-1).
5. Using graphing, spread sheet, and other utility programs as tools in appropriate projects.
6. Investigating and comparing several counting, calculating, and other symbol-manipulating devices. Exploring binary and other number bases.
7. Inventing your own language and coding and decoding with *Jabbertalky* (Automated Simulations). In Cryptogrammar every letter of the alphabet is substituted for another letter. Jabbergrammar lets children add, change, or delete words from a sentence creation program, creating new vocabulary lists.
8. Engaging in challenging problem solving with programs such as those in Chapter 9 as well as simulations (e.g., "Layer Cake" in *Body Builder* from CTW for younger children; *Rocky's Boots* from the Learning Company for primary grade children).
9. Working with software specifically designed for the gifted and talented (more will be available all the time; the Worthington Schools, 752 High Street, Worthington, OH 43085 have created a series of math and science software for gifted children, including such topics as probability and computer operation).

Several projects have shown that access to computers *and* supervision are necessary, without all these elements, gifted children often played computer games and did not develop significant abilities (Kolstad & Lidtke,

1983). G/T programs should provide guidance in the undertaking of meaningful projects that provide for enrichment of the curriculum.

Experiences for gifted children should include expectations of both convergent and divergent thinking and should contain subject matter that is so current that it is on the cutting edge of the discipline. Computer technology allows for this as well as or better than any other vehicle. However, as with other advanced work, the teacher needs to plan and guide the child's efforts. One such successful program might provide the interested reader with suggestions (Doorly, 1980).

Communication. Gifted children are often isolated—from peers and adults with similar interests. A modem and communications programs could expand their world. They might communicate with agemates for sharing in both the social and intellectual spheres. They could participate in teleconferences with others interested in the some topics. This might involve peers but could also involve other hobbyists and experts of any age. The lack of face-to-face contact need not be detrimental and may, in some cases, be beneficial. One educator tells the story of his intermediate grade son who was involved with an interesting "conversation" with a person in a different state via computers. However, when the other person revealed that he was a college professor and the child "confessed" his age, communications broke down; the professor became condescending and the child suddenly began making grammatical errors!

Gifted children might also communicate with mentors. First, data bases and specially designed programs could help these children search for and *find* mentors in their area of interest. Second, they could use the computer to communicate with the mentor. Through electronic message services and teleconferencing, these children could also interact with teachers in several subject areas. They could also take university courses offered from a distance via computer. Finally, they could use data bases and on-line libraries to uncover new information.

THINK ABOUT

1. Should exceptional children receive more, less, or the same amount of computer time as others?
2. Given limited computer facilities, what application—CMI, CAI, IEP construction, as a prosthetic device, for data-base use, or record keeping—or a combination of applications do you believe would be most valuable in aiding special children?
3. Gather information and prepare a report on the programs discussed that are designed to help prepare IEPs. If this process is increasingly efficient, should IEPs be mandated for every child?
4. Will computers increase our ability to mainstream handicapped people? How?.
5. Defend or attack the following statements:
   a. Gifted children have a special need to be challenged; they should receive priority in access to computer facilities.

b. It is better for a handicapped person to live life honestly, even if that means he or she is incapacitated to a degree, than to live dependent on a machine—or worse, virtually to *be* part machine.
c. Appropriate personal computer facilities should be provided for handicapped children at home and at school at public expense from the time their handicap is identified.
d. Computer use will only encourage gifted children to become "computer eggheads," socially inept and detached from the "real world."

ANNOTATED BIBLIOGRAPHY

Brudner, Harvey J. (1982). Light on: Microcomputers, special education, and CMI. *Educational Technology, 22*(7), 25–26.

    The author lists several publishers that are developing systems that can help to write IEPs and CMI systems that manage the work of entire classes in reading and mathematics (other similar publishers are listed in *Electronic Learning,* February 1984, 41–42). He argues that wider utilization of CMI in individualizing the education of *every* child is the single most important need in the area of educational application of computers. What do you think?

Ricketts, Dick (ed.) (1983). Computers and special needs. *The Computing Teacher, 10*(6).

    This issue features several articles about computers and special needs children.

17

LOOKING FORWARD

Larry sits down in front of a cathode ray tube. He turns it on. Millions of bits of information flash before his eyes and enter his ears every minute. He absorbs both details and the main concepts while making brief reactions, pushing buttons on the control unit. Not only is he not overwhelmed by the experience, he is bored by it and leaves it to do something more interesting. When his mother asks him about it, he explains why it was boring, recalling both main ideas and details with amazing accuracy. Larry is only 5 years old.

Does this scene seem possible? Or outlandish? Actually, it's a common occurrence today. Larry was watching Saturday morning TV, which produces myriad specks of sight and sound information that change thousands of times every second. And he, like most of us, understood what was going on very well. For if it is presented in the right way, we are very good at sensing, interpreting, and reacting to information. Will computers of the future interact with us in ways that take advantage of these talents of ours? Will the nature of information and its communication change, changing us with it? If so, will the changes be positive ones?

LOOKING OUT: ARE THERE DANGERS IN THE COMPUTER WORLD FOR CHILDREN?

Physical Dangers

Is exposure to computers and their video terminals safe? Every new technology spawns worries that center first on the possiblity of physical harm. Computers have generated a wide range of fears, of everything from eyestrain to radiation. To set the matter to rest, there are no physical dangers from viewing computer screens. Radiation levels of computers are far below any current standards; the background radiation is usually far greater than is the video display unit itself. Fluorescent light emits more radiation (e.g., Letourneau, 1981; "Terminals," 1981). Eyestrain or other pains are merely a result of any type of work that requires a fixed position and visual concentration.

It would appear that we should have few worries about biological hazards. If any child in our care is spending so much time viewing a computer (or television) screen that he experiences eyestrain or backaches, the problem is not so much physical as emotional.

Emotional and Cognitive Dangers

What if a child spends too much time with computers? What might these emotional problems be? Might children actually feel safer and more accepted by a computer than by other people? Little is known about this, although there are reports of adult "hackers" who have become overly entranced by the machine. Teachers of young children are experienced at observing behaviors which indicate that individuals are not adapting well socially. They should, of course, use this skill to ensure that their students do not use computers as a substitute for human interaction. In most classrooms, however, this is an unlikely situation. Remember, too, the positive social interaction that computers can facilitate if used correctly (see Chapter 14).

Will computers turn children into robots? It should be clear that while this fear could have some remote validity, its realization would require the insidious assistance of programmers, parents, and teachers. Used correctly, computers can expand children's autonomy, independence, and creativity. However, computers are still based on a logical-scientific model. The limitations of this view, and the importance and power of the artistic and humanistic views, need to be kept firmly in mind. Even some of the best uses of computers, such as putting the child in control through programming, have limitations. For example, spending undue amounts of time controlling some part of the world might lead to an overemphasis on instrumental, power-based relationships. A mechanistic view of the world tends to emphasize means, not goals. Thinking and rationality are to be encouraged, but they should never be separated from intuition and feeling.

Even worse, computer applications that are not well conceived might do for thinking what mass transportation did for walking and what television did for reading and creative play. This is especially true if cute, but low-level, programs with no connection to the curriculum are used. Computer activities should generate, not replace, the need for thought.

The issue of video games is unresolved. Many say that they constitute a harmless way to play, to release energy, to learn to solve problems quickly, and to build eye-hand coordination. Others maintain that true play is curious, open ended, and creative. Video games, they say, are preprogrammed, closed, and deadening. Play is constructive. Video games are most often destructive.

It is difficult to know which view is correct. However, the eye-hand coordination argument is weak—the movements made in game playing are limited, repetitive, and unrefined. They usually do not involve movements needed for other, more complex tasks. It is hard to believe that introducing more violence—no matter how unrelated to true violence—into the environment of children will help them to build a positive picture of the world. The most important concern is, What experiences are lost to hours of shooting spaceships?

Finally, there are human experiences such as love and respect for which computers should not be substituted. The principles of the first chapter state that educators should be wary of every computer application that is substituted for an actual experience. As Abraham Maslow said: to a person who has only a hammer, the whole world looks like a nail. A computer, and any computer language, is also a tool, and it also shapes our view of the world (Weizenbaum, 1976). The fear is that to those who have only computers, the world looks like information to be processed and quantified. Computers should not be used too much, and other tools should be used by children and their teachers. There is an essential question of balance. As stated previously, it is not likely that early childhood educators will abandon the intuitive, humanistic view of the world. More likely dangers are the next ones.

Practical and Political Dangers

Will computers be available to everyone equally? There are several disturbing trends against which educators should guard. Often, computers are used as tools by advantaged children, while those not so blessed either do not have access to computers or use computers only as drill machines. Biases in society tend to encourage boys to use and enjoy computers more than girls. Biases in some school systems tend to favor mathematics classes at upper levels, ignoring the potential of computers to assist in the learning of other subjects and to enrich the educational experience of young children.

LOOKING AHEAD: THE FUTURE

Glimpses of Utopia

In *Education and Ecstasy,* George Leonard describes a utopia in which lifelong learning and lifelong creative change exist as the main purposes of life. Computers play an essential role. In one section of the futuristic school, the Basics Dome, children sit at individual learning consoles that form a ring within the dome. The children face outward toward a laser-produced three-dimensional learning display.

When a child first sits down, the computer taps into her learning history. The child puts on combination earphones and brainwave sensors. The latter analyze the wave patterns of the learner and influence the on-going dialogue between her and the computer immediately. If she is responding neurologically, the dialogue moves on. Pace is adjusted. Learning is efficient and steady. General states of emotion, consciousness, and short-term memory are taken into consideration.

After reading these patterns, the computer quickly reviews the child's last session. If she wants to continue, she pushes the "yes" key on the modified typewriter keyboard. If she presses "no," the computer searches rapidly for other material appropriate to her level of learning, flashing alternatives in front of the child until she presses "yes."

Taking into consideration a full bank of basic cultural knowledge (which most children learn from ages 3 to 6), other interesting material that allows for individual discovery, the child's brain wave pattern, the child's typed or spoken responses, and even the material from the displays of the child's friends sitting around her, the computer constantly creates and re-creates an appropriate dialogue. A 4-year-old girl is dialoguing about primitive cultures. A 6-year-old boy is deep into a simple calculus session. A 3-year-old girl is learning standard spelling and is trying out alternative forms (this experimentation gradually leads most children into a key project—inventing their own languages). For instance, the computer asks for the spelling of a cat in response to the girl's recognition of a displayed cat and her verbalization of the word "cat." After she provides the standard spelling, she is asked for a few alternative spellings (e.g., "kat" or "katte"). The following dialogue ensues.

COMPUTER: A cat is a kat is a katte.
GIRL (TYPING): A katte is a kat is a cat.
COMPUTER: Copy cat.
GIRL: Koppy Kat.

At that time the girl notices the display from the child in the next console. This is taken into account by the computer. For a few moments the microworlds of several children interact and influence each other. The jungle from the "primitive cultures" dialogue of the other girl spills over into the 3-year-old's display. She types, "A cat hiss a kat hiss a katte." The computer says, "Wild!!!" Reacting to a leopard in the scene, she types "A tiger is a tigger./A gunne has a trigger." The leopard becomes a tiger before her eyes. The two girls exchange delighted glances.

COMPUTER: Why not "leopard"?
GIRL: "Leopard" doesn't rhyme with "trigger."
COMPUTER: Okay. How about some alternate spellings for "leopard"?
GIRL: That's easy. Leppurd.

The computer compliments her, but reminds her that she does not have to stay with sound correspondence. She tries, "Leap-heart."

Leonard postulates that human potential is great, learning is sheer delight, learning is life's ultimate purpose and that educators can use computer technology to actualize that potential and that ecstasy. It is critical to note that Leonard's vision includes many other learning and growing situations besides the Basics Dome. Just as essential is the purely human contact. He gives an example of a group of children and adults dramatizing an historical episode, discussing it (and crying from empathy) afterward.

Socrates as a personal tutor. A person whose writing gives you the feeling that he is very comfortable with a rapidly changing world, Christopher Evans (*The Micro Millennium,* 1979) paints a picture of futuristic education that is as convincing as it is dramatic. His teaching computers will be genuinely "smart," in that they will adjust their responses in a variety of ways, giving the impression that they are interested in teaching and that they understand the subject matter and the student's grasp of it. "Lessons" will be true dialogs. Teaching devices must, according to Evans, be made available to all children; otherwise, the bright, the advantaged children will benefit from the mind-stretching and information-giving potentials of the machines, while the less fortunate will be left, again, far behind. These teaching computers must be carefully prepared to motivate every child. Information is now locked in books, available only to those with the keys to their use. In Evans's future, "books will come down from their shelves, unlock and release their contents, and cajole, even beseech, their owners to make use of them" (p. 129). When they reach the stage of ultraintelligent machines (more intelligent than people) their role as teachers will be unequaled. "It will be like having, as private tutors, the wisest, most knowledgeable and most patient humans on earth: An Albert Einstein to teach physics, a Bertrand Russell to teach philosophy, a Sigmund Freud to discuss the principles of psychoanalysis, and all available where and when they are wanted" (p. 229).

Other Futures: Darkness at Noon?

Even if much of this is realizable, is it all desirable? These issues also need to be thoroughly examined. There are, of course, many scenerios that we can dimly perceive as we try to look through the veil of the future. Not all are utopian. What actually happens depends on many forces—one of which is the impact of teachers like you. The darker pictures are not meant to make you depressed or uneasy but are possibilities we can work together to avoid.

Future 1. Computers made a big impact—about 5 to 10 years ago. Now they are sitting in storerooms, decaying beside the other unused teaching machines. They made no more lasting impact than did movies and television. One or two teachers in a building use them for remedial help in reading and mathematics, although the programs have not been updated in quite a while.

Future 2. Schools have benefited from the application of computer technology, although the inertia of society has tended to channel their application into teaching the traditional curriculum more efficiently. Some educators are insisting that computers, used innovatively, can make a major change in the thinking and learning of children. The few implementations of their ideas seem interesting, but have not made a large impact on most schools.

Future 3.   Schools are controlled mainly by curriculum writers, computer scientists, educational psychologists, programmers, and administrators, in that order. Advances in cognitive psychology and computer science have allowed the construction of "intelligent systems" that can test, prescribe, teach, and retest students, keeping track of all their studies with impressive efficiency. Because the cost of developing ultracomplex curricula is tremendous, there is a trend for decisions as to the nature and content of the programs to be made at the national level, as the curriculum becomes more standardized and education more centralized. Students learn as much or more at home as they do at school, except that the school provides certain important social and physical activities. The influence of teachers has lessened considerably, largely due to the way in which educational computing grew. The school adapted it too slowly—students learned about it, and from it, at stores, clubs, and home. Institutions and forces outside of schools stepped in and met the growing demand.

Future 4.   Students learn almost everything at home. (Farfetched? Estimates are that 70 percent of the more than $1 billion educational software market of the next few years will be home users.) With cables connecting every home to every other home and institution, schools have become unnecessary, dinosaurs in a technological age. Due to the availability of huge communication networks and the dwindling supply of energy, people live, work, and learn at home. Contacts with other children and with teachers still exist via telecommunications. Social and physical needs are met through play with other neighborhood children. Heavily funded interest groups are lobbying to have the national curricula reflect their point of view.

Future 5.   Schools have become centers for learning and communicating for entire neighborhoods. Computer-enhanced facilities are used by children and adults throughout the day. Classes are held, but their organization has been substantially changed, and attendance is usually not mandatory. Children explore and learn about their world through a variety of formats and experiences, some of which are highly technological, some of which are not at all. Computers are used to drill, instruct, solve problems, simulate, and stimulate. Each student has a work station where he or she can put in and receive information, solve problems, and "play." First graders develop their own cartoon shows with computer graphics and child-oriented computer language. Some third graders do more advanced art, music, and writing. Virtually no children "fail," as all can find, with help, those activities in which they excel, and they have the encouragement and supportive environment to pursue those activities.

Teachers in these schools are thankful that their predecessors worked hard to become computer literate—some at the beginning, some in the middle of their careers—taking the responsibility upon themselves to give students the education they needed within the schools. They avoided any technological panacea and looked carefully at every new computer application.

There are many possible futures. Every concerned educator should be knowledgeable about, concerned with, and involved in, the applications of technology to education. By becoming authors of the future scenario, they can ensure that the future will not take the shape of that foretold by Isaac Asimov (1976). He describes an 11-year-old girl who hates her expert learning machine. Finding a book ("what a waste," says her friend, for it must be discarded, unlike his television screen), she reads about the schools of the past. Although her mother explains that learning must be adjusted to fit the mind of each boy and girl, she was entranced by the schools of the past. When her mechanical teacher flashed a problem on the screen, she thought about the kids of those days and *The Fun They Had*.

If educators do not accept the challenge, others will. If other sources accept leadership, then computer education will be in the hands of those without dedication to, and expertise in, the provision of educational opportunities befitting a democracy. The first ramification is the possibility of a decrease in the quality of education for every child. The second is the possibility of a societal movement toward overreliance and submission to the "expert" (either computer or technocrat), what Hansgen (1982) has termed "the tyranny of expertise." "Those who use the computer, if left unchecked, will probably acquire a great amount of power" (Frates & Moldrup, 1980, p. 18).

Looking Ahead: CAI

Computer instruction of the future will undoubtedly combine present-day CAI techniques with knowledge gained through artificial intelligence research. The result, ICAI, or intelligent computer-assisted instruction, will be able to (a) infer students' strengths and weaknesses from their responses, (b) compare those responses with those of an expert to figure out what the student needs to learn, and (c) "understand" enough about teaching and learning to figure out when and how it should intervene and what it should teach. Computer tutors such as these might even help children to learn programming. For example, a girl (whose responses are underscored) might be coached in learning Logo:

```
I am going to draw a napolean.
I don't think that I have ever seen a napolean.  Perhaps you
could draw one on the tablet, just to give me the idea.
Oh, I see, napolean is a stick man, only with a funny head!
That's his hat.
Oh! OK.  Do you have a plan?
Well, sort of.  I thought I would start with his hat and
work downward.
Are you going to use any subprocedures?
No.
Hmmm.  I notice that you already have a program to draw a
triangle.  Perhaps you could use that?
```

```
Ok.  That can be his hat.  Here is the definition.

    TO NAPOLEON

      TRIANGLE

      BACK 50

      LEFT 120

      FORWARD 100...
```

(She runs NAPOLEON, finding that the triangle repeats forever.)

```
It has a bug!  It's just drawing the same old triangle, over

and over.  How come?

Well, let's see.  How could we find such a bug?

I give up.

Well, what is the first thing your procedure does?

I don't know.

What is the first subprocedure called by NAPOLEAN?

Yes,  Print out TRIANGLE.

    TO TRIANGLE

      FORWARD 100

      RIGHT 120

      TRIANGLE

      END

Do you see the problem?

Yes.  Isn't there some way I can make it stop?

Yes.  Do you remember how we did it for SQUARE?  Perhaps you

could use that as a pattern to work from.
```

Looking Ahead: Controlling the Computer

How about programming? Which language will be used? Will everyone program computers? Answers to these questions can be speculative only, but it would seem that, just as today, people will program at varying levels. Some will, of course, still design and program computers at a technical, "machine language" level. At the other extreme, some may only employ "user-friendly" programs that ask them what they want done. However, even for those somewhere in between who wish to write programs for the computer, the task may be very different from today's process. Many will use tool programs such as word processing programs, database management systems, and the like. However, these programs, and programming languages themselves, will be radically advanced. People will be able to talk to the computer and design programs, compositions, or data bases in natural languages. However, as we have seen, our conversations can often hide ambiguity. How will this be handled?

First, because people of the future will have worked with computers almost since birth, planning and problem solving will be more natural and more organized for them. Second, where their intents or ideas are a bit "fuzzy," the computer they are conversing with will ask them what they meant, carrying on a dialog that will force them to think through their problem, their goals, and their methods of solution carefully. Thus, computer programmers may write initial systems that, once written, can grow and adapt with the user.

Some of the pioneers in the construction and use of the Logo language are already making steps toward a new, even more "user-friendly," language that also overcomes some of the disadvantages of Logo (e.g., limited data storage capabilities and inability to integrate many users and/or many types of systems). Called Boxer, it is visually oriented so that "what you see is what you have." The spatial relationships among words and phrases enclosed in boxes on the screen directly represent meaningful relationships within the language. What is seen, then, is a close representation of the computational system itself. Also, the various uses of a computer such as text processing, programming, and file management are built into the system simultaneously.

As an example, a teacher might type the names of his students into the computer. He then could enter one of the student's data boxes by moving the cursor into it and hit a key, "entering" that box (i.e., that box would expand to fill the screen). There he could enter another data box, say, "Math." Here he might enter new information directly, such as a new unit, or he might enter yet another box to add to or change an existing grade or other piece of information. Notice that the spatial arrangement directly mirrors the hierarchical arrangement of information. Also note that the editing system is always present (information can be added or changed at any time). Helpful "menus" are no longer special, auxiliary features but, rather, are built into the program. They can be used, constructed, or edited by the user. Data can also be shared among different modules, and one module can "ask" another to "do something" for it. Statements can be typed in and executed one at a time and later built up into a program of the user's choice. While Boxer demands higher capabilities than most microcomputers possess at the time of this writing, it should be available soon.

So in one way, we have come full circle to the little story that introduced this chapter. A computer language is already being written that capitalizes on our strengths—intuitions and abilities in perceiving and understanding ideas presented spatially. If educators are proactive, tomorrow's children will be provided with increased interaction with others, increased opportunities for exploration and access to information, and an enriched learning environment. Children will use computers as general-purpose tools, just as they are used in the real world.

New ideas are coming. Look out for the negative ones. Look ahead to the positive ones.

FIGURE 17–1 Tomorrow's children will be provided with increased interaction with others for exploration and access to information in an enriched environment. (Photo by Douglas Clements.)

ANNOTATED BIBLIOGRAPHY

Brandt, R. (1983). Preparing for the future. *Educational Leadership, 41*(1).
　　This issue is dedicated to the future and technology. How do the views expressed changed your view of yourself as a teacher?
Deken, J. (1982). *The electronic cottage.* New York: William Morrow.
　　This book contains interesting insights in the computer revolution of the near future (as well as readable explanations about how computers work).
Pritchard, W. H., Jr. (1982). Instructional computing in 2001: a scenario. *Phi Delta Kappan, 63,* 322–325.
　　Another possible future. What do you think?
Toffler, A. (1980). *The third wave.* New York: William Morrow.
　　Toffler is famous for helping us think about the future and our place in it. What insights into your and your students' future do you gain from reading his book?

APPENDIX

The addresses of many of the *main* producers of educational software and hardware as well as journals and other organizations are listed in the following pages. Space constraints do not allow a complete listing; see also listings in computer magazines and books, references such as the *Classroom Computer News Directory of Educational Computing Resources* (see address for that magazine below), or ask for assistance at your local computer store or library.

PRODUCERS OF EDUCATIONAL SOFTWARE

Addison-Wesley Publishing Co.
2725 Sand Hill Rd.
Menlo Park, CA 94025

Americal Peripherals
122 Bangor Street
Lindenhurst, NY 11757

Automated Simulations
1043 Kiel Court
Sunnyvale, CA 94086

Avant-Garde Creations
P.O. Box 30160
Eugene, OR 97403

Bell & Howell
7100 N. McCormick Rd.
Chicago, IL 60645

Bertamax, Inc.
Suite 500
101 Nickerson St.
Seattle, WA 98109

Bolt, Beranek and Newman
50 Moulton St.
Cambridge, MA 02238

Borg-Warner Educational Systems
600 W. University Dr.
Arlington Heights, IL 60004-1889

Boston Educational Computer
78 Dartmouth St.
Boston, MA 02116

Britannica (Encyclopaedia Britannica Educational Corp.)
425 North Michigan Ave.
Chicago, IL 60601

Broderbund Software, Inc.
1938 Fourth St.
San Rafael, CA 94901

C & C Software
5713 Kentford Circle
Wichita, KS 67220

Children's Computer Workshop
(CCW, an activity of CTW)
1 Lincoln Plaza
New York, NY 10023

Computer Curriculum Corp.
P.O. Box 10080
Palo Alto, CA 94303

Computing Adventures Ltd.
9411 North 53rd Avenue
Glendale, AZ 85302

CONDUIT
P.O. Box 388
Iowa City, IA 52244

Control Data Corp.
8100 34th Ave. South
P.O. Box 0
Minneapolis, MN 55440

Counterpoint Software
4005 West 65 St.
Minneapolis, MN 55435

Creative Publishing
P.O. Box 10328
Palo Alto, CA 94303

CTW (Children's Television
   Workshop)
One Lincoln Plaza
New York, NY 10023

Davidson & Associates
6069 Groveoak Place, #12
Rancho Palos Verdes, CA 90274

Digital Research
160 Central Ave.
Pacific Grove, CA 93950

DLM (Developmental Learning
   Activities)
P.O. Box 4000
One DLM Park
Austin, TX 75002

Disk Depot
731 W. Colorado Ave.
Colorado Springs, CO 80905

Disney Electronics
6153 Fairmount Ave.
San Diego, CA 92120

Dr. Daley's Software
Water St.
Darby, MT 59829

Dynacomp, Inc.
1427 Monroe Ave.
Rochester, NY 14618

Educational Activities, Inc.
P.O. Box 392
Freeport, NY 11520

Educational Administration Data
   Systems, Inc.
P.O. Box 7005
Springfield, IL 62791

Educational Media Assoc.
342 W. Robert E. Lee
New Orleans, LA 70124

Educational Progress Corp.
4235 S. Memoria Dr.
Tulsa, OK 74145

Educational Teaching Aids
159 West Kinzie Street
Chicago, IL 60610

EduFun (see Milliken)

Edu-Soft
P.O. Box 2560
Berkeley, CA 94702

Edutek Corp.
P.O. Box 11354
Palo Alto, CA 94036

EduWare Services, Inc.
28035 Dorothy Dr.
Agoura Hills, CA 91301-0522

Electronic Courseware Systems, Inc.
309 Windsor Rd.
Champaign, IL 61820

Evanston Educators
1718 Sherman Ave.
Evanston, IL 60201

Floppy Enterprises
716 E. Fillmore Ave.
Eau Claire, WI 54701

Hammett
Hammett Place
P.O. Box 545
Braintree, MA 02184

Hartley Courseware
P.O. Box 431
Dimondale, MI 48821

Harvard Associates, Inc.
260 Beacon St.
Somerville, MA 02143

Hayden Software
600 Suffolk St.
Lowell, MA 01853

D. C. Heath and Company
125 Spring St.
Lexington, MA 02173

HEI, Inc.
Victoria, MN 55386

Holt, Rinehart and Winston
383 Madison Ave.
New York, NY 10017

I/CT
Taylor Associates
10 Stepar Place
Huntington Station, NY 11746

K-12 Micromedia
Box 561
Valley Cottage, NY 10989

Kangaroo
332 South Michigan Ave.
Suite 700
Chicago, IL 60604

Krell Software
1320 Stony Brook Rd.
Stonybrook, NY 11790

Laureate Learning Systems, Inc.
1 Mill Street
Burlington, VT 05401

Lawrence Hall of Science
University of California
Berkeley, CA 94720

The Learning Company
545 Middlefield Rd., Suite 170
Menlo Park, CA 94025

Learning Systems Ltd.
P.O. Box 9046
Fort Collins, CO 80522

Learning Unlimited Corp.
200 Park Offices Bldg., Suite 207
Research Triangle Park, NC 27709

Learning Well
200 South Service Rd.
Roslyn Heights, NY 11577

Logo Computer Systems
220 5th Ave., Suite 1604
New York, NY 10018

Math City
4040 Palos Verdes Dr. North
Rolling Hills Estates, CA 90274

Mathware
919 14th St.
Hermosa Beach, CA 90254

McGraw-Hill
1221 Ave. of the Americas
New York, NY 10020

MECC (Minnesota Educational
  Computing Consortium)
2520 Broadway Dr.
Saint Paul, MN 55113

Melcher Software
P.O. Box 213
Midland, MI 48640

Mercer Systems
87 Scooter La.
Hicksville, NY 11801

Merry Bee Communications
815 Crest Dr.
Omaha, NE 68046

Micro Learningware
Hwy. 66 So., P.O. Box 307
Mankato, MN 56002

Micro Power and Light Co.
12820 Hillcrest Rd. #224
Dallas, TX 75230

Micro-Ed, Inc.
P.O. Box 24156
Minneapolis, MN 55424

Microgram
Box 2146
Loves Park, IL 61130

Microphys Programs
2048 Ford St.
Brooklyn, NY 11229

Micropi
Box 5524
Belligham, WA 98227

Microsoft Consumer Products
400 108th Ave. NE
Bellevue, WA 98004

Midwest Software
Box 214
Farmington, MI 48024

Milliken Publishing Co. (EduFun)
1100 Research Blvd.
P.O. Box 21579
St. Louis, MO 63132

Milton Bradley
Springfield, MA 01101

Modern Education Corporation
P.O. Box 721
Tulsa, OK 74101

NOVA Software
P.O. Box 545
Alexandria, MN 56308

NTS Software
680 Arrowhead Ave.
Rialto, CA 92376

Opportunities for Learning
8950 Lurline Ave.
Chatsworth, CA 91311

Polytel
2121 S. Columbia, Suite 550
Tulsa, OK 74114

Prentice-Hall, Inc.
Sylvan Ave.
Englewood Cliffs, NJ 07632

Program Design, Inc.
95 East Putnam Ave.
Greenwich, CT 06830

Psychotechnics, Inc.
1900 Pickwick Ave.
Glenview, IL 60025

Quality Educational Designs
P.O. Box 12486
Portland, OR 97212

Queue
5 Chapelhill Dr.
Fairfield, CT 06423

Random House School Division
2970 Brandywine Rd.
Atlanta, GA 30341

Reader's Digest Services
Educational Division
Pleasantville, NY 10570

Reston Publishing Co.
11480 Sunset Hills Rd.
Reston, VA 22090

Rhiannon Computer Games for Girls
3717 Titan Dr.
Richmond, VA 23225

Right On Programs
P.O. Box 977
Huntington, NY 11743

Scarborough Systems
25 North Broadway
Tarrytown, NY 10591

School Office Software Systems
3408 Dover Rd.
Durham, NC 27707

Scholastic, Inc.
902 Sylvan Ave.
Englewood Cliffs, NJ 07632

SRA (Science Research Associates)
155 Wacker Dr.
Chicago, IL 60606

Scott, Foresman and Co.
1900 East Lake Ave.
Glenview, IL 60025

Sensible Software, Inc.
6619 Perham Dr.
West Bloomfield, MI 48033

Sierra On-Line
Sierra On-Line Bldg.
Coarsegold, CA 93614

Silicon Valley Systems
1652 El Camino Real #4
Belmont, CA 94002

Sirius Software
10364 Rockingham Dr.
Sacramento, CA 95827

Skillcorp, Inc.
1711 McGaw Ave.
Irvine, CA 92714

Softswap
San Mateo County Office of Education
333 Main Street
Redwood City, CA 94063

Software Arts
27 Mica Lane
Wellesley, MA 02181

Software Productions
2357 Southway Dr.
P.O. Box 21341
Columbus, OH 43221

Software Publishing Corp.
1901 Landings Dr.
Mountain View, CA 94043

Southwestern Publishing Co.
5101 Madison Rd.
Cincinnati, OH 45227

SouthWest EdPsych Services
P.O. Box 1870
Phoenix, AZ 85001

Spinnaker Software
215 First St.
Cambridge, MA 02142

Sterling Swift Publishing Co.
1600 Fortview Rd.
Austin, TX 78704

SubLOGIC Communications Corp.
713 Edgebrook Dr.
Champaign, IL 61820

Sunburst Communications, Inc.
Room YB7
39 Washington Ave.
Pleasantville, NY 10570

SVE (Society for Visual Education)
1345 Diversey Parkway
Chicago, IL 60614

Tamarack Software
Water St.
P.O. Box 247
Darby, MT 59829

TYC (Teach Yourself by Computer
   Software)
40 Stuyvesant Manor
Geneseo, NY 14454

Teaching Tools
P.O. Box 12679
Research Triangle Park, NC 27709

Teaching Tools Microcomputer
   Services
P.O. Box 50065
Palo Alto, CA 94303

TEKSYM Corporation
145404 County Road 15
Minneapolis, MN 55441

Terrapin Inc.
380 Green St.
Cambridge, MA 02139

T.H.E.S.I.S
P.O. Box 147
Garden City, MI 48135

TSC/Houghton Mifflin Co.
One Beacon St.
Boston, MA 02108

Universal Systems for Education, Inc.
2120 Academy Cir., Suite E
Colorado Springs, CO 80909

Vocational Education Productions
California Polytechnic State University
San Luis Obispo, CA 93407

John Wiley & Sons, Inc.
605 Third Ave.
New York, NY 10158

Xerox Educational Pub.
245 Long Hill Rd.
Middletown, CT 06457

MAGAZINES AND JOURNALS

AEDS Journal and *AEDS Monitor*
1201 16th St., NW
Washington, DC 20036

Arithmetic Teacher
NCTM
1906 Association Dr.
Reston, VA 22091

Byte
70 Main St.
Peterborough, NH 03458

Classroom Computer News
Intentional Educations, Inc.
341 Mt. Auburn St.
Watertown, MA 02172

Compute!
515 Abbott Dr.
Broomall, PA 19008

The Computing Teacher
International Council for Computers
   in Education
University of Oregon
1787 Agate St.
Eugene, OR 97403

Creative Computing
P.O. Box 789-M
Morristown, NJ 07960

Educational Computer Magazine
3199 De La Cruz Blvd.
Santa Clara, CA 95050

Educational Technology Pub.
140 Sylvan Ave.
Englewood Cliffs, NJ 07632

Electronic Education
Suite 220
1311 Executive Center Dr.
Tallahassee, FL 32301

Electronic Learning (and *Teaching and Computers*)
Scholastic, Inc.
902 Sylvan Ave.
Box 2001
Englewood Cliffs, NJ 07632

Instructional Innovator
AECT
1126 16th St., NW
Washington, DC 20036

Scholastic, Inc. (*Electronic Learning, Teaching and Computers,* etc.)
730 Broadway
New York, NY 10003

School & Home Courseware Journal
11341 Bulldog Lane, Suite C
Fresno, CA 93710

T.H.E. Journal
P.O. Box 992
Aston, MA 01720

TLC (Teaching, Learning, Computing)
P.O. Box 9159
Brea, CA 92621

WINDOW
469 Pleasant St.
Watertown, MA 02172

PRODUCERS OF HARDWARE

Apple Computer
10260 Bandley Dr.
Cupertino, CA 94017

Atari, Inc.
1265 Borregas Ave.
Sunnyvale, CA 94086

Commodore Computer Systems
1200 Wilson Dr.
West Chester, PA 19380

Heathkit Educational Systems
Dept. 558-872
Benton Harbor, MI 49022

IBM Personal Computers
P.O. Box 1328-D
Boca Raton, FL 33432

Koala Technologies
3100 Patrick Henry Drive
Santa Clara, CA 95050

Mattel
P.O. Box TLC
Madison Heights, MI 48071

Milton Bradley Co.
Springfield, MA 01101

NEC Home Electronics
1401 Estes Ave.
Elk Grove Village, IL 60007

Radio Shack
1800 One Tandy Cntr.
Fort Worth, TX 76102

RB Robot Corportation
18301 W. 10th Ave., Suite 310
Golden, CO 80401

Sinclair Research Ltd.
50 Staniford St.
Boston, MA 02114

Software Productions
P.O. Box 21341
Columbus, OH 43221

Synetix, Inc.
10635 NE 38th Place
Kirkland, WA 98033

Timex Computer Corp.
Waterbury, CT 06720

Zenith Data Systems
1000 Milwaukee Ave.
Glenview, IL 60025

ORGANIZATIONS DEDICATED TO SOFTWARE EVALUATION

Apple Journal of Courseware Review
Apple Educational Foundation
20525 Mariani Avenue
Cupertino, CA 95014

California Library Media Consortium
    for Classroom Evaluation of
    Microcomputer Courseware
San Mateo County Office of Education
Redwood City, CA 94063

EPIE Institute
P.O. Box 620
Stonybrook, NY 11790

Far West Laboratory for Educational
  Research and Development
1855 Folsom Street
San Francisco, CA 94103

The Micro Center
Dept. M G
P.O. Box 6
Pleasantville, NY 10570

MicroSIFT
Northwest Regional Educational
  Laboratory
International Council for Computers
  in Education

% Dept. of Computer and
  Information Science
University of Oregon
Eugene, OR 97403

School Microware Reviews
Dresden Associates
Box 246
Dresden, ME 04342

Technical Education Research Centers
  (TERC)
Computer Resource Center
8 Eliot St.
Cambridge, MA 02138

ORGANIZATIONS DEDICATED TO THE EXCEPTIONAL STUDENT

Apple Computer Clearinghouse for
  the Handicapped
Prentke Romich Co.
Box 191, R.D. 2
Shreve, OH 44676

Closing the Gap
Route 2
P.O. Box 39
Henderson, MN 56044

Computeronics Gifted Child Project
925A Miccousukee Rd.
Tallahassee, FL 32303

Creative Educational Services
36 River Ave.
Monmouth Beach, NJ 07750

ERIC Clearinghouse on Handicapped
  and Gifted Children
CEC
1920 Association Drive
Reston, VA 22091

Evans-Newton, Inc.
7745 E. Redfield Rd.
Suite 100
Scottsdale, AZ 85260

Gifted Child Project
Leon County School Board
2757 West Pensacola
Tallahassee, FL 32304

HEX
Richard Barth
11523 Charlton Drive
Silver Spring, MD 20902

Instructional Systems Group
Scott Instruments Corp.
1111 Willow Springs Dr.
Denton, TX 76201

Learning Tools, Inc.
686 Massachusetts Ave.
Cambridge, MA 02139

Maryland Computer Services
2010 Rock Spring Rd.
Forest Hill, MD 21050

National Rehabilitation Information
  Center
4407 Eighth Street, NE
The Catholic University of America
Washington, DC 20017

Project CAISH
3450 Gocio Road
Sarasota, FL 33580

Project Micro-Ideas
1335 N. Waukegan Road
Glenview, IL 60025

SECTOR
Exceptional Child Center
UMC 68
Utah State University
Logan, UT 84322

SpecialNet
% NASDSE
Suite 404E
1201 16th Street, NW
Washington, DC 20036

Trace Research and Development
Center

University of Wisconsin-Madison
314 Waisman Center
1500 Highland Ave.
Madison, WI 53706

Western Center for Microcomputers in
Special Education
Suite 275
1259 El Camino Real
Menlo Park, CA 94025

Zygo Industries
P.O. Box 1008
Portland, OR 97207-1008

DATA BASES AND NETWORKS

CompuServe Information Service
5000 Arlington Centre Blvd.
Columbus, OH 43220
Communications network for
general purpose.

Dialog Information Services
3460 Hillview Avenue
Palo Alto, CA 94304
Communications network with
educational data bases.

Directory of Online Information Resources
CSG Press
11301 Rockville Pike
Kensington, MD 20895
Not a data base, but a directory to
data bases.

ERIC
Educational Resources Center
National Institute of Education
Washington, DC 20208

MicroSIFT
300 SW 6th Street
Portland, OR 97204
Clearinghouse for software.

RICE/BRS (Resources in Computer
Education/Bibliographic Retrieval
Services)
1200 Route 7
Latham, NY 12110
Data base on software for education.

The Source
Reader's Digest Educational Division
Pleasantville, NY 10570

Source Telecomputing Corporation
1616 Anderson Road
McLean, VA 22102
Communications network with
consumer services, data bases, and
electronic mail.

GENERAL ORGANIZATIONS

American Educational Research
Association (AERA)
1126 16st Street, NW
Washington, DC 20036
Includes special interest group for
CAI.

Association for Computers and the
Humanities (ACH)
Queens College
Flushing, NY 11367

Association for Computers in
Mathematics & Science Teaching
P.O. Box 4455
Austin, TX 78765

Association for Computing Machinery
(A.C.M.)
1133 Ave. of the Americas
New York, NY 10036

Association for Educational
Communications and Technology

(AECT)
1126 16th Street, NW
Washington, DC 20036

Association for Educational Data
Systems (A.E.D.S.)
1201 16th Street, NW
Washington, DC 20036

Association for the Development of
Computer-Based Instructional
Systems (ADCIS)
Western University Computer Center
Bellingham, WA 98225
Goal: To facilitate communication
between developers and consumers
of computer materials.

Boston Computer Society (BCS)
Educational Resource Exchange
Three Center Plaza
Boston, MA 02108

Computer Technology and Reading
International Reading Association
800 Barksdale Road
P.O. Box 8139
Newark, DE 19711

Computer-Using Educators (CUE)
% Don McKell
Independence High School
1775 Educational Park Drive
San Jose, CA 95113

Dataspan
% Karl Zinn
109 East Madison Street
Ann Arbor, MI 48104

EPIE Institute
P.O. Box 620
Stony Brook, NY 11790
Educational technology consumer
group.

ERIC Clearinghouse on Elementary
and Early Childhood Education
University of Illinois
College of Education
Urbana, IL 61801

ERIC Clearinghouse on Information
Resources
Syracuse University
School of Education
130 Huntington Hall
Syracuse, NY 13210

Educational Computing Consortium of
Ohio (ECCO)
4777 Farnhurst Road
Lyndhurst, OH 44124

Educational Technology Center
% Alfred Bork
University of California
Irving, CA 92717
Middle school computer materials.

Far West Laboratory
1855 Folsom Street
San Francisco, CA 94103
Information service on many aspects
of computers in education.

Human Resources Research
Organization (HumRRO)
300 North Washington Street
Alexandria, VA 22314

International Council for Computers
in Education (ICCE)
Computer Center
East Oregon State College
LaGrande, OR 97850
Educational users group.

Microcomputer Resource Center
Teachers College
Columbia University
New York, NY 10027

Minnesota Educational Computing
Consortium (MECC)
2520 Broadway Drive
St. Paul, MN 55113

National Audio-Visual Association
(NAVA)
3150 Spring Street
Fairfax, VA 22031

National Council for the Social Studies
(NCSS)
3501 Newark Street, NW
Washington, DC 20016

National Council of Teachers of
English
Dr. Bernard O'Donnell
111 Kenyon Road
Urbana, IL 61801

National Council of Teachers of
Mathematics (NCTM)
1906 Association Drive
Reston, VA 22091

National Logo Exchange
P.O. Box 5341
Charlottesville, VA 22905
Information and newsletters on the
educational use of Logo.

National Science Teachers Association
(NSTA)
1742 Connecticut Avenue, NW
Washington, DC 20009

Softswap
San Mateo County Office of Education
333 Main Street
Redwood City, CA 94063
Software exchange; "public domain"
software.

Technical Education Research Center
(TERC)
3 Eliot Street
Cambridge, MA 02138
Technical educators users group.

Young People's Logo Association
(YPLA)
P.O. Box 855067
Richardson, TX 75085
Information and newsletter on
Logo.

GLOSSARY

Algorithm A step-by-step procedure or strategy for solving a problem. In elementary mathematics, children apply algorithms to compute sums, differences, products, and so on. They also learn algorithms for alphabetizing words. Many types of algorithms can be designed for computers to carry out.

Alphanumeric Data consisting of any letter of the alphabet, numeral, or character.

Arithmetic-Logic Unit That section of the computer that performs all the arithmetic and logical operations.

Artificial Intelligence The study of the possibilities and implications of developing computer systems that can perform "intelligent" tasks so that they appear to "think" like humans. This might involve playing games, interacting in a human language, or the like.

Assembly Language An intermediary computer language that uses mnemonics (memory aides) to write machine language instructions in a more understandable form.

Authoring Languages High-level computer languages that are designed for use by those who wish to write CAI materials (e.g., teachers or personnel trainers). See CAI, PILOT.

BASIC (Beginner's All-purpose Symbolic Instruction Code) A popular, high-level computer language, widely available on most inexpensive microcomputers. While it is often the first language taught to children, there are other languages (see Logo) that might be more appropriate.

Binary A system based on only two possibilities. Computers can store information only as "off" (the absence of an electrical voltage) or "on" (the presence of electricity). So patterns of electrical current represent binary codes in which "off" represents 0 (zero) and "on" represents 1 (one). A group of these, in turn, represent other characters, like letters (see byte). It should be noted that it is not necessary to understand the binary number system in order to use computers with understanding.

Bit (Binary digIT) Either of the numerals 0 or 1, the only numbers in the binary number system. Computers use these two digits to represent all data (see binary).

Bug An error in a computer program.

Byte A group of consecutive bits, often 6, 8, or 16, that are treated as a single unit of information by the computer. A byte, then, represents one character such as a letter, numeral, punctuation mark, special character (e.g., > or }), or function (e.g., a carriage return).

CAI (computer-assisted instruction) A method of teaching that uses a computer to present instructional materials. Students interact with the computer in a learning situation that might involve drill and practice, tutorials, simulations, or the like. Sometimes referred to as CAL (computer-assisted learning).

Cathode Ray Tube (CRT) The picture tube of a television set and the display screen for most microcomputers. A cathode ray (an electron beam) strikes a phosphorescent screen to display information such as text or graphics. Also called a monitor, display, or video screen.

CBI (computer-based instruction) The use of computers in education, either to teach (see CAI) or to help manage instruction (see CMI).

Central Processing Unit (CPU) The "brains" of the computer, it consists of the arithmetic-logic unit and the control unit (see arithmetic-logic unit, control unit).

Character A letter, numeral, punctuation mark, or any other symbol used to represent information (see also byte). A computer stores and manipulates characters. The size of a computer's memory is designated as the number of characters it can store (see K).

Chip See microprocessor.

CMI (computer-managed instruction) Use

of computers in the management of instruction (as opposed to CAI programs that are designed to teach students). For example, computers might keep records, test results, and progress reports, generate materials, or test students and prescribe appropriate work.

Command An instruction given to a computer.

Computer A device capable of accepting information, processing that information by performing prescribed arithmetical and logical operations upon it, and producing the results of this processing. A general purpose tool.

Computer-Assisted Instruction *See* CAI.

Computer Language Instructions to a computer in a form it can "understand" (i.e., carry out). "High-level" languages contain English-like words and are easier to understand.

Computer Literacy Knowledge of the technology, capabilities, applications (uses and abuses), limitations, and impact of computers. Often separated into two levels, computer awareness and full working knowledge.

Computer-Managed Instruction *See* CMI.

Computer System *See* system.

Control Unit One of the two main components of the central processing unit, the control unit translates computer programs, directs the sequence of operations, and initiates correct commands to the computer circuits. It directs the step-by-step operation of the whole computer system.

Courseware Software (computer programs) designed specifically for classroom use (*see* software).

CPI Characters per Inch.

CPU *See* central processing unit.

CRT *See* cathode ray tube.

Cursor A symbol, often blinking, that indicates where the next character will be displayed on the CRT. Often, it can be moved around on the CRT to refer to or identify a location.

Data Any information to be processed by a computer program (as opposed to programs that are instructions that tell the computer how to manipulate or process the data).

Data Bank A large collection of data. A large data bank may hold as much information as a large library. Often many people use common data banks.

Data-Base Management System Computer programs designed to store, maintain, and retrieve information (*see also* data bank).

Debugging Searching for and correcting errors in computer programs.

Disk A device used to store magnetic information on a circular plate.

Disk Drive A mechanical device that can store information on, and retrieve information from, a disk or diskette. This information may consist of data or programs.

Disk Operating System *See* DOS.

Disk (also diskette or floppy disk) Similar to the disk, but smaller and more flexible, with less storage density. Along with cassette tape, the most common secondary storage device for microcomputers. The diskette permits more rapid retrieval of information. Permanently stored in a square jacket for protection, it resembles a phonograph record (especially the thin, flexible ones).

Documentation Materials designed to aid the user of a computer program. It may include written directions and descriptions, examples, flowcharts, listings of the program, sample outputs, and so on.

DOS (disk operating system) A language or program that operates the disk system, keeps track of storing and retrieving information, creates and opens files, copies files, and generally lets the computer know what devices are available and how to use them. It allows communication between the computer and the software and/or user.

Dot Matrix A technique of printing characters (text) or graphics using small dots.

File A collection of information that is treated as a unit; may be a data file (information to be processed by a program) or a program file (a computer program).

Floppy Disk *See* disk.

Format The way in which text is visually organized.

Graphics Any shapes, dots, lines, and colors that are drawn using a computer. May involve pictures, graphs, maps, diagrams, or the like.

Hard Copy Printout on paper of data, programs, or solutions.

Hardware The physical equipment of a computer system, consisting of electrical, electronic, magnetic, and mechanical devices. For example, keyboards, CRTs, printers, the central processing unit, circuit boards, and primary storage.

Heuristic Describes an exploratory method of problem solving with repeated evaluations of progress toward the goal; for example, guided trial and error. (Contrast with algorithm.)

High-Level Language *See* computer language.

High Resolution The ability of a cathode

ray tube (display screen) to display highly detailed graphics such as pictures.

Information Processing Describes all the operations performed by a computer. The handling of information according to rules of procedure to accomplish classifying, recording, retrieving, calculating, or the like.

Information Retrieval The storage and recall of large amounts of information. (*See also* data bank.)

Input Data and programs to be processed by the computer. Also the process of transferring data from an external source to an internal storage medium.

Input/Output Devices (I/O devices) The parts of a computer system that allow people to communicate with the central processing unit. Input devices insert data to be processed into the computer; for example, keyboards or card readers. Output devices include CRTs, printers, or card punchers.

Instructions Symbols used to communicate with the computer that constitute orders or directions. Computer programs.

Interface An electronic link between components of a computer system that allow communication between these components and between the mechanical system and humans.

I/O Devices *See* input/output devices.

K (kilobyte) Used to represent the number 1,024 (2 raised to the tenth power). The letter originates from the prefix "kilo" (1,000). The size of a computer's memory is often stated in terms of a number of K of bytes of information; for example, 64K.

Keyboard An electric typewriterlike input device for typing information into a computer. Many microcomputers combine the central processing unit and the keyboard into one unit.

Language *See* computer language.

Letter Quality Professional quality printing from a formed character printer.

Light Pen Used to select numbers, letters, or the like on a CRT.

List Logo's way of storing information. A list is an ordered sequence of words and/or other lists. Because lists can consist of other lists, complicated structures can be created.

Logo A computer language designed by Seymour Papert at M.I.T. to be used by grade school children. Includes "turtle graphics." Logo can be easily extended. It is said to encourage problem solving by children.

Machine Language The language or instructions that a computer is constructed to carry out; usually binary code. The only language the computer can "understand" and respond to directly without first translating the input.

Mainframe A large computer system with powerful capabilities. Some schools tie into a university's mainframe computer through telephone lines to implement CAI programs.

Memory A computer's storage. Usually, it involves primary storage for rapid access to a limited amount of data and secondary storage for larger amounts of data. (*See* primary storage, secondary storage.)

Menu A list of choices exhibited in a computer program to guide the user.

Microcomputer The smallest self-contained computer system with a central processing unit consisting of a single chip or a small number of chips. Designed for single users.

Microprocessor (chip) A type of integrated circuit that contains microscopic switches etched into a small piece of silicon. These switches record the presence or absence of electrical current (see binary). It is the computing equivalent of thousands of transistors and other electronic components and carries out the processing of the data. A handful of chips, each small enough to rest on a fingertip, contain most of the circuitry for a microcomputer.

Microworld In Logo, a well-defined, focused learning environment in which a child can explore and discover. Similar in some respects to a well-designed learning center.

Modem (MOdulator/DEModulator) A device that allows information to pass from one computer to another over telephone lines.

Monitor *See* cathode ray tube. Also refers to a program that supervises the sequencing of operations by the computer.

Minicomputer A medium-sized computer design for a variety of uses, many languages, and several input/output terminals.

Network Communication lines that connect various computer components together for large-scale computing and information sharing. A computer system consisting of a central computer and a number of users.

Output Information that is reported by a computer. Also a device that allows the computer to report to humans (*see* input/output devices).

Pascal A high-level computer language that is becoming increasingly popular for use with older people. It is more structured than is BASIC, so programs are often more readable and clearly organized. It allows the user to extend the language by defining new procedures.

Peripheral Devices Accessories and/or extra equipment that are added to the computer system to increase its capabilities. For example, game paddles, voice synthesizers, any input/output devices, and printers.

Personal Computer *See* microcomputer.

PILOT A computer language designed for use by those who wish to write CAI materials (e.g., teachers or those in business responsible for the training of personnel).

Primary Storage Information handling devices that hold data and programs in memory during a program's execution. See RAM, ROM.

Primitive A built-in Logo procedure, such as FORWARD or BUTLAST.

Printer An output device for printing data onto paper.

Procedure A step-by-step set of instructions that tells how to do something. The building block of a Logo program.

Procedural Language High-level programming language designed for the efficient expression of procedures that can be used to solve wide classes of problems.

Program Instructions used to direct a computer to perform a specific set of operations so as to accomplish a given task. A plan for solving a problem written in a computer language so that it is "understood" by the computer. *See also* software.

Programmer A person who prepares a set of instructions (software) for a computer.

Prosthetic An artificial device used as a replacement for a missing part of the body.

RAM (random access memory) A section of the primary memory of microcomputers. RAM chips store programs and data input from the keyboard or from secondary storage. It is called random access because it permits direct communication with any location in memory, and the time required is independent of the location of the last bit of information that was stored or retrieved. The location then can have information read from it or written into it. RAM can be used over and over again, but when the system is turned off the data are lost. (Compare with ROM.)

ROM (read only memory) A section of the primary memory for microcomputers. Retains certain information indefinitely (i.e., does not lose data when the system is turned off). Used to store programs that do not change such as a BASIC language interpreter or disk operating system. (Compare with RAM.)

Secondary Storage A peripheral device used to store computerized data. Examples include magnetic disks or magnetic tapes and reels.

Simulation A representation of "real-life" physical conditions or situations through models. A mathematical model is used that gives the effect of a copy of a real action. Also, the use of such models to learn about the situations, especially when actual participation would be impractical or dangerous (e.g., flight simulation, selling products, a prehistoric ecology).

Software Computer programs that are required to enable computers to process information and solve problems. Along with hardware, these constitute the computer system. Although it usually refers to professionally written programs, it sometimes is used to name any computer program. Examples include language translators that allow the use of BASIC, Logo, PILOT, Pascal, and so on. Another type consists of CAI or CMI programs. A good library of computer software is necessary for worthwhile educational use of microcomputers.

Storage *See* memory.

Structured Programming A technique for designing and writing computer programs in which the program is constructed in independent segments arranged in a hierarchy, using a minimum number of branches and statement types so as to produce better organized, more readable programs.

Syntax In computing, this refers to the structure of instructions within a computer program; a syntax error is a mistake in programming procedure, such as a spelling error in a command word, or the omission of a needed number or space.

System A computer and other electronic equipment, along with computer programs (software), which work together to input, process, and output data.

Turtle A computer-controlled robot that can move and draw pictures. Also, a triangular graphic representation of such a robot.

Variable Something that may have several values and that can alter the outcome of a program.

Video Display A view or display of data or graphics on a CRT (TV screen). Other displays do not use a CRT (e.g., plasma displays or LEDs).

Word Processing Computerized typing and composing. Allows the user to list, repeat, edit, store, and print text. It can be used to rearrange words, sentences, paragraphs, and larger sections of text. It may include a dictionary that can check for misspelling.

Write Protected A term that indicates that information cannot be written onto or erased from a disk. Involves an adhesive tab on the jacket of the disk.

REFERENCES

Abelson, H. (1982). *Logo For the Apple II.* Peterborough, NH: BYTE/McGraw-Hill.

Abelson, H., & Goldenberg, P. (1977). *Teacher's guide for computational models of animal behavior.* Cambridge, MA: MIT A. I. Laboratory.

Aeschleman, S., & Tawney, J. (1978). Interacting: A computer-based telecommunications system for educating severely handicapped preschoolers in their homes. *Educational Technology, 18*(10), 30–35.

Alderman, D. L., Swinton, S. S., & Braswell, J. S. (1979). Assessing basic arithmetic skills and understanding across curricula: Computer-assisted instruction and compensatory education. *Journal of Children's Mathematical Behavior, 2,* 3–28.

Anderson, R., & Klassen, D. (1981). A conceptual framework for developing computer literacy instruction. *AEDS Journal, 14,* 128–150.

Asimov, I. (1976). The fun they had. In *The best of Isaac Asimov.* Greenwich, CT: Fawcett.

Atkinson, R. C., & Fletcher, J. D. (1972). Teaching children to read with a computer. *The Reading Teacher, 25,* 319–327.

Badiali, B. J. (1982, September/October). Micros make time for readability. *Educational Computer Magazine,* pp. 26–27.

Baker, F. B (1971). Computer-based instruction management systems: A first look. *Review of Educational Research, 41,* 51–70.

Baker, F. B. (1978). *Computer managed instruction: Theory and practice.* Englewood Cliffs, NJ: Educational Technology Pub.

Baker, F. B. (1981). Computer-managed instruction: A context for computer-based instruction. In H. F. O'Neil, Jr. (Ed.), *Computer-based instruction: A state-of-the-art assessment.* New York: Academic Press.

Baker, E. L., Herman, J. L., & Yeh, J. P. (1981). Fun and games: Their contribution to basic skills instruction in elementary school. *American Educational Research Journal, 18,* 83–92.

Ball, M. (1972). *What is a computer.* Boston: Houghton Mifflin.

Ball, M., & Charp, S. (1978). *Be a computer literate.* Morristown, NJ: Creative Computing Press.

Bamberger, J. (1982). Logo music. *Byte, 7*(8), 325, 328.

Bamberger, J. (1983). The computer as sandcastle. In *Chameleon in the classroom: Developing roles for computers* (Tech. Rep. No. 22) (pp. 34–39). New York: Bank Street College of Education, Center for Children and Technology.

Barnes, B. J., and Hill, S. (1983). Should young children work with microcomputers—Logo before Lego? *The Computing Teacher, 10*(9), 11–14.

Barrett, B. K., & Hannafin, M. J. (1982). Computer in educational management: Merging accountability with technology. *Educational Technology, 22*(3), 9–12.

Beardon, D., Martin, K., & Muller, J. (1983). *The turtle's sourcebook.* Reston, VA: Reston Publishing Co.

Behr, M. J., & Wheeler, M. M. (1981). The calculator for concept formation: A clinical status study. *Journal for Research in Mathematics Education, 12,* 323–338.

Berger, M. (1981). *Computer in your life.* New York: Thomas Y. Crowell.

Berthold, H. C., & Sachs, R. H. (1974). Education of the minimally brain damaged child by computer and by teacher. *Programmed Learning and Educational Technology, 11*(3), 121–124.

Billings, K. (1983). Research on school computing. In M. T. Grady & J. D. Gawronski (Eds.). *Computers in curriculum and instruction* (pp. 12–18). Alexandria, VA: Association for Supervision and Curriculum Development.

Bitter, G. G. (1982, September). The road to computer literacy: A scope and sequence model. *Electronic Learning,* pp. 60–63.

Bitter, G., & Watson, N. R. (1983). *Apple Logo primer.* Reston, VA: Reston Publishing Co.

Blanchard, J. S. (1980). Computer-assisted instruction in today's reading classrooms. *Journal of Reading, 23,* 430–434.

Boudrot, T. E. (1983, February). The magical typewriter: A step-by-step guide for choosing and using a word processing program in your classroom. *Electronic Learning,* pp. 84–87.

Bozeman, W. C. (1978). Human factors considerations in the design of systems of computer managed instruction. *AEDS Journal, 11,* 89–96.

Bozeman, W. C. (1979). Computer-managed instruction: State of the art. *AEDS Journal, 12,* 117–137.

Bracey, G. (1982, November/December). What the research shows. *Electronic Learning,* pp. 51–54.

Braude, M. (1969). *Larry learns about computers.* Minneapolis, MN: T. S. Dennison.

Brebner, A., Hallworth, H. J. McIntosh, E., & Wontner, C. (1980). *Teaching elementary reading by CMI and CAI.* Columbus, OH: ERIC. (ERIC Document Reproduction Service No. ED 198 793).

Brown, N. P. (1982). CAMEO: Computer-assisted management of educational objectives. *Exceptional Children, 49*(2), 151–153.

Brudner, H. J. (1982). Light on: Microcomputers, special education, and CMI. *Educational Technology, 22*(7), 25–26.

Burns, P. K., & Bozeman, W. C. (1981). Computer-assisted instruction and mathematics achievement: Is there a relationship? *Educational Technology, 21,* 32–39.

Burrowes, S. (1983). Some Logo drawing ideas. *The Computing Teacher, 10*(8), 64–65.

Cartwright, G. F., & Derevensky, J. L. (1976). An attitudinal research study of computer-assisted testing as a learning method. *Psychology in the Schools, 13,* 317–321.

Cavin, C. S. (1982). Microcomputer generation of interactive quizzes. *Educational Technology, 22*(2), 31–32.

Center for Social Organization of Schools (1983a, April). *School uses of microcomputers: Reports from a national survey* (Issue No. 1). Baltimore, MD: Johns Hopkins University.

Center for Social Organization of Schools (1983b, June). *School uses of microcomputers: Reports from a national survey* (Issue No. 2). Baltimore, MD: John Hopkins University.

Chambers, J. A., & Sprecher, J. W. (1980). Computer assisted instruction: Current trends and critical issues. *Communications of the ACM, 23,* 332–342.

Chanoine, J. R. (1977). Learning of elementary students in an individualized mathematics program with a computer assisted management system. *Dissertation Abstracts International, 38,* 2626A.

"Citizens Committee" attacks use of computers to teach basic skills. (1982). *Educational Technology, 22*(6), 7–9.

Cleary, A., Mayes, T., & Packham, D. (1976). *Educational technology: Implications for early and special education.* London: John Wiley & Sons.

Clement, F. J. (1981). Affective considerations in computer-based education. *Educational Technology, 21,* 28–32.

Clements, D. H. (1983). Supporting young children's Logo programming. *The Computing Teacher, 11*(5), 24–30.

Clements, D. H., & Gullo, D. F. (in press). Effects of computer programming on young children's cognition. *Journal of Educational Psychology.*

Collins, A. (n.d.). *Teaching reading and writing with personal computers.* Cambridge, MA: Bolt Beranek and Newman.

Crouse, D. B. (1981). The computerized gradebook as a component of a computer-managed curriculum. *Educational Technology, 21*(5), 16–20.

Daiute, C. (1982, March/April). Word processing. Can it make good writers better? *Electronic Learning,* pp. 29–31.

D'Angelo, J., & Overall, T. (1982). Learning with Logo. In C. Hernandex-Logan & M. Lewis (Eds.), *Computer support for education.* Palo Alto, CA: R & E Research Associates.

Dayton, D. K. (1981). Computer-assisted graphics. *Instructional Innovator, 26,* 16–18.

DeVault, M. V. (1981). Computers. In E. Fennema (Ed.), *Mathematics education research: Implications for the 80's.* Alexandria, VA: ASCD, 1981.

Doerr, C. (1979). *Microcomputers and the 3 R's.* Rochelle Park, NJ: Hayden.

Doorly, Ann. (1980). Microcomputers for gifted microtots. *G/C/T, 14,* 62–64.

du Boulay, B., O'Shea, T., & Monk, J. (1981). The black box inside the glass box: Presenting computing concepts to novices. *International Journal of Man-Machine Studies, 14,* 237–249.

Durkin, D. (1980). *Teaching young children to read.* Boston: Allyn and Bacon.

Dwyer, T. (1980). Heuristic strategies for using computers to enrich education. In R. Taylor (Ed.), *The computer in the school: Tutor, tool, tutee* (pp. 87–103). New York: Teachers College Press.

Edwards, J., Norton, S., Taylor, S., Weiss, M., & Dusseldorp, R. (1975). How effective is CAI? A review of the research. *Educational Leadership, 33,* 147–153.

Eisenberg, B. (1977, November/December). Final exams—Let the computer write them. *Creative Computing,* 103–106.

Ellis, J. A. (1978). A comparative evaluation of computer-managed instruction and instructor-managed instruction. *Proceedings of the Association for the Development of Computer-Based Instructional Systems.*

Embry, D. (1983, March-April). Music CAI. *Educational Computer Magazine,* pp. 30–31.

Ethelberg-Laursen, J. (1978). An experiment in Danish schools. *Mathematics Teaching, 82,* 24–25.

Evans, C. (1979). *The micro millennium.* New York: Viking Press.

Fiske, Edward B. (1982, April 18). Grammar school use of computers isn't elementary. *Buffalo Courier-Express,* pp. C-1, C-4.

Fletcher, J. D., Suppes, P., & Jamison, D. T. (1972). *A note on the effectiveness of computer-assisted instruction.* Stanford, CA: Stanford University. (ERIC Document Reproduction Service No. ED 071 450).

Forman, D. (1982, January). Search of the literature. *The Computing Teacher,* pp. 37–51.

Fowler, W. (1980). *Infant and Child Care: A Guide to Education in Group Settings.* Boston: Allyn and Bacon.

Fox, B., & Wilson, M. (1982). *Microcomputer administered receptive language testing: A new alternative.* Manuscript submitted for publication.

Frase, L. T., Macdonald, N. H., Gingrich, P. S., Keenan, S. A., & Collymore, J. L. (1981, November). Computer aids for text assessment and writing instruction. *National Society for Performance and Instruction,* pp. 21–24.

Frates, J., & Moldrup, W. (1980). *Introduction to the computer: An integrative approach.* Englewood Cliffs, NJ: Prentice-Hall.

Fricke, J. (1976). *CAI in a school for the deaf: Expeded results and a serendipity or two.* Scranton, PA: Scranton State School for the Deaf.

Frost, J. L., and J. B. Kissinger. (1976). *The young child and the educative process.* New York: Holt, Rinehart and Winston.

Gelman, R., & Gallistel, C. R. (1978). *The child's understanding of number.* Cambridge, MA: Harvard University Press.

Geoffrion, L. D., & Goldenberg, E. P. (1981). Computer-based exploratory learning systems for communication-handicapped children. *Journal of Special Education, 15*(3), 325–331.

Goldenberg, E. P. (1979). *Special technology for special children.* Baltimore, MD: University Park Press.

Goldreich, G., & Goldreich, E. (1979). *What can she be? A computer scientist.* New York: Lothrop.

Goldstein, I., & Miller, M. (1976). *AI based personal learning environments: Directions for long term research.* AI Memo 384. Cambridge, MA: MIT Artificial Intelligence Laboratory.

Goodman, D., & Schwab, S. (1980, April). Computerized testing for readability. *Creative Computing.*

Gorman, H. (1982). The Lamplighter Project. *Byte, 7*(8), 331–332.

Graves, D. (1979). Research update: What children show us about revision. *Language Arts, 56*(3), 312–319.

Graves, D. (1983). *Writing: Teachers & children at work.* Exeter, NH: Heinemann Educational Books.

Grimes, L. (1981, November). Computers are for kids: Designing software programs to avoid problems of learning. *Teaching Exceptional Children,* pp. 49–53.

Hansgen, R. (1982). *The consequences of a technological society: The tyranny of expertise.* Technology Concentration Papers. Toronto: National Council of Teachers of Mathematics.

Harris, L. (1982, May/June). Which way did it go? *Classroom Computer News,* pp. 35–36.

Hart, D. G. (1981/1982). Computer managed instruction: An approach. *International Journal of Instructional Media, 9*(1), 11–12.

Hartley, S. S. (1978). Meta-analysis of the effects of individually paced instruction in mathematics. *Dissertation Abstracts International,* 38, 4003A. (University Microfilms No. 77–29, 926).

Hasselbring, T., & Owens, S. (1983, Summer). Microcomputer-based analysis of spelling errors. *Computers, Reading and Language Arts, 1*(1), 26–31.

Hastings, D. (1980, April). Pre-school math. *Microcomputing,* pp. 77–78.

Haugo, J. E. (1981). Management applications of the microcomputer: Promises and pitfalls. *AEDS Journal, 14,* 182–188.

Hawkins, J. (1983). Learning Logo together: The social context. In *Chameleon in the classroom: Developing roles for computers* (Tech. Rep. No. 22) (pp. 40–49). New York: Bank Street College of Education, Center for Children and Technology.

Hedden, R. (1981, November). Calling all teachers. *Microcomputing,* pp. 306–310.

Hedges, W. D. (1980–81). Teaching first graders how a computer can sort. *The Computing Teacher, 8*(5), 24–25.

Heller, R. S., & Martin, C. D. (1982). *Bits 'n bytes about computing: A computer literacy primer.* Rockville, MD: Computer Science Press.

Hines, S. (1983, July/August). Computer programming abilities of five-year-old children. *Educational Computer,* pp. 10–12.

Hofstetter, F. T. (1979, April). Microelectronics and music education. *Music Educator's Journal,* pp. 39–45.

Hofstetter, F. T. (1983). Computers in music education: The GUIDO system. In M. Grady & J. Gawronski (Eds.), *Computers in* curriculum and instruction. Alexandria, VA: Association for Supervision and Curriculum Development.

Hollingsworth, S. (1982). *The effects of CAI and PT as supplements to the basal reading program.* Missoula, MT: University of Montana.

Horack, V. M. (1981). A meta-analysis of research findings on individualized instruction in mathematics. *Journal of Educational Research, 74,* 249–253.

Horn, C., & Collins, C. (1983). *COM-LIT: Computer literacy for kids.* Austin TX: Sterling Swift.

Hughes, K. (1981, November). Adapting audio/video games for handicapped learners: Part 1. *Teaching Exceptional Children,* pp. 80–86.

Humphrey, M. M. (1982, April). "All the scientists in the world smushed into one": What kids think about computers. *Creative Computing,* pp. 96–98.

Hungate, H. (1982, January). Computers in the kindergarten. *The Computing Teacher,* pp. 15–18.

Hunter, B. (1981–82). Computer literacy in grades K-8. *Journal of Educational Technology Systems, 10*(1), 59–66.

Hunter, B. (1984). *My students use computers: Computer literacy in the K-8 curriculum.* Reston, VA: Reston Publishing Company.

Hunter, D. (1983, August). Robots come home. *Softalk,* pp. 144–157.

Ingram, J. A. (1981, September). Tame that blackboard jungle. *Microcomputing,* pp. 92–91.

Jamison, D., Suppes, P., & Wells, S. (1974). The effectiveness of alternative instructional media: A survey. *Review of Educational Research, 44,* 1–67.

Jernstedt, G. C. (1983). Computer enhanced collaborative learning: A new technology for education. *T.H.E. Journal, 10*(7), 96–101.

Johnson, D. (1981). A grade assignment program—AGAP. *The Computing Teacher, 9*(2), pp. 29–34.

Joiner, L., Vensel, G., Ross, J., & Silverstein, B. (1982). *Microcomputers in education: a nontechnical guide to instructional and school management applications.* Holmes Beach, FL: Learning Publications.

Jones, B. J. (1983). Computer uses in the arts and humanities. In M. Grady & J. Gawronski (Eds.), *Computers in curriculum and instruction.* Alexandria, VA: Association for Supervision and Curriculum Development.

Judd, D. H. (1981). Avoid readability formula drudgery: Use your school's microcomputer. *Reading Teacher, 35,* 7–9.

Kearsley, G., Hunter, B., & Seidel, R. J. (1983). Two decades of computer based instruction projects: What have we learned. *T.H.E. Journal, 10*(4), 88–96.

Keller, J., & Shanahan, D. (1983). Robots in the kindergarten. *The Computing Teacher, 10*(9), 66–67.

Kieren, T. E. (1973). *The use of computers in mathematics education resource series: Research on computers in mathematics education.* Columbus, OH: ERIC. (ERIC Document Reproduction Service No. ED 077 734).

Kimmel, S. (1981, October). Programs for preschoolers: Starting out young. *Creative Computing,* pp. 44–46; 50–51.

Klahr, D., & Robinson, M. (1981). Formal assessment of problem-solving and planning processes in preschool children. *Cognitive Psychology, 13,* 113–148.

Kleiman, G., & Humphrey, M. (1982, May). Learning with computers. *Compute!,* pp. 105–108.

Kleiman, G., Humphrey, M., & Lindsay, P. (1983). Microcomputers and hyperactive children. In D. Harper & J. Stewart (Eds.). *Run: Computer Education.* Monterey, CA: Brooks/Cole.

Knight, C. W. 2nd, & Dunkleberger, G. E. (1977). The influence of computer-managed self-paced instruction on science attitudes of students. *Journal of Research in Science Teaching, 14,* 551–555.

Koelewyn, A. C. (1983). TESTSCORER: A computer program for grading tests. *Educational Technology, 23*(5), 31.

Kolstad, R., & Lidtke, D. (1983). Gifted and talented. In H. Dennis & J. Stewart (Eds.), *Run: Computer Education* (pp. 222–227). Monterey, CA: Brooks/Cole.

Kraus, W. H. (1981). Using a computer game to reinforce skills in addition basic facts in second grade. *Journal for Research in Mathematics Education, 12,* 152–155.

Kuchinskas, G. (1983, Summer). 22 ways to use a microcomputer in reading and language arts classes. *Computer, Reading and Language Arts, 1*(1), 11–16.

Lally, M. (1981). Computer-assisted teaching of sight-word recognition for mentally retarded school children. *American Journal of Mental Deficiency, 85,* 383–388.

Lally, M., & Macleod, I. (1982). Development of skills through computers: Achieving an effective, enjoyable learning environment. *Impact of Science on Society, 32,* 449–459.

Lally, M., & Macleod, I. (1983). Computer-based handwriting exercises: From laboratory to classroom. In *The Proceedings of the Second Educational Computing Conference,*

City University, London, April 1983. Paper #18, 12 pp.

Larsen, S. G. (1982). *Computers for Kids* [different versions available for different computers]. Morristown, NJ: Creative Computing Press.

Lavin, R., & Sanders, J. (1983, April). *Longitudinal evaluation of the C/A/I Computer Assisted Instruction Title 1 Project: 1979–82.* Chelmsford, MA: Merrimack Education Center.

Lawrence, J., & Lee, R. E. (1961). *Inherit the Wind.* London: English Theatre Guild Ltd.

Lecarme, O., & Lewis, R. (Eds.). (1975). *Computers in Education: Proceedings of the IFIP 2nd World Conference.* New York: American Elsevier Publishing Company.

Leeper, S. H., Dales, R. J., Skipper, D. S., and Witherspoon, R. L. (1974). *Good Schools for Young Children.* New York: Macmillan.

Leonard, G. (1968). *Education and ecstasy.* New York: Delacorte Press.

Lesgold, A. M. (1983). A rationale for computer-based reading instruction. In A. C. Wilkinson (Ed.), *Classroom computers and cognitive science* (pp. 167–181). New York: Academic Press.

Lester, F. K. (1983). Trends and issues in mathematical problem-solving research. In R. Lesh & M. Landau (Eds.), *Acquisition of mathematics concepts and processes.* New York: Academic Press.

Letourneau, E. G. (1981, September). Are video terminals safe? *Canadian Medical Association Journal, 125,* 533–534.

Levin, J. A. (1982a). Microcomputer communication networks for education. *The Quarterly Newsletter of the Laboratory of Comparative Human Cognition, 4*(2).

Levin, J. A. (1982b). Microcomputers as interactive communication media: An interactive text interpreter. *The Quarterly Newsletter of the Laboratory of Comparative Human Cognition, 4*(2).

Lindahl, R. (1983, October). Electronic spreadsheets: What they are; what they can do. *Electronic Learning,* pp. 44–50.

Lipson, J. I. (1976, January). Hidden strengths of conventional instruction. *Arithmetic Teacher, 27*(5), 11–15.

Long, S. M. (1982). The dawning of the computer age: An interview with Ronald Palamara. *Phi Delta Kappan, 63,* 311–313.

Luehrmann, A. (1980, July). Computer illiteracy—A national crisis and a solution for it. *Byte,* pp. 98; 101–102.

Luehrmann, A. (1982a, May/June). Computer literacy: What it is, why it's important. *Electronic Learning,* pp. 20; 22.

Luehrmann, A. (1982b). Don't feel bad about teaching BASIC. *Electronic Learning, 2*(1), 23–24.

Lutz, J. E., & Taylor, P. A. (1981). A computerized home-based curriculum for high-risk preschoolers. *AEDS Journal, 15,* 1–9.

Macleod, I., & Overheu, D. (1977). Computer aided assessment and development of basic skills. *Exceptional Children, 24,* 18–35.

Madgidson, E. M. (1978). Issue overview: Trends in computer assisted instruction. *Educational Technology, 18*(4), 5–8.

Malone, T. W. (1980). What make things fun to learn? A study of intrinsically motivating computer games. *Dissertation Abstracts International, 41,* 1955B. (University Microfilms No. 8024707).

Martin, J. H. (1981). On reading, writing, and computers. *Educational Leadership, 39,* 60–64.

Martin, K. (1981). The learning machines. *Arithmetic Teacher, 29,* 41–43.

Mayer, R. E. (1979). *A psychology of learning BASIC computer programming: Transactions, prestatements, and chunks.* Series in Learning and Cognition Technical Report No. 79-2. Santa Barbara, CA: Department of Psychology, University of California.

Mayer, R. E. (1980). *Contributions of cognitive science and related research on learning to the design of computer literacy curricula.* Report No. 81-1. Series in learning and cognition. Santa Barbara, CA: Department of Psychology, University of California. (ERIC Document Reproduction Service No. ED 207 551).

Mayer, R. E. (1981). The psychology of how novices learn computer programming. *Computing Surveys, 13*(1), pp. 121–141.

McIaac, D. N., & Baker, F. B. (1981). Computer-managed instruction system implementation on a microcomputer. *Educational Technology, 22*(10), 40–46.

McKinley, R. L., & Reckase, M. D. (1980). Computer applications to ability testing. *AEDS Journal, 13,* 193–203.

Meichenbaum, D. (1977). *Cognitive-behavior modification: An integrative approach.* New York: Plenum Press.

Michaels, D. (1968). *The unprepared society.* New York: Basic Books.

Milner, S. (1973, February). *The effects of computer programming on performance in mathematics.* Paper presented at the annual meeting of the American Education Research Association, New Orleans, Louisiana. (ERIC Document Reproduction Service No. ED 076 391).

Minsky, M. (1970). Form and content in computer science. *Journal of the Association for Computing Machinery, 17,* 197–215.

Moe, A. (1980). Analyzing text with computers. *Educational Technology, 20*(7), 29–31.

Moffett, J., & Wagner, B. J. (1983). *Student-centered language arts and reading: K-13: A handbook for teachers* (3rd ed.). Boston: Houghton Mifflin.

Molnar, A. R. (1978). The next great crisis in American education: Computer literacy. *AEDS Journal, 12,* 11–20.

Molnar, A. R. (1981). The coming of computer literacy: Are we prepared for it? *Educational Technology, 21*(1), 26–28.

Morgan, C. (1982, August). Editorial. *Byte,* pp.

Moser, J. M., & Carpenter, T. P. (1982). *Using the microcomputer to teach problem-solving skills: Program development and initial pilot study* (Working Paper No. 328). Madison, WI: University of Wisconsin—Madison, Wisconsin Center for Education Research.

Moursund, D. (1976, November/December). What is computer literacy? *Creative Computing,* pp. 2, 6, 55.

Muller, B., & Kovacs, D. (1983, Spring). An electronic mailbox. *Teaching and Computers,* pp. 38–41.

National Council of Teachers of Mathematics. (1980). *An agenda for action: Recommendations for school mathematics in the 1980's.* Reston, VA: National Council of Teachers of Mathematics.

Nelson, T. (1981, November). Mail chauvinism: The magicians, the snark, and the camel. *Creative Computing, 7*(11), 128, 130, 134–135, 138, 140, 142, 144, 150, 156.

Nimnicht, G., O. McAfee, & J. Meier. *The new nursery school.* New York: General Learning Corporation, 1969.

O'Brian, L. (1978). *Computers—A first look.* New York: Franklin Watts.

O'Donnell, H. (1982a). Computer literacy, part I: An overview. *Reading Teacher, 35,* 490–494.

O'Donnell, H. (1982b). Computer literacy, part II: Classroom applications. *Reading Teacher, 35,* 614–617.

Olds, H. (1981). How to think about computers. In B. Sadowski (Ed.), *Using computers to enhance teaching and improve teacher centers.* Houston: National Teacher Centers Computer Technology Conference.

Oliver, P. (1983, February). Technology and education: Issues and answers. *Electronic Learning,* pp. 63–66.

O'Neal, S., Kauffman, D., & Smith, D. L. (1981–82). Cost effectiveness of computerized instruction. *International Journal of Instructional Media, 9*(2), 159–165.

Overton, V. (1981, Spring). Research in instructional computing and mathematics education. *Viewpoints in Teaching and Learning, 57,* 23–36.

Papert, S. *Mindstorms: Children, computers, and powerful ideas.* New York: Basic Books, 1980.

Papert, S., diSessa, A., Watt, D., & Weir, S. (1979). *Final report of the Brookline Logo Project: Project summary and data analysis.* Logo Memo 53, MIT Logo Group.

Papert, S. A., & Weir, S. (1978). *Information prosthetics for the handicapped* (Logo Memo No. 51). Boston: M.I.T. Artificial Intelligence Laboratory.

Pea, R. D. (1983). Logo programming and problem solving. In *Chameleon in the classroom: Developing roles for computers* (Tech. Rep. No. 22) (pp. 25–33). New York: Bank Street College of Education, Center for Children and Technology.

Pea, R., Hawkins, J., and Sheingold, K. (1983, April). Developmental studies on learning Logo computer programming. *Abstracts from the Biennial Meeting of the Society for Research in Child Development, 4,* 207. (Summary)

Perfetti, C. A. (1983). Reading, vocabulary, and writing: Implications for computer-based instruction. In A. C. Wilkinson (Ed.), *Classroom computers and cognitive science* (pp. 145–163). New York: Academic Press.

Perlman, R. (1976). *Using computer technology to provide a creative learning environment for preschool children.* Logo Memo 24. Cambridge, MA: M.I.T. Artificial Intelligence Laboratory.

Petty, W. T., Petty, D. C., & Becking, M. F. (1981). *Experiences in language* (3rd ed.). Boston: Allyn and Bacon.

Piaget, J. (1973). Comments on mathematics education. In A. G. Howson (Ed.). *Developments in mathematical education.* Proceedings of the Second International Congress on Mathematical Education. London: Cambridge University Press.

Piestrup, A. M. (1981). *Preschool children use Apple II to test reading skills program.* Portola Valley, CA: Advanced Learning Technology. (ERIC Document Reproduction Service No. ED 202 476).

Piestrup, A. M. (1982a). *Early learning of logic and geometry using microcomputers. Final report.* Portola Valley, CA: Learning Company. (ERIC Document Reproduction Service No. ED 202 476).

Piestrup, A. M. (1982b). *Young children use computer graphics.* Cambridge, MA: Harvard University, Graduate School of Design. (ERIC Document Reproduction Service No. ED 224 564).

Prinz, P., Nelson, K., & Stedt, J. (1982). Early reading in young deaf children using microcomputer technology. *American Annals of the Deaf, 127,* 529–535.

Pritchett, B. (1981, February). Computers and descriptive linguistics. *Creative Computing,* pp. 76–77.

Quinn, J., Kirkman, J., & Schultz, C. J. (1983). Beyond computer literacy. *Educational Leadership, 41*(1), 38–39; 67.

Ragosta, M., Holland, P., & Jamison, D. (1981). *Computer-assisted instruction and compensatory education: The ETS/LAUSD study.* Princeton, NJ: Educational Testing Service.

Rice, J. (1981). *My friend the computer.* Minneapolis, MN: T. S. Denison & Co.

Rice, J., & O'Connor, S. (1981). *Computers are fun.* Minneapolis, MN: T. S. Dennison.

Roblyer, M. D. (1981, October). When is it "good courseware"? Problems in developing standards for microcomputer courseware. *Educational Technology,* pp. 47–54.

Ross, S., & Campbell, L. (1983). Computer-based education in the Montessori classroom: A compatible mixture? *T.H.E. Journal, 10*(6), 105–109.

Rowe, M. B. (1978). *Teaching science as a continuous inquiry* (2nd ed.). New York: McGraw-Hill.

Rowe, N. (1978, January/February). Grammar as a programming language. *Creative Computing,* pp. 80–86.

Rubin, A. (1980). Making stories, making sense. *Language Arts, 57,* 285–298; 334.

Rubin, A. (1982). The computer confronts language arts: Cans and shoulds for education. In A. C. Wilkinson (Ed.), *Classroom computers and cognitive science.* New York: Academic Press.

Saracho, O. N. (1982). The effects of a computer-assisted program on basic skills achievement and attitudes toward instruction of Spanish-speaking migrant children. *American Educational Research Association Journal, 19,* 201–219.

Scandura et al. (1978). Using electronic calculators with children ages 5–7, four mini-experiments. *School Science and Mathematics, 78,* 545–552.

Schofield, J. M. (1981). *Microcomputer-based aides for the disabled.* London, England: Heyden & Son Ltd.

Schuyler, M. R. (1982). Readability formula program for use on microcomputers. *Journal of Reading, 25,* 560–591.

Seidman, R. H. (1981). *The effects of learning a computer programming language on the logical reasoning of school children.* Paper presented at the Annual Meeting of the American Education Research Association, Los Angeles, CA, April 14, 1981.

Sewell, D. F., Clark, R. A., Phillips, R. J., & Rostron, A. B. (1980). Language and the deaf: An interactive microcomputer-based approach. *British Journal of Educational Technology, 1*(11), 57–68.

Shostak, R. (1982, March). Computers and teaching English: Bits 'n' pieces. *The Computing Teacher,* 57–58.

Shult, Douglas L. (1981). Appendix C: A review of research of calculator effects on mathematical abilities. In D. Moursund, *Calculators in the classroom: With applications for elementary and middle school teachers.* New York: John Wiley & Sons.

Shumway et al. (1981). Initial effect of calculators in elementary school mathematics. *Journal for Research in Mathematics Education, 12,* 119–141.

Smith, A. (1980). *Goodbye, Gutenberg: The newspaper revolution of the 1980's.* New York: Oxford University Press.

Smithy-Willis, D., Riley, M., & Smith, D. (1982, November–December). Visual discrimination and preschoolers. *Educational Computer Magazine,* pp. 19–20.

Soloway, E., Lochhead, J., & Clement, J. (1982). Does computer programming enhance problem solving ability? Some positive evidence on algebra word problems. In R. Seidel, R. Anderson, & B. Hunter (Eds.), *Computer literacy.* New York: Academic Press.

Spencer, D. (1982). *Computer awareness book.* Ormond Beach, FL: Camelot Publishing Co.

Spencer, D. (1983). *Microcomputer coloring book.* Ormond Beach, FL: Camelot Publishing Co.

Spuck, D. W., & Bozeman, W. C. (1978). Pilot test and evaluation of a system of computer-managed instruction. *AEDS Journal, 12,* 31–41.

Spuck, D. W., & Owen, S. P. (1974). Computer managed instruction: A model. *AEDS Journal, 8,* 17–23.

Statz, J. (1974). The development of computer programming concepts and problem solving abilities among ten-year-olds learning Logo. *Dissertation Abstracts International, 34,* 5418B–5419B. (University Microfilms No. 74-10, 180).

Stauffer, R. G. (1980). *The language-experience approach to the teaching of reading* (2nd ed.). Cambridge, MA: Harper & Row.

Steffin, S. (1983, April). The instructional applicability of Logo. *Classroom Computer News,* p. 88.

Stoodt, B. (1981). *Reading instruction.* Boston: Houghton Mifflin.

Swett, S. (1983, September). Every teacher is

a computer instructor; every student is a programmer. *Teaching and Computers*, pp. 18–21.

Swigger, K., & Cambell, J. (1981). Computers and the nursery school. *Proceedings of the National Educational Computing Conference.* Iowa City, IA: National Educational Computing Conference.

Swigger, K. M., Campbell, J., & Swigger, B. K. (1983, January/February). Preschool children's preferences of different types of CAI programs. *Educational Computer Magazine*, pp. 38–40.

Taylor, R. (1975). Computerless computing for young children or what to do till the computer comes. In O. Lecarme & R. Lewis (Eds.), *Computers in education: Proceedings of the IFIP 2nd World Conference.* New York: American Elsevier Publishing Company.

Ten basic skill areas. (1977). *The Arithmetic Teacher, 25*(1), 18–24.

Teoh, W. (1981, October). Grades: A class record updating system. *Creative Computing*, pp. 166–168, 170, 172–177.

Terminals only secondary cause of health efects, researchers say. (1981, April). Occupational Safety and Health Reporter, 10 (45), 1431–1432.

Tinker, B. (n.d.). Logo's limits: Or which language should we teach? *Hands On!, 6*(1), 1, 4–6.

Visonhaler, J. F., & Bass, R. K. (1972). A summary of ten major studies on CAI drill and practice. *Educational Technology, 12,* 29–32.

Walker, N., & Boillot, M. A. (1979). A computerized reading level analysis. *Educational Technology, 19*(1), 47.

Wall, E. (1982). *Computer alphabet book.* Nokomis, FL: Bayshore Books.

Watkins, M. W., & Webb, C. (1981, September/October). Computer assisted instruction with learning disabled students. *Educational Computer Magazine,* 24–26.

Watt, D. H. (1981, October). Computer liter-

acy: What should schools do about it? *Instructor,* pp. 85–87.

Watt, D. (1982, June). Word processors and writing. *Popular Computing,* pp. 124–126.

Way, F. L. (1969). The DOVACK model. *Educom, 4*(5), 6–7.

Weir, S. (1981, September). Logo and exceptional children. *Microcomputing.* pp. 76–82, 84.

Weizenbaum, J. (1976). *Computer power and human reason: From judgment to calculation.* San Francisco: W. H. Freeman.

West, C. E. (1983). Computers in the 80's. In M. T. Grady & J. D. Gawronski (Eds.), *Computers in curriculum and instruction.* Alexandria, VA: Association for Supervision and Curriculum Development.

Wexelblat, R. L. (1981). The consequences of one's first programming language. *Software—Practice and Experience, 11,* 733–740.

White, M. A. [Cassette Recording]. (1982). *The new media and the American family.* Racine, WI: The Johnson Foundation.

Whitmore, J. R. (1980). *Giftedness, conflict, and underachievement.* Boston: Allyn and Bacon.

Wilkins, P. W. (1975). The effects of computer assisted classroom management on the achievement and attitudes of eighth grade mathematics students. Dissertation Abstracts International, 36, 3379A.

Williams, J., Thorkildsen, R., & Crossman, E. K. (1983). Application of computers to the needs of handicapped persons. In D. Harper & J. Stewart (Eds.), *Run: Computer Education.* Monterey, CA: Brooks/Cole.

Wilson, M. S., & Fox, B. J. (1982). *User's manual for FIRST WORDS.* Burlington, VT: Laureate Learning Ssytems.

Yeager, R. F. (1977, May). *The reading machine.* Paper presented at the meeting of the International Reading Association, Miami Beach, FL. (ERIC Document Reproduction Service No. ED 142 990).

Young, R. M. (1976). *Seriation by children: An aritificial intelligence analysis of a Piagetian task.* Basel: Birkhauser Verlag.

INDEX